In the Steps of Rosa Luxemburg

Historical Materialism Book Series

More than ten years after the collapse of the Berlin Wall and the disappearance of Marxism as a (supposed) state ideology, a need for a serious and long-term Marxist book publishing program has arisen. Subjected to the whims of fashion, most contemporary publishers have abandoned any of the systematic production of Marxist theoretical work that they may have indulged in during the 1970s and early 1980s. The Historical Materialism book series addresses this great gap with original monographs, translated texts, and reprints of "classics."

Haymarket Books is proud to be working with Brill Academic Publishers (www.brill.nl) and the journal *Historical Materialism* to republish the Historical Materialism book series in paperback editions. Current series titles include:

Alasdair MacIntyre's Engagement with Marxism: Selected Writings 1953–1974, edited by Paul Blackledge and Neil Davidson

Althusser: The Detour of Theory, Gregory Elliott

Between Equal Rights: A Marxist Theory of International Law, China Miéville

The Capitalist Cycle, Pavel V. Maksakovsky, translated with introduction and commentary by Richard B. Day

The Clash of Globalisations: Neo-Liberalism, the Third Way, and Anti-Globalisation, Ray Kiely

Critical Companion to Contemporary Marxism, edited by Jacques Bidet and Stathis Kouvelakis

Criticism of Heaven: On Marxism and Theology, Roland Boer

Criticism of Religion: On Marxism and Theology II, Roland Boer

Exploring Marx's Capital: Philosophical, Economic, and Political Dimensions, Jacques Bidet, translated by David Fernbach

Following Marx: Method, Critique, and Crisis, Michael Lebowitz

The German Revolution: 1917–1923, Pierre Broué

Globalisation: A Systematic Marxian Account, Tony Smith

The Gramscian Moment: Philosophy, Hegemony and Marxism, Peter D. Thomas

Impersonal Power: History and Theory of the Bourgeois State, Heide Gerstenberger, translated by David Fernbach

Lenin Rediscovered: What Is to Be Done? in Context, Lars T. Lih

Making History: Agency, Structure, and Change in Social Theory, Alex Callinicos

Marxism and Ecological Economics: Toward a Red and Green Political Economy, Paul Burkett

A Marxist Philosophy of Language, Jean-Jacques Lecercle, translated by Gregory Elliott

Politics and Philosophy: Niccolò Machiavelli and Louis Althusser's Aleatory Materialism, Mikko Lahtinen, translated by Gareth Griffiths and Kristina Köhli

The Theory of Revolution in the Young Marx, Michael Löwy

Utopia Ltd.: Ideologies of Social Dreaming in England 1870–1900, Matthew Beaumont

Western Marxism and the Soviet Union: A Survey of Critical Theories and Debates Since 1917, Marcel van der Linden

Witnesses to Permanent Revolution: The Documentary Record, edited by Richard B. Day and Daniel Gaido

In the Steps
of Rosa Luxemburg

Selected Writings of Paul Levi

*Edited and introduced
by David Fernbach*

Haymarket Books
Chicago, IL

First published in 2011 by Brill Academic Publishers, The Netherlands
© 2011 Koninklijke Brill NV, Leiden, The Netherlands

Published in paperback in 2012 by
Haymarket Books
P.O. Box 180165
Chicago, IL 60618
773-583-7884
www.haymarketbooks.org

ISBN: 978-1-60846-234-6

Trade distribution:
In the US, Consortium Book Sales, www.cbsd.com
In Canada, Publishers Group Canada, www.pgcbooks.ca
In the UK, Turnaround Publisher Services, www.turnaround-psl.com
In all other countries, Ingram Publisher Services International, ips_intlsales@
ingramcontent.com

Cover design by Ragina Johnson. Cover image from *Abstract Composition*,
1917 by Alexandra Exter.

This book was published with the generous support of Lannan Foundation
and the Wallace Global Fund.

Printed in the United States.

Entered into digital printing January 2019.

Library of Congress Cataloging-in-Publication data is available.

Contents

Part Three
The Soviet Question

Part Four
The German Republic

Introduction

The two paths by which socialist parties came to power in the twentieth century were, on the one hand, by confining themselves to a limited set of reforms, and on the other, by taking power without an electoral-democratic mandate. Both can be seen as departures from Marx's anticipated revolution of a proletarian majority, but also as adaptations to local conditions that advanced the cause of the working class to a certain degree. In the world of today, the one seems inadequate and the other unfeasible. Revolution against the existing power-structure offers the only way to stop the stampede into planetary disaster, yet this can hardly succeed except as the act of a majority. However different conditions today are from those of the early twentieth century, it is not just out of historical interest that it is worth studying the politics of majority-revolution where this came closest to success: in Germany in the years immediately following the First World-War.

This politics is associated above all with Rosa Luxemburg, despite her death in the first phase of this period of revolution. Already before the War, she had done more than anyone to revitalise Marxism against the mainstream of the SPD, whose professed orthodoxy concealed a politics of passive anticipation. After the disaster of 1914, it was around her that the core of revolutionary opposition formed, taking the name of Spartakus that she coined for it.

The Spartacus group remained small until a mass-movement of workers and soldiers broke out in the second half of 1918, by which time the great example of the Bolshevik Revolution was making itself felt. But, when Germany's revolutionary socialists came to form a new party in December 1918, this was under the tutelage of the Spartakusbund, and it took the name Kommunistische Partei Deutschlands (Spartakus).[1]

Two weeks later, Rosa Luxemburg and Karl Liebknecht were dead, followed in March 1919 by Leo Jogiches. For the next two years, the orphaned KPD was led by Paul Levi, who sought to continue Luxemburg's politics of majority-revolution and succeeded in building the KPD into a mass-party of a third of a million members. But, despite Levi's own enthusiasm for the Bolshevik Revolution and the newly formed Communist International, his good relations with Lenin and his readiness to learn from Russian experience, the KPD came under increasing pressure to adopt unsuitable tactics decided in Moscow. The watershed of the 'March Action' in 1921 led to a break between Levi and the KPD, followed in short order by the 'Bolshevisation' of the German Party, and an explicit rejection of the 'Luxemburgist' heresy.

Paul Levi was 36 years old when he became, not by his own choice, the leading figure in the KPD. As Clara Zetkin said in her *Conversations with Lenin*, 'Following the murder of Rosa, Karl and Leo he had to take it over [the leadership of the Party], though he often enough resisted it.'[2] What were Levi's special qualities, so that Lenin would say, after Levi had supposedly 'lost his head', that 'he at least had something to lose: one can't even say that about the others [in Germany]'?[3]

Levi was born on 11 March 1883 into a securely bourgeois family, typical of assimilated Germans of Jewish origin in its dedication to literature and the arts, and to the values of liberal democracy.[4] He grew up in Hechingen, a small

---

1. After the merger with the left Independent Social Democrats in November 1920, the Party was known as the Vereinigte Kommunistische Partei Deutschlands, then, from April 1921, as the Kommunistische Partei Deutschlands (Sektion der Kommunistischen Internationale). It is generally referred to here as the KPD.

2. Cited after Gruber (ed.) 1967, p. 354.

3. Reported in Trotsky 1975, p. 19.

4. The material on Levi's early life here draws especially on Beradt 1969 and Quack 1983. Charlotte Beradt's book is extremely patchy, lacks an analytical framework, and is especially inadequate on Levi's KPD period. The subject of Sybille Quack's is explained by its subtitle, 'Paul Levi – Rosa Luxemburg. Political Work and Personal Relationship'. Both authors had access to the Paul Levi collection now at the Archiv der Sozialdemokratie in Bonn, which is the necessary starting point for any further

town in the Swabian hills, where his father owned a textile-mill. He attended the Gymnasium in Stuttgart, and his twin passions of socialism and law were formed before he left school. His university-studies took him to France as well as other German cities, and he retained a certain admiration for Clemenceau – defender of Dreyfus and of the republic. The subject of his doctoral thesis at Heidelberg was 'Complaints and Actions against the Administration', but he was widely read even by the standards of his time, and, in the 1920s, was to produce original interpretations of the trial of Socrates and of the Cataline conspiracy. From 1906, he practised as a lawyer in Frankfurt, and contributed sufficiently to the work of the SPD to be elected a town-councillor in 1914. He made no original claims as a theorist, though his introduction to Luxemburg's posthumous pamphlet on the Russian Revolution develops an interesting position on the dictatorship of the proletariat as a form of state. But, as leader of the KPD, Levi proved a skilful tactician, and when he subsequently found himself back in the SPD, he still sought to advance the proletarian cause in the way he believed Luxemburg would have done in the circumstances.

Levi was uncompromisingly an intellectual, even something of an aesthete. He collected Chinese porcelain, and this figured significantly on the chargesheet drawn up by Karl Radek on behalf of the Comintern. At meetings of the KPD Zentrale,[5] if business dragged, he would pull out a copy of the London *Times* to read. Tall and lanky, elegantly dressed, a keen skier and automobilist, he was equally removed from any Jewish stereotype and from being a 'man of the people'. To his KPD-comrades, he seemed somewhat solitary, and most of them did not feel very warm in their relations with him.[6] He never married, and enjoyed the freedom of a bachelor-existence, though, at his funeral, 'alongside left-wing journalists and writers stood fur-clad young women, more than one of whom could have worn widow's weeds'.[7] But he

---

research. Charlotte Beradt also edited a useful collection of Levi's writings, Beradt (ed.) 1969.

5. The leading instance of the KPD was in early years known as the Zentrale, with around a dozen members. This corresponds to what, in later Communist practice, was the political committee or politburo.

6. Zetkin, cited after Gruber (ed.) 1967, p. 354. The view is confirmed in other sources.

7. Gruber (ed.) 1967, pp. 391–2. His account of Levi's funeral is based on a verbal report from Levi's friend Heinz Pol. In Fernbach 2009, I suggested that, from today's perspective on sexual politics, Levi's close friendships with women might appear in a different light.

could lapse jovially into the Swabian dialect of his childhood-environment, and, in Saxony, was to win friendship and admiration for his dedication to his working-class constituents.

In September 1913, Rosa Luxemburg was charged in Frankfurt after a speech in which she called on workers to refuse to fire on their class-brothers if the threat of war materialised. Paul Levi was recommended to her as a lawyer, and became right away a staunch disciple. The case itself was a cause célèbre when it came to trial in February 1914, and Rosa Luxemburg's defence a bravura performance. What remained a close secret, until her letters to Levi were unearthed in the 1980s, is that, for a while, the pair had a passionate love-affair. The correspondence – only her side survives – shows hasty meetings, joint speaking tours, holiday-plans. A few brief extracts will give its complex tenor:

> Darling, that was so nice: on Monday you preached on imperialism in Frankfurt, on Tuesday I did in Charlottenburg.[8]
>
> What do you think, darling, how fantastic! It's a prosecution from war-minister von Falkenhaym for insult to the officer-corps and NCOs, because at the Freiburg meeting on 7 March I proposed proceedings against the abuse of conscripts and told how these 'defenders of the fatherland' are kicked around.[9]
>
> My love, yesterday the desire for a word from you made me sick, first thing today your letter arrived. I was already prepared for unpleasant decisions. Rosen[feld] and others here believe I may be imprisoned any moment...[10]

By the outbreak of War, the relationship seems to have mellowed into a sympathetic friendship; but Paul would have had, as Rosa's lover, a privileged access to her mind. In this woman half a generation older, Paul found the word of Marxism made flesh, and, though this unique apprenticeship was apparently unknown even to her closest circle, Levi's close intellectual relationship to his mentor was certainly recognised, and played no small part in his qualification for the KPD-leadership.

---

8. 3 May 1914; Luxemburg 1984, p. 434.
9. 13 May 1914; Luxemburg 1984, p. 435.
10. Mid-May 1914; Luxemburg 1984, p. 436.

Levi belonged, from the start, to the small group that responded to Rosa Luxemburg's call to oppose the War, and was one of the twelve delegates to the meeting in March 1915 that founded the 'Internationale' group, subsequently known as Spartakus. He was called up the following month, while giving a series of lectures against the War, and was sent with a local regiment to the Vosges. He decided to escape from the army by starving himself, and, eventually, was discharged on medical grounds. He then moved to Switzerland, where he worked with Lenin and Zinoviev (under the pseudonym Hartstein), helping to found *La Nouvelle Internationale* and joining the bureau of the Zimmerwald Left; he was one of the few Germans at this time to call for a break with the 'centrists'. In April 1917, when Lenin and his party arranged to travel through Germany on the famous 'sealed train', Levi signed a declaration approving this on behalf of the German internationalists. His activities in the following months are unclear, though it was slanderous for Radek to charge later on that Levi 'does not go into hiding to risk his life for the ideas of the Spartacus League, as was done by Johann Knief, [Wilhelm] Pieck and Karl Becker. Paul Levi lives and travels abroad, engaging in Spartacist activities as a sideline'.[11] Karl Radek had been Levi's neighbour in Davos in the winter of 1916–17, where they heard the news of the Russian February Revolution and travelled immediately to see Lenin in Zürich.[12] Luxemburg's hostility to Radek is legendary; when he arrived in Berlin on 29 December 1918, as the Bolsheviks' emissary to the Spartacus congress, Jogiches and Levi had to prevail on Luxemburg to at least treat him civilly, such was her contempt. This was the context for her often-quoted remark to Radek, 'We need no commissar for Bolshevism.'

Levi returned to Germany after the Bolshevik Revolution, and from March 1918 was mainly in Berlin, as one of the three editors of the *Spartakusbriefe* after the arrest of Leo Jogiches. He also maintained his connections with Stuttgart, where Clara Zetkin lived, where the Spartacists had a majority among

---

11. Karl Radek, 'The Levi Case', in Gruber (ed.) 1967, p. 344. Radek was a master of journalistic distortion from the time he lived in Germany before the War. In 1914, he joined a dissident faction in the SDPKPL – the Polish Marxist party that Luxemburg and Jogiches still controlled – which sided with the Bolsheviks in the Russian organisational dispute; shortly before the War, Luxemburg sought his expulsion from the SPD on grounds of personal dishonesty.
12. Beradt 1969, p. 19.

the local Independent Socialists (USPD), and where Levi helped organise deserters from the armed forces.[13]

Rosa Luxemburg's continuing mentorship of Levi in the final months of her life, and her regard for his political acumen, is apparent in a number of ways. In summer 1918, she smuggled out of Breslau Prison the first in a series of articles, 'The Russian Tragedy', which the editors of the *Spartakusbriefe* (Ernst Meyer, Paul Levi and Eugen Leviné) reluctantly published – without signature, and with a distancing note. In September, Levi visited Luxemburg in Breslau, mandated to persuade her not to insist on publishing the intended sequels. Levi seems to have shared at this time the uncritical admiration for the Bolsheviks' success that was typical of the younger Spartacist generation.

A further factor was the opening of a Soviet mission in Berlin following the peace of Brest-Litovsk, which substantially aided the work of the Spartacists at this time.[14] Luxemburg reluctantly agreed to refrain for the time being from public criticism of the Bolsheviks, though she continued to work up her articles into a pamphlet and wrote to Levi, 'I am writing this pamphlet for you, and if I convince only you, I shall not have done the work in vain.'[15] It was to take the lessons of experience before Levi was fully convinced.

With the November Revolution and Luxemburg's release from prison, Levi worked closely with her on the daily *Rote Fahne*, addressing meetings and as a member of the Spartacus Zentrale. Levi was the one Spartacus leader beside Luxemburg and Liebknecht whose name appeared regularly in public print, and it was in these weeks that he established himself as a capable orator. As

---

13. Cf. Jacob 1999, p. 90. Rosa Luxemburg's friend and assistant, Mathilde Jacob, reproduces here a political report Levi sent to Luxemburg in prison in the days before the November revolution. Levi here raises the question of the strategic goal of the workers' movement: 'As I see it, the following points have to be considered in the immediate future, as the questions are now becoming acute: question of soviets or constituent assembly, question of dictatorship of the proletariat. The arming of the Berlin workers seems to be considerably more favourable lately. Weapons have been acquired, approx. 2,500.'

14. 'In March 1918...the people's delegates from the Russian Federal Soviet Republic came as diplomatic representatives to Berlin....A feverish cooperation between Russian and German comrades commenced. Besides the old stock of revolutionary Social Democrats others now flocked in, attracted partly by the large salaries which the Russians paid and partly by the position of power' (Jacob 1999, p. 85). The Soviet mission was closed down by the German government at the beginning of November, when revolution was already impending.

15. 'Introduction to Rosa Luxemburg's pamphlet, *The Russian Revolution*, below, pp. 220–1.

the SPD's *Vorwärts* put it, 'Karl Liebknecht, a certain Levi and the big-mouth Luxemburg, who never stood at a lathe or in a workshop, are in the process of ruining everything that we and our fathers aspired to.' Or, in the words of a scurrilous leaflet, 'Judah has reached for the crown. We are to be ruled by Levi and Rosa Luxemburg.'[16]

At the KPD's founding conference on 30–1 December 1918, Levi reported for the Zentrale on the most sensitive of current questions, participation in the forthcoming elections to the National Assembly. Despite his skilful handling of the issues, the leadership was defeated on this question by 62 votes to 23. Given the hesitancy with which Luxemburg and Liebknecht had decided on an organisational break with the USPD in the first place, the prevalence of the ultra-Left put in question the very project of a separate party, and Jogiches had even voted in these circumstances against the formation of the KPD – two weeks before he himself became its leader.[17] Though Jogiches had successfully run the Spartacists' illegal organisation from summer 1916 to his arrest in March 1918, he preferred to remain behind the scenes, and was too much the Polish foreigner to appear as leader of a German party – even the KPD. The Zentrale agreed that, while Jogiches would lead the Party, Levi should be its outward representative, and, when Jogiches was killed on 10 March 1919, Levi's assumption of his position was unchallenged. As Clara Zetkin was later to explain to Lenin, Levi 'is no ambitious political careerist. It was his fate and not his wish that he assumed the leadership of the Party at a young age and without great political experience or profound theoretical education'.[18]

That Levi was still alive was largely due to his imprisonment when the white terror began, prison proving the safest place to be.[19] And if he 'had to' take over the Party, this was a function of two factors: his own qualifications and the limitations of his possible rivals. His skills were already evident as writer, orator, and organiser; his tactical aptitude still had to be proved. Only two

---

16. Beradt 1969, p. 21.
17. It was at the conference of the Spartakusbund on 29 December, the day before the founding congress of the KPD, that Jogiches voted against the proposed new party.
18. Cited from Gruber (ed.) 1967, p. 354.
19. Mathilde Jacob describes the circumstances of her own and Levi's arrest, when Luxemburg and Liebknecht were already in hiding. At the newspaper-office, 'The troops encircled me like wild animals....Though I did get out, it was in company of brutalised soldiers who took me to my flat. Waiting there for me in my office sat Paul Levi...and we were taken together to the Moabit prison. Probably his arrest at that time saved his life; he often maintained that later on' (Jacob 1999, p. 101).

other candidates could have been seriously considered. Leviné was brilliant in a different way, with a revolutionary panache reminiscent of Trotsky, which Levi would not seek to match. But Leviné had struck a semi-detached position at the founding congress, and was not voted onto the Zentrale. He had taken too high a risk with the *Vorwärts*-occupation during the *Spartakus-woche*, and went on to oppose Rosa Luxemburg, just days before her death, on the question of the new International to be formed in Moscow, which she and Liebknecht both agreed was premature. Of the younger leaders, Ernst Meyer had done most for Spartacus during the war-years, but his strength was that of a scholar and editor, and it is typical that, at the founding conference, he was charged with greeting the delegates and guests, rather than leading one of the six debates.[20] Levi was the obvious successor, and he was soon to prove his political acumen on the Party's desperate problem of tactics.

The Party leader

Following the defeats of its first weeks and months, the infant KPD was an easy target for government repression. A state of siege was proclaimed in Berlin in March, after an unsuccessful general strike was coupled with renewed street-fighting. The party-offices were occupied by the military, and Levi retreated with the leading comrades first to Frankfurt, then to Hanau, finally managing to produce *Rote Fahne* for some weeks in Leipzig until General Maercker's troops occupied the city on 11 May.[21] Ten days earlier, the Bavarian soviet-republic had been crushed, and Leviné was shot after a mockery of a trial. Until December, the Party was formally outlawed under the state of siege declared in Berlin and its other strongholds. The leadership were unable to hold their followers to a reasoned tactical line, and the Zentrale was itself divided. The newly recruited rank-and-file showed a laudable readiness for combat, but the cost was that they became tagged for the majority of class-conscious workers as 'putschists'. Opposition to electoral and trade-union work was still the prevailing sentiment.

---

20. These were: 'The Crisis in the USP' (Liebknecht); 'The National Assembly' (Levi); 'Our Programme and the Political Situation' (Luxemburg); 'Our Organisation' (Hugo Eberlein, standing in here for Leo Jogiches); 'Economic Struggles' (Paul Lange); 'International Conference' (Hermann Duncker): Weber 1993, p. 49.

21. This is vividly described in Jacob 1999, pp. 108–9.

The other factor in the equation was the development of the USPD. The Independent Social-Democratic Party had been formed in April 1917, after eighteen Reichstag members refused to vote further war-credits and were expelled from the SPD. This party uneasily grouped together, under the dominant issue of peace, long-time revisionists such as Eduard Bernstein and Kurt Eisner, the 'Marxist Centre' around Karl Kautsky, as well as radicals such as Georg Ledebour[22] and Wilhelm Dittmann not yet prepared to rally to the Spartacist message of revolution. Rosa Luxemburg had been dismissive of the Independents' lack of resolve, though the Spartacists joined the new party as an organised group. It was a foregone conclusion that, after the War, the Independents would break up into their component factions. But, in November 1918, the USPD stood for a *Räterepublik* (republic of workers' councils), and its left wing steadily gained ascendancy in the following two years. The first wave of revolution might have passed, but radical socialism was still spreading among the working class, and, by 1920, even the centrists had to pay lip-service to 'the dictatorship of the proletariat'.[23]

Levi concluded that the partisan divisions in the working-class movement did not properly reflect the basic tactical options. While the USPD had a revolutionary wing that could be won for Communism, the KPD was itself riven between a wing that sought a mass-base as the only effective agent of revolution, and the 'left-wing communists', as Lenin was to call them, who cultivated putschist illusions which isolated them from the mainstream of the working class. Levi embarked on a complex manoeuvre: the goal was to win over the greater part of the USPD, but the necessary precondition for this was to break with the KPD's own ultra-Left. Painful as it was to criticise the martyred Leviné, Levi staked out his position in the summer of 1919, in his comments on the Munich soviet:

> [A]n Independent/Majority-Socialist/anarchist 'soviet-republic', established with insufficient support among the masses, [replaced] by a communist soviet-republic with the same shortcoming...means to replace one nothing with another ... an aimless drifting in the political whirlpool....If the masses proceed with actions which are only pseudo-revolutionary and in reality

---

22. On Georg Ledebour, see below, p. 105, note 11.
23. The most detailed study of the USPD is Morgan 1975. But, for the revolutionary period as a whole, Broué 2005 is unsurpassed.

can only lead to setbacks, it is our duty to step forward with warnings and criticism....To place ourselves, however, at the head of the movement, though it can only lead to trouble – that obligation we do not have....Was it necessary to say all this? Yes, for the sake of clarity and our future.[24]

At a clandestine national conference on 16 August, 'Comrade Paul' explained:

The revolution has apparently reached a dead end, such that we must speak of a dying back of the revolution. We stand now at the end of the epoch that opened on 9 November [1918] and led to a defeat for the revolution....We have entered a creeping stage in the revolution, and will no longer be able to count on great mass movements.[25]

While broad strata of the working class were still being radicalised and could be drawn to the Communist Party, Levi stressed that these best and surest elements wanted nothing to do with potential putschists any more than with anti-parliamentarians and anti-trade-unionists.

Levi met fierce resistance in the Party. As the founding congress had shown, the leftists were a majority in the rank and file, and could potentially take over the leadership if they were not blocked in time. In October 1919, the KPD's second congress was held, moving daily through a succession of south-German venues, one step ahead of military repression. Here, Levi, with a bare majority on the party Zentrale, made a successful coup. In his opening address he attacked as 'syndicalists' the various elements of the opposition – anti-parliamentarians, opponents of the trade-unions, and anti-centralists. Those who would not subscribe to the official line were expelled, almost half of the Party's membership, which was given at the congress as 106,656. A few months later, they formed the short-lived Communist Workers' Party (KAPD). At the KPD-congress, Levi still presented his aim as winning USPD left-wingers individually, but, before the USPD held its own congress in November, Levi approached the leaders of its left wing, who agreed to co-operate on a unifying tactic.

At this time, communications with Moscow were still limited; despite the founding of the Comintern in March 1919, it was only the following year that the Bolshevik leaders could offer regular advice to their foreign comrades.

---

24. Cited after Beradt 1969, p. 37.
25. Cited from the Paul Levi archive in Beradt 1969, p. 32.

But there was no sign at this stage of an impending conflict. At the high tide of the revolutionary movement in Germany, a synthesis of 'Luxemburgist' and 'Leninist' traditions seemed possible, despite the past tactical differences between their two protagonists. Levi and his Spartacist friends accepted the need for a communist party that grouped the revolutionary vanguard of the working class, excluding reformists and centrists, and could practise a disciplined tactic through to the seizure of power. Lenin, on the other hand, accepted that the Bolshevik experience had been too Russian to generalise to the countries of advanced capitalism, and recognised the need to build mass revolutionary parties. Radek was still in Germany until the end of the year and supported Levi in his approach to the Independents, as he had in the drastic pruning of the KPD. Though Lenin had been sharply hostile to the left Independents, he backed Levi's moves when Radek returned to Moscow and explained the situation to him.[26] Neither Germans nor Russians at this point saw the issue in rigid terms of 'Bolshevism versus Luxemburgism'. Both Levi and Lenin, and Radek as their intermediary, saw the KPD's line as the best tactic for the revolutionary forces in Germany. And, though Levi's radical surgery might seem, in hindsight, an ominous precedent for subsequent splits that the Comintern engineered to ensure a 'small but pure' core faithful to Moscow, this split proved itself in practice as leading forward to a mass communist party.

The campaign of denigration against Levi long predated his expulsion from the KPD in 1921; the discontented leftists had already sought to bury him in a torrent of abuse: 'the Judas of the German Revolution', 'parliamentary stockjobber', 'political prima donna' were among their favoured epithets.[27] Even without these malcontents, however, Levi still faced an uphill struggle on the Zentrale for the course he sought to pursue. This was made clear with the Kapp Putsch of March 1920, when the Freikorps, whose dissolution was required by the Versailles Treaty, occupied the government-district in Berlin

---

26. 'This precise problem of winning the masses who followed the Independent leaders provided Lenin with the example which enabled him to demonstrate the necessity of compromise outlined in *"Left-Wing" Communism*. Against those who were for "small hard solid nuclei", he wrote that recent events in Germany had confirmed his opinion that "German revolutionary social democracy...came closest to being the party the revolutionary proletariat needs in order to achieve victory"' (Broué, 2005, p. 413).

27. Beradt 1969, p. 34.

for four days, before a nation-wide general strike defeated their would-be dictator. Levi was once more in prison at the time, and, in his absence, the first slogan of the party-leadership was 'Not a finger for the republic'. From his prison-cell, Levi wrote:

> It is criminal to write, 'The proletariat won't lift a finger for the republic.' Do you realise what this means? It means turning our back on the greatest action of the proletariat....The important thing now is that the putsch should be defeated without compromise....As we have often promised before, in the event of a counter-revolutionary putsch, then action even together with the SPD. And now, 'Don't lift a finger'! Every strike has its demands. The Communist Party has to put these demands, *Vorwärts* certainly won't. The demands are...arming of the proletariat for the defence of the republic, i.e. distribution of weapons to the politically organised workers...immediate imprisonment of the leaders of the putsch by a proletarian special court, as a military court [would be] a comedy. Republic of councils, congress of councils, are not demands whose fulfilment we can work towards, especially as they are not demands on our opponents.[28]

Nor was this leftism that denied the value of republican gains confined to Levi's opponents in the KPD. The battle against Kapp had been led from a Berlin cellar by the septuagenarian trade-union leader Karl Legien, a dyed-in-the-wool reformist, and a social patriot during the War. But, alienated by the Prussian-sergeant mentality that had marked the Noske régime, Legien proposed, from his temporary position of strength, a government-coalition of the two socialist parties, on a programme of democratisation of Germany's institutions, social legislation and nationalisation of the mines. 'Had Legien's plan been realised,' Franz Borkenau perceptively wrote, 'it might have changed the fate of Germany.'[29] At the decisive meeting on 18 March, the KPD was represented by Wilhelm Pieck and Jacob Walcher – both, at the time, followers of Levi. They undertook that, if the proposed government kept to its programme, the Communists would act as a 'loyal opposition'. Walcher expressed himself in clumsy terms more pertinent to a trade-unionist, and Levi faced the prospect of the Zentrale rejecting this

---

28. *Die Kommunistische Internationale*, vol. 2, no. 12; cited after Beradt 1969, p. 37.
29. Borkenau 1962, p. 155.

plan; but it was scuppered instead by the left Independents, now in their own throes of revolutionary enthusiasm, who took up the same all-or-nothing attitude as the 'left-wing Communists'.

The defeat of the Kapp Putsch at least gave new strength to the working class. The Independent vote soared in the elections of June 1920, and the majority of this party was keen to join the Communist International.[30] The SPD was itself forced to slough off its most discredited leaders such as Noske and Südekum. At the Second Congress of the Comintern in July/August 1920, a delegation from the USPD represented the Party as a whole, though it was made clear to them that only its left wing would be acceptable in the new International. To Levi's surprise, however, a delegation was also invited from the KAPD, the 'syndicalists' whom Levi had expelled the previous year. Lenin had recalled even before the congress how 'in 1907–08 the "Left" Bolsheviks on certain occasions...carried on more successful agitation among the masses than we did'. When the KPD delegation threatened to leave, the KAPD were kept at arm's length, but although Lenin still endorsed the tactics of the KPD under Levi's leadership, including unity with the left USPD, his priority was 'the amalgamation in a single party...of all those in the working-class movement who sincerely and conscientiously stand for soviet government and the dictatorship of the proletariat'.[31] Levi did not conceal at the congress his principled antipathy to putschism, and, when Lenin asked him about the prospects of an uprising of the German working class as response to the victory of the Red Army – momentarily at the gates of Warsaw – Levi allegedly shrugged his shoulders. In October, the majority of the USPD accepted the Comintern's 'Twenty-One Conditions' and joined the renamed United Communist Party of Germany (VKPD). The membership of the united party was given three months later as 449,700, of whom about 370,000 were from the former Independents. The Communists also now had a significant presence in the Reichstag,

30. In this first Reichstag election under the Weimar constitution, the USPD won 4,896,095 votes (18.8%) against 5,616,164 (21.6%) for the SPD. The KPD won a mere 441,793 votes (1.7%), just enough to send Levi and Clara Zetkin to the Reichstag. It is notable that, at this time of revolutionary ferment, the proportionate vote for the workers' parties was little more than its prewar peak, one explanation being that women had the vote for the first time. Despite her disinterest in political feminism, Luxemburg's awareness of this 'gender-gap' problem is clear from her letter to Zetkin of 18 November 1918.
31. '"Left-Wing" Communism', in Lenin 1964b, p. 108.

and a number of regional newspapers. At the unification-congress, Levi greeted the merger 'with a deep inner satisfaction':

> We stand together once again with a large group of comrades, with whom we are linked by the work of very many years, and from whom we were separated not because we pursued different goals, but because we believed we had to attain one and the same goal by different roads. The United Communist Party has been founded out of our own forces and our own struggles.[32]

The USPD-decision had been swayed by a rousing speech from Zinoviev, the Comintern chairman, who declared: 'Either one is Menshevik or Bolshevik, there is no third way';[33] even a significant section of the Independents' left wing, however, still found the Twenty-One Conditions unacceptable. Up to the unifying congress with the KPD, there was no criticism from the Comintern of Levi's policy. Immediately after, however, the trouble began. First, Moscow accorded the KAPD the status of a sympathising party, which Levi could only see as pulling the movement in a false direction. He publicly rebuked the Russian comrades for this under the heading 'An Intolerable Situation'. Against such interference in German affairs, Levi wrote:

> If the objection is made that our tactics lack the emotional charge and broad gestures of the traditional revolutionary, our response is that what from the outside may seem the petty work of individual functionaries in the factory or trade-union is dearer to us than all revolutionary psychopathy....No provision in the statutes of the Communist International obliges us...to declare all decisions of the Executive Committee as strokes of genius.[34]

Levi's response in the new year of 1921 was to propose a positive new tactic. Despite unification having created a mass-party, this did not by itself 'permit the VKPD to control totally, and without concern for other strata of the proletariat, the destiny of the German Revolution'. It was not only through propaganda that the Party would win a majority of the workers, but, by leading them in action through which they would 'grasp their own interests through

---

32. 'Der Parteitag der Kommunistischen Partei', *Die Internationale*, vol. 2, no. 26.
33. Sinowjew 1921.
34. 'Eine unhaltbare Situation', *Rote Fahne*, 24 December 1920. Cited after Beradt 1969, p. 44; Broué 2005, p. 467.

taking part in the struggle', as the Bolsheviks had done in the Soviets of 1917. In particular: 'It is absolutely incorrect to treat the proletarian masses who are still on our right today with less consideration and patience than we have for the proletarian comrades in our class who believe themselves to be to our left.'[35] The opportunity for this arose right away, with a local initiative in Stuttgart, where the Communist metalworkers won their non-Communist fellow-unionists for a joint struggle around basic demands – from 'lower food-prices' through to 'the disarming of reactionary gangs and the arming of the workers'.[36] Levi and Radek together convinced the rather reluctant Zentrale to issue an 'Open Letter', calling on other parties and trade-unions 'to announce in public meetings that they are willing to defend themselves together against capitalism and reaction, and to defend jointly their common interests'.[37] It also called for trade-relations to be opened with Russia as a way of alleviating the current economic distress.

It was predictable that the 'Open Letter' would come under scathing attack from the KAPD. But this turn to the united front was also opposed by the 'left' wing of the KPD itself, forming around Ruth Fischer, Arkady Maslow and Ernst Friesland. And, in Moscow, where Radek had returned at the turn of the year, Zinoviev and Bukharin won the 'small bureau' of the Comintern's Executive Committeee (ECCI) to condemn the 'Open Letter' on 21 February – against opposition from Radek that was subsequently supported by Lenin.

But, despite Radek's standing together with Levi on the 'Open Letter', more important issues had now arisen, which led Radek, who had particular responsibilities for German affairs on the ECCI, to go along with Zinoviev's 'left' course and seek to force Levi's resignation as KPD leader. The starting point here was Levi's support for Giacinto Serrati, the leader of the Italian Socialist Party, which had opposed the War and was now an accredited section of the Communist International. Serrati was prepared to expel from his party the reformists under Turati; he accepted, on principle, the 'Twenty-One Conditions' for Comintern membership, though requesting time and flexibility for their application. The ECCI preferred however to break with Serrati and the PSI majority, and switch its support to the smaller faction under Gramsci and

---

35. 'Taktische Fragen', *Rote Fahne*, 4 January 1921; Broué 2005, p. 468.
36. Broué 2005, p. 469.
37. Broué 2005, p. 470.

Bordiga that split away to form the Italian Communist Party. This manoeuvre was carried through by Matthias Rákosi and Christo Kabakchiev at the PSI's Livorno congress, where Levi refused to support the ECCI-representatives and publicly expressed his support for Serrati.

Levi's discussion of Livorno in *Rote Fahne* on 22 January brought an immediate response from Radek, now back in Berlin, who defended the ECCI's position in the paper four days later. In the meantime, at a stormy meeting of the Zentrale on the 25th, Radek claimed that Levi's article was 'a deliberate attack on the ECCI', and threatened: 'Before you can attack us, we shall get in ahead of you and draw the sword against you.'[38] When senior members of the Zentrale such as Clara Zetkin and co-chair Ernst Däumig (ex-USPD) stood by Levi, Radek took a more compromising tack, even accepting on 2 February a resolution proposed by Zetkin that stressed the need to improve communications and relations between the ECCI and its member-parties. Behind the scenes, however, the ECCI was cultivating the leftists on the Zentrale, and, on 4 February, Friesland attacked the resolution as evading the real problem, which was the transformation of the KPD into a party of action.[39]

The break with Moscow

As Broué writes, 'from that time onwards, Levi fought the battle on the political plane with great clarity'.[40] In a series of articles in *Rote Fahne*, he argued that the international situation was not now propitious for a proletarian offensive, that it was essential for the VKPD to win trade-unionised workers, that revolution depended on the will of the proletariat in each country, and that the tactics appropriate for Western Europe were necessarily different from those that had proved successful in Russia. It was a dangerous sign that the ECCI saw the way to build communist parties 'not by progressive educa-

---

38. Broué 2005, p. 479. In a private letter to Radek, Levi asked, 'Does the Executive or its German representative see my removal from the post of chair of the Party as necessary or simply desirable?'. It did not help matters that this letter was published by the USPD paper *Freiheit* on 20 January 1921, after being either 'stolen', as the Zentrale claimed, accidentally dropped in the Reichstag corridor, or indeed leaked by Levi himself.

39. 'Zur Kritik der Partei', *Rote Fahne*, 4 February 1921; Broué, p. 484.

40. Broué 2005, p. 488.

tion, but by mechanical splits'.[41] In an article 'We and the Executive' [i.e. the ECCI] he wrote:

> There exist two ways, with these masses organisationally linked with the Third International, to reach a higher level of communist experience and communist will. One lies in educating them through fresh splits, and the other in politically educating these masses who have come towards us, going through this revolutionary period with them, and in this way reaching a higher level, with the masses and amongst the masses.[42]

On 24 February, Levi spoke to his comrades on the Zentrale on 'The Beginnings of the Crisis in the Communist Party and the International'.

> [I]f the Communist International functions in Western Europe in terms of admission and expulsion like a recoiling cannon...then we will experience the worst possible setback.... [Our Russian] comrades did not clearly realise that splits in a mass-party with a different intellectual structure from, for example, that of the illegal Russian party...cannot be carried out on the basis of resolutions, but only on the basis of political experience....We have already had the experience in Germany of what Communists are in a revolution, in action, as a small circle of Communists without that wide circle of comrades around them who have a Communist orientation and are willing to accept Communist leadership.[43]

Radek now re-aligned himself with the 'Berlin leftists' on the Zentrale, and claimed that the VKPD needed a more active new leadership. On 22 February, Rákosi – stopping in Berlin en route from Italy to Russia – addressed the full Central Committee of the German Party, defending the Livorno decision and maintaining that 'splits, ten times over if need be, whether in Italy, France or Germany' were needed 'in the interest of political clarity'.[44] His rhetoric won over the Committee by a small majority; Levi and Däumig resigned from the Zentrale together with Zetkin and two other members, with Heinrich Brandler emerging as the Party's effective leader.

---

41. Broué 2005, p. 489.
42. 'Wir und the Exekutive', *Rote Fahne*, 6 February 1921.
43. Below, pp. 108–11.
44. Broué 2005, p. 486.

There can be little doubt that the leftism on the Zentrale corresponded to a mood of impatience in much of the VKPD rank and file, especially the militant workers who had joined it from the USPD, with high expectations of what affiliation to the Comintern would bring. More important, however, were the tactical debates under way in Moscow, where Zinoviev rejoiced that the 'rightist' Levi had been 'exposed'.

It was at this point that Béla Kun arrived in Berlin as the Comintern's special emissary. His mass-executions of White prisoners in the Civil War had infuriated Lenin, who sent him off on a mission to Turkestan; on return, he now proved a close supporter of Zinoviev. Opposed as he was to the proposed New Economic Policy, Zinoviev apparently hoped that struggles abroad might obviate the need for this compromise. The theory of the 'revolutionary offensive', discredited the previous year in the Polish campaign, was revived with the pretext of relieving the immediate pressure on Soviet Russia.

In the first two weeks of March, Kun lobbied individual members of the Central Committee in favour of the new policy. Zetkin was so alarmed by what he said to her that she refused to meet him again without the presence of a witness. When the Committee met on 16–17 March, Brandler and Frölich explained that an Anglo-American war could soon be expected, sanctions on Germany were imminently to be stiffened, and there was a 90 per cent chance that the Silesian referendum on the 20th would lead to armed conflict between Germany and Poland. In this context, the Zentrale proposed 'a complete break from the past', 'forcing the revolution' and doing all possible to provoke a breach between Germany and the Entente.

Though the new leadership may not have sought to take action quite so precipitously, news arrived while the meeting was still in progress that the Oberpräsident of Prussian Saxony, Hörsing (a Social Democrat), planned to send troops to occupy various industrial zones in central Germany that were Communist strongholds, and where the workers had kept the weapons they had acquired at the time of the Kapp Putsch. The Zentrale immediately decided to launch 'partial actions' in this region that would create a local civil war. This not only required manipulating the working class in these districts to believe that seizure of power was on the agenda, but stoking the struggle by a variety of ruses, including bombing the Party's own offices in order to blame the Right, using unemployed workers to drive employed colleagues out of the factories, and so on. The VKPD now coordinated its actions with the KAPD, and Max Hoelz, a KAPD-activist, started an urban guerrilla in the region. But, even in the occupied districts, the general strike was only partially successful, and the appeal for its national extension met with a very poor response.

Levi was in Vienna when the March Action broke out, led by the purged Zentrale under Heinrich Brandler and August Thalheimer. With the 'passive weakling' Levi no longer in the way, dynamite-attacks gave the signal for an uprising that had no hope of success, but was justified because it would serve to keep the class-struggle on the boil. In the event, however, the Communists' call for a general strike went completely unheeded outside their own ranks, in marked contrast to the previous year's action against the Kapp Putsch. After a week of violent clashes, not only were several hundred workers dead and thousands imprisoned, but the membership of the United Communist Party that Levi had achieved was cut by half, and entire local organisations destroyed.

The manipulative character of the March Action became public knowledge in May, when party-documents were seized from Clara Zetkin at the Polish frontier and reproduced in the SPD *Vorwärts*. At the Krupp works, for example, when workers would not heed the call to strike, Communist unemployed had been sent into the factories to drive them out by force. And, in central Germany, the intended heart of the action, 'The mood of the workers was so unsatisfactory that the opinion prevailed that artificial means must be used to inflame the people.... Attempts must be made to incite the workers by assassinations until they start to fight.'[45]

Before publicly attacking this disastrous campaign, Levi wrote privately to Lenin on 27 March:

> Anyone familiar with my views knows that I experienced my withdrawal from the leadership of the Communist Party as a happy event rather than the opposite.... What has been attained by the March Action, however, is that we stand in open opposition to the big organisations of the working class and the majority of the proletariat.... I am approaching you with this personal request to consider the situation.... For the time being I shall not go further than perhaps write a pamphlet to explain my views...[46]

---

45. Borkenau 1962, pp. 215–20. Zetkin was taking these documents to Moscow as evidence of the disastrous tactics forced by the Comintern on the KPD.
46. Cited from the Paul Levi archive after Beradt 1969, p. 48.

Undoubtedly, the disaster of the March Action made waves even in Moscow. But this was a time of extreme political tension in Russia, just after the Kronstadt revolt, and more pressing concerns occupied Lenin for the moment. 'Dear friends,' he wrote on 16 April to the German Zentrale,

> Unfortunately I was so busy and exhausted in the last few weeks that I was unable to read anything from the German press... Why not wait? Congress here 1 June.[47] Why not a private discussion here before the congress? Without public polemic, without expulsions, without pamphlet over differences. We have too few tested forces... at all costs avoid resignations or sharpening contradictions.[48]

By this time, however, Levi had published his pamphlet *Unser Weg*, after twice being refused a hearing by the Zentrale:

> It works perfectly well for an anarchist club if the will of the leader commands and the believers follow unto death. For a mass-party, one that does not just seek to set the masses in motion but is itself a mass, this is quite insufficient.... Only their own will, their own understanding, their own determination, can move the masses.... An action that corresponds simply to the political needs of the Communist Party, and not to the subjective needs of the proletarian masses, is ruined in advance.... [T]he struggle of the unemployed against those in work, the struggle of Communists against proletarians, the emergence of the lumpenproletariat, the dynamite attacks – these were all logical consequences.[49]

As for the party-Zentrale, as the failure became evident there was a majority of five to three for breaking off the action. But the five refrained from pressing their point against the Comintern representatives, for fear of being accused of a lack of revolutionary will.

> And what were the reasons of the three diehards? I am not certain that all shared the same view, but the reason expressed by one of them was that now that the action was lost, it had to be pursued as far as possible, so that after it was broken off they would have no need to defend themselves against the 'Left', but only the 'Right'.... The comrades now lying dead in

---

47. The Third Congress of the Comintern did not, in the event, open until 16 July.
48. Cited from the Paul Levi archive after Beradt 1969, p. 49.
49. 'Our Path', below, pp. 145–8.

central Germany were not told, when they were sent to their deaths, that their corpses would be used as dynamite for the Party.

Turning to the Comintern policy as a whole, Levi explained:

> Western Europe and Germany thus become a test-bed for all kinds of duodecimo statesmen.... We believe that more or less in all countries where these emissaries are working, discontent with them is the same.... They never work with the Zentrale of the country in question, always behind its back and often even against it.... The ECCI works more or less like a Cheka projected beyond the Russian frontiers – an impossible state of affairs. The clear demand that this should change, and that the leadership in certain countries should not be taken over by incompetent delegates with incompetent hands, the call for a political leadership and against a party police, is not a demand for autonomy.... If we do succeed, however, as we hope and wish, in rescuing the Communist idea in Germany and so proving that there are still revolutionary forces that can seize the hour, let the International not put obstacles in our path if we return to the past of the Communist Party and the doctrine of its founder. She depicted the route we have to take in the following words: 'The unification of the broad popular masses with an aim reaching beyond the whole existing social order, of the daily struggle with the great world transformation – that is the task of the Social-Democratic movement, which must successfully work forward on its road of development between two reefs: abandonment of the mass-character or abandonment of the final aim; the fall back to sectarianism or the fall into bourgeois reformism; anarchism or opportunism.[50]

Levi's pamphlet made headlines both within Germany and abroad. On 16 April 1921, *Rote Fahne* confirmed: 'Paul Levi Expelled from the Party'. It fell to August Thalheimer, under the heading 'The Highest Law', to explain the expulsion in terms that express the militarist and totalitarian philosophy that was already taking over the new International:

> With Paul Levi, the German Communist movement is overcoming a part of its own past. A leader of high and shining talents, but a leader who did not surrender himself completely to the cause that he served...which, in

---

50. Ibid., pp. 165–5. The Rosa Luxemburg quotation is from *Social Reform or Revolution?* (1899); Hudis & Anderson (eds.) 2004, p. 165.

the given historical circumstances, means more than life itself, it means surrendering one's complete personality to the Party....With this separation, the iron law of discipline is imposed at the top as well as in the ranks.[51]

As was stressed again when Levi appeared before the Party's executive – a privilege soon withdrawn for future dissidents – his expulsion was not for his opposition to the March Action, but for 'breach of discipline'. Indeed, by this time, Kun's 'theory of the offensive' had been rejected in Moscow, even before at the Comintern's Third Congress in July. In Trotsky's words, directly referring to Levi's second pamphlet *What Is the Crime: the March Action or Criticising It?*, 'It is our duty to say clearly and precisely to the German workers that we consider this philosophy of the offensive to be the greatest danger. And in its practical application to be the greatest crime.'[52] And Lenin explained to Clara Zetkin, 'The "offensive theory" is not a theory at all, it's an illusion, nothing but romanticism.'[53] In stark refutation of the 'theory of the offensive', the theses adopted at the Third Congress insisted that the revolutionary wave in Europe was over, and world-capitalism had, for the moment, stabilised.

Levi chose not to attend the Congress, and Zinoviev refrained from reading out the letter Levi had sent him protesting at his expulsion. But, as Zetkin recounted in her memoir, Lenin was loath to dispense with Levi's talents, and prepared to offer him a way back into the fold:

> If Levi subordinates himself to party discipline – he can write anonymously for the party press, produce some good pamphlets – then, after three or four months, I will demand his rehabilitation in an open letter. We should not lose Levi, for his sake and that of the cause.

'Levi literally cried with pain at the idea that the Party was lost', Zetkin explained to Lenin. 'He had written his pamphlet in the spirit of the legendary Roman, who throws himself willingly into the opening abyss, to save his country by sacrificing himself.'[54] For a few months after the Congress, Levi believed that, with the change in the Comintern line, he would still be accepted back on his own terms. In August, he wrote to Mathilde Jacob:

---

51. Cited after Beradt 1969, p. 53.
52. Trotsky 1945, p. 277.
53. Cited after Gruber (ed.) 1967, pp. 353–4.
54. Cited after Gruber (ed.) 1967, p. 354.

With us are the better part of those with whom Communist politics can be made. I am convinced that if we stand fast, the ECCI will give us all we ask and more, as they are beginning to understand that without our group the Party is finished.[55]

His supporters included not only a large group of rank-and-file 'Levites' who were expelled from the KPD after its Jena Congress in September, but also the majority – thirteen including himself – of the Party's Reichstag delegation. By the end of the year, however, he accepted that the battle was over. In his hatchet-job on 'The Levi Case' published in September, Karl Radek predicted that Levi would now retire to private life:

He had contemplated desertion a thousand times before: to retire...to a cosy home, where he could devote himself after the completion of higher legal work to the contemplation of his collection of vases....The bourgeois youth, driven to the side of the proletariat by the stench of his decaying class, becomes a renegade.[56]

To the end of his life Levi was indeed attacked in these terms by his old party, but nothing could have been further from his mind than to withdraw from the socialist cause, and a new phase in his career was now to begin.

Levi did not seek to form a splinter-party, though, for a few months, he gathered his supporters, including the expelled Reichstag members, into the Communist Workgroup (KAG) and continued the struggle to reform the KPD from without. The KAG demanded for the German Communists material independence from the Comintern, joint control of literature, security from open and covert attacks, a policy of collaboration with all revolutionary German workers and the maintenance of the organisational unity of the trade-unions. (This last point directed against the 'Red Trade-Union International', which the Comintern had just formed.) 'Our task,' wrote Levi, 'is to promote the process of coming together...without pursuing anti-Bolshevism'.[57] The KAG was immediately declared by the Comintern a 'hostile organisation', though Levi maintained links with several groups, including trade-unionists,

55. Beradt 1969, p. 57.
56. *Die Kommunistische Internationale*, vol. 2, no. 17, September 1921; Gruber (ed.) 1967, pp. 345–6.
57. Beradt 1969, p. 64.

who remained in the KPD. But, threatened with growing isolation, in April 1922 the 'Levites' rejoined the USPD, already preparing its merger with the SPD that was accomplished a few months later.

'A revolutionary socialist of the Rosa Luxemburg school'

Levi's expulsion from the KPD undoubtedly led to a period of serious reflection on his part, and marks a watershed in his political career. But it would be superficial to see this simply in party-terms: that he had reverted from 'Communist' to 'Social Democrat'. For the Spartacus group that had formed the KPD three years before, the party represented a wager that, in a situation of Europe-wide proletarian turbulence, giving the principles of revolutionary Marxism a distinct new organisational form would provide a basis to which the mass of the working class could be won. It was soon clear, however, that this would be a far more long-term struggle, and, even after the union with the left USPD, the KPD still represented only a small portion of the organised working class. Meanwhile, the crisis in Russia that came to a head with the Kronstadt revolt led to a new course and a marked change in the relationship between the Comintern and its member-parties. In Russia itself, the tack towards capitalism of the New Economic Policy was combined with the ban on factions within the Bolshevik Party; internationally, the Comintern parties were to be 'Bolshevised', bringing them more firmly under control from Moscow.

Levi had reluctantly accepted the Twenty-One Conditions of autumn 1920, though describing them privately as 'legalese'. But, after the disaster of the March Action, he believed it essential that the European Communist parties should remain free to develop their own strategies, and this soon proved quite incompatible with the demands of the Comintern leadership in Moscow.

He could not refrain in this situation from a reconsideration of the Bolshevik Revolution as a whole, starting from Rosa Luxemburg's own concerns expressed in 1918. Clara Zetkin had returned from the Comintern's Third Congress with the plan for a full edition of Rosa Luxemburg's works – excluding, however, her unpublished pamphlet on the Russian Revolution, which was embarrassing from the Bolshevik point of view. For Levi, however, it was precisely the issues on which Luxemburg had criticised Bolshevik policy that had now come to the fore and demanded its publication.[58] In an extensive introduction that he wrote for the pamphlet, he focused on two of these issues in particular: land-ownership and democracy. It might have been unavoidable in the circumstances for the Bolsheviks to allow individual peasant-ownership of land, but the New Economic Policy had shown how this inevitably pulled Russia in a capitalist direction. Levi tied this to the question of democracy in an innovative way. He saw no guarantee that the soviet-form of government must express by its essential nature the rule of the proletariat, even in the Leninist system that distinguishes between the working people in general, the industrial proletariat as their 'front rank', and the Communist Party as the 'advance detachment' of the proletariat. A party cannot be walled off from the society around it, and peasant and capitalist influence would make itself felt within the soviet-government itself.

In this context, Levi made short shrift of the arguments with which official Communist dismissed the Kronstadt revolt:

> But there is one thing that we do know for sure, which is that neither tsarist generals nor French money nor Menshevik slogans are a sufficient explanation of how it was possible that the most loyal sons of the Revolution, the most devoted supporters of the Bolsheviks, who had so long been the élite of revolutionary fighters, proven in a hundred battles, rose up against those whom they formerly supported. This fact can only be explained by a profound crisis within the proletariat itself, a serious conflict that has arisen between the 'advance detachment' [i.e. the Communist Party] and the 'front-rank' [i.e. the working class], perhaps indeed within the 'advance-detachment' itself.[59]

In Germany, though the adventure of the March Action did not damage the KPD as fatally as Levi had feared, the 'Bolshevisation' to which it was now subjected tied it increasingly to shifting Russian requirements rather than the needs of the German workers' movement. Levi remained, as Carl

---

58. Though Luxemburg's manuscript had been lost in the chaos of revolution – it turned up in 1929 – the edition Levi published from her unfinished notes proved accurate in essentials. This was facilitated by his access to her library and manuscripts; these had been safeguarded after Rosa Luxemburg's death by Mathilde Jacob, who had subsequently worked as Levi's assistant and followed him out of the KPD.

59. 'Introduction to Rosa Luxemburg's pamphlet *The Russian Revolution*', below, pp. 244–5.

von Ossietsky would describe him, 'a revolutionary socialist of the Rosa Luxemburg school'. But it was precisely in this sense that he no longer saw the advance of revolution by way of winning the working class for the KPD. In its own way, the KPD had walled itself off from the society around it. The majority of workers still saw the SPD as their party, and it was here that he would have to find his place, working to develop revolutionary consciousness and always striving for united action across party lines.

Levi's critique of the Soviet Union sharpened as its new course at home and abroad took shape. In a 1924 essay, he speculated on the future course of the Bolshevik experiment. The Russian Revolution had undoubtedly given the German Revolution a decisive impetus, even if it was historically premature and many of its methods had been wrong. But:

> The Bolsheviks have not managed to halt the development at the point at which they took power. They are no longer the party that gathers social forces and leads them to a goal, but rather the expression of forces that are not proletarian, and whose goal is not socialist.

The most vital tendency in Russia was an almost savage nationalism, and, once the powerful economic energies of the country were developed, this nationalism threatened 'a new and bloody chapter of imperialism for Europe and the world'. 'For the first time in history, class-sentiment is being wielded as a means of diplomacy.'[60]

When Trotsky began to develop his own critique, Levi was interested enough to write a preface to the German edition of his pamphlet *The Lessons of October*, but glossed this in a characteristically 'Luxemburgist' sense:

> [T]he freedom that the Bolsheviks, like the tsars, claim for themselves reduces the amount of freedom for others and in this way loses all its qualities. And the Bolsheviks thus suffer the same burdens from their freedom as they once suffered from their unfreedom...not only rigid persecution but also rigid rule, condemn people to the life of a sect, and thus ultimately to political negation.[61]

---

60. *Sachverständigen-Gutachten und was dann? Zur innen- und aussenpolitischen Orientierung*, Berlin 1924; cited after Beradt 1969, p. 92.
61. Ibid., pp. 264–5.

On the rise of Stalin, Levi simply said to his friends: 'Genghis Khan has come to power.'[62]

While still hoping to rejoin the KPD, Levi had founded in summer 1921 a monthly magazine to which he gave the same name as his celebrated pamphlet, *Unser Weg*. Its subtitle changed from 'A Periodical for Communist Politics' to 'A Periodical for Socialist Politics' when his group rejoined the USPD. In the reunited Social-Democratic Party, however, a different kind of publication was needed, and, from February 1923, Levi produced the *Sozialistische und politische Wochentliche*.[63] This was no longer the journal of a group, but his own personal mouthpiece, and became popularly known as the 'Levi-Korrespondenz'. Here, he commented weekly on national and international events, bringing out, in particular, material on the Reichswehr and paramilitary groups, political trials and other reactionary phenomena. In an early issue, commemorating the fortieth anniversary of Marx's death, Levi chided equally those who sought to expunge from Marx's political doctrine the aspect of democracy and those who failed to recognise the aspect of force. He persistently championed the unity of proletarian forces which both SPD and KPD from their opposing perspectives rejected. His attention came to focus especially on the defence of the republic, which he consistently presented from the standpoint of the working class:

> The German republic is not firmly established....A counter-revolutionary Reichswehr is robbing it of free breath. A rebellious caste of officials lames its arms and legs. Cowardly assassination creeps like poison through its veins....The one thing that the Revolution has brought the German workers is in danger....The Social-Democratic Party will be able to hold together working class and Republic, the one for the other, only if it leads a clear, determined, and unambiguous policy for the working class...[64]

His comments on the Hitler Putsch of November 1923 also show a depth of perception that few at that time could match:

---

62. Beradt 1969, p. 93.
63. Mathilde Jacob signed for the *SPW* as the legally responsible publisher. Levi finally discontinued the *SPW* in 1928, merging it into the independent socialist publication *Der Klassenkampf*.
64. 'Why We Are Joining the USPD', below, pp. 297–8.

In its execution, this putsch is more grotesque and ridiculous than any previous attacks on the republic, but its consequences strike the Republic more seriously than any other....Previous attacks were all just shots from a pistol, metaphorically if not literally. This is the first movement which, grotesque as it may seem, grows out of a deep social movement, and we have to look it in the face. The deep shattering of the social edifice by the War and postwar is only now entering the consciousness of those affected by it....The Republic, for them, is almost identical with the cause of their sufferings. And to complete the misfortune: this republic has come to be identified with socialism to the degree that on the day...when those masses who now confront us as distant and hostile should rightly turn to us, socialism is devoid of any attractive force....It is no wonder then that hungry bodies and souls should begin to wander back to old dreams: this great layer of the desperate and the newly dispossessed is the social foundation....It supplied the so-called Hitler Putsch with the social resonance that the Kapp Putsch lacked.[65]

Levi had maintained his KPD Reichstag mandate of 1920 via the KAG and USPD back to the SPD. For the general election of May 1924, he was adopted by the district of Zwickau in 'red Saxony', which he continued to represent until his death. This was one of the poorest constituencies, semi-rural as well as industrial, and Levi regularly held meetings in remote villages, gave education-classes, and conducted petty legal cases. The SPD-fraction restricted his interventions in the Reichstag, though he was allowed to speak on issues of civil liberty and to represent the Party on the Reichstag's legal committee. This was one area in which modest gains could be made, and, when the SPD-press was increasingly barred to him, he found new outlets for his views in left-liberal publications that were often more sympathetic to this cause. Two pamphlets of his on military reform were also reference-points in party-debate. Levi found the discipline that turned the SPD-fraction into a voting machine for the leadership increasingly irksome, and said as much in his weekly articles. He had been seen by the SPD-leadership as a trouble-maker ever since the Independents had merged back into the Majority Party. According to them, he had already split two parties, and presented a similar

---

65. *SPW*, 19 November 1923; Beradt 1969, p. 87. Levi was one of the six 'arch-traitors' whose assassination the Nazis immediately called for in their one-day putsch.

risk to the SPD. But Levi made it clear from the point he rejoined the Social Democrats that the working class now needed unity, not division. He resisted calls from friends of his such as Carl von Ossietsky to organise a new left faction, such as would emerge again after his death with the Sozialistische Arbeiterpartei. Never inclined by temperament to the role of a party-leader, in the late 1920s he felt less at home with party-politics in general, and came to prefer his legal practice as a vehicle for political struggle.

In the 1920s, the number of 'treason'-trials in Germany was over a thousand per year. Even compared with the situation in the prewar-years, the authorities were ever ready to use draconian legislation to clamp down on writers and newspapers that disclosed information embarrassing to the government. This became Levi's particular speciality, and he won a wide reputation for his conduct of a string of important cases. The so-called 'Kuster/Jacob trial', one of the most celebrated, was typical in that it involved a journalist's disclosure of violations of the Versailles Treaty by the Reichswehr. The journalist, Berthold Jacob, and the public prosecutor here, Paul Jorns, were both to feature again in Levi's final and most dramatic case. Levi was also called on for cases of censorship and obscenity, successfully defending the film *Battleship Potemkin*, but unsuccessful in his defence of George Grosz: 'When I raised my eyes to the judges,' Levi wrote, 'I was immediately sure of a defeat; one of the judges had the exact features that Grosz had caricatured.'[66] Bertolt Brecht was another client, and despite the Communists' repeated attacks on their 'renegade' former leader, Willi Münzenberg and others prominent in the Party were happy to draw on Levi's legal skills.

The article 'Colleague Jorns' appeared anonymously in *Das Tagebuch*, whose publisher, Josef Bornstein, was sued for libel by Paul Jorns's superior, the Reich's chief public prosecutor. Jorns had been the prosecutor for the military court before which the murderers of Rosa Luxemburg and Karl Liebknecht appeared in 1919. Only one of the soldiers who fired at the pair had been convicted, and had immediately fled with false papers; one other, who struck them with his rifle-butt, was imprisoned for two years. The KPD had not pursued its own investigation, even when more settled conditions in Germany permitted this. Despite the limitations of his discoveries, the article's author, Berthold Jacob, had pressed to publish before the ten-year period for possible

---

66. *Literarische Welt*, vol. 26, no. 32; Beradt 1969, p. 116.

prosecution expired. Combining his privileges as defence-counsel and Reichstag deputy, Levi gained access to the hidden files, and dug out information to prove that Jorns had colluded in a flagrant miscarriage of justice. By the time Jorns appeared as a witness, Levi so dominated the proceedings that the prosecutor inadvertently referred to Jorns as 'the accused'. His summing-up speech, which Ossietsky called 'the greatest speech in German since Lassalle', was widely distributed as a pamphlet. Beyond the reputation of Jorns himself, Levi was able for the first time to present a thorough record of the murders of the two Spartacus leaders, 'the first case [in Germany] in which murderers killed and knew they could escape justice'.[67]

Even so, the publisher Bornstein was subsequently fined 500 marks for the unprovable allegation that Jorns had deliberately obstructed the course of justice. Jorns continued in office, and went on to become a senior legal official under the Nazi régime. In January 1930, he appealed against the original finding, and Levi was compelled, reluctantly this time, to re-enter the lists. On the third day of the hearing, he fell ill with pneumonia, and was taken to bed with a high fever. In his delirium, the murder of Rosa Luxemburg seems to have haunted him: 'We threw her over the bridge, she was still floating', he murmured, repeating what one of the soldiers had said in evidence.

Levi lived in an attic-flat on the fifth floor, and, in the early hours of 9 February, the nurse attending him came into his bedroom to find the window open and her patient fallen to his death.[68] Among the plethora of obituaries, Albert Einstein described him as 'one of the wisest, most just and courageous persons I have come across',[69] but two others particularly stand out. For the Jew-baiting *Der Stürmer*, Levi was 'driven to suicide by his racial stench'; while the *Rote Fahne*, still bearing the motto 'Founded by Rosa Luxemburg', wrote: 'Scarcely anyone hated the revolution as fanatically as Levi.' When the customary tribute to a deceased member was paid in the Reichstag, two parties demonstratively walked out: the Nazis and the KPD.

Paul Levi's life is just one small piece in the jigsaw of German history, but a piece that fits closely together with a larger piece: that of his lover, friend, and teacher Rosa Luxemburg. In so far as his biography helps illuminate any

---

67. Beradt 1969, pp. 119–26.
68. Beradt 1969, p. 147.
69. Beradt 1969, p. 127.

broader historical question, it is how the workers' movement in Germany might have developed differently had Luxemburg survived the events of January 1919.

With hindsight, the revolutionary movement in Germany was at its height at the end of 1918, and the *Spartakuswoche* was already a resistance to the burgeoning counter-revolution. Levi recognised this trend within a few months; it took longer to perceive from the Moscow meridian. But it was here that Luxemburg's classical Marxism faced its fundamental dilemma. Majority-revolution, the taking of power by a class, albeit with a necessary political leadership, assumes that the greater part of the working class will want this power. Luxemburg had expressed this beyond any ambiguity in the Spartacus programme: 'The Spartacus League will never take over governmental power except in response to the clear, unambiguous will of the great majority of the proletarian mass of Germany.'[70] The leftists, however, and especially those most eager to learn from the Bolshevik experience, saw this right away as a hostage to fortune.[71] As the wave of revolution ebbed, Paul Levi was forced to make the choice that Rosa Luxemburg had not had to face: press forward to revolution even in the absence of majority-support, or retreat to at least a temporary accommodation with bourgeois democracy. If Lenin shared Levi's disapproval of the 1921 March Action, it was, ultimately, on different grounds; for Lenin, the KPD had simply over-reached itself, while, for Levi, the means resorted to threatened to lead to a different end.

The choices made by Levi in the 1920s cannot arbitrarily be attributed to a hypothetically surviving Rosa Luxemburg. But they certainly indicate the points where she would likewise have had to choose. It seems likely that she, too, would have broken with the 'left communists' for the sake of union with the radical Independents. And it is hard to imagine that she, any more than Levi, would have accepted the Comintern's manipulation of proletarian militancy, and its counterpart in the Bolshevisation of the German Party. But would she then have sought to maintain a separate 'Spartacus' organisation, or rejoined the remerging Social Democrats?

70. 'What Does the Spartacus League Want?', in Hudis and Anderson (eds.) 2004, p. 356.
71. See Nettl 1966, vol. 2, pp. 790–1.

Rosa Luxemburg would surely have put up more of a struggle than Levi against a return to the SPD – not just by dint of character and conviction, but because she would have been better placed to do so. With her authority against the Comintern, the 'Leninist' party in Germany might have shrunk to an insignificant sect, with Spartacus hegemonising such revolutionary momentum as remained. Yet, even in this contingency, Rosa Luxemburg could not have escaped the question Levi was aware of as early as the Kapp Putsch: to defend the Weimar Republic or overthrow it. He made his choice early on: the achievements of the November Revolution were a working-class gain to be defended, providing at least a basis for further advance. Whatever Rosa Luxemburg's choices in this hypothetical scenario, it is certain that her politics would have taken a different course from the line that led from the March Action, through the 'German October' of 1923, to the suicidal policies of 'class against class'. And, as the threat of fascism intensified, Spartacists would have had less difficulty than 'Leninists' in joining hands with Social Democrats and liberals in a 'historic compromise' that might well have averted the plunge into the abyss.

Part One

Leading the KPD

Address to the Founding Congress of the KPD*

I am aware that it's no easy task to argue in favour
of the elections to the National Assembly.[1] I am also
aware that we ourselves are to blame for the difficult
situation. It was impossible for us to discuss unin-
hibitedly in the press whether we were for a national
assembly or a council-system. In this context, the
decision as to what our position is now that the
decision for the National Assembly has been made
has fallen into the background. The main problem
now is the mood that is making itself felt against
the National Assembly...people are trying to show
that a revolutionary spirit prevails in the provinces
and should be transposed to Berlin, where they are
already starting to depart from the proper path. The
question must be considered coolly and calmly.

* Translated from the stenographic report reproduced in Weber 1993. [The Spartakusbund held its conference in Berlin on 29 December 1918, transformed into the
founding conference of the Kommunistische Partei Deutschlands (Spartakusbund) on
30–1 December. Despite Levi's skilful handling of this difficult task, the leadership
weas defeated on this question by 62 votes to 23.]
1. [On 10 November 1918, after the abdication of Kaiser Wilhelm II, executive power
passed to the Council of People's Deputies made up of three members from the SPD
(the party-leader Friedrich Ebert, Philipp Scheidemann, Otto Landsberg) and three
from the USPD (Hugo Haase, Wilhelm Dittmann, Emil Barth). A Congress of Councils
convened on 16–21 December decided to hold elections to a national assembly for
19 January 1919. On 29 December 1918, the USPD-members resigned from the Council
of People's Deputies, and were replaced by Gustav Noske and Rudolf Wissell from
the SPD. When the National Assembly convened on 13 February 1919, a government
was formed under Scheidemann as chancellor, supported by the SPD, the German
Democratic Party and the (Catholic) Centre Party. It was Scheidemann who had
reluctantly proclaimed the Republic from the Reichstag balcony on 9 November, to
forestall the proclamation of a workers' republic by Karl Liebknecht. In the elections
to the National Assembly, the SPD won 37.9% of the vote and the USPD 7.6%.]

All power should be based on a council-government as against a national assembly. We agree on this. The proletariat is forced to emerge from this chaotic situation and create new forms for dealing with economic and political affairs. It goes without saying that the idea of a council-constitution, coming from the east, conceived by the revolutionary proletariat in the east, was bound to have a powerful fascination on the minds of the German proletariat. It goes without saying, too, that the proletariat is deeply aware that it is only on the basis of the council-system that it can achieve a genuine grip on political power, a genuine seizure of power in both state and society. It goes without saying, and everyone agrees, that only the model of a council-constitution [offers] that marvellous unification in which will and deed go hand in hand, in which the proletariat is not just limited to casting votes through representatives in a parliament and leaving the whole executive power to a staff of specialists and officials, that this alone gives it the possibility of penetrating the whole state and economic structure with a socialist spirit. And it also goes without saying, for all of us, that only in this assertion, only in the living seizure of the whole state and economic structure, will the idea of socialism grow in the proletariat itself. It is also only in this living struggle that the sense will be aroused that it is possible for it to fill the vessel of socialism with a socialist spirit. And besides, party-comrades, if we were to have even a minute of doubt, even just theoretically, as to whether we should prefer a council-constitution or a national assembly, then political development in Germany would be immediately such that it would be bound to end in defeat for the proletariat.

The National Assembly is the banner of counter-revolution. The National Assembly is conceived as a fortress that the counter-revolution is seeking to build, and in which it wants to withdraw with all its defences intact: with Ebert and Scheidemann, with all its generals, with Hindenburg and Gröner,[2] with all its economic powers, with Stinnes and Thyssen and the directors of the Deutsche Bank, it intends to seek its survival in the National Assembly. It

---

2. [Marshal Paul von Hindenburg became chief of the general staff in 1916 after a distinguished military career. His popularity with the public was a major asset for the German Right, both at this time and when he was elected president in 1925 and again in 1932. Wilhelm Gröner, as quartermaster-general of the armed forces, supervised the German retreat and surrender in October/November 1918, and assured Ebert the support of the army. August Thyssen and Hugo Stinnes were leading industrialists.]

needs the National Assembly as the anchor to which it will be able to tie once more its floating bark.

Comrades, we are perfectly clear about all this. There is not the least difference between you and us on this score. We know quite exactly that the path of the proletariat to victory can only pass over the corpse of the National Assembly. I use the word corpse, though in Berlin it has in a certain sense come into disrepute. We also have no doubt about something else. The National Assembly will be, quite in accordance with the wishes of the bourgeoisie, quite in accordance with the wishes of its agents Ebert and Scheidemann, a ready instrument in the hands of the counter-revolution. There is no doubt that, in this National Assembly, the representatives of the determined revolutionary tendency will find themselves in a minority. Party-comrades, despite this, we propose to you that the elections to the National Assembly should not be ignored. We propose to you that we should contest these elections to the National Assembly with all our powers.

[SHOUTS: 'Never! No!']

Let me continue! You can say your 'Never!' when I've finished. We propose to you that we enter these elections and fight them through with all the resolution and energy and readiness for struggle, I tell you, that you have shown in every struggle, for every position that the counter-revolution has up to now confronted you with.

[SHOUTS: 'Waste of energy!']

Comrades! You say waste of energy. Yes, the comrade is right. If positions that the counter-revolution sets up before us can be taken without an expenditure of energy, without our storming them, then Comrade Kahlert is correct. As long as the bourgeoisie is not prepared to do this, as long as it forces us to struggle, it is then our task to take up the struggle with the bourgeoisie for every position in which it is to be found.

[INTERJECTION: 'By revolution!']

All your interjections essentially come to the same thing, and you will perhaps allow me to discuss in advance those objections that are not too far off course. You say that entry into the National Assembly and participation in the elections is a useless expenditure of energy. If I understand you correctly, you mean that it will be just a talking shop, as the Reichstag was. They will sit down and talk to each other, give fine speeches and go their various ways, and this means nothing for the revolution. But don't believe this is such an original objection, or that we didn't take it into account. This objection is not too far off course. I ask you to consider the following: think of the history of parliamentarism in the German Reichstag. Where did its weakness lie? Its weakness and the weakness of the Social Democrats in the Reichstag consisted in the fact that they were supposed to act as revolutionaries in parliament at a time when no revolutionary situation existed. Read for example the speeches of Bebel in the Reichstag from the 1890s, or even the early years of this century. They were supposed to make revolution when there wasn't any revolution. They limited themselves to speaking about it and prophesying the threatening revolution, and the glaring contradiction between a revolutionary phraseology and the lack of a revolutionary situation in the working class and the state was bound in the end to drive the Social-Democratic fraction into that outward inactivity for which we all abhor the German Reichstag.

But what is the situation today? If your representatives enter the National Assembly, are they just going to keep still and prophesy the coming revolution? Isn't the situation rather one in which, even if there are only a couple of your representatives there, they can march into that chamber and speak like Frederick the Great's ambassador in London: 'Behind me march the millions of German people!' Can they not, if they enter today, throw onto the scales a quite different force, not just moral but also physical? You say that the proletarians should do everything. They should come out on the streets with hand-grenades. Yes, comrades, but does the one thing exclude the other? Isn't what you are telling me the necessary and self-evident complement of action in parliament?

That is precisely the difference between what you see in parliament and what we understand by it. You see in parliament only the crippled figure that parliament was and had to be, so long as the proletariat was not in a revolutionary situation. Today we have a different situation. Your representatives would enter parliament today not to give speeches, not to chat, not to propose motions for improvements, not to negotiate in commissions with other representatives, not to tack this way and that. They will have to stand and struggle with the threat of open force that stands behind these proletarian representatives.

[INTERJECTION: *'Then we could have stayed in the USPD!'*]

No, esteemed comrades, no, comrades, what ultimately divides us from the USPD, and what divides the comrades who made the interjection from us, is precisely that we say that the USPD was never at any time prepared to cast onto the scales the great weight of revolutionary readiness for sacrifice, of revolutionary force, that it shrinks from the ultimate consequences of revolutionary struggle, and that, on this account, it will not be prepared in the future to draw those ultimate consequences and conclusions that must be drawn and from which none of us shrink back.

And I say, party-comrades, if today you give the bourgeoisie the possibility of forming a national assembly, of meeting there, while you remain outside, what options do you have? You have the option of coming out with armed force, and, if you can manage it, chasing its representatives away. The option is there. Suppose that you have the physical power, whatever it might be, that is needed, that you have physical power at the place where the National Assembly meets. And what happens then? Then the National Assembly is chased away, and all your burning desires are fulfilled. And tell me one thing: will you have broken the real power of the bourgeoisie, the real power of the counter-revolution, by this chasing away? I say not! You can chase away the National Assembly. You can imprison four hundred German bourgeois and shut them away somewhere safe, and yet the counter-revolution will still continue on its march, exactly as if these four hundred men were still there.

Your position is a different one. You have to penetrate into every trench that the bourgeoisie builds against you, and storm the trench in tough struggle, hand to hand. You also have to struggle and again struggle against all attacks in this parliament, and I say, struggle in a different way than before, than with speeches. You have to appear with the consciousness that behind you stands the power of the proletariat. Only in these struggles, party-comrades, can you morally overcome the enemy, and only in these struggles will things come to the point that, if you should be forced to overcome the enemy physically, the outcome of the physical struggle will be that the bourgeoisie will suffer a political defeat in a stronghold that it has itself erected, which will really be the end for it. You can say if you like that this is not a political defeat. But you can overcome them in struggle, that is the point at which the bourgeoisie will permanently lose its power-position in Germany. In Russia, as you know, the Bolsheviks always took part in elections to the National Assembly. The

Bolsheviks did this, although they knew that they would be only a tiny minority in the National Assembly. And only when a situation developed in the course of the elections that meant that objectively the National Assembly was overtaken by the actual condition that Russia had reached, did they chase away the National Assembly.

[INTERJECTION: *'Let's get on with it!'*]

You say, let's get on with it. What makes you so sure that the whole of Germany today is already at such an advanced stage of revolution as the comrade believes? Of course, it may be. We can do it in Berlin, in Rhineland-Westphalia conditions may be right, perhaps also in Upper Silesia. But are these three districts Germany? I say no! I say that, behind this power that the National Assembly is seeking to erect, and the dissolution of which you see as the complete political collapse of the bourgeoisie, there must be more than these three centres that I just mentioned, and that you believe give a picture of German conditions.

The Bolsheviks initially, when no one stood behind them, took part in elections to their National Assembly, and only when the process of decomposition had progressed so far that at the end of the whole campaign and when the National Assembly met they had the power behind them, only at that moment did they concentrate on chasing away the National Assembly. It is not true that the Russians invented a tactic like you imagine, that at the beginning they said, when these people come together we'll chase them away. On the contrary, they prepared themselves to enter the National Assembly, in order to speak and act there.

It seems to me that the whole conception that prevails here is still a highly external and crude conception of the concepts of revolution and counter-revolution, which believes that you can make revolution, and that you can strangle the counter-revolution, by seizing on one or other of its symptoms. That's not the way things are. You have to attack every position in which you come face to face with the bourgeoisie. You have to take possession of any position in the electoral struggle.

Party-comrades! I only ask you to imagine the consequences that would result if we did not take part in the national elections. I ask you to consider the following: the comrade from Wilhelmshaven, who is so fond of making interjections, will please consider this, that there certainly may be a large number of people who stuck with us right through the War. It may be that these would understand a boycott of the elections. But think of the immense number who are now taking part in the elections for the first time, whether they were drawn into the maelstrom of political activity for the first time by the revolution, or that immense throng of young people and women who have acquired the right to vote for the first time. If you now give out the slogan of a boycott of the elections, you will never at any time succeed in reaching that powerful throng who sympathise with us inwardly, who stand with us inwardly, and whom we could get to join with us in a short space of time; they will stand aside from us. And we shall as you say, Comrade Rühle,[3] not pursue any kind of tomfoolery with them, we shall rather drive them into the camp of those who really will use them for their tomfoolery. That will be the success of your whole tactic. Comrades, you basically seem to have already made up your mind. I would just like to say something to you in all seriousness, and ask you not to decide on the basis of preconceived opinions that you've brought with you from home.

The question is serious. We all see the situation as being one in which decision on this question can determine the fate of our movement for months ahead. We insist completely on the deep and decisive importance of this question. We do not mean, party-comrades, that if you decide this question differently from ourselves, it will be the death of the German Revolution, of course not. But it will hinder our movement for a good while to come. Just consider the following situation. The National Assembly is convened. For months to come, it may well dominate the whole political picture of Germany, and you cannot prevent this. It will stand at the centre of the political movement in Germany. You will not be able to prevent all eyes from looking at it, and even your best supporters having to orient themselves towards it, inform themselves and ask what is going on in the National Assembly. It will enter the consciousness of the German proletariat, and against this fact do you really want to stand and act outside?

Party-comrades! You want to dissolve the National Assembly. What would you say, for example, if the National Assembly was meeting in a town like Schilda?

[INTERJECTION: *'Then it would have condemned itself!'*]

---

3. [Otto Rühle had been an SPD-deputy in the Reichstag and followed Liebknecht in opposing the War. He joined the KAPD when this was founded in 1920.]

Nothing condemns itself if it represents such a powerful force as the German bourgeoisie. The German bourgeoisie is constituting itself, gathering its whole power, creating an organ with the object of suppressing the revolution once more, and then you come along and say, it condemns itself. It does not condemn itself. It is our duty to go into that building, it is our duty to hurl firebrands into those positions, our duty to take up the struggle as much as we would do in any other situation where the bourgeoisie confronts us head on. The bottom line is this: where the bourgeoisie constructs its positions, where it concentrates all its forces one more time, where it is ready to take up the struggle again, are we going to say that we won't get involved? And I tell you, with this decision you will do yourselves and our movement the greatest damage.

Letter to Lenin (1919)*

Esteemed Comrade Lenin, I am taking the first opportunity to let you have a brief report on our situation.

The detailed circumstances of the events in Berlin you will see from a small pamphlet that I am also sending you at this time.[1] Berlin is still experiencing the most savage form of terror, we are personally forced to live illegally, and we have had to move part of our activity which is difficult or impossible underground, such as publication of the newspaper, the office, etc. to Leipzig while the terror in Berlin is at its worst.

Apart from this, I believe I can say that, despite the ravages of the white guards, the movement has not suffered. The anger is unbounded, and above all the strike-movement that got under way has not been brought to a halt even by the Berlin bloodbath. It is already starting up again afresh. In Rhineland-Westphalia, the movement has broken out again, Wurtemburg will follow in the next few days, Upper Silesia is in ferment, etc.

We see these partial strikes, which all have a political character, as, in a certain sense, unwelcome. They are

---

* This letter, dated 27 March 1919, is translated after Beradt (ed.) 1969, from a copy in the Paul Levi archive.

1. [This was Levi's pamphlet *Generalstreik und Noske-Blutbad in Berlin*, published under a pseudonym. Gustav Noske, effectively minister of defence in 1919–20, deployed the Freikorps to crush the revolutionary workers in the early months of 1919.]

certainly very powerful in the particular districts of the Reich in which they break out, but as long as they remain partial, the government has the resources to repress the political movement again. Since we see the possibility of victory only in a general strike across the whole of Germany, we do nothing to call for partial strikes, and, in certain cases, we do everything we can to restrain people from giving the government any kind of opportunity for spilling blood. We can hold back the proletarians from this – but not the government. Not from simply striking: the workers literally walk out of the factories themselves, so great is their bitterness. On the other hand, we cannot, of course, act as a brake on the strike-movement; especially since the general strike will to all appearance be triggered in Germany by an ever quicker succession of partial strikes. There is, however, to a certain degree, a syndicalist current present in Germany: it is sometimes not easy to hold our people back from such follies. Especially since even within our organisation we have certain attempts from that camp, which led directly to a coup d'état[2] within our organisation.

The murder of Leo[3] in particular, and the interruption for over a week in the appearance of a newspaper due to the events I described, concentrated people's minds: we have therefore called a conference for tomorrow in order to clarify what our position is towards syndicalism and the question of the general strike.

In party-politics the situation is as follows:

The position of the Ebert-Scheidemann government has been shattered. It only survives by grace of the bourgeoisie, and all signs point to this grace not being extended very much longer.

In the broad layers of the proletariat, they are on their last legs. The slaughters that they caused throughout the whole of the Reich, the lack of results that is apparent now to everyone, have had the effect that even the section of the bourgeoisie that hopes to damp down the revolution by way of concessions (e.g. *Frankfurter Zeitung*, *Vossische Zeitung*) is dissatisfied with this lack of results.

---

2. [An attempted 'coup d'état' by the strong ultra-left faction.]
3. [Leo Jogisches was murdered by Freikorps soldiers on 10 March 1919.]

It goes without saying that the Independents, as well as ourselves, are drawing the greatest advantage from this development, especially since they have now once again made themselves out to be extraordinarily radical, and, by radical speeches, are trying to make people forget how they collaborated with the *whole* policy of Ebert and Scheidemann as long as they were tolerated by them in government[4] – both domestic and foreign policy. They collaborated in making the councils powerless. They ratified the summoning of the National Assembly.

They also collaborated in the whole policy against Russia; indeed, they were its original inspirers. We assume you know that already on 12 November [1918], i.e. the day after the session of the Berlin Workers' and Soldiers' Council that decided to resume relations with you, the Reich government, with the agreement of the three Independents, decided not to commence negotiations with you; this was decided on the proposal of Kautsky himself, with the argument that 'we would make ourselves unpopular with the Entente', that the Berlin plenipotentiary council's invitation to the first council-congress was blocked by the government, that Haase and Dittmann voted for this, that, on 12 December, the Independent members of the government all decided to propose to the Entente a common struggle against Bolshevism.

'Public opinion' in Germany, as you know, has now undergone a change. There is an 'eastern orientation'. Now, the Independents are again calling as loud as they can for unity with Russia.

Kautsky himself has, meanwhile, travelled to Russia. There can be no doubt that this wretch now intends to play the role of 'mediator' with Russia in Germany.

It follows from all this that the greatest obstacle for us at present is the ambiguity and lies of the Independents. In domestic policy, it would thus be of greatest interest for us if you could treat Kautsky so that it can be recognised clearly here what you think of these elements. The best for us would be if you let us have an official declaration as to how you assess Kautsky and the policies of the USPD (domestic and foreign).

---

4. See above, p. 35, note 1.

If negotiations with the Ebert-Scheidemann government are necessary in your interest (something that we cannot judge), we would prefer it if a bourgeois could act as intermediary; then, at least, the USPD would be deprived of the possibility of creeping around here with your 'friendship'.

With best greetings,
Yours, Hartstein[5]

5. [A pseudonym that Levi had used since the Spartacus period.]

The Munich Experience: An Opposing View*

I believe that, before one begins a discussion, it is best to focus on the facts that one discusses with somewhat greater precision than Comrade Werner has done. The history of the Munich Soviet Republic[1] may be concisely rendered in the following manner: Majority-Socialists, Independents and anarchists decide on a 'Soviet Republic' in the Café Stephani and environs, whose sovereign empire reaches from Schwabing to Pasing and from Laim to Freimaring. The Communists oppose this soviet-republic with the most trenchant criticism. This soviet-republic did not suffer from premature birth, as Comrade Werner[2] claims, but was rather a *prodigiosum aliquid*,

* Published in *Die Internationale*, I, no. 9/10 (4 August 1919). Translation from Gruber (ed.) 1967.

1. [With the fall of the monarchy on 7 November 1918, workers' and soldiers' councils were formed in Munich, and a socialist coalition-government under the Independent Kurt Eisner. Elections to a Bavarian state-assembly were held in January 1919, with the Majority-Socialists the largest party, but, when Eisner was on his way to its first meeting on 21 February, intending to offer his resignation, he was assassinated by the monarchist Count Anton von Arco-Valley. Political chaos was combined with economic paralysis; on 7 April, a group of left intellectuals including the playwright Ernst Toller proclaimed the Soviet Republic of Bavaria, and the SPD government under Johannes Hoffmann retreated to Bamberg. Four days later, an attempted coup by the exiled government's defence-minister Ernst Schneppenhorst swept away this 'first' soviet-republic, and the direction of resistance under Eugen Leviné and Max Levien led to a 'second', Communist soviet-government. By the end of March, the revolutionary struggles in north Germany had been crushed by the Freikorps, whom Ebert now sent against Bavaria. The troops entered Munich on 1 May, killing some 700 people in a white terror. Leviné was executed for 'high treason', though Levien managed to escape.]

2. ['Comrade Werner' was Paul Frölich, member of the KPD Zentrale and, at this time, a supporter of the left faction.]

that is, a freak; as a human child cannot issue from the womb of a female gorilla, so little can a soviet-republic issue from the womb of a Majority-Socialist/Independent/anarchist coffee-house clique.

This soviet-republic was just in the process of passing over into the Elysian Fields – meaning into the memoirs and feuilletons of its generally poetically gifted leaders – when the Hoffmann government staged a putsch against it on 13 April. The purpose of this putsch was less concerned with giving the *coup de grâce* to the mortally sick patient than with its revival, in order to give Schneppenhorst and others a fine opportunity for a bloodbath. This was the second phase. The position of our Party during this second phase involved taking over and directing the defence against the putsch. Out of this defensive action grew without special restraint the third phase: the Communist Soviet Republic.

How could the Party conduct itself in relation to these three phases?

I trust that we are all agreed on the first phase. This 'soviet-republic' was the result of a putsch, a very clumsy one at that, not staged by the working masses, but by a handful of literati who are now appealing for a full measure of mercy on the part of the tribunals. They deserve it in accordance with the proverb: Forgive them who know not what they do.

Confronted with this situation, Comrade Werner believes that it was incumbent upon the Communists to 'apply the brakes'. I do not share that opinion. A Communist never holds back. When he calls a spade a spade, a putschist a putschist, when he exposes illusions for what they are, when he reveals the impotence, incompetence, and the immaturity of political actions – he does not 'retard' but *leads* the revolution. Only people who believe that wherever there is noise there must also be a revolution will call this applying the brakes.

Accordingly, our Party stood with its trenchant criticism in the forefront of the Revolution; so far, there existed everywhere complete agreement on the conduct of our Munich comrades, or rather it existed until Comrade Werner began to defend the Munich action.

Until now, we had all been of the opinion that the Munich comrades had viewed the soviet-republic of Toller, Mühsam, etc. as one of those comedies whose rapid collapse was required in the interest of the progress of the revolution. The Munich comrades themselves clearly recognised that this Munich

Republic lacked any relationship with the Bavarian and particularly with the German proletarian revolution.

In his reflections on the question of free will, Comrade Werner embraces a personal and political determinism. I do not touch this question here as a philosophical speculation: in everyday matters, I can manage without it. 'To make revolutionary politics means to act in accordance with a clear, well-defined revolutionary will', says Comrade Werner. My formulation is shorter: to make revolutionary politics means to act rationally in the interest of the revolution. In this manner, I skip around Werner's problem of the will. When Comrade Werner then continues to say that 'the "firmly defined will" is not solely determined by general tactical precepts and guiding principles, but is dependent upon the situation', he is actually quite correct. But it is not the 'will' which is dependent upon the situation, but the *decision*. Thus things fall into place even without determinism.

Back to the situation. As outlined above, we have, on the one hand, a dying soviet-republic, and deficient maturity on the part of the whole German proletariat for the task of the seizure of power, and, on the other hand, the impossibility of establishing a soviet-republic in Munich. Out of this situation, developed with physical necessity the politics pursued by the Munich [comrades] until 13 April. Comrade Werner believes that the existence of the pseudo-soviet-republic imposed certain obligations on us. Not that I know of. 'The pseudo-soviet-republic did not expire as a result of our criticism.' This may be true, but what our criticism did not accomplish, Toller, Mühsam, Landauer, etc. accomplished of their own accord. 'However weak, it constituted a real government.' True, but what kind of government! If it was revolutionary, we had to be part of it; if it was not, it might as well go to the devil and make room for another that at least did not arouse illusions in the proletariat.

'The only factor which gave it a treacherous appearance was that it called itself a soviet-republic.' This 'only' of Comrade Werner speaks volumes, for behind this 'only' hides the most important fact: it just was not a soviet-government.

This Munich soviet-government was actually a nothing, neither fish nor fowl, neither roast nor salad. But, from the nothingness of this government, Comrade Werner infers that we were compelled to take up the open fight against it, with all its consequences, culminating in the 'seizure of power which we ourselves considered altogether too narrowly based'. What does that mean? It means to replace an Independent/Majority-Socialist/anarchist 'soviet-republic', established with insufficient support among the masses, by a communist soviet-republic with the same shortcoming – and, according to Comrade Werner's own description, inevitably so – as the other. This means to replace one nothing with another. Comrade Werner calls that 'to act in accordance with a clear, well-defined revolutionary will'. Others call it something else, call it in fact an aimless drifting in the political whirlpool. I do not believe in fate in politics, in a fate inflicted on us by mighty gods, let alone in a fate concocted by six bar-cronies in a corner of the Café Luitpold.

But I am looking ahead, and I do not want to have the Munich comrades suffer for the defence which Comrade Werner inflicts on them. Considering the unequivocal attitude of Leviné it cannot be assumed that the Munich comrades vacillated to the point indicated in Werner's description; in fact, the really difficult situation arose for them during the second phase, with the Hoffmann putsch.

I distinguish, in this second phase, two alternatives. One was the defence of the 'pseudo-soviet-republic'. As has been generally agreed, the Toller-Mühsam soviet-republic was a nothing, from which I draw the conclusion that one does not defend a nothing. The fatherland of Toller-Mühsam was distinguished only in degree, not in principle, from that of the house of Wittelsbach. If the action of the Munich comrades had been nothing but a defensive gesture on behalf of the ungracefully dying Toller-republic, it would be in, my opinion, inadmissible both from a logical and tactical point of view.

But the comrades who describe it simply as such a defensive action of the soviet-republic do it injustice. It was a trifle more. It was a defensive action on behalf of certain real positions of power attained by the proletariat during the months of the revolution, particularly in Munich. Should the Munich proletariat have defended them with gun in hand? In view of the unfinished state of revolutionary development at that time we followed the tactic of evading an armed struggle throughout Germany even in the face of an offensive act by advance of the counter-revolution, because a victorious conclusion of an armed struggle appeared impossible. This tactic was applied with all our consent in Bremen, in Braunschweig, in Leipzig, in Gotha, Erfurt, indeed everywhere. But, I admit, matters in Munich were different. As far as I can judge the situation from a distance, the position of the Munich proletariat was such that it did not have to stand by while its rights created by the revolution were being wrested from its hands. The Bavarian government, on the basis of its own strength, was unable to move against it. Waiting before the gates, however, were Noske, Haase, etc., eager to move in. But, here, the Hoffmann government was limited as well. In view of certain Bavarian peculiarities, it could not afford to open the gates willy-nilly to the 'Prussians' and other foreigners. In addition, the mere fact that the Munich proletariat held on to its revolutionary position might not have been a sufficient reason for the Hoffmann people to take refuge with the 'Prussians'. The Hoffmann government might well have been obliged to come to terms with the Munich proletariat.

Accordingly, I believe that the Munich comrades made the correct decisions during the second phase as well.

Then came the third phase.

The defence 'resulted in a victory and this victory had to be liquidated. There was no longer a turning back.' What does Comrade Werner mean by the liquidation of the victory?

Does he mean by 'liquidation of victory' that one lays hold of everything delivered up by the moment without consideration as to whether one can hold on to it?...But should the liquidation of the victory not have meant instead the determination of what corresponded to the inner development of the revolution? In that case the result would have been different.

'There was no longer a turning back. The most essential prerequisite existed; the victorious action of the masses. The soviet-republic had become the only alternative.' Well, Comrade Werner. Indeed! At the end of his exposition Comrade Werner states that the action of the masses constitutes the essential prerequisite not only for the establishment of a Munich but of a Bavarian soviet-republic. At the beginning of his exposition, Comrade Werner spoke differently.

> We Communists considered a soviet-republic consisting of Bavaria alone an absurdity....A soviet-republic without the areas of large-scale industry and the coalfields is impossible in Germany. Besides, the Bavarian proletariat is only in a few large industrial plants genuinely disposed toward revolution....A Bavarian soviet-republic appeared to us for this reason from the beginning a mistaken undertaking.

Thus spoke Comrade Werner at the beginning. He seems to belong to that category of people who are wiser before entering a discussion than after. Too much meditation does not agree with him. For the time being, I side with Comrade Werner's earlier view and raise the question: Did anything happen between 6 and 13 April which changed these true prognoses of a Bavarian soviet-republic? No, nothing at all. The Bavarian soviet-republic was on 13 April as much an absurdity as on the 6th, and the 'victorious action' at the large plants of Maffei, Krupp. etc., was not a sufficient basis, constituted no 'essential prerequisite' for a Bavarian soviet-republic, on 13 April as little as on 6 April.

But, I repeat: injustice is being done to the Munich comrades if one judges them on the basis of Comrade Werner's defence. Their decision was not as blatantly wrong as it must appear from Comrade Werner's defence. The difficulty of their decision did not lie in the sphere of political calculation – here, the case was as clear as daylight – but in that of political psychology. We are often required to tread along different paths from those of the masses. The masses have as yet not completely comprehended our programme – otherwise we would already have reached our goal. They often continue along other paths than those desired by us, in which case we have recourse to criticism. No one among us has any scruples on this score, because the difference between us and the masses usually consists of our wish for action, while the masses remain passive.

It is for this reason that it is particularly hard for us when the reverse is the case, when the masses proceed with action while we have to tell them that the action is useless or injurious to the interest of the revolution. Before we declare ourselves opposed to the action, we have to make doubly and triply sure whether we cannot turn it to our advantage. But there can be no serious doubt that this must be our position. If the masses proceed with actions which are only pseudo-revolutionary and in reality can only lead to setbacks, it is our duty to step forward with warnings and criticism, as was done by the Munich comrades. To place ourselves, however, at the head of the movement, if the masses move ahead nevertheless, though it can only lead to trouble – that obligation we do not have. Not only for our own sake, but also for the sake of the masses who will thus be enabled, in the face of the setback and the disappointment, to seek support in the derided critics of yesterday...

The Munich comrades failed to take into account one additional factor. The grievous dénouement of the Munich action involved essentially no setback for us in Germany, aside from the terrible loss of some of our best comrades-in-arms.[3] The German revolutionary working-class movement hardly suffered as a result of the Munich events. For unknown reasons, however, it appears that Munich has stirred up abroad, particularly in Russia and Hungary, illusions about the possibilities for revolution in Germany, which fail to be substantiated by the conditions of the whole German revolutionary movement, but which could actually become highly dangerous for Hungary, Austria, and even Russia. We are presently involved not only in a German but in a worldwide revolution, and in viewing every possibility for action we should not lose sight of the possibility of a reaction not only at home but against the world-revolution.

Was it necessary to say all this? Yes, for the sake of clarity and our future. Is it possible to reproach anyone? No, I do not lift a stone against any person.

---

3. [This statement of Levi's may sound surprising, in view of the considerable resonance that the Munich soviet has had for the Left down the years. But confirmation is given by Broué 2005, who dispatches it with a mere three paragraphs (pp. 280-1) in his thousand-page book.]

The Political Situation and the KPD
(October 1919)*

[...] Given all this, German economic life presents a completely hopeless picture. And this hopelessness becomes particularly clear if we examine the hopes that the German bourgeoisie gives itself. It has two hopes in particular. One of these is the American loan. To speak cautiously, it has to be said that the loan that Germany would have to ask to set its economy to rights amounts to several hundred billion, and not even rich America is in a position to afford this, especially as the American bourgeoisie, to the extent that it is in a position to make loans, will first of all have to help its former allies, especially France, Italy and Belgium.

The other hope is that the German bourgeoisie will operate virtually as a subcontractor for British and American capital, in other words import raw materials, produce goods for wages and then re-export them. This path too is inaccessible, simply because the German bourgeoisie cannot take it if it is not to deny its own existence. If it just becomes an Anglo-American subcontractor, it will have completely ceased to be master of its own capital.

* Translated from the pamphlet *Die politische Lage und die K.P.D. Rede von P. Levy* [sic] *auf dem Oktober-Parteitag nebst den vom Parteitag angenommenen Leitsätzen* (KPD, December 1919). Levi's speech began with a lengthy analysis of the international economic and political situation that is omitted here. The 'Basic Principles' at the end were supplemented by similar principles on parliamentarism and on the trade-unions.

If you look at this whole picture of the economic and political situation, you have to conclude that the crisis that has shattered Germany economically and politically has not come to an end with the Versailles peace-treaty and the ratification of the German constitution. The worst consequences of the crisis that the War brought about are still only now on the horizon. We are not at the end of the great crisis that the War visited on Germany and the world, but at its beginning. We are, objectively, only at the beginning of the crisis, and, subjectively as well, we are only at the beginning of the crisis. For all the major strata of society that formerly kept their distance from the German Revolution will only now notice what the War and the crisis mean for them. Only the tax-demand, the enforced reduction of their salaries, their rising impoverishment, will tell the middle class and the civil servants what the capitalist war has brought them. It is not the fact that we make them speeches that will drive these layers into the revolution; the consequences that they feel in their own persons are what will bring them towards us in the camp of revolution.

And, in all this, the question is, how should the proletariat conduct itself in this situation, how should the Communist Party conduct itself? The overall situation of the proletariat is clear. Up to now, it has suffered external defeat after defeat, the counter-revolution has advanced from one stage to another. Its position and its task is indicated in Marx's words:

> Revolutionary progress cleared a path for itself not by its immediate, tragic-comic achievements, but, on the contrary, by creating a powerful and united counter-revolution; only in combat with this opponent did the insurrectionary party mature into a real party of revolution.[1]

This describes the task of the Communist Party clearly. It must form the nucleus of the determined party of revolutionary overthrow.

The counter-revolution has powerfully constructed itself. With greater barbarism than ever it uses the state of siege and Noske's guards, murder and imprisonment, muzzling of the press and judicial terror, 'people's courts' and military courts, forces of strike-breakers and treacherous moral assassination. Politically and economically, intertwining the two like fascines of a rampart, the counter-revolution has built up its defence; the task of the Communist

---

1. 'The Class Struggles in France', Marx 2010b, p. 35.

Party is to lead the troops that will take this fortress. And we must ascertain, without prettifying and without hate and without exaggeration, the extent to which the Party is ready for this task, and we must conclude, without haste and without exaggeration, that the Party is not yet up to this task. The Party finds itself in a state of complete breakdown; the Party has fundamentally departed from the clear path that Marxist theory prescribes to it. The Party has fallen into a most serious sickness, which I can describe in one word: syndicalism. This syndicalist sickness has not been brought into our Party from outside, it has developed inside the Party, and it has its base in Hamburg.

It is now my task to prove this to you. Only if you are convinced of this sickness will you let yourselves be convinced that we have to use all possible means to cure the Party of this sickness.

What is the core of the syndicalist theory? Syndicalism proceeds from the fact that the proletarian is exploited economically in the factories. On this fact, which is quite correct in itself, syndicalism builds its theory. A simple recipe. If all proletarians refuse to let themselves be exploited any more, then all political oppression, all unfreedom and subjugation will disappear right away. And how are the proletarians to abolish economic exploitation? Here, too, we have the simplest means in the world: the proletarian no longer allows himself to be exploited, he goes on strike, he seeks to bring his comrades out with him in a general strike, and, from this general strike, or it may even be a series of strikes, comes the 'great day' on which, as a result of the destruction of the economy by strike-action, the bourgeoisie collapses, immediately and completely, like Minerva appearing from the head of Zeus.

There are three characteristics in particular by which syndicalism stands in opposition to Communism.

Syndicalism sees revolution as a purely economic process. If the proletarians, as the syndicalists say, are exploited only in the factories, then they can also liberate themselves only in the factories. We Communists, on the other hand, say: 'Of course exploitation only takes place in the factories, but the means by which the bourgeoisie forces the proletariat into exploitation are political means.' State-power with all its forms of expression, police and military, press and courts, parliament and propaganda, are the means by which it bows the proletariat's neck under the yoke. We have to fight these political means with political means; the first step in the proletariat's struggle for liberation is for us the conquest of political power and its exercise in a dictatorial way. Syndicalism refuses the struggle for political power, whereas we give it pride of place.

Secondly, because syndicalism sees revolution as a purely economic struggle, it rejects all political means on the part of the proletariat as harmful, and it rejects, above all, the political party. We Communists however, because we wage a political struggle, see the political party as the life principle of the revolution, and the Communist Party as the leader of revolutionary struggle.

Thirdly, the syndicalists see the general strike as the alpha and omega of the revolution; the revolution begins and ends with it. Constantly making propaganda for the general strike, gathering the masses for the general strike, creating an organisation that can lead the general strike: that is revolutionary activity. We Communists, however, say that there is no single recipe for revolution. Revolution means ongoing political and economic struggle. Struggle in all forms and struggle with all means. No means is too petty and none is too great. You cannot propagandise one means as the only one, because one means arises from another, because the greatest action grows out of the smallest, because the class of the proletariat is not created for one means, but must be developed for the use of all means, because even the peaceful means of the general strike, 'direct action', cannot accomplish the revolution, but the general strike must develop into the general uprising, the uprising of the whole proletariat. In other words, you cannot mechanically make revolution with a prized patent-method; revolution is, rather, the organically self-forming process of liberation of the whole proletarian class, with all means, by all paths, in all places.

And a fourth point: because we Communists see revolution as the overall political struggle of the proletariat, which can only achieve its goal by bringing together the combined forces of the proletariat, we seek to bring these together by the strictest centralisation of the Communist Party that is to lead the struggles. Syndicalism, which sees in revolution only economic 'liberation' and economic struggle, sees its task as already fulfilled if the workers of the factories come out in struggle for the factory. We Communists are thus centralist, whereas the syndicalists are federalist.

And we shall now see whether Hamburg is still Communist or not.

The foundation of the Hamburg theory is that the political revolution is now finished, and that, in place of the political revolution, what has started now is the economic revolution.

This is what Wolffheim[2] says in his pamphlet *Betriebsorganisation oder Gewerkschaft* [Factory-Organisation or Trade-Union]: 'The German revolution, which was completed in its political forms on 9 November last year...' – in other words, the revolution is now finished in its 'political forms' – and

> the proletarian revolution is essentially an economic revolution, which has the task of transforming the whole economy, the whole economic form, from the bottom up. If the political revolution took place in the streets, this is not possible for the economic revolution. It cannot be carried out by armed action, but rather has to take place where the economic process has its roots – in the factories.

This revolution is therefore an economic process, and also has an economic goal, which Wolffheim describes as follows:

> To destroy the capitalist economy...by a continuous chain of revolutionary mass-strikes with ever-greater extension, gripping one branch of industry after another, and finally forcing the capitalist class to a confession of its bankruptcy. It is already bankrupt today, but it has not yet given up the attempts to recover afresh, has not yet admitted its incapacity. It cannot do so, as this would mean committing suicide.

I shall leave aside the nonsense contained in the last two sentences, the idea that the bourgeoisie cannot confess its bankruptcy, after it is said that the goal of the revolution is precisely to force the bourgeoisie to confess this. I shall just focus on the overall view that is given in these lines of the nature and course of the revolution. According to this, the political revolution is dead, i.e. the revolution that strives for the political goals of the dictatorship of the proletariat is accomplished. Its place is taken by an economic revolution which has its locus in the factories, i.e. in the seat of the economic process, and which only requires economic means, i.e. the revolutionary mass-strike, and achieves its goal not by the conquest of political power, but rather by

---

2. [Fritz Wolffheim, after contact with the IWW in California in 1912–13, was active during the War in Hamburg, and defended syndicalist ideas in the KPD until the expulsion of the ultra-Left after the Heidelberg Congress. Though a founder of the KAPD, he was expelled in August 1920 for 'national Bolshevism', and later drifted towards the left wing of the Nazi Party.]

the destruction of the economy and a confession of bankruptcy on the part of the bourgeoisie.

This idea reflects the image that the syndicalists have of the revolution. A purely economic process, which ignores all politics and everything political.

It will be clear to you, in this connection, what a different character the question of anti-parliamentarism has as represented by the Hamburg people. And only in this connection can you see the full sharpness of the contradiction that exists between us and the Hamburgers on the question of parliamentarism.

The majority of you believe that we can for a while, given the present situation of the revolution, renounce the use of parliamentary means. This is something that we can discuss and come to an understanding about. For it is also possible from our point of view that such renunciation might be appropriate at a particular stage of the revolution. And the question is simply whether or not we are in such a situation. Between the Hamburg people and us, however, the contradiction is that the Hamburgers, as syndicalists, scorn the use of any parliamentary means, because parliamentary means are political means, because this diverts the proletariat, the syndicalists say, from the economic revolution and leads to a view of the revolution as a political process, as a struggle for political ends.

The Hamburgers refuse parliamentarism because it is political. And you, who reject parliamentary activity today, reject it although it is political.

And, along with all political means, the syndicalists and the Hamburg people deny the most important political means that the proletariat can make use of, i.e. the party.

In this connection, the question of the general workers' union takes on a quite particular significance, which we shall discuss at this conference in another context. For the Hamburg people, the general workers' union means the form of organisation that not only has to bear and lead the form of economic revolution, but is called on at the same time to kill off the political party, which, in the syndicalist conception, is at least superfluous, if not harmful.

I would like to anticipate one point here. The general workers' union, i.e. in the Hamburg way of speaking 'the proletarian class-organisation that should embrace all proletarians', which the Hamburgers have imported as something brand-new from America, is neither a Hamburg nor an American patent. It is not the latest thing in the field of the workers' movement and workers' organisation. It has its place not at the end-point of the development of the working class but, rather, at its beginnings. The idea of 'one big union' arose in England with the Chartist movement, and fell into oblivion along with the Chartist movement itself. And the fact that, in America today, the idea of 'one big union' that would embrace all proletarians still has its supporters is not a sign of the advanced state of the American workers, but rather of how, in the particular conditions of the United States, the American working class is theoretically, economically and politically backward. The fact that the revolutionary section of the American working class remains trapped in these illusions is simply a reflection of the backwardness of the American workers' movement in general, as is also expressed in the fact that, on the other hand, they still tolerate someone like Gompers[3] and allow themselves to be led by him.

What then is the task of this 'one big union' in the Hamburg view, as against the party? I have an article here, signed by the painter Heinrich Vogeler, which the *Kommunistische Arbeiterzeitung* published on 30 September 1919. There you can read: 'The fact that the growth of the workers' union leads to the death of all parties is logically determined by its growth. For, on this basis, the complete unification of the proletariat is effected, as in America.'

If an editor of this Hamburg *Arbeiterzeitung*

[INTERJECTION FROM LAUFENBERG:[4] *'Fritz Wolffheim is the editor'*]

added here a note that this view of the future role of the party is not shared by the editorial team, Comrade Wolffheim, who added this note, is clearly unaware that in an earlier issue of his paper, he himself – I assume – wrote similarly about the role of the workers' union and the party.

In the issue of 31 July 1919, the Hamburg *Arbeiterzeitung* said:

> The proletarian class-organisation can only be a unitary economic and political organisation if its construction is complete. Until this point in time, it needs a political party of its own, which sees its main goal in propaganda for the unitary organisation and the council-system. The Communist Party propagates the unitary proletarian organisation and the council-system in order to abolish itself as a political party when its demands are realised.

---

3. [Samuel Gompers, founder of the AFL in 1886 and its president until his death in 1924.]

4. [Heinrich Laufenberg was chair of the workers' and soldiers' council in Hamburg in 1918–19, and a follower of Wolffheim at least through his 'national-Bolshevik' period.]

> With the realisation of the proletarian class-organisation, the Communist
> Party will cease to exist alongside it as a party.

The Hamburg school has delivered its verdict here on our political party; all
it is good for is to disappear.

And, if even the Hamburg syndicalists admit that this party won't be
destroyed from one day to the next, they are none the less already set today
on destroying the vital nerve of our party. For one thing, by seeking to expel
the Party from its particular field of revolutionary action and reduce it to a
mere propaganda-society. I am not using the term 'propaganda-society' with
any malign intent, it is literally what the Hamburg school stand for.

Wolffheim, for example, already in the sentences quoted above, says that
the party's only task is that of propaganda for the unitary organisation and
the council-system. And, if Comrade Wolffheim wants to argue against me
that this is – as he put it – 'an unfortunate formulation', I point out to him that
he said precisely the same thing at the Bremen district-conference.

According to the report of the Bremen Communists from 27 September 1919,
Wolffheim maintained there that the Communist Party has been transformed
from a party of action, which it had been last November [1918], into a party of
propaganda. Actions have now become fully and completely a matter for the
mass of workers. They are led by the general workers' union, and politically
oriented by the Communist Party.

And, so, the task of the Communist Party should now be to supply leaflets,
to supply articles and slogans, in sum to supply propaganda to get the presently unclear mishmash of proletarians who 'acknowledge the council-system', these 'unconscious proletarians', to unite into a general workers' union,
with an object that no one can recognise. Not only is the aim of our party to
be crippled, but it is also to be crippled already in its form of existence. The
disguised form in which the Party is to be killed off is federalism.

The syndicalists know perfectly well why they preach federalism as the
form of political organisation. They know perfectly well that federalism
means death for the unity and determination of the Party and for the resolute
political action of the proletariat, and it is following from the knowledge and
desire that the political party has to be killed off that the Hamburgers preach
federalism.

They write as much in the issue of 31 July 1919:

> All workers engaged in a factory join with the fully or nearly proletarian
> employees in a factory-organisation that is linked with the factory-
> organisations of all factories in the same industry on a federal basis according
> to industrial zones across the whole country. All federalistically combined
> organisations of all industries unite on a federal basis into the great unitary
> proletarian class-organisation, which, in its federalist sections, wages the
> economic partial struggle as a whole, the final political struggle.

This then is the doctrine that the Hamburgers have learned from twelve
months of revolution in Germany, from the thousands of corpses and a series
of defeats of the German Revolution, which is because the proletariat has
not yet risen in a united action: that the proletariat has to decompose into
federalist patterns that are not united.

And how do the Hamburg syndicalists see the course of the revolution as
a whole? They have understood how to clothe themselves in the lion's skin
of arch-radicalism, and it is high time to see whether this lion's skin actually
hides a lion or a donkey. We can obtain information on this from Comrade
Wolffheim's spiritual twin brother, Comrade Laufenberg.

In his pamphlet on the revolution in Hamburg, Comrade Laufenberg
repeats the arguments that he made in December 1918. He says here the
following:

> If we intend to continue the revolution in an orderly way, and secure the
> political power of the working class, if we want to avoid the sharpening
> of class contradictions and perhaps even civil war, there is only one path
> that offers itself...
>
> In order to forestall both possibilities [i.e. of loss to Right and Left] and
> the civil war that would necessarily arise from this, it will be necessary, on
> the one hand, to maintain the political rule of the working class in its full
> scope, in order to ensure socialisation. On the other hand, however, it will
> be necessary to secure the bourgeoisie the possibility, in accordance with its
> numerical importance, to join in influencing the course, manner and form of
> socialisation. The summoning of the Constituent Assembly fundamentally
> means a challenge to the political power of the working class and will lead
> to the restoration of the political power of the bourgeoisie, if the working

class does not enter the electoral struggle resolved and united as a class. Those who stand for the political power of the working class, therefore, should not seek to seize this assembly, for which the bourgeoisie literally cry out, but alongside the ruling organ of the working class, alongside a central council of councils, a parliament arising from general elections may come into place, which under the control of the workers' government and with firmly circumscribed authority secures the bourgeoisie a certain room for manoeuvre, and enables it to give expression to its interest as the process of socialisation proceeds.

That, then, is the arch-radicalism of the Hamburg people, and what stands behind the hollow cries of principled anti-parliamentarism with which the Hamburgers have been shaking the Party for the last several months.

In the guiding principles about parliamentarism that the Zentrale has prepared for you, you will read: 'The KPD thus fundamentally rejects parliamentarism as a means for the exercise of class-rule.' Here, we have made our standpoint towards parliamentarism quite clear. Today, when we are reaching for political power, we have to make use of any political means, including that of parliament. But, once the proletariat has power, we reject sharing this power with the bourgeoisie in the way that the Hamburgers maintain. What the Hamburgers want is not the mishmash that the USPD wants, it is something quite different again. The USPD wants the council-system to be anchored in parliament. Comrade Laufenberg has a new patent, the anchoring of parliamentarism in the council-system, so as to allow the bourgeoisie 'to give expression to its interest as the process of socialisation proceeds'. Would Karl Kautsky or Rudolf Hilferding put it any differently?[5] What stands behind all the noise that the Hamburg people make, the full-blooded radicalism that they claim and profess? Nothing more than the dream of a peaceful revolution, a revolution hand in hand with the bourgeoisie, a revolution with the council-system on the one hand and parliament on the other, a revolution on a path of understanding with the bourgeoisie as to the interests of the bourgeoisie in the progress of socialisation. The line we have to draw here is not against the Left, but rather against the Right.

---

5. [Kautsky and Hilferding were the intellectual leaders of the USPD at this time.]

We have literally here what Karl Marx described in the following words:

> Since the petty bourgeoisie dream of a peaceful implementation of their
> socialism – allowing possibly for a second, brief February revolution [of
> 1848] – the coming historical process appears to them as an application of
> systems, which the thinkers of society, either in company with others or
> as single inventors, devise or have devised. In this way they become the
> eclectics or adepts of existing socialist systems, of doctrinaire socialism,
> which was the theoretical expression of the proletariat only as long as it
> had not yet developed further and become a free, autonomous, historical
> movement.[6]

Systems that the Hamburg 'thinkers' have devised, either in company or as
single inventors, indeed dominate the Hamburg-type of politics. In place of
the great historical process of revolution we have a system. The revolution
is dissolved into a process of organisation. Why have the Hamburgers lost
sight of the revolution? Comrade Wolffheim offers the following answer:

> If the German proletarians were not accustomed to following their leaders
> in everything, if astonishment had not led them to lose the power of speech
> and the ability to think, then they would at least have raised the question
> at that moment [i.e. on 9 November] as to what do now to maintain the
> power they had conquered.... The proletarians did not reach the idea that the
> conquered power now also had to be anchored, to be newly organised.

This is the result of the German revolution according to Wolffheim's conception. The proletarians 'did not conceive the idea', and did not find the
'right form of organisation'. And this is why they could not keep power on
9 November.

For us Marxists, the revolutionary process is not so simple. The organisational form that the proletariat is capable of at a particular moment cannot be
the product of people's minds, no matter how clever they are, not even such
as the Hamburg 'thinkers'. And if the proletarians did not 'conceive' the necessary idea on 9 November, it was not because the Hamburg 'thinkers' could
not give them this idea; the real reason lies deeper.

---

6. 'The Class Struggles in France', Marx 2010b, p. 122.

If the organisational form and conceptions of the German proletariat were inadequate in the revolution, this is based historically in the millennia of proletarian slavery, it is based historically in this class, in its process of liberation, only being able to come to a consciousness of its path through long and difficult struggle, and in the fact that only the violent school of revolution could raise the struggles and victories, the defeats and bloodshed, the uprising and retreat of the proletariat, to a level of conception of its task and its duties, so that it understands how to seize power and how to exercise it.

This is our conception of the course of the revolution. The work of revolution cannot be performed by a form of organisation that some know-all in Hamburg has brought from America as the latest invention, but only by the will, the belief, the readiness for sacrifice and the clarity of the broad masses themselves, from which the necessary 'thoughts' and 'organisational form' arise completely of themselves.

And how can the masses be led to this great object? Here, again, we Marxists have our own opinion. And our opinion is that it is not a group of know-alls and clever minds, inventing systems of organisational form 'singly or in company', who can lead the proletariat in this struggle for liberation. The leaders of the proletariat are those very proletarians who have acquired the deepest understanding of the condition and aims of the proletariat, and have the most energetic and firmest will to achieve these aims. They have to unite in a party, and this party is the Communist Party. This is where the leading stratum of the proletariat joins together, those who in every individual action, every day and every hour, stand at the head of the proletariat in its battles, show it the way and point out its goals.

This is the historical task that our party has, and anyone who, after twelve months of revolution, wants to destroy this leading stratum that has formed and is still being formed, wants to destroy it in favour of a hazy brew of proletarians who lack a clear consciousness of their aims and condition, commits high treason against the revolution and wants all the mountains of corpses, all the sacrifices and sighs that the proletariat has experienced in these months, to have been undergone in vain.

And I say again: the situation of our party has become one in which it cannot continue in the way that it has. The Party is threatened with collapse, it has become crippled. Opinions are confused, we are no longer clear in our own ranks, and, without clarity, we are not a party, we are just a disordered heap that cannot even lead itself, let alone lead anyone else. And there must be a change in all this. Whatever may happen, even the worst, cannot be worse than what already is.

For this reason, the Zentrale is proposing to you the guiding principles that have already been brought to your attention. They contain nothing new, they contain what should be taken as given by those united in a political party. They contain the profession of Communism and the profession of the Communist Party.

We are laying these proposals before you in full awareness of what their acceptance or rejection will mean. We all have to decide over the life and existence of the Party, and more besides. For it is not just the eyes of our party-comrades who are turned to your decision. The questions that you decide today are of the greatest importance for the whole of the Third International. In every country, especially in France and Italy, the same debates are under way as those that are needed today in our ranks. And I venture to say that we have allowed the syndicalist outcry so much room for manoeuvre in our party that it has already done the Third International considerable harm. What prevented the adherence of the Swiss Socialist Party to the Third International? Nothing else than the fact that the right wing there were able to say that the Third International was 'on principle' anti-parliamentary.

We also help the Third International here in our own country if we take a clear position. This is certainly a different International from how the Hamburg people conceive it. For the Hamburg syndicalists also have their own opinion on the International.

In the article by Heinrich Vogeler that I mentioned, a sentence appears that was not criticised by the editor Fritz Wolffheim, that was approved. It reads: 'The workers' union will prepare the international unification of the proletariat with syndicalist means of struggle for the communist classless society.'

For us Communists, the International is something quite different. For us, it is the unification that brings the proletarians of all countries together, clearly and constantly, with Communist means on political paths, with the great aim of the political uprising of the proletarians of all countries, the proletarian world-revolution.

We need to achieve clarity at any cost. We know that difficult hours are ahead of us. There is nothing worse than the struggle between hostile brothers. And, yet, even if we had to undergo something a thousand times worse, the revolution that has already demanded so much of us will find us ready, even when it requires the hardest sacrifices. Whatever confronts us, we will bear for the sake of the German Revolution, for the proletariat, for the International.

Tune cede malis, sed contra audentior ito!

No evil gives way, unless you step boldly towards it!

Guiding Principles of Communist Precepts and Tactics

1. The revolution, which is born from the economic exploitation of the proletariat by the capitalists and from the political oppression by the bourgeoisie for the purpose of maintaining the relationship of exploitation, has a double task: removing the political oppression and abolishing the capitalist relationship of exploitation.

2. The replacement of the capitalist relationship of exploitation by the socialist order of production has, as its precondition, the removal of the political power of the bourgeoisie and its replacement by the dictatorship of the proletariat.

3. At all stages of the revolution that precede the proletariat's seizure of power, the revolution is a political struggle of the mass of proletarians for political power.

   This struggle is conducted with all political and economic means.

   The KPD is aware that this struggle can only be brought to a victorious conclusion with the greatest political means (mass-strike, mass-demonstrations, insurrection).

   In this connection, the KPD cannot renounce on principle any political means that serves in the preparation of these great struggles. Such means to be considered also include participation in elections, whether to parliaments, local assemblies, legally recognised factory-councils, etc.

   Since, however, these elections have to be subordinated to the revolutionary struggle, as merely preparatory means, the use of these means can be abandoned in particular political situations, i.e. if revolutionary actions that are already underway or in the course of decision make the use of parliamentary means superfluous, either temporarily or permanently.

   The KPD therefore rejects, on the one hand, the syndicalist view of the superfluity or harmfulness of political means, while, on the other hand, it rejects the view of the USPD that revolutionary gains can also be introduced by way of parliamentary decisions or negotiations with the bourgeoisie.

4. Already before the conquest of power, greatest importance should be placed on the construction of existing council-organisations and the creation of new ones.

   In this connection, it is of course to be kept in mind right away that councils and council-organisations cannot be created by statutes, electoral regulations, etc., and nor can they be maintained by statutes, electoral regulations, etc.

   Instead, they owe their existence solely to the revolutionary will and the revolutionary action of the masses, and are the ideological and organisational expression of the will to power on the part of the proletariat, in the same way as parliament is this expression on the part of the bourgeoisie.

5. The revolution, which is not a single stroke, but rather the long and tough contention of a class that has been oppressed for millennia and hence is not, right from the start, fully conscious of its task and its power, is subject to rise and fall, ebb and flow. It changes its means according to the situation, it attacks capitalism now from the political side, now from the economic side, and now from both. The KPD combats the view that an economic revolution leads to a political one.

   The means of economic struggle have particular importance, since they open the eyes of the proletariat to the real causes of its economic and political misery in a quite particular way. The value of these means of struggle is all the greater as the understanding grows in the proletariat that these economic means of struggle also serve the political aim of revolution.

   It is the task of the political party to secure for the proletariat the unimpeded use of these economic means, not hindered either by a counter-revolutionary trade-union bureaucracy, even where necessary at the price of the destruction of the form of the trade-union and the creation of new forms of organisation.

   The view that a particular organisational form could be the way of creating mass-movements, i.e. that the revolution is a question of organisational form, is rejected as a relapse into petty-bourgeois utopianism.

6. The economic organisation is where the broad masses are gathered. This is where an important part, though not the only part, of the masses who wage the revolutionary struggle are to be found.

The political party, on the other hand, is called to lead the revolutionary mass-struggle. The KPD assembles the most advanced elements of the proletariat, those who are clearest about its aim; its vocation is to stand at the head of revolutionary struggles.

In the interest of unity, intellectual education and conviction, this leading stratum must be united in the political party.

The syndicalist opinion that this unification of the proletarians with the greatest clarity is unnecessary, that the party has rather to disappear in favour of an economic organisation of the proletariat, or to dissolve into it, or that the party has to abandon its leadership in revolutionary actions in favour of factory-organisations etc., and confine itself to propaganda, is counter-revolutionary, since it seeks to replace the clear understanding of the vanguard of the working class by the chaotic drive of the mass that is in ferment.

The party can however only do justice to this task if, in revolutionary periods, it is united in the strictest centralisation. Federalism in such times is simply the disguised form of the rejection and dissolution of the party, since federalism in actual fact lames the party. Just as for the political organisation of the proletariat, so strictest centralisation is likewise required for its economic organisation. Federalism in economic organisations makes united actions of the workers impossible. The KPD rejects federalism of any kind.

7. Members of the KPD who do not share these views as to the nature, organisation and action of the Party have to be excluded from the Party.

The Lessons of the Hungarian Revolution*

In no. 21 of the *Internationale*, Comrade Radek has bequeathed to us what he has learned from the Hungarian Revolution. His pleasure herein is two-fold: firstly – *discendi voluptas* – to show that he has learned something from it, secondly – *docendi voluptas* – to show that others have not learned as much as he. He enjoys this second pleasure with the same frigid superiority with which the mountains of eternal snow look down upon the lower peaks. The lesser minds are 'credulous critics' – in which case, honest belief is presumably contrasted with the poor understanding – and 'political disputants', etc. Since, according to my knowledge, no one except myself has 'reasoned' in Germany in this manner, I have the honourable task to bring this 'dispute' to a conclusion, with due consideration to what Comrade Radek had to say about it.

First the facts.

On 22 March 1919, the soviet-government was proclaimed in Budapest. On 24 March 1919, I wrote in the Hanau *Freiheit* – the *Rote Fahne* had again become an object on which Gustav Noske tested the freedom of the press – an article on the Hungarian events which read in part as follows (after the bankruptcy of the Hungarian bourgeoisie had first been described):

---

* Published in *Die Internationale*, II, no. 24 (24 June 1920). Translation from Gruber (ed.) 1967.

In this situation the proletariat enters the stage, summoned by Count Károlyi and the Hungarian bourgeoisie itself. The Soviet Republic is proclaimed in Hungary and the proletariat seizes power. The call resounds to the proletariat of the world but particularly to those who are today's shock-troops of the world-revolution, the Russian brothers.

This is actually a moment of impressive greatness. A low-bent and broken people, deprived of all light and air, all prospects and hope, hurls itself into the arms of the International, sounding the tocsin so that its shrill sound rings throughout the world.

And yet, in the face of all the might and majesty of these events, we should not disregard the historical context, the manner in which this was all brought about. And here it must be said: the new revolution in Hungary, replacing the bourgeois democracy with the soviet-government, is not the immediate result of a battle given by the Hungarian proletariat to the Hungarian bourgeoisie and the Hungarian Junkers. It is not the result of a struggle between the proletariat and the bourgeoisie in which the latter has been vanquished, but is simply the result of the fact that the Hungarian bourgeoisie kicked the bucket – there is hardly a more appropriate expression. It perished in shame and dishonour and the only force which remained was the proletariat.

This is precisely the case we had in mind in the framing of our programme when we said that 'the Communist Party is unwilling to seize power simply because' – speaking of Germany – 'the Ebert-Scheidemann government is stuck in a blind alley or because it has ruined itself.'[1]

This case has just now materialised in Hungary and it almost seems to us as if the first moves of this new Hungarian revolution already demonstrate the correctness of our views. As far as we are concerned, the possibility for the dictatorship of the proletariat exists not when the bourgeoisie collapses but when the proletariat rises – when, in other words, it has acquired in the process of a constant revolutionary struggle the intellectual maturity, the determination and the insight to realise that salvation lies in its dictatorship

---

1. Rosa Luxemburg, 'What Does the Spartacus League Want?'; Hudis and Anderson (eds.) 2004, p. 356, gives a slightly different translation.

alone; it will become possible when the last proletarian is filled with the belief in socialism.

To illustrate: the German proletariat held power on 9 November. It was the strongest factor contending for power in the Reich; before its determination everything bent low. Why did it not hold on to this position of power? Because its power too did not rest on a victory but on the bankruptcy of 9 November; because the proletariat as a whole, as a mass, lacked the insight on that day that it had to establish the dictatorship. The will of the German proletariat was excluded because it had ceased already on 10 November to possess a will, because it had begun already on 10 November to return to the bourgeoisie by way of the 'unity of all socialists' – meaning by way of Ebert-Scheidemann – that power which had just slipped from its hands.

And what about the present events in Hungary? The proletariat gains power as a result of the collapse of the bourgeoisie. Does it have the intellectual maturity nevertheless? We are seeing only one thing; in the beginning of this revolution too stands the 'unity of all socialists'; the same scoundrels who betrayed the Hungarian proletariat as Ebert-Scheidemann betrayed the German proletariat now rave for the soviet-republic and the dictatorship of the proletariat.

That is the danger which is awaiting the Hungarian Revolution already today and which we have to point out for the sake of our brothers in Hungary and for the sake of the German movement.

I do not think that there exist many today who will find this analysis, made two days after the events, faulty in its main outline. I further think that all subsequent critics – in the best sense of the word, naturally – are able to diagnose nothing more than what had been said at that time. Even Radek does no more. For when he writes in his article: 'What followed the downfall of the Hungarian Soviet Republic, the cowardly and vile betrayal on the part of the Social Democrats...will cure the Hungarian proletariat once and for all of all its illusions regarding the Hungarian Social Democrats', it is nothing more than the assertion that such traitors had been included in the foundation of the soviet-fortress. Radek, in fact, speaks freely about the 'tactical error' committed in this connection by Béla Kun and his friends.

It should thus be possible to admit that what I wrote has been justified by the course of events and that my scepticism on 24 March 1919 was not just general 'defeatism' – saying 'I told you so' when things went wrong – but, rather, pointed out the Achilles heel of the Hungarian Revolution.

I find myself thus in the curious situation of having to defend myself against having been correct, and I will therefore address myself to the reasons adduced by Comrade Radek to show why right has been wrong and wrong been right.

To begin with, I am, even in polemics against my friend Radek, a friend of clarity. And clarity, in this case, means asserting that the proletariat of Hungary and thus the proletariat of the world suffered a defeat in Hungary. One should not conceal this fact by explanations like the following: '...there cannot exist the least doubt that this fight had much deeper consequences than the credulous critics of the Hungarian Revolution assume'. This is on the same plane as those German professors and literati who assert that the German defeat has strengthened the 'inner nature' of the Germans, etc. It is nothing more than the assertion that every evil, even the worst, has its propitious side. Since, however, we Communists can solve our critical and leading task only if we decline to participate in such comforting nonsense, it is incumbent upon us to recognise the fact of defeat.

Having recognised this fact we have to examine the following questions:

1) Could the impending defeat of 22 March have been anticipated?
2) Is it the duty of Communists to join in tactics which presumably were bound to lead to defeat?

I am proceeding with the answer to the first question not without a feeling of uneasiness. For I know that to judge an action bad after it has gone badly easily invites the impression of 'self-righteousness' and 'knowing-all' at the expense of others, and nothing is more alien to me than that. In fact, I go even further and admit that I do not even know whether I would have acted differently, had I been any one of the Hungarian friends, than they did; for it is a known fact that the judgement of any politician in the midst of the action is not the result of a sober evaluation but is dependent in varying degrees on intangibles, such as the intellectual atmosphere of the given moment, which deflect purely theoretical judgement and either weaken or strengthen the acuity of judgement. What I am saying here is thus not 'cleverness', though Comrade Radek would love to have it viewed as such, but a critical examination of what happened in Hungary; it has equally nothing to do with putting on airs, for I base myself not on the proclamation of the soviet-republic in Hungary, but on our party-programme and its author.

But to come to the point, the key to my criticism lies in the sentence of the Spartacus programme: 'The Communist Party is unwilling to seize power simply because Ebert-Scheidemann are stuck in a blind alley or have ruined themselves.'[2]

According to Radek, this sentence was wholly justified as a rejection of the putschist elements of the German Communist Party, but 'Rosa Luxemburg would certainly have rejected having this sentence recited like a *sura* of the Koran.'

In this view, I am in agreement with Comrade Radek. I too think little of the sacerdotal inclinations of Rosa Luxemburg, in fact as little as of his own or my own. On the other hand, I value the political qualifications of Rosa Luxemburg too highly to believe that she was simply engaged here in political casuistry, in drawing up at a moment of opportunist caprice a sentence designed for Germany, December 1918. I rather assume that this sentence in the party-programme constitutes a deduction from a political principle. We would thus proceed logically, in my view, if we attempt to locate this principle; if this succeeds, we have to explore further whether it is applicable to Hungary and to decide the Hungarian case accordingly. This logical procedure should have been all the more obvious since it only involved Comrade Radek's reading of the following sentence in which Rosa Luxemburg outlined the positive presuppositions for the assumption of power by the Communists:

> The Spartacus League will never take over governmental power except in response to the clear, unambiguous will of the great majority of the proletarian mass in Germany, never except by means the proletariat's conscious affirmation of the views, aims, and methods of struggle of the Spartacus League.[3]

---

2. [In this quotation (see n. 18 above), Levi replaced 'Spartacus League' by 'Communist Party' to avoid anachronism.]

3. 'What Does the Spartacus League Want?', in Hudis and Anderson (eds.) 2004, pp. 356–7.

Thus the principle guiding Rosa Luxemburg has been fairly satisfactorily expressed: that is, that the positive criterion, so to speak, for the seizure of power by the proletariat lies within the *proletariat* and is expressed in the revolutionary stage of development in which the proletariat finds itself.

On the basis of this principle, Rosa Luxemburg came to a conclusion about the November and December situation in Germany in 1918. What is decisive is not the negative action on the part of the bourgeoisie but the positive action on the part of the proletariat.

In reply, Comrade Radek has ready a simple recipe. He writes:

> The idea of a simple collapse of the bourgeois/Social-Democratic coalition, without the collapse of the bourgeois state at the same time being a process of the gathering of the proletarian forces, is entirely unhistorical.

In that case, I dare to have this unhistorical idea. Comrade Radek's concept involves simply the following: the bourgeoisie, on the one hand, and the proletariat, on the other, constitute, in a sense, a system of connecting tubes in which the outflow of one is the inflow of the other, or a minus in the one *mechanically* calls forth a plus in the other. I, on the other hand, believe that all thinking along mechanical lines is especially unhistorical, and I am, moreover, of the particular opinion that there is not necessarily a correlation between the degree of purpose and determination of the proletariat and the degree of carelessness and disorganisation of the bourgeoisie. I think we have evidence for this in the above-cited example of Germany in November 1918, where a momentary total powerlessness and carelessness of the bourgeois was not balanced by a corresponding degree of clarity and determination but an equally great powerlessness and carelessness on the part of the proletariat. The case cited by Comrade Radek, in which the downfall of the bourgeoisie involves, at the same time, a consolidation of the proletariat in such a manner that the moment of cessation of bourgeois power coincides with the ascent of the proletariat to it is *perhaps possible* but *not at all inevitable*; it might, indeed, be more appropriate to say that, normally – as far as it is at all possible to speak of norms in history –, there is a twilight-zone between the bourgeois night and the proletarian day. It is in the condition of such twilight, when the power of the bourgeoisie is already so diminished in certain cases that the seizure of power by a small minority becomes conceivable, that the first great and positive task devolves upon us Communists: the organisation of the proletariat as a class in soviets. I maintain that the result of this phase of the organisation of the proletarian class – which cannot proceed either according to some formula according to a 'soviet-system', but will be an up-and-down movement of battles, demonstrations, actions, etc. – will be decisive in determining the moment of the seizure of power by the Communists, and that Rosa Luxemburg said nothing more nor less.

All Hungarian comrades, as well as Radek and myself, are after all agreed on the fact and the manner of the mistake of the Hungarian comrades.

> This error, [says Radek] is obvious. Hungarian Social Democracy, belonging to the most corrupt creatures of the Second International, was bankrupt. The masses escaped from its leadership. The left elements of the Party decided on a desperate step, the formation of the soviet-republic....If the Communist Party did not want to leave the masses in the lurch, it had to agree to the formation of the soviet-government jointly with the Social Democrats.

Comrade Radek establishes, in this sentence, two facts which ought to be treated separately. Firstly, he refers to the fact that Hungarian Social Democracy had failed and that the masses were moving leftward in the direction of communism. The process of organisation and consolidation of the proletarian class on the basis of communism had thus entered a particularly crucial stage, and even I readily admit that the firmness and determination of the masses at such a stage may grow in a very short time, perhaps within days, to the point where it provides a sound foundation for a soviet-republic. At such a time, everything depends on the *manner* in which this process of consolidation proceeds, and what we Communists have to do in order to make it as lasting and thorough as possible.

The Hungarian comrades had now taken the road toward alliance with the Social Democrats, who declared themselves in agreement with the Communist programme – that is, accepted the 'basis of the given situation' – and who, with almost all their leaders at their head, became Communists overnight. Radek fundamentally approves this approach and this is his second assertion in the sentence quoted above. He adds:

> The coalition with Social Democracy was necessary; but the Communists should have maintained the gallows next to the government-buildings in order, if necessary, to demonstrate to their dear allies the concrete meaning of proletarian dictatorship. By dropping the necessary caution,

the Communist Party was in the hands of the vacillating elements of the Social Democrats.

I realise quite well that the allusion to the gallows as an instrument of government makes an unusually strong and manly impression, and that all those who doubt the omnipotent effect of this instrument of power easily provoke the contrary impression. But, as much as I am aware of the resulting danger, I have to say this: I think that, under the dictatorship of the proletariat, thorough and drastic measures against the bourgeoisie are necessary; I can even imagine difficult situations in which the proletariat is forced to maintain its own power in the face of the fainthearted or traitors in its own ranks by means of drastic measures. But, to propose the gallows, at the moment of the establishment of soviet-power, as the method of unifying and amalgamating the proletariat; to undertake the organisation and consolidation of the proletariat not on the basis of the 'clear, unambiguous will of the great majority of the proletariat', 'its conscious affirmation of the views, aims, and methods of struggle' of the Communists (according to Rosa Luxemburg), but on the basis of mutual hangings, all this strikes me – I do not want to use strong words – as a very unfortunate method for the unification of the proletariat. Neither do I think that this method has ever been practised, nor that there exist prospects for its use. I am not aware that the Russian Soviet Republic, for example, added the gallows to the hammer and sickle as the third link of its emblem; I do not think that this omission was due to accident or to shamefacedness, but simply to the fact that the Russian Soviet Republic was erected on the basis of different foundations than those proposed for Hungary by Comrade Radek. The bond holding the proletarian class as such together perhaps cannot be a garland of roses, but it certainly cannot be the noose of the executioner.

I therefore think that the approach suggested by Comrade Radek does not need to be discussed seriously. I consider it fundamentally wrong and believe that, in all similar cases, no other approach is possible than that carried out by the Munich comrades under the leadership of Leviné,[4] which corresponds to the spirit of the Spartacus programme. And this spirit involves asking the working class itself through the election of factory-councils, or better yet,

---

4. See Introduction, p. 8, and 'The Munich Experience', above, pp. 47–53.

the election of workers' councils, and the direction of these elections under such slogans as stand in the sharpest possible contrast to the current 'socialist' leadership of the working class. The more trenchantly these slogans are formulated, the more effective they will be. If the working class adopts these slogans, then the ditch which it builds against its present leadership will be correspondingly deep; it will become conscious of stepping across the Rubicon. If the proletariat, on the other hand, rejects such slogans formulated by us, if it hesitates in crossing the Rubicon, then we Communists should not act as if it were ready to cross the Rubicon. Naturally, I lack the precise knowledge of Hungarian conditions to indicate what slogans the Communists should have raised in a concrete situation. But I can easily imagine that demands, such as, for example, the arrest of Garbai, Weltner, and Kunfi could have been raised.[5] With this method, it seems to me the error might have been avoided that no one else recognised and expressed as clearly as Béla Kun himself when he said, 'It went too smoothly.' And, on the basis of this sentiment of Béla Kun, on the basis of the present exposition, together with what I wrote on 24 March 1919 as an application of these thoughts, I answer to the question as to whether the coming defeat could be anticipated with a 'Yes...'

---

5. [Sándor Garbai, a leading Social Democrat, was the first chairman of the Revolutionary Governing Council in Hungary; his Social-Democratic colleague Zsigismund Kunfi became education-minister. Jacob Weltner was a trade-union leader.]

The World-Situation and the German Revolution*

[...] Even if German militarism today may be
weaker than before the War, it is still more unconscionable and irresponsible than before the War, and
desperadoes are no less dangerous externally than
internally. France is therefore pressing for the armed
strength of Germany to be destroyed. What is the
position of America and England on this question?
Both want Germany to be economically exhausted
and to exploit it economically as much as they like.
They see Germany's armed strength as the guarantee against what they call Bolshevism, which they
see as the greatest threat to the economic exploitation of Germany.

You see, then, how each state in the capitalist world
is thrown back and forth between the Scylla of militarism and the Charybdis of Bolshevism. This antagonism has already split the Entente into two distinct
camps: France, which wants to dispel the danger of
militarism right away, and England-America, which
want to make use of militarism to press back Bolshevism; France that is making a deal with what is
called the German Revolution, i.e. the Independents,
etc., and England that is collaborating with Kapp
and Lüttwitz. And so, today, I see France as not only

---

* Translated from *Die Weltlage und die deutsche Revolution. Rede, gehalten auf dem 4.
Parteitag der K.P.D. (Spartakusbund) in Berlin am 14 April 1920 von Paul Levi*, KPD
(Spartakusbund) 1920. As with Levi's speech at the October 1919 congress, this also
began with a substantial analysis of the international situation.

isolated on the question of its economic rehabilitation, but even on the question that was the main one throughout the War, the destruction of German militarism. England is satisfied with having destroyed the German fleet. The rest of German militarism can remain, it is only a threat to isolated France. Looking at the French situation from the point of view of the French bourgeoisie, it is impossible not to allow oneself a certain feeling of sympathy with this tragedy. For four years of war, they strove for victory with extraordinary persistence and energy – we can concede as much even to the class-enemy – and now, having won the War, they see all the fruits that they hoped for vanish, and are facing the same misery in which the conquered find themselves. France will naturally do its utmost to banish this danger, and this is why, most recently, it has already gone over to conducting its *own* actions against German militarism. What this means is as follows: France now sees the latest date having arrived at which it can still implement the disarmament of German militarism, which is the main question for France.

And the danger of disarmament, the danger of the dissolution of the whole military establishment, was what gave the immediate occasion for the events at the centre of the latest German developments, i.e. the Kapp Putsch. If Noske was at the defence-ministry and Ebert in the presidential palace on the Wilhelmstrasse, this was something that the Junkers had already put up with for a year and a half, and they could have put up with it for another six months, until both were dismissed by the Junkers in the normal course of events. But the disarmament-question could not tolerate any further delay; France insisted on its promissory note. And, so, the Junkers were forced to make the attempt of organising resistance to the French demands off their own bat, i.e. calling for a military dictatorship in Germany. It was therefore the urgent extreme need of the Junkers that gave the occasion. This plan was worked out in the fullest detail. The Kapp Putsch, triggered by a dangerous constellation abroad, was no more than the logical development of the mistake that the German Revolution had itself made on its very first day. The mistake of the German Revolution was the belief in November 1918 that a system could be changed by a simple change of personnel. This is all that happened in November, and nothing more. The Kaiser and the princes disappeared, and the monarchical topping was replaced by a 'democratic' or 'republican' one. But the internal construction of the state, above all the pillars on which it rests, the bureaucracy, the military, and above all the economic pillars of capitalism, remained completely undisturbed, and, indeed, so far as they were disturbed, they were improved again as speedily as possible. For, if, to a certain extent, German militarism was weakened by the November events, by the disintegration of the old army, the German bourgeoisie repaired this mistake with an extraordinary vigour and ability. Indeed, it made up for this mistake to such a degree that, as far as domestic affairs are concerned, it was in a better position than before. Before November 1918, it had an army made up of all strata of the population, which was highly permeable to all currents and tendencies of the broad masses of the proletariat. And, in the last years of the War, the mood of the proletarian masses coloured the army in such a way that, from one day to the next, it ceased to be an arbitrary tool of the bourgeoisie. But what came into being after November 1918 was a specific organisation designed for struggle against the proletariat: this was the white guard that was established with all available means, with the means of ideological seduction and the stimulus of material means, which was made dependent on the bourgeoisie and hostile to the proletariat.

We can confidently say that what came after 9 November 1918 was worse for the progress of the revolution than what existed before 9 November 1918. And the fact that the proletarian revolution only began from 9 November, that the broad layers of the proletariat were then forced into motion and gradually came to recognise the proper goal of the revolution, the suppression of the capitalist system, this fact provided the white guards with the activity they needed. Not only the activity of being launched against the proletariat time after time, called on to conduct a bloodbath and being given Iron Crosses for their heroic deeds in Berlin and Leipzig, but, above all, that, from time to time, and then permanently from about April 1919, the military was itself called on to rule; it was explained to them that a military administration, i.e. administration under the state of siege, was really the best form of state-administration in general. The sabre was not put down from then on. When the state of siege was finally lifted in December 1919, that lasted just three weeks, until Ebert and Bauer were once more at a loss and again explained that no better government was possible than the state of siege. And, so, everything at home was in place for the Kapp Putsch. This was not simply the result of the negligence of the proletariat, which had been satisfied in November 1918 with a change of a few heads, it was the direct result of the system of government established after 9 November 1918, known as the Noske system. A system that time and again, and in the final analysis, simply comes down to the machine-gun and appeals to the hand-grenade as its ultimate wisdom, must, in due course, itself capitulate in the face of these helpers that it constantly calls upon.

The Kapp Putsch thus did not pose any really new problem. The problem of the German Revolution remained, even on 13 March 1920, exactly the same as it had been on 9 November 1918. The basic question of the Revolution had returned to that of 9 November 1918, the question that we can initially formulate very simply: should the *one* support of the capitalist system in Germany, militarism, continue or not?

But, if the question is the same, the way it is posed is rather different. For, at that time, in November 1918, this question was still disguised by pacific phrases, and exhaustion with the War was an over-riding factor: at that time, there was hatred of the imperialist machine of conquest and the flood-tide of thieves, cheats, loud-mouths and shirkers that the Kaiser's army had become. Now, in March 1920, the question the proletariat faces is clearly raised in all its nakedness: do you want militarism, which is the means of the bourgeoisie for suppressing its wage-slaves?

It is a very typical hallmark of this German revolution that people thought, in November 1918, that they could avoid responsibility for this question. The executive of the Berlin workers' councils had called for the formation of a red army, but it backed down in the face of the threats of the soldiers' councils. The attempts of the Red Soldiers' League shattered on the lack of consolidation of the proletarian mass. The task that could at that time only be solved by the councils was not fulfilled. Nothing happened on the side of the proletariat.

The bourgeoisie relied, first of all, on those front-line troops that were still 'reliable', but these disintegrated on their first contact with the proletariat. What began in November 1918 was a state of suspense, in which neither of the two contending classes had a military power. This state of suspense came to an end with the January battles of 1919, with the proletariat defeated and the bourgeoisie emerging with the knuckle-dusters of its volunteer Freikorps on its fists.

Where were these new military forces recruited? The officers were the old Imperial ones, who had learned nothing and forgotten nothing. They had their old lord and master in Wilhelm, and their new clown in Noske. And the men? These were, in fact, a new stratum. They were no longer the workers of town and country, but the large masses of those who had been economically and morally wrecked by the long war. They were 'decomposition-products of the lowest strata of the old society', they were – and I in no way use this term here by way of insult, but purely in a sociological sense – they were 'lumpen-proletarians' who offered living proof of the correctness of the Marxian prognosis that they would, now and then, be drawn into the movement of a proletarian revolution, but that their whole life-situation made them ready to sell themselves to reactionary undertakings.

The proletariat was now confronted with this question and with this stratum. And it was settled, at the same time, that the question of the new staffing and purging of the officer-corps was only one part of the whole question, and not the most important one. The nub of the military question in Germany does not lie with the officer-corps, but with the men.

As long as the weapons remain in the hands of the stratum that we have now, then they will be at the disposal of any reactionary coup at any time; all that the organisers of a coup need is money. For the strata that now have weapons in their hands are socially rootless. Weapons belong in the hands of the stratum that socially and economically shores up the whole edifice, the factory-proletariat.

If, in November 1918, the German Revolution hedged around this core-question, it has now made sure that it has to be resolved one way or the other. For how was it possible, in November 1918, not to take this question seriously, and then solve it in such a fashion that, with the lumpenproletariat as the basis, the Imperial officer-corps in the middle and the Social Democrat Noske at the head, a social chimera emerged? Only because between these two poles, the Junkers and the big bourgeoisie, on the one hand, and the clear-sighted proletariat, on the other, stretched the very broad layer of petty bourgeois and quasi-proletarians who did not see this question at all. And this broad stratum, which at that time, if for instance you take the elections to the National Assembly as a measure, was the overwhelming great majority of the whole German people and also of the whole German proletariat, has now been reduced, in my opinion, to a minimum. This is how things stand today: on the side of the bourgeoisie, a quite clear, strictly organised, conscious and energetic group, which is not, as in November 1918, under the pressure of military defeat and in a temporary state of agony, but, rather, is quite ready for action and has all its resources strictly organised in its hands. And, on the other hand, the proletariat.

Whether we Communists as a party have increased or decreased does not have a bearing on the matter. One thing we can say: as a result of our work this pole, the proletariat, has developed clarity and determination to a far greater level than in November 1918. In particular, I must say that the movement of 13 March [1920] and the following days was one of the most edifying and important in the German Revolution, certainly more edifying than that of 9 November 1918. With volcanic power, the flames of revolt flared up in milieus that had previously been quite foreign to the Revolution. Circles were drawn in, and – perhaps, for the time being, just quite instinctively – grouped around the conscious nucleus of the proletariat, circles that previously stood on the side of the bourgeoisie. Just as when a new star forms where there had been mist around a core in the middle, the formation of a star then depends on two factors: that the core is quite firm, and that the mist settles ever more firmly around the core until it becomes part of the core itself. Today, the core is larger and firmer than in November 1918. It is no longer limited to a few people from the Spartacus League, but stretches well beyond the narrow circles of our party. And ranged around this core are those who were still, both before and during the November Revolution, in the great semi-obscurity that stretched between the bourgeoisie on the one hand and the proletariat on the other.

This semi-obscurity still persists. There is a small stratum that is still in the middle, between the great opposing parties that divide Germany, and has not decided on which side it finds its place. Petty bourgeois who find their position undermined, small pensioners who still have to live, house-owners, etc. Certain strata, who, by nature and by their economic constitution, find themselves in this twilight position. But, today, this stratum is almost insignificant. It has become so small that, in the long run, it can no longer be the basis of a government. These strata, who are still at present the basis of the government, are like a narrow spit of land which the waves are breaking against on both sides. And, so, it is clear that the struggles in and around the coalition-government cannot just be dismissed with the word 'party-manoeuvrings'. There is little time now for party-manoeuvrings. No, they are the natural and necessary expression of the decay and decomposition of those strata that, up till now, still supported the coalition-government. The Kapp episode has reinforced the process of concentration, and, just as only a minimum now remains in the Centre, so there is an increase on both Left and Right. I just want to explain here how this process of concentration has increased on the left side. Although the action of 13 March, in my view, was, in many respects, not sufficiently clear about its goals, or sufficiently energetic, the overall effect of the action was extraordinarily favourable for the whole revolutionary movement, and for our party. For the whole movement, because, as I already said, I see it as one of the most important advances that wide strata have been won for the Revolution. Certainly, the intermediate railway-, post-, prison- and court-staff have not become Communists, and the mass of them will not very quickly become Communists; but they have, nonetheless, fought for the first time on the side of the proletariat. Previously, they always fought against the proletariat. Today, need has placed them on the side of the proletariat, and the fact that they have stood *once* in struggle alongside the proletariat creates certain assurances that these circles will no longer be such completely passive tools in the hands of the bourgeoisie. Now, certain strata have been linked with the fate of the proletariat, and they are of considerable importance for the construction of the Revolution. We have spoken often enough of how important for us the position of these railway-, post-, telegraph- etc. officials can be. Thus, the whole movement had something about it that was of greatest benefit for the Revolution; but, in my opinion, the movement has also been an important advance in the position of our party. It is already an advance in so far as the greater part of our supporters across the country found, on their *own* initiative, the quite correct and pertinent slogans, right from the first minute, and, in every respect, we moved decisively in grasping the character of the movement and proclaiming slogans for it. Our comrades proclaimed the slogan of arming, they raised the strike via a general strike to an open challenge to militarism; and, even where they were victorious, they stuck with what had to be the goal considering the German revolutionary movement as a whole, i.e. they did not pursue the movement further to local council-republics. They proclaimed the slogan of workers' councils; they kept their eyes on the *whole* German movement, and, as far as our party is concerned, they all recognised immediately the moment that represented the high point and then the decline of the movement. I believe that we can recognise here, where, for the first time, the comrades across the country operated successfully and decisively, not on the basis of a 'command' from the Zentrale, but, rather, on their own initiative, the fruits of the intensive self-education that we Communists have undergone in the last years.

I must say that a few wrong turnings were taken. I see it as a need for the Party that we recognise those wrong turnings for what they were, that we do not have to stand by them. I would like to propose to you a resolution along these lines, with all circumspection in its form. However favourably the movement took shape in its first moment, its image became, to a degree, muddied and confused by the intervention of the syndicalists and our former opposition, and also by the Hoelz affair. In my view, we have to say that a revolutionary struggle is impossible without the strictest discipline. In my view, the Hoelz case was not as bad as that of the Rhineland.[1] As I judge the conditions in the Vogtland, there does not seem to have been there a strong council-organisation. So it is understandable that certain individuals believed they could settle the fate of the proletariat with some three or four hundred men. And, in my opinion, it is also nothing special about the proletarian revolution, but has been the case at all times, both within and outside revolutions, that many people, who personally are in no way the worst and who quite certainly are not highway-robbers, believe that their own interventions in world-history can undertake the liberation of the proletariat from their own point of view. I see the Rhineland-Westphalia situation as much the worse; for the situation there, as I see it, was that conditions had developed as far as they could develop before the proletariat advances to a council-republic. Our comrades, naturally, avoided this goal, but, in Rhineland-Westphalia, a complete council-system was established, which functioned well and which also, as far as I can judge, well reflected the desire of the workers in Rhineland-Westphalia. If, within the council-system, and against the will of the workers, certain comrades believed that they could make the proletarian revolution over the heads of this representation, that was bound to lead to events that could only be damaging for the whole proletariat.[2]

---

1. [Max Hoelz organised armed groups in the Vogtland region in 1919, which expanded to a substantial urban guerrilla at the time of the Kapp Putsch.]

2. [The workers of the Ruhr had obtained a substantial quantity of weapons, and continued to escalate the struggle after the Kapp Putsch had been defeated. It was not until early April that the Reichswehr succeeded very brutally in restoring order. See Broué 2005, p. 349ff.]

Rhineland-Westphalia was given an object-lesson in how ominous this was bound to be. You will remember what role sabotage played in our party-debates. In the Ruhr district, we had a classic test of the doctrine of salvation by sabotage. There, the workers' councils, when Rhineland-Westphalia was isolated, took the decision to stand on the basis of the Bielefeld agreement. One may debate as to whether this decision was right or wrong – I personally believe it to have been right – but, in any case, the decision was made, and gave expression to what I see as a misguided mood in the whole working class, not to escalate open struggle. It was already a mistake if the comrades of the red army, certainly inspired with the best of wills, decided not to obey this decision and to struggle off their own bat. They resorted to arms independently. But, all the same: at least they still enjoyed the sympathy of the working masses, and the workers were still prepared to come out on general strike when the first Noske guards set foot in Rhineland-Westphalia. But then came the threat of sabotage. You have to imagine what effect this had on the masses of mineworkers. Workers, where father, grandfather and even great-grandfather had already worked in the pits; suddenly these disappeared, from one day to the next, the shaft was blown up. There may well be people who see this feeling as outmoded, stemming from a time long past. I personally believe that underlying it is a quite sound thought, that even the finest council-republic is no use if the mines are blown up. But this, too, we don't need to debate. The fact is that the masses experienced the threat of sabotage not as directed against capitalism, but against them, and they began to see the Noske guards, who had already been hailed to them as saviours from sabotage, no longer as the main enemy, but, in places, even as a kind of liberator. The determined will for a general strike was broken by the advance of the troops: it was not the mines that were sabotaged, but the determined defensive action of the proletarians. This was the final result of the sabotage-preachers. In Rhineland-Westphalia, we have the typical case of how making revolution off your own bat can lead to serious harm for the proletariat. We have to say this in the interest of the proletariat itself.

That is the development that the proletariat underwent in this action. On the whole successfully, and the result of this strengthening is that the contradictions between bourgeoisie and proletariat have become so sharp, and the middle-stratum between them so narrow, that the immediate collision of classes can begin any day. We have thus entered once more on a phase of vigorous political life; we assume that the long months of political ebb and quietude are at an end. We are forced to seek our position and our leadership in this more vigorous political life.

First of all, the most recent action in Germany once again created workers' councils, at least in large parts of the country. In my opinion, it is our most important task to do all that we can to keep these councils alive and spread them. The tasks that confront the proletariat in the immediate future are so numerous that there is no shortage of material to politically inspire the councils. There is the question of foreign policy, the question of food-supplies, the debates with the SPD and USPD, with the factory-councils etc. A task that is completely sufficient, and, in my opinion, of the greatest importance especially in the smaller districts in which workers' councils have been formed, is to bring local affairs also into the council. For precisely local matters, discussion of local questions, which, in small places, are experienced with much greater liveliness than in the cities, give the proletariat the right idea of the importance of political questions. Here, far more clearly than in the big cities, the workers' council can take the lead on every question, and develop into the assembly-point of the proletariat.

A particular important task that the councils have is that of weapons. For, if we talk about the Kapp Putsch, we are forced to speak almost more about the future than about the past. With the revolutionary situation coming to a head, with the concentration on both sides, the danger is only strengthened that the reactionary camp resorts to new military coups, all the more so as the time is rapidly approaching when certain sections of the army have to be dissolved.[3] This will accelerate the danger. We have to say quite clearly everywhere that the armed power of the Kapp people can only be broken if it is countered by the armed power of the proletariat. I am of the opinion that a decisive importance on this question falls to the workers' councils. The question can be resolved purely locally in different ways, either by workers' militias being set up by the local authorities under pressure from the council, or by the proletariat solving the question of weapons in a direct practical fashion. The workers' council plays the decisive role when it not only takes the lead in the action,

---

3. [Under the provisions of the Versailles Treaty, the German army was to be reduced to 100,000 men, the Freikorps disbanded, and a number of officers charged with war-crimes arrested.]

but also controls the distribution of weapons to the workers. In other places, control-instances for the local storing of weapons will be created. On these burning questions, the workers' council plays a central part.

In the next few months, as well, political life will be dominated by the elections. We can see it as a misfortune that the electoral movement falls precisely at a time of intensified political life. You may think that this is disastrous, since, in this way, political activity is directed into the wrong area. I must even say that, in a certain sense, there is something correct in this idea. There will be many proletarians who believe that they fulfill a revolutionary duty in this way. I share this point of view, however, only in so far as, in a situation in which such wrong turnings are possible in the proletariat, we can still less afford to be absent. The way that things will develop in practice is like this: if there is not, for example, a new putsch from the right, then German political life will be dominated in the next six months by the elections. I prefer not to go into all the arguments for or against parliamentarism here, and for or against the advantages of participation. The arguments, as I had the satisfaction of seeing, have not got any better since the Heidelberg Congress. The result of all this is that the question for our Party now is simply: is the political situation such as to make participation necessary? I say: yes. For, no matter how you regard the election-movement and what follows, in the light of the Kapp Putsch and its effect on the masses, this election-movement will be a tremendous step towards self-understanding. In a certain sense, there are masses of proletarians who will only take stock of the Kapp Putsch in context of the elections. I believe no one can deny that, in November 1918, the overwhelming majority of the proletariat stood behind the Majority-Socialist party. In the last year and a half, the proletariat has inwardly separated from its former leaders and turned more or less clearly towards communism.[4] We should not forget that such a movement within the great masses of the proletariat does not occur by the proletariat waking up one morning and finding that it is no longer Majority-Socialist but rather USPD or Communist. The process, rather, proceeds in terms of a general feeling; it needed a certain event to arouse

---

4. On the 1919 general election, see above, p. 13, note 30. In the election of 6 June 1920, the SPD remained the largest party, but its vote fell sharply to 21.7%, while the USPD rose to 17.9%. The KPD, contesting the election for the first time, polled 2.1%, sending four deputies including Levi and Zetkin to the Reichstag.

the proletariat to the knowledge that its feeling had changed. All actions are moments of self-understanding of this kind. In the action, when large parts of the masses are faced with the question 'what now?', tremendous masses awaken to clear knowledge of what was formerly just a feeling. There can be no doubt that in the present situation, if new situations do not anticipate this, the election will also be the moment, for many proletarians, at which they take notice, at which, by the simple fact that they take a different voting slip from last time, they awaken to a knowledge of what they have become. This process can then be, for thousands of proletarians, the experience by which they notice that they have changed. It was precisely the weakness of the action of 13 March that, in Berlin, for example, the leadership was still in the hands of the trade-unions and Majority-Socialists, but precisely this can now be turned to use, if the proletariat once more looks back with recognition at the whole last movement, where did the Kapp business come from, who raised it and protected it, etc.?

I am especially sure, therefore, after the experiences that we had in January 1919, how our decision must be made. I need only recall that, today, we are all more or less of the opinion that the January decision of 1919, not to participate in the elections to the National Assembly, was a mistake, and affected us no less severely than the January events and even the murder of Karl Liebknecht and Rosa Luxemburg. For that decision simply banished us for a whole year to political obscurity, and it took its revenge in the way that we let people decide on the fate of our party who, as it emerged, were not Communists and had not read the Spartacus programme. Certainly, we worked and can even see fruits, but, in the wider world, it was as if we did not exist. No party can make such a mistake a second time. That we survived it a first time is miraculous enough. If we Communists join in the election-movement, it is important for us not to lose sight for a moment that our goals lie outside of parliament. Catching votes and winning seats are of secondary importance for us, if they matter at all. The decisive thing is that we show our political face for what it is. We shall distinguish ourselves favourably from all others, and make headway, if we stand firm on this point. We are presenting you with a draft for an appeal in which we seek to express this line. We are not making empty promises, not telling the usual electoral lies, by saying that we are Communists and that we see the achievement of our aims only outside of parliament. The more clearly we Communists present ourselves, then, even if we only receive few votes, we fulfill our task all the more. For, if we remain conscious of the task that Marx handed down to us, the task of showing, in every act of political life, the aims of the proletarian revolution, we can even enter into the election-business that has fallen into discredit with determination and unconcern. We shall emerge from the electoral movement as we went in, and more influential than the Communists of January 1919, who left the proletariat in the lurch at a critical moment by declaring that they were already so much cleverer than the masses, that it was no longer necessary for them to do what twenty million proletarians did at that time and will also do again this time.

The Beginning of the Crisis in the Communist Party and the International*

[Levi cites Zinoviev's speech at Baku, where he said: 'Pursuing Communist world-politics means leading these revolutionary movements of all countries onto a clear course, creating Communist parties in these countries that will prepare the fall of the bourgeoisie intellectually and organisationally with their own strength and their own will, as they are anchored unbreakably in the masses of workers.' He continues:]

Comrades, if I read you this passage and compare it with what I read you before from Kautsky and Ledebour, you will have a pleasant sound in your ears. I say quite deliberately: in my view, we are already beyond the stage at which we have to prepare the fall of the bourgeoisie intellectually and organisationally.

[INTERJECTION: *'Very true!'*]

We are directly in the struggle in which we work, blow by blow, for the fall of the bourgeoisie.

[INTERJECTION: *'Quite right!'*]

And so we see the front that the Communist International refers to not just as a front of Communist parties, we see it – and, here, I deliberately refer to what I have always championed – we see it also as the front

---

* Translated from *Der Beginn der Krise in der Kommunistischen Partei und Internationale. Rede von Paul Levi auf der Sitzung des Zentralauschusses der V.K.P.D. am 24. February 1921* (Remscheid, 1921).

of the oppressed against the front of the oppressors. The front of the oppressed – this must certainly be said – is not a unity. The front of the oppressed includes all conceivable forces, from nationalist through to Communist.

[INTERJECTION: 'Quite right!']

In the front of the oppressed, there are expressly nationalist movements

[AGREEMENT]

as we have in India and Ireland. In the front of the oppressed, there are small peasants who generally do not start out with any political idea, who have only a hunger for land. And, in the front of the oppressed, there are also the conscious Communists of Western Europe; and the great task of the Communist International is to bring together and lead together these forces of very different kinds. The Communist International cannot content itself with influencing these forces merely through propaganda; rather, we were and are of the opinion that the Communist International also has the duty of binding the revolutionary forces who are not Communist organisationally in some kind of way. And it is from this idea that we completely agreed with the creation of sympathisers. This should be the form in which the Communist International, which, in itself and at its core, seeks above all simply to be *the* Communist Party of the whole world, can bind to it, and group around it, those forces that do indeed stand in the camp of the oppressed, but are not Communists. And, from this idea of sympathisers, which we agreed with and still agree with, and which we accept has an important function in the overall struggle of the oppressed against the oppressors, from this idea, a conflict has arisen with the Executive Committee of the Communist International, the conflict about the KAPD.[1] We say that, in Western Europe, where the front of the oppressed is made up principally of Communists, who are the élite of the revolution, the Communist International has the duty of strengthening this élite and not doing anything that could weaken the front of Communists. In Western Europe, where the struggle is not over nationalistic secondary aims or nationalistic primary ones, but where the struggle is for communism, the struggle of the Communist International is equivalent to the struggle of Communists. And, from this idea, we see the admission of the KAPD not

---

1. [See Introduction, pp. 13–15.]

only as a mistake that was made in view of the particular situation of the KAPD, a mistake in so far as it gave the KAPD new life at a point at which it would otherwise have not had any more life, but we also see a different attitude from the one that we had. The declarations of the Zentrale and my article in the *Rote Fahne* have now been criticised. And, here, I would like to bring the critics up to date on a certain matter: we received the communication of the decision to admit the KAPD to the Communist International not directly, but indirectly, and, initially, quite without any commentary. And, I have to say: if something like this occurs, it is quite naturally our immediate duty to take a principled stand towards it. It was and is our view that the duty of the Executive should have been to explain for itself this position of principle towards the KAPD. And this duty on the part of the Executive was recognised by the Executive Committee itself in the telegram that came subsequently: 'The Executive requests its smaller bureau to publish a letter to the German workers explaining the motive behind this decision.'

This letter has still not arrived. It should have been the first thing to arrive following the decision, and would have relieved us of the whole troublesome and unpleasant task of ourselves taking a position and ourselves making a hostile declaration towards the KAPD. But we *had* to do this, to show our face, and we did do so in our fundamental position against the KAPD. We were obliged to do so, as, after the struggle we had waged with the KAPD about our fundamental position, we could not allow the KAPD to be admitted with our making a public commentary. Our Berlin comrades particularly regret that the protest we then published was not followed by any positive statement. I would like to say to them: the same active position that you yourselves wanted, i.e. that we should demand concrete measures from the Executive, is already there in our protest-statement. After the Executive Committee of the Communist International had decided to admit the KAPD, we wanted the Executive Committee to give the relationship of the KAPD to the Communist International a concrete form, expressed first of all in an 'adjustment' of the KAPD's language; given that the Executive Committee could now apply its influence and disciplinary power, it should have compelled the KAPD to remain, in Germany itself, within the front that it accepted in Moscow. It is our opinion that, if that had come from Moscow, the development would have been extraordinarily swift, and the KAPD would have seen that membership of the Communist International does not mean sending a commission to Moscow but accepting a certain front in Germany. This we already explained in the first letter to the Executive Committee. We cannot erase the fact that the KAPD has been admitted, this matter can only be resolved by the Executive Committee maintaining towards the KAPD the organisational consequences of its membership, and compelling it either to remain in the front or to separate off again.

Comrades, if we consider the front of the oppressed against the oppressors, we do not just have to establish the historical line that this front takes, we do not just have to consider the historical tasks, but we must concern ourselves with what the present tasks of this front are. And I come here to a matter that has played a certain role in the last few years under the question: 'offensive or defensive tactics for the Party?'. I already spoke about this offensive tactic in Berlin, in a statement that was, in my view, misunderstood. I do not want to repeat this here, but ask you to read the speech in the material that you have before you. I say: the tactic of the Communist International must, in any case, be an offensive tactic in the present situation. Why I say this results from what I explained at the start: the Entente is stuck fast, it is experiencing a crisis and has been forced by this crisis on to the defensive, and so it is the moment for us to go over to the offensive. And what does the offensive mean? It means that we do not damp down any of the conflicts that arise, but, rather, bring them to a head, sharpen them, and do all that we can to force the bourgeoisie not to delay its conflicts but to fight them out directly and immediately. This was also, as well as the idea that I mentioned previously, one of the ideas that guided us in the position we took towards the demands of the Entente.[2] The slogan 'Alliance with Soviet Russia'[3] forces Germany, and forces France and England, into conflict; the Paris demands can, of course, still be further delayed, the possibility technically exists; our task is to bring matters to a head so that the German bourgeoisie is forced into a violent resolution of its differences and forced to fight out the conflict now and at this moment. Our view was that there is no slogan better suited to arouse the interest of the German proletariat and more actively bring it into this foreign policy than that of alliance with Soviet Russia. We are convinced that this is the only slogan with which to lead the proletarian masses into activity in the international

2. [The KPD had opposed the Versailles Treaty.]
3. [See Introduction, p. 15.]

context, and it is also the only slogan that most rapidly will bring the conflict to a head in the context of bourgeois politics. And so, comrades, I must say that we never had a clearer conscience than when we proclaimed this slogan. It was a situation in which we did not expect an action to ensue the next day, but we did see a situation with the possibility of action, of proletarian action, and we proclaimed the slogan, I believe, at the earliest moment that it was possible, the slogan with which to lead the masses onto the streets when conditions were right. And, now, this slogan, which therefore, in my opinion, was the most active and was proclaimed in good time, has encountered particular misfortune. First of all by the Munich comrades having been so foolish as to go far beyond the goal and extending it to the bourgeoisie. This is undoubtedly a mistake. But we also see the Berlin comrades as having made a mistake.

[INTERJECTION: *'Quite right!'*]

How the Berlin comrades see things, I would like once again to show from the article I mentioned, in which Friesland[4] says:

> We do not want any actions that are too far-fetched, as have been proposed
> to the German workers and to the Executive. We want the working masses
> to be shown the clear, unambiguous path of the German Revolution, even
> if this is heavy going…

Once again, therefore, sticking completely to propagandistic activity, and in a situation in which we are not calling people onto the streets right away, but tomorrow, in certain circumstances, perhaps on 3 or 4 March, if Simons returns, we shall call the workers onto the streets. In this situation, the Berlin people reproach us for giving out a slogan 'for an action that is too far-fetched'. And there is something else to point out in this connection: the Munich people did indeed do us harm with what they did, and this is a serious wrong turn: but it is unclear whether it is more or less serious than the other one, if the Berlin comrades in such a situation attack a party-slogan, which can directly lead to action and will lead to action, with such a criticism, and, in this way, inhibit it.

---

4. [Ernst Friesland, also known as Ernst Reuter, was a leader of the left faction in the KPD, but, after replacing Levi as general secretary, he moved rightward and was expelled from the Party in 1922. After returning from exile in 1945, he was mayor of West Berlin during the Cold War.]

[INTERJECTION: *'Quite correct!'*]

And, for this reason, I would like to say one thing right away: if the *Rote Fahne* was consistent, as we would like it to be, it would not have accepted the article at all. That didn't happen, and I myself was not in favour of it. It is clear that, in a young party such as ours, wrong turns are bound to happen. But we should not close our minds to this: at a point in time when the important thing was to call the masses to action, we had to begin once more to recite the ABC. And, so long as we have to do this, we cannot yet be up to the level of the task that we have to fulfill.

[INTERJECTION: *'Especially not in Berlin!'*]

And then, comrades, it is quite clear that the Communist forces, the forces of the international workers' organisation, as I have previously described them, must and do have certain organisational forms, and that these organisational forms do not just express our position in the context of the Communist International, but also its relationship to the proletarian masses that are not yet within the sphere of the Communist International.

Comrades, I believe that if we consider this, we bear in mind two points. The one is that the greatest obstacle to the development of the Communist forces in Western Europe was not the bourgeoisie, but rather the workers' organisations; all revolutionary movements so far have broken against this wall.

[INTERJECTION: *'Very true!'*]

For this reason, I believe that, to be sure, the relationship of Communists to the unorganised masses is of great importance, and there are revolutionary situations in which the unorganised masses are directly of decisive significance. But we, in Western Europe, with our strong workers' organisations, must never lose sight of our relationship to these workers' organisations. Our relationship to the organised masses, in comparison to our relationship to the unorganised ones, is perhaps quite the other way round in Western Europe from how it was for example in Russia etc., where the relationship of the organised Communist party to the unorganised was of overwhelmingly great importance in the whole context of the proletarian forces – far, far greater in scope than with us in Western Europe. And, from this idea, there also follows a second: this movement of the organised working masses finds no better expression, in my mind, than the fact that the Second and

Two-and-a-Half Internationals,[5] which, as I have said, always stick together, and will soon be together again, are in a certain process of concentration. Until some six months ago, this was not the case. Until about six months ago, we were completely on the offensive, and they were on the floor with their bones broken. But, in the last half-year, they are beginning to stir again, beginning to gather themselves, beginning to make conscious resistance to the Communist wave, and are ready in certain conditions, as for example with the trade-unions in Germany, to go over already to the offensive. And, for this reason, comrades, the relationship we have to these organised masses is of greatest importance for us. A situation in which we appear as open enemies of these organised masses would seriously restrict us in our movement, and perhaps for a long time to come.

[AGREEMENT]

We must not appear as enemies of these organised masses, but as friends. In this relationship, which is of extraordinary importance for us in Western Europe, we believe that the Executive Committee of the Communist International has not fully appreciated our perspectives. We shall get into a hostile relationship to these organised masses if we appear as the splitters. It cannot be denied that there is a deep sense of belonging together in the proletarian masses, and anyone who gets branded as a splitter without this appearing justified in the eyes of the masses, places themselves in a very difficult situation. And, comrades, we believe that the Executive Committee of the Communist International, from this point of view, has been mistaken on the question of the trade-unions. It is true that the German syndicalists were expelled from the Communist International. Moreover, they were grateful for this honour and have remained outside the Communist International. But the fact remains that the Communist International wanted them back. Secondly, certain connections – I have not managed to shed light on this

---

5. [The International Working Union of Socialist Parties, also known as the 'Two-and-a-Half International', was founded in Vienna in February 1921; its affiliates included the USPD, the Social-Democratic Party of Austria, and the Independent Labour Party. The merger of the USPD with the SPD in September 1922 seriously weakened the organisation, and, in 1923, the IWUSP merged with the Second International to form the Labour and Socialist International.]

matter – certain connections have been made to the Arbeiter-Unionen.[6] The Gelsenkirchen Free Workers' Union has been admitted with our agreement, because this organisation is strongly influenced by us. But, as well as this, other connections have been made to other Unions, and the way in which the Executive has dealt with this question of the trade-unions, which is of the utmost importance for us, is generally unfortunate. I assure comrades, I believe that none of the comrades on the Zentrale knows how many commissions there are and have been in Germany, which feel called to work on the trade-union question in Germany. It is a quite unreasonable situation: one comrade reaches a quite reasonable relationship with us, then another comrade comes and issues different guidelines on this very difficult question. And so I say that, with these connections that have been made between the Communist International and these associations, the Executive Committee has managed, on the one hand, to disguise the real nature of the Communist International from the broad proletarian masses, and, secondly, it has made a connection with those who are decried as splitters among the working class. It was with this in mind that we took the decision on the trade-union question that we sent to Moscow and published at the same time.

Comrades, it was at this juncture that the Italian situation arose, which has attracted such extraordinary attention, and which, in fact, has been, in recent days at any rate, a question of the greatest interest and greatest importance in principle. I want first of all to give a historical presentation of the Italian question, how things developed. We had, first of all, decided, back in the unruly days of January, not to send any delegate to Livorno. A few days before the congress was to take place, the news arrived that passes had been distributed and that a delegate needed only four or five days to travel there and back. It was decided that I should go to Livorno: I had to leave early on Wednesday and was supposed to be back the following Tuesday, when there was a meeting of the Reichstag fraction. When the decision was made that I should go to Livorno, I explained, first of all, my view of the Italian situation, as this was known to me from reading the newspapers, with the object that you would later have understood my point of view. At that point, the Zentrale agreed with this view. I communicated my viewpoint in writing to

---

6. [The 'workers' unions' of the syndicalists.]

Comrade Clara Zetkin, as she was unable to be there, and she responded in writing and continues, I believe, to share my point of view. Then, I travelled out on Wednesday, after having had on Tuesday evening, from eight until one in the morning, a discussion with the representative of the Executive who was in Berlin at that time, in which we dealt with the Italian question in minute detail. I read out the key passages from the letter from Comrade Zetkin that I had received the same morning, and received agreement to act in this sense: we should seek to keep Serrati, but we had definitely to demand of him that the Turati people be excluded. This decision was made accordingly, and, comrades, I emphasise right away: the Zentrale was aware in this decision that this line would, in certain circumstances, not coincide with that of the Executive Committee. For it was decided, with a view to this possibility, that I should certainly take no step in Livorno that would put me at odds with the representatives of the Executive Committee there. Thus, I left for Livorno with God's blessing and the decisions of the Zentrale. Both turned out to be equally fragile. On Sunday, a telegram arrived from Moscow that the representative of the Executive read out to us, stating that the new decision of the Executive was: sharp struggle against Serrati. The representative of the Executive – and Comrade Däumig here can attest to this – wanted a similar telegram to be sent to me, so that I was informed of the new conception of the Executive. The telegram was sent off on Sunday, but, because I left Livorno on Sunday, it failed to reach me. I then returned from Livorno and had the impressions that I had received there confirmed, and these impressions only strengthened the decision we had previously made. As a result of this, I published the article that you likewise know, without signing it; for I do not believe that, at that stage, either on the Zentrale or on the editorial board of *Rote Fahne*, anyone whom I spoke with represented a different view. It was, at that time, the view of all comrades whose views mattered. I then arranged to meet the representative of the Communist International on the following Sunday, and already received serious criticisms, though, at this point, they remained within friendly forms. On the Monday, the representative[7] of the Executive began to publish in *Rote Fahne* the three articles signed 'P.B.', in which he polemicised not against the Zentrale, but against me personally, as the unsigned author of the article. I want to say one thing right away: the

---

7. [I.e. Radek. See Introduction, p. 16.]

entire material published in the three articles is old material. Not all of it was known to me, but I was familiar with part of it and it was *all* known to the representative of the Executive Committee when we discussed together what our position should be.

[INTERJECTION: *'Hear, hear!'*]

The Executive representative then demanded a session of the Zentrale. This took place, and did not follow the forms that we had previously practised. Previously, we would debate with one another; this time, there were quite sharp personal clashes, so that I said that I had come to debate and not to trade insults; as long as this went on, I had nothing to say and left.

The following morning, I received a letter from the representative of the Executive Committee in which he took back and apologised for the personal insults, but in which certain things were wrongly represented. To take one thing first of all: even if one's opinion is that the view of the Zentrale at this time on the Italian situation was wrong, I believe that I was justified in writing an article like the one I published on the Italian question. If it is no longer possible to publish one's own view in the form that I did, then any kind of criticism is finished.

[AGREEMENT]

In sum, it was no occasion for personal invective. Despite this, the representative of the Executive explained the following evening: 'With this article you are opening a deliberate campaign against the Executive. We shall anticipate you and draw the sword against you.' I asked quite calmly: if you draw the sword, 1) with what means do you intend to struggle against me, and 2) with what aim? He gave the same day a confused answer, and, also in the letter that I received the next morning, the response was confused. I wrote a reply to the letter that, by unfortunate circumstances, found its way to *Freiheit*,[8] in which I in no way pleaded for the blessing of the Executive, but, rather, in which I sought from the representative of the Executive a clear and unambiguous reply to my questions.

And, now, comrades, we – I believe also Comrade Clara Zetkin and others – have not been shaken by arguments that were old and brought nothing new. That was not the case with other comrades. They vacillated in their conviction, and so the attitude of the Zentrale since then on this question has not

---

8. [The newspaper of the USPD (Independents).]

been very impressive. The matter first acquired importance by the representative of the Executive compelling us to accept a resolution. This was already very foolish. We had no need to pass a resolution on the Italian question; it was quite unnecessary for us to interfere by a resolution in a matter that was up to the Executive to settle organisationally. The published resolution was then passed, and I stress that this resolution too was, once more, accepted unanimously, and this is the resolution that I stand by today, although it since has been abandoned by some comrades who accepted it at that time.

And, now, comrades, I want to present the Italian situation, but first to anticipate one thing. Many comrades have said: yes, our previous decisions were based on one-sided reports that I or other people had made, etc. We have shown you the report from Comrade Marbosi as well as the report that I sent to the Executive Committee immediately after my return from Italy. I believe you will see that, *in nuce*, the judgement of the situation, the judgement of Italian conditions, is not so far apart. In what I want to say about the Italian situation, I shall not just base myself on my personal impressions, but, rather, on what Comrade Marbosi has said. He expressed himself as follows:

> The situation was that the great majority of Italian workers are for the Third International. And so they were very confused because all sides said that they accepted the Twenty-One Conditions. The workers are not so canny as to see the deceit....

When I came to this passage in Comrade Marbosi's report, it reminded me of debates from earlier times, and I have to read out to you, to illustrate this similarity, what Wolffheim said to the Hamburg people then:

> If the German proletarians were not accustomed to following their leaders in everything, if astonishment had not led them to lose the power of speech and the ability to think, then they would at least have raised the question at that moment [i.e. on 9 November] as to what do now to maintain the power they had conquered....The proletarians did not reach the idea that the conquered power now also had to be anchored, to be newly organised.[9]

---

9. [See above, p. 64.]

In just the way that Wolffheim saw the November Revolution and its failure
as arising from a lack of ability to think, and the speechless astonishment of
the German proletariat

[INTERJECTION FROM FRÖLICH: *'You're arguing against yourself!'*]

in just the same way, Comrade Marbosi sees the situation in Italy in terms of
the confusion of the workers. I take one thing from what Comrade Marbosi
says, which was unchallenged and was the foundation of all my conclusions: the majority of the Italian proletariat and of the workers organised in
the Italian Socialist Party were *for* the Third International, and, equally, the
unchallenged fact that, today at any rate, this majority is not in organisational
terms within the Communist International. This is the one basis from which I
proceed. The other thesis on which I base myself was expressed by Comrade
Marbosi as follows: 'We would have been able to reach the masses, but only
by also taking their leaders. And that we refused to do.'

And, then, if I proceed from these two propositions, I want to put forward
my idea of the Italian question once again. It is correct that the majority of
Italian Communists support the Third International and acknowledge their
adherence to it, but, organisationally, they remain outside of it. And this raises
the fundamental question: how are we to proceed with the construction of a
Communist party in Western Europe? One thing first of all: the Communist
International can be one of two things; it can either be an organisation of Communists in the strictest and most exclusive sense, or it can be the organisation
of the masses whose political understanding is not something firmly fixed,
but who are led by Communists and, above all, are prepared to accept Communist discipline. These two possible conceptions of the Communist International have not been more clearly expressed than by Comrade Gorter[10] in the
Kommunistische Arbeiterzeitung no. 162, when he wrote:

> After the defeat and disarmament of the German proletariat, it and the
> world-proletariat is faced with the question: how, by what tactic, can the
> unarmed proletariat be victorious in Western Europe and more generally in
> a highly developed capitalist country?...Two answers came from Western
> Europe itself, which was in the best position to judge this: a revolutionary-
> opportunist one [says Gorter] and a Marxist-revolutionary one [says

---

10. [Herman Gorter, a Dutch poet and socialist, moved to Germany in 1920 and
helped to found the KAPD.]

Gorter]....The first is a tactic that could only lead to the attraction of non-Communist elements on a massive scale, and to the revolution running into the ground....We sent Moscow our advice in favour of a tactic that was completely opposed to this. We counselled the choice of a tactic that would make the Communist parties of Western Europe genuinely revolutionary by their completely transforming the trade-unions, establishing new ones, and keeping the outbreak of revolution separate from elections. This tactic would have made the Communist parties much stronger internally, would have schooled the whole proletariat through struggle over genuinely basic questions, and made it ready and able for revolution....Either revolutionary opportunism or revolutionary Marxism....And the Third International has chosen the same tactic, the opportunist one! ...The dreadful result of this tactic is that, as I already explained in Moscow at the session of the Third International, that it is leading the German Revolution and thus the world-revolution into the marsh....For we can rule out that elements that are not truly Communist but have now joined the Third International, indeed, that are literally pursued with all means (Zinoviev at Halle, Clara Zetkin at Tours), that these will lead the great masses to revolution.

Here, the two principles are clearly counterposed. For us, it is not a question of attracting masses who do not think at all for themselves, – that is a polemical exaggeration of Gorter's –, but we rather need masses that already have a revolutionary development and experience behind them, and an experience that already prepares them for certain acts, for acts that, in some circumstances, are very difficult. And an example of such an act, in which these proletarians showed their determination, we see among others in the split in this party that the workers of the USPD carried out at Halle.

Finished Communists do not exist in this world. There is nobody who does not daily learn in the struggle and in the situation. There are no leaders who know everything better in advance, who know precisely how things are, and there are no masses who simply trot behind; instead, there is a mutual political learning and experiencing, in the course of which, we shape our tactics, our knowledge, and practice. In the Communist International, the following tactic had been practised at least since the Second Congress in Moscow: to try, in the above sense, to absorb masses with political experience into the Communist parties and the Communist International. Comrades, if one splits parties, as we Communists have done, which are organisationally not connected with us, then it is possible to draw the line either narrowly or widely. The Executive of the Communist International, for example, drew the line in Germany in accordance with our wishes in such a way that the Ledebour people were excluded and everybody left of Ledebour[11] and Rosenfeld[12] admitted to our side. One might quarrel over whether, for example, the line in France should have been drawn more tightly or not. I want to tell you, Comrade Frölich, that when Zinoviev arrived in Germany[13] – and this not my impression alone – he had totally changed; we who, in Moscow, had still been, in his eyes, semi-Independents had to hold him by his coat-tails in order to check him. But, to continue, whether the line should have been drawn somewhat more tightly in France is another question. In Italy, we are concerned with something altogether different. In my article on the subject, I wrote the following with full consciousness:

> With the Italian party-congress, an event has occurred which is new in the history of the Third International. What has happened is not the splitting of a party of the Second International for the purpose of a union of its Communist members with the Communist International, but a party already belonging to the Communist International has been split in order to be able to continue as a member of the Communist International. One may comfort oneself by saying: the split was necessary...

I am saying that we are dealing here with a case where we did not split another party in order to create the basis for a mass-party, but where we split a party which is organisationally connected with us. And this raises a

---

11. [Georg Ledebour was a journalist and SPD Reichstag deputy who had opposed the War and was a founder of the USPD. He formed close ties to the revolutionary shop-stewards' movement which was generally distrustful of politicians, and, after the November Revolution, was elected to the executive of the workers' and soldiers' councils. He played an active role in the Spartacus uprising, but remained in the USPD, even after the greater part of its left wing joined the KPD in November 1920, and almost all the remainder merged back into the SPD in 1922. He remained a leading figure on the German Left until forced to flee from the Nazis to Switzerland, where he continued political work until 1946, calling, at the age of 96, for the unification of the SPD and KPD.]

12. [Kurt Rosenfeld, a lawyer who had defended Rosa Luxemburg, was a founder of the USPD and, after the War, a Reichstag member and Prussian minister of justice. After rejoining the SPD, he was along with Paul Levi a leading member of its left wing.]

13. [This was for the Halle Congress of the USPD in November 1920. See Introduction, p. 14.]

major question of principle, a question, I think, of crucial importance to the Communist International. If we have connected these masses organisationally with us, these masses who are, as I said, as little finished Communists as all of us are, and who experience the process of communism as their political life, what do we do to promote and realise their education? And, here, comrades, one thing should be crystal-clear: there exist two ways in which to achieve a higher degree of communist experience in these masses organisationally connected with the Third International. One way to carry out this education involves new splits; the other way implies that we train politically the masses who have found their way to us, experience with them the present age, the revolution, and in this way reach a higher stage together with and within the masses. That is the problem and with it a problem has been opened up which is not new in the history of socialism. It is the old problem regarding the formation of socialist parties.

I do not want to conceal anything: the old difference between Rosa Luxemburg and Lenin emerges here again, the old difference which involved a question: how are Social-Democratic parties – in the parlance of the day – formed? History has produced its judgement. Lenin was right: socialist and communist parties could also be created through the strictest screening proposed by him. In a time of illegality, he produced a good party by means of the strictest screening and by the mechanical process of adding one communist to another; and perhaps, comrades, if we were confronted with a period of illegality of ten years, we might also vote in favour of this way. But we do not count on a period of ten years.

[INTERJECTION FROM FRÖLICH: '*1905 was the revolution!*']

The revolution that showed the capability of the Communist Party was in 1917, the process took until then. I am saying that, if we had such a period ahead of us, maybe we would choose this way, although even then the one vast difference about which I just spoke would still remain: the organisational emphasis, in addition to all the other considerable differences between the past Russian period and the present German and European period. But, above all else, we do not expect such a period and, for this reason, we are of the opinion that we can only win over the masses, make Communists out of them, create a big party, and engage in Communist politics, if we maintain the closest relations with the masses, drawing them nearer to us ever more tightly instead of splitting them off.

[INTERJECTION: *'Why not accept the KAPD, then?'*]
You are completely right, the moment that the KAPD wants to join with us,
I will be the last to be against that. I have nothing against it! They can join
with us tomorrow, I have nothing against their entry as party-members. I
say: the whole contrast will be clear to you, if I quote the following from
Rosa Luxemburg's essay from 1904:

> The conditions for Social-Democratic activity are radically different. This
> derives historically from the elemental class struggle. It operates within the
> dialectical contradiction that here it is only in the struggle itself that the
> proletarian army is itself recruited and only in the struggle that it becomes
> conscious of the purpose of the struggle. Organisation, enlightenment and
> struggle are here not separate moments mechanically divided in time, as in
> a Blanquist movement, they are merely different facets of the same process.
> On the one hand, apart from the general basic principles of struggle, there
> is no ready-made predetermined and detailed tactic of struggle that the
> Central Committee could drill into the Social-Democratic membership. On
> the other hand, the process of struggle that creates the organisation stipulates
> a constant fluctuation in the sphere of influence of Social-Democracy. From
> this it follows that Social-Democratic centralization cannot be based either
> on blind obedience or on the mechanical submission of the party's militants
> to their central authority and, further, that an impenetrable wall can never
> be erected between the nucleus of the class-conscious proletariat that is
> already organised into tightly knit party cadres and those in the surrounding
> stratum who have already been caught up in the class struggle and are in
> the process of developing class consciousness.[14]

And, so, I am saying, comrades, that, in the case of Italy, the road has been
taken for the first time to conduct the education of the Communist masses
within the Communist International, not through an organic development
but through a mechanical split. That I am not simply looking at the dark side,
that I am perceiving, in fact, the underlying principle – as may be expected
from the Russian comrades – and a well-thought-out principle at that, which

---

14. 'Organisational Questions of Russian Social Democracy'; Hudis and Anderson
(eds.), p. 252.

will have its effect, I infer again from the explanations of Comrade Marbosi.[15] Speaking of France he said: 'There too we have many undesirable people, as for example Lafont, who was expelled from Russia by Trotsky and who is now a member of the Communist Party, and Cachin,[16] who is a member of the Masons...'. He continued: 'Aside from the fact that we wanted to create a precedent, this question is not just an Italian question. This can be currently seen in the negotiations with the French Party and with the Czechoslovakian Party...'.

The principle to create parties within the Communist International not through organic growth with the masses but through deliberate splits is thus now to be applied to the French Party; and, I am telling you, comrades, with all the seriousness at my command – may the representative of the ECCI return to Moscow and report on it – that, if the Communist International functions in Western Europe in terms of admission and expulsion like a recoiling cannon; if the correction in France – where, I admit, the line was possibly drawn too loosely – is to be carried out not through the unification and direction of the masses who would then proceed with the correction on their own, but through repeated splitting, then we will experience in Western Europe the worst possible setback. And, I add that the principle adopted in this instance is a principle which can be and will be applied to all parties. Among us Germans too there are opportunists; Friesland may possibly say I am one of them, but I know others as well. There are opportunists in our midst; we will experience splits to the right and left in Germany too, in the same way as I had considered the right split in Italy vis-à-vis Turati absolutely necessary, because it could be carried out by keeping the masses, who are in favour of the Third International. To continue: it is possible that we too may have splits in Germany both right and left; if, however, the process of the training and creation of still more stalwart cadres – and all of us are in need of more training – is to achieved by means of repeated splits, then I say, comrades: Communism will not survive the next split in Germany.
[APPLAUSE]

---

15. [Levi is referring to two articles by Rákosi published in the *Rote Fahne*, no. 95 (26 February 1921) and no. 99 (1 March 1921), in which Rákosi defended his and Kabakchiev's actions in Italy and the policy of splits in general.]

16. [Despite Rákosi's stricture against Marcel Cachin, he remained a loyal member of the PCF, and editor of *L'Humanité*, until his death in 1958.]

It will suffer for many, many years from the remedy. I am telling you, comrades, the elections to the provincial diets and the picture they convey – I believe that as many voters of the former USPD turned to the SPD as to us – speak volumes. I am not speaking about the number of seats which we might have gained through the elections, but I am speaking about the mood of these masses, who preferred to return to the party of Ebert and Noske rather than to come to us Communists.[17] These are very serious lessons, and to be considered for our conduct in the elections and for the results of a split as necessary as that of the USPD was.

And, now, comrades, I would like to return briefly to the Italian question.[18] I maintain that it was possible in Italy to separate the right wing from the Party without losing the masses. I appeal in this connection to no one else than Marbosi himself, who says quite clearly in the section to which I have already referred: 'We would have swept the masses along with us – but we could have done so only by taking the leaders, that is, the Serrati people, into the bargain. For this reason, we let go of the masses…' – this makes the case quite clear to me. I had stated in a resolution I submitted, in which I strictly avoided, as in all other statements, all identification and solidarity with the person of Serrati: 'No price is too high for the unity of the Italian Communists, short of the continued membership of the Turati people.' I have always been of the opinion that, if the masses could be retained within the Communist party of the International only by taking Serrati into the bargain, then the price was not too high. Comrades, I cannot help myself, but I think that, on the whole question of the Italian split, there has developed an all-too-mechanical view in the minds of our Russian friends and of the representatives present in Italy as well. I do not know whether our Russian friends are unanimous, for, according to reports received by me, Zinoviev is said to have taken a different position, but to have been outvoted. But it seems to me that the comrades did not clearly realise that splits in a mass-party with a different intellectual structure from, for example, that of the illegal Russian Party – which performed brilliantly in its own way – cannot be carried out on the basis of resolutions, but only on the basis of political experience.

---

17. [After the USPD split at the Halle Congress in October 1920, a little more than a third of its 800,000 members joined the KPD and roughly the same number joined the SPD.]

18. [See Introduction, pp. 15–16.]

If we had confronted the comrades of the USPD with a resolution from Moscow and declared: 'Now get out of the Party', then we would not have mustered the 400,000 members we did on the basis of a political struggle lasting a year or more. In the course of this struggle, the masses personally had experienced and understood the deep political differences, understanding at the same time that the Party had to draw the necessary conclusions. If we had come only with a resolution in Germany, we would simply have flopped. It was a mistake on the part of the Italian comrades as well as of the ECCI, because the political differences had not been clearly enough worked out; they were not strong enough against the Turati people, though I continue to be of the opinion that they would have been sufficient. But, in the understanding of the masses, there existed no cause for a split with the Serrati people. But read the draft of the Stöcker-Thalheimer[19] resolution, in which particular reasons are explained: reasons that are cooked up, desk-work, not a single reason that was alive in the Italian masses, so that any honest proletarian was bound to say: yes, I have to separate from the Serrati people. I tell you: it may be the fault of the Italian Communists that they did not explain this opposition strongly enough, if the split with Serrati was indeed necessary, but it was also the fault of the ECCI. Things cannot be done this way. Until the middle of 1920, Serrati was outwardly in Italy, before the Italian masses and the Party, the representative of the ideas of the Communist International, still sitting in Moscow as a member of the presidium of the Congress; and, a quarter of a year later, the masses are told Serrati is a traitor. The masses do not re-adjust their ideas that quickly; they have to recognise, from the concrete questions of their daily struggle, that a split is necessary. If they fail to do that and we split nonetheless, then, I say, we burden ourselves with the heavy opprobrium of splitters.

[APPLAUSE]

---

19. [Walter Stöcker became chair of the KPD after Levi's resignation. He led the Party's Reichstag fraction, and was convicted in the Reichstag fire-trial; he died of typhus in Buchenwald. August Thalheimer, with a reputedly deep knowledge of Marxism, had been active in the Spartakus group and was a member of the KPD Zentrale. He supported the 'theory of the offensive' in 1921, but was blamed with Brandler for the failure of the revolutionary attempt of 1923. He died in exile in Cuba.]

We know that splits were and are necessary, but we must avoid splits in which the burden of blame falls on us simply because the masses do not know that a matter of life and death is involved.

And, so, comrades, as we see, the Italian question now presents, with the consequences that the representative of the Executive Committee has explained, a question of the most serious kind also for our German party. We must be completely clear how we intend to further build up and construct the German Communist Party, whether we want to remain and grow with the masses together, irrespective of splits right or left, or whether we want to aim at a higher form of Communist organisation, in which, after some coexistence, we again split off the cream that has formed. And I say quite openly, there are signs in the Party that this is the path being considered. I say this openly, the comrades in the Party who are thinking once again of this kind of faction-forming may not yet be thinking of the end-result, but they will lead to a split. I want to say to the comrades: in our party, organisationally and otherwise, everything is in flux, there is no comrade who would be prevented from taking the post of any other comrade; there is no occasion for a faction forming in our party. If someone has better ideas, they should take over the leadership [INTERJECTION: *'Very true!'*],

and should remain in the masses and with the masses; in this young party, however, to start with faction-forming and, once again, take a course that we know where it must lead with iron necessity, this, I say, I should like to warn the comrades against. We have already had the experience in Germany of what Communists are in a revolution, in action, as a small circle of Communists without that wide circle of comrades around them who have a Communist orientation and are willing to accept Communist leadership. We have precisely been familiar, comrades, of how powerless we essentially were, how our best ideas and good ideas simply shattered against the paper-wall of organisation between us and the masses. And we do not want to follow this path any more, for the sake of the masses and for our own sake. For the sake of our own formation and our own survival, we have to remain in a mass Communist party of this kind. The Communists and the masses cannot leave one another: 'If they keep closely entwined, they'll both do all right.' And, because I see today a path being embarked on that must, with iron consequences, lead to this parting, and because this parting is indicated in the view of the Italian question, for this reason, it has become a question of survival for us, and this is why we ask you in all seriousness to consider the standpoint that you want to take.

[BRAVOS AND APPLAUSE]

Letter to Loriot[*]

Dear Comrade Loriot,

I read about you from time to time in the papers, and a comrade has asked our Zentrale to follow up your request and let you know something about conditions in Germany.

The position of our party in Germany is dominated at the moment by the merger with the sections that have split off from the USPD. We all see this process as one of greatest importance. This split and the merger with us is a conclusion to two years of history of the German Revolution. The situation in Germany was actually that, right from the very first days of the Revolution, ever-larger layers of the German proletariat listened to the words of the Communists. The Communist Party itself, however, was illegal from a few days after its foundation in January 1919; it had to retreat into clandestinity under the blows of the counter-revolution, under the onslaught of Noske's troops and the persecution of the police. For a year and a half, it could hardly appear in public anywhere or at any time, its whole existence was illegal. This had the effect that the influence the KPD exerted

---

* This letter dated 23 November 1920 is translated after Beradt (ed.) 1969, from a copy in the Paul Levi archive. [The French Socialist Fernand Loriot had opposed the War from 1915, and helped to win the majority of the SFIO to the Third International in 1920. He withdrew from a leading position in the PCF in 1922, and left the Party in 1926, becoming an editor of the independent left journal *La Révolution prolétarienne*.]

was not directly expressed in the ranks of the Party, but, rather, in a strengthening of the ranks of that party which could work legally and thus gather in it organisationally all the masses who were gripped by Communist ideas, i.e. the USPD. The power and strength of the so-called left wing of the USPD grew in proportion to the growth of the Communist idea in Germany, and you could read the growth of the Communist idea from the development of the USPD just like on a manometer. In January 1919, the Communist idea within the masses of the USPD was still so weak that the foundation of the Communist Party scarcely had any effect on the organisation of the USPD. In March 1919, it was already strong enough that the right wing of the USPD had to abandon up to a point its slogan of democracy, and make a compromise with the left wing on the 'anchoring of the councils in the constitution'. The left wing was still sufficiently weak that it had to agree to this compromise. By November 1919, the left wing had grown strong enough to come to the Leipzig Congress with a majority for adhesion to the Communist International, but it was still sufficiently weak that it was trapped again in another compromise. In October 1920, the left wing was strong enough to have a majority at the Halle Congress for the Communist International and for the Moscow conditions, and, at the same time, strong enough to draw the organisational consequences from this position, i.e. to exclude the right wing from the Party. So, if we now find ourselves together with the left wing of the USPD, this is the union with a considerable throng of proletarian fighters who had not only fought with us in all the great actions of the German proletariat, but who had won, in these long battles, a schooling in political matters that makes them Communists in the best sense of the term. The unification and the ensuing foundation of the Unified Communist Party of Germany is thus a concentration of proletarian forces in the best sense of the word.

All this is not to deny that the bourgeoisie has also concentrated itself politically to an extraordinary degree. The German bourgeoisie today is no longer confined to dominating the state-apparatus, but has organised strong military forces, partly for internal reasons and partly for external ones. A whole flock of armed organisations are found now across Germany. Petty bourgeois, intellectuals, and, above all, farmers have been armed in their hundreds of thousands, and, despite the disarmament-legislation and everything else, the bourgeoisie is stiff with weapons. On top of all this, the self-confidence of the bourgeoisie has increased extraordinarily. This is best seen in the way that the position of the Majority Social Democrats has changed. Until some six months ago, the Majority-Socialists were asked for their collaboration in government, but, then, it was explained to them quite openly, with a scornful smile, they were no longer needed.[1] For the bourgeoisie, they've gone downhill. But the bourgeoisie cannot say this of the proletariat. In the proletariat, the Majority-Socialists still have a stronger position than one might have expected, in view of the acts of Noske, and also in view of the organisational toughness of the German proletariat, quite apart from the fact that the Majority-Socialists will also experience a certain growth in the immediate future by crushing the part of the USPD that stands between them and us.

Because the Social Democrats no longer pursue open collaboration with the bourgeoisie, or can no longer pursue this, and have gone into opposition, the further revolutionary process within the proletariat is taking a different guise. The centre of gravity of the Revolution now lies in the conflict between Communists and Social Democrats. And this is no simple process, but, because of the extremely strong organisational anchorage of the German Social Democrats – in part through the Party, but especially through the trade-unions – this is a very tough struggle in which every single position has to be wrestled for.

The collapse of the whole economy, the rising unemployment and hunger, obviously help our agitation. In absolute terms, we should expect the sum of impoverishment that we see in Germany today to be unbearable for the proletariat. But something similar is at work here as what we saw during the War. Anyone who predicted in 1914 what the German proletariat would have to put up with in the way of deprivations by 1918 would have been told that this was impossible. It was possible because it came about gradually. Similarly now: the sum of misery that prevails among the proletariat in Germany today is almost unimaginable, and is only tolerated by the proletariat because it was just gradually piled on the shoulders of the German proletariat, one pound after another.

The German bourgeoisie, however, while gathering its forces politically, has also not yet given in to despair economically. The difficulties that it faces in the way of reconstruction are enormous, and ultimately quite insoluble.

---

1. [In June 1920, Hermann Müller, the fourth Social-Democratic Chancellor in eighteen months (following Ebert, Scheidemann, and Gustav Bauer) gave way to Konstantin Fehrenbach of the Centre Party.]

Despite this, the German bourgeoisie is seeking to create, by powerful amalgamations, new organisations and transformations of its productive forces, a productive basis on which it believes it will be able to go on operating. These processes within the German bourgeoisie are of greatest significance, and perhaps I will be able to send you further material about these matters shortly.

Further, the German revolutionary development is also governed by the international constellation. Germany is first of all the country between Russia and the counter-revolutionary West. To this extent, the question of Western policy against Soviet Russia is of the greatest importance for Germany. Of course, the German proletariat is also more slow-moving on these things than one might wish. But there was one point when the German proletariat seemed to have concretely understood the question: in the middle of this year, when the Russian armies stood before Warsaw. Then there was at least a movement, even if it hardly led to any concrete results. The international situation, however, may soon be similar again to how it was last summer, as I expect that after the defeat of Wrangel,[2] France will be tempted right away to continue the struggle through Poland.

This is a rough picture that I can give you of the German situation. I will be happy to help if you want more detailed information on any particular points.

I hope that the time will not be too long until you can move your forces freely again in a free republic.

With best wishes, Paul Levi

---

2. [Pyotr Nikolayevich Wrangel, the last commander-in-chief of the White armies in the Civil War, was finally defeated in southern Russia in November 1920.]

Part Two

The March Action

Our Path: Against Putschism[*]

> Heavens above, what is going on here! Genuine
> remorse, even if enforced, or nothing of the kind?
> Do you really know what you have done? The best
> action, the noblest and highest cause... a cause that
> God just for once put in your hands, you have treated
> like muck in a pigsty.
>
> – Gerhart Hauptmann, *Florian Geyer*

At the time that I planned this pamphlet, Germany
had a Communist Party with half a million members.
When I came to write it eight days later, this Communist Party was shaken to its foundations, and its
very existence put in question.

It may seem risky in such a serious crisis as that
in which the Communist Party presently finds itself,
to come out with such an unsparing criticism. But it
needs little reflection to conclude that this criticism
is not only useful but necessary. The irresponsible
game played with the existence of a party, with the
lives and fates of its members, must be brought to an
end. It has to be ended by the will of the members,

---

[*] The title page of the original edition reads:
'Unser Weg
Wider den Putschismus
von Paul Levi
Mit einem Artikel von Karl Radek als Anhang'
[The appended Radek article was 'Die Lehren eines Putschversuchs' ('Lessons of
a Putsch Attempt'), directed at the Vienna action of June 1919, and partly translated
in Gruber (ed.) 1967. Levi's intention was to show how Radek had argued in similar
vein against the Austrian Communists.]

given that those responsible for it still refuse to see what they have done. The Party must not be dragged with eyes closed into anarchism of a Bakuninist kind. And, if a *Communist* Party is to be built up again in Germany, then the dead of central Germany, Hamburg, the Rhineland, Baden, Silesia and Berlin, not to mention the many thousands of prisoners who have fallen victim to this Bakuninist lunacy, all demand in the face of the events of the last week: *'Never again!'*

It goes without saying that the white terror now raging must not be used as a cloak behind which those responsible can escape their *political* responsibility. Nor should the anger and insults now raised against me be a reason for refraining from this criticism. I address myself to the members of the Party in this spirit, with an account that must tear the heart of anyone who worked to build up what has now been torn down. These are bitter truths, but 'what I hand you is medicine, not poison'.

Written 3–4 April, 1921
Paul Levi

I

Working-class debate about the revolution immediately raises the question of tempo. Opinions spread between those of little faith, at one extreme, who see the whole question as 'still on the horizon', and, at the other extreme, the optimistic ones who believe the revolution could 'break out tomorrow' if some people somewhere were not putting the brakes on. When such questions are discussed, however, it is rare for people to indicate the concrete factors that are decisive for this faster or slower pace, so that the question as to the timescale of the revolution fails to rise above the level of whether a particular date would be too soon or too late. In prison, the day is always long, walking in the woods in spring it is always short, even though it is the same day of twenty-four hours. In fact, the pace of the revolution depends on two kinds of factors: objective and subjective. The objective factors are the strength of the contradiction between relations of production and the system of distribution, the possibility and ability of the existing system of production continuing to function, the condition of the proletariat, how acute is the antagonism between proletariat and bourgeoisie, the intensification of crises within the world-bourgeoisie, and so on.

It would be superfluous here to repeat again what has so often been said. Rising unemployment, the growing impoverishment of the proletariat as well as the commercial and intellectual middle class and civil servants, the ever greater bankruptcy of the state, the reorganising of bourgeois states into new and hostile interest-groups, the world-contradiction of the oppressors against the oppressed of all countries, with the latter being, for the first time in world-history, united into a conscious body, thinking and planning on a world-political level in the Communist International with Soviet Russia at its head: these are the objective factors.

In the present case, however, we need to consider the subjective factors, or rather *the* subjective factor which today is always decisive in the formation of objective conditions: How far is the revolutionary class willing and able, indeed mature enough, to take power? How far has the counter-revolutionary class been spiritually worn down and exhausted so that power can be taken from its hands? These two forces, the conquering will of the revolutionary class, and the defensive will of the counter-revolutionary class, are not two distinct things. Each is, rather, a function of the other; the struggle of parties is the reflection of this, possession of state-power its goal, and the strength of the use of state-power its measure.

It is a well-established fact, that in this sense, despite its growing economic decay, the German bourgeoisie has managed a certain consolidation. In November 1918, state-power was a 'no man's land'. It had slipped from the bourgeoisie, yet no one would claim today that the proletariat took it up. The bourgeoisie, despite the numbing blow it had received, was the first to get back on its feet; Noske's mass-slaughters of January and March 1919 were the milestones, the Weimar constitution the outwardly recognisable sign, that it felt itself master once more. Since that time, the rule of the German bourgeoisie – its political rule – has not experienced any further serious shock: the Kapp Putsch, which might have led to such a shock from either right or left, passed without serious damage to it.

This victory of the bourgeoisie is, of course, not an absolute one, but to the highest degree something relative, maintaining its character as a victory only so long as the forces of the revolutionary class do not overtake it. That the forces of the proletariat are in the process of doing so is quite assured. Not just because there are far more proletarian fists than bourgeois leather-gloves: the bourgeoisie is under pressure from the ever growing economic decay, and completely pervaded by a sense of the hopelessness and inescapability of its situation, living from one day to the next devoid of further hope. The proletariat is the only class bearing on its breast the star of hope and thus of victory: both physical and (as Napoleon would have put it) moral factors are on the side of the proletariat, and thus of its victory.

Everything thus depends on the state of the revolutionary forces and their development. Is this happening quickly or slowly? Marx himself gave a certain answer to this. In *The Class Struggles in France*, he wrote:

> Revolutionary progress cleared a path for itself not by its immediate
> [...] achievements, but, on the contrary, but creating a powerful and
> united counter-revolution; only in combat with this opponent did the
> insurrectionary party mature into a real party of revolution.[1]

Nothing could express the intensity and rapidity of revolutionary development in Germany more clearly than this. What Marx referred to here was the development of the revolutionary power in struggle against a stabilised counter-revolutionary power. In Germany however, in this present revolution, the revolutionary forces are more or less keeping pace with the development of the forces of counter-revolution. This is expressed in two ways. The strength of a revolutionary class, the proletariat, grows in proportion to the strength and number of its clearest, most conscious and decisive vanguard. In November 1918, the Communists in Germany formed a group, but not a large one. In February 1921, they were a force half a million strong. The other phenomenon in which the growing strength of the revolutionary forces finds expression is that the German proletarian class has already received terrible blows in the two and a half years of the German Revolution. It has lost blood in streams. Once, twice, and again a third time, it has suffered heavily from this, yet, on each occasion, it has taken only a short time for it to rise up again with new forces, with a giant's stature and strength. No class in the world has ever managed this before. The development of the revolutionary forces in Germany – no matter how much this may surprise the impatient heads among us – is proceeding at an unexpected and tremendously rapid pace. The proletariat, which, for four years, ran behind the Kaiser but today

---

1. Marx 2010a, p. 35.

counts half a million Communists, has acquired a new face both intellectually and politically.

The impatient ones, however, will ask what use all this might be if the proletariat has still not conquered power. And, now, we come to the real problem: what can the Communist Party do in this situation, in order to conquer state-power?

II

Many Communists commit two mistakes in their thinking. The first is to see in the contending classes only the proletariat. In reality, however, it is not revolutionary tactics to keep examining and measuring oneself in the mirror; far more important is the relationship of the Communists to all other classes and strata in struggle against capitalism, who all work together for the fall of the bourgeoisie. Of all these classes and strata, of course, only the proletariat is the one that by virtue of its conditions of existence 'abolishes the old relations of production, and along with these relations of production marked by class antagonism, abolishes classes altogether';[2] the proletariat is the only really revolutionary class. It is only the working class whose goal as a class is directed at a change in the present relations of production and of all relations that follow from this. At a later stage of the revolution, indeed, a contradiction must necessarily emerge, even if temporarily, between the proletariat and those classes and strata that today stand alongside it, but *in no way* does this justify the proletariat treating these classes and strata as non-existent, as incapable of alliance with it, let alone as enemies.

Yet precisely this has most frequently been the case. There are many Communists who see outside the proletariat only 'a single reactionary mass'. This 'single reactionary mass' was a slogan dreamed up by Lassalle, and like many others, has more of a good sound than a sound meaning. Marx bitterly criticised it in this very sense, showing that it was completely devoid of content. In his 'Critique of the Gotha Programme' of 1875, he wrote:

> In the Communist Manifesto [...] the bourgeoisie is conceived of as a revolutionary class – as the bringer of large-scale industry – in relation to

---

2. 'The Communist Manifesto', in Marx 2010a, p. 87.

the feudal lords and the lower middle class, who want to retain all the social positions created by obsolete modes of production. These do not, therefore, form a single reactionary mass *together with the bourgeoisie*.

On the other hand the proletariat is revolutionary in relation to the bourgeoisie because it has itself sprung up on the ground of large-scale industry; it is struggling to divest production of its capitalist character, which the bourgeoisie seeks to perpetuate. The Manifesto adds, however, that the lower middle class is becoming revolutionary 'in view of (its) impending transfer into the proletariat'.

From this point of view, therefore, it is once again nonsense to say that in relation to the working class it 'forms a single reactionary mass', 'together with the bourgeoisie' and with the feudal lords to boot.[3]

As well as these ideas of theory and principle, tactical considerations also come into play in times of revolution. In non-revolutionary times, these non-proletarian and non-bourgeois elements are the least conscious of their class-position. In the slow course of development, they fail to see and understand how their goals and those of the bourgeoisie are distinct and opposed. This is the very reason why, like the impoverished artisans in Germany, they are so frequently and bitterly seen as an appendage of the bourgeoisie or the feudal classes, and even identified *with* them. But revolutions dissolve all social veils of this kind. They act like a solvent to separate those who do not belong socially together. They break with tradition and force both individuals and classes to see the reality behind the appearance. The class-antagonism between the bourgeoisie and the classes exposed to proletarianisation – if not yet actually proletarianised – becomes flagrant.

What is the composition of these strata? In Germany, they are extraordinarily multifarious, more so than in Russia. Certainly, all the strata present in Germany were also present in Russia, but their centre of gravity there was the land-poor peasantry. In both number and power, this outweighed all other petty-bourgeois and semi-proletarian strata, so that it could be said that, in Russia, whoever had the peasants had half the proletariat.

In Germany, no single intermediate class is so preponderant. Here, the rural proletariat is itself divided both socially and geographically into the land-poor

---

3. Marx 2010c, p. 349.

small peasants of the south and the estate workers of the north. Then there are artisans of the most varied levels, from the bow-legged village-tailor in Upper Bavaria working for the peasants for his meals and 50 pfennig a day, through to the self-employed craftsman with electrical tools. There is also a third stratum that is incomparably more important in Germany, that of clerical workers and civil servants, impoverished intellectuals, etc. All these experience the revolution in their own lives. Consider for example the development of the German railway-workers in the two years of revolution. Or read the recently published booklet by the Saxon government-adviser Schmidt-Leonhardt, *Das zweite Proletariat*. None of these are proletarians, at least not in their class-existence, but they are all anti-bourgeois, and they have to be taken into account.

What is the significance of these strata? As long as they belong to the bourgeoisie, they signify hands which the bourgeoisie uses to beat the proletariat; if this tie is broken, but they still stand at a distance from the proletariat, they signify at least an extraordinary obstacle to the seizure of power by the proletariat; if they sympathise with the proletariat, then they make this seizure of power easier or even make it possible for the first time.

It goes without saying, in this connection, that no Communist thinks of waiting until these strata have become Communist themselves. Lenin put this question as follows in his article on 'The Constituent Assembly Elections and the Dictatorship of the Proletariat':

> [O]nly the proletariat can *lead the working people* out of capitalism to communism. It is no use thinking that the petty-bourgeois or semi-petty-bourgeois masses can decide in advance the extremely complicated question: 'to be with the working class or with the bourgeoisie'. The *vacillation* of the non-proletarian sections of the working people is inevitable; and inevitable also is their own *practical experience*, which will enable them to *compare* leadership by the bourgeoisie with leadership by the proletariat.[4]

Further on, Lenin writes: '[I]t was this vacillation of the peasantry, the main body of the petty-bourgeois working people, that decided the fate of Soviet rule and of the rule of Kolchak and Denikin.'[5]

---

4. Lenin 1965a, p. 267.
5. Lenin 1965a, p. 268.

Thus, these strata *may* be decisive in certain situations. It is the task of the Communists to win influence over them. But how should they do so?

In Russia, where this middle-stratum was less complicated, consisting essentially of just the peasants, the question was similarly more straightforward. Whoever gave the peasants land had their support. The Bolsheviks were the only ones resolved, not just to *give* the peasants land – everyone was 'resolved' on this – but to create the precondition for it by *taking* the land from the proprietors, and this made it possible for the Bolsheviks to gather this middle-stratum under their banner.

The German Communists have not as yet found a way to even approach these middle-strata.

An agrarian programme, even one that satisfies both peasants and farm-workers, is not sufficient, as the peasants and farm-workers are not decisive here as they were in Russia. Nor is it enough to assure the artisans that their death as a class is certain from the laws of the capitalist economy; for even if someone is going to die, you do not win them as a friend by prophesying their death each day. It is also insufficient to maintain that intellectuals and officials are already proletarians, but simply unaware of this; this is not adequate for the particular character of this social stratum. There is no doubt that Communists must seek to get closer to these strata on questions that interest them *as a whole*.

In Russia, there were two such questions besides the agrarian question. The one with overriding importance was the question of peace, which at the present time does not come into consideration for Germany. The other was the national question, which, of course, had a completely different content in Russia than it does in Germany.

The very term 'national question' immediately arouses feelings of disquiet among some people in Germany. Remembering national Bolshevism, a danger that they narrowly escaped, they can no longer bear to hear the word 'national'.[6] But the reason national Bolshevism was un-Communist was not because of its concern with the national question, but because it sought to

---

6. [National Bolshevism was a widespread current after the German defeat of 1918, standing for a united struggle of all classes in Germany together with Soviet Russia against the Entente. It was represented particularly by the Hamburg Communists Heinrich Laufenberg and Fritz Wolffheim, who formed the KAPD after their expulsion from the KPD in August 1919, though they broke with it soon after.]

solve the national question by a pact of 'all classes of the people', by the road of fraternisation of the proletariat with the bourgeoisie, of the Communists with Lettow-Vorbeck.[7] *That* was what was un-Communist. But neither is it Communist to refuse now to examine the national question. At the very start of the Revolution, a Berlin littérateur tried to get rid of the national question by founding an 'anti-national socialist party'. Getting rid of the national question in this way is simply like saying: 'There are no more donkeys in this world, because I'm an ox.'

The national question *exists*, and Karl Marx, as an internationalist, was the last person not to see it and take it into account politically. The 'abolition' of the nation is not the object of a decree, still less of a party resolution, it is rather a process:

> Since the proletariat must first of all acquire political supremacy, must rise to be the leading class of the nation, it is, so far, itself national. [...] National differences, and antagonisms between peoples, are daily more and more vanishing [...]. The supremacy of the proletariat will cause them to vanish still faster. [...] In proportion as the exploitation of one individual by another is put an end to, the exploitation of one nation by another will also be put an end to. In proportion as the antagonism between classes within the nation vanishes, the hostility of one nation to another will come to an end.[8]

At the present time, therefore, the nation is for the proletariat still an existing entity; comrades who, because we are internationalists in our final goal, refuse already today to see the national question and to treat it as something existing, commit just the same mistake as those who, holding that in our final goal we are against parliaments and for soviets, refuse to see parliaments now, or, holding that we are for the abolition of the state, treat the state as no longer existing and, like the anarchists, want nothing to do with politics. The comrades in question are likewise anti-politicians, simply that they transfer this to the field of foreign policy.

The national question exists, I repeat, it exists in Germany in the form of 'the exploitation of one nation by another', and this is the most burning question for all those middle-strata in Germany. Only in this way will we win over

---

7. [Paul von Lettow-Vorbeck, Prussian general and commander in German East Africa; as a Reichswehr general he put down the Hamburg uprising of 1919.]
8. Marx 2010a, pp. 84–5.

these strata. And, for this reason alone, it should be the task of Communists to come out, at the most critical moments for the national question, with slogans that signify to those middle-strata a solution of their national pains. The slogan of alliance with Soviet Russia would have been such a slogan,[9] and should have been given out as a *national* slogan, i.e. not as a slogan under whose shadow Communists and Prussian Junkers would embrace as brothers, but, rather, as a slogan under which the Communists, and proletarians in general, would act together with those middle-strata in a struggle against the Junkers and the bourgeoisie, who sabotage this *only escape-route*, as they are trying to ensure their continued existence as an exploiting class by betraying their country, negotiating with the Western bourgeoisie to hand over portions of German territory to France (the Rhineland) or deliberately fragmenting the country (Bavaria); by this demand we would further the proletarian struggle.

It is no more than foolish talk for a small troop of Marxist sycophants to raise the cry that demanding alliance with Soviet Russia from a bourgeois government would be something counter-revolutionary or – still worse – opportunist, not a 'revolutionary slogan'. One might remind these careful individuals that the Bolsheviks conducted their entire political propaganda before the seizure of power with 'opportunist slogans' such as these. They demanded from the bourgeois government the immediate conclusion of peace, even though *no* Bolshevik was unaware that a peace concluded by a bourgeois government would not be peace, and that a genuine peace could be concluded only from proletariat to proletariat. They conducted their propaganda under the slogan: land to the peasants, and *even carried out the distribution of land*, though *no* Bolshevik was unaware that the final goal of communism is not the division of land into private peasant-property, but more or less the opposite of this. This is what they did, and what they had to do. Was this a task of Marxism? In no way. Revolution is not a Communist Party matter, and not a Communist monopoly. To use Marx's phrase in a letter to Kugelmann, it is a 'people's revolution', i.e. a violent process in which all working people and oppressed forces come into flux, are aroused and come into opposition – each in their particular way – against the oppressors, in which process, the highest art of the Communists is to bring all these forces together and lead them towards

---

9. [See Introduction, p. 15.]

one goal, the overthrow of the oppressors. For only in so far as they understand this are the Communists what they are supposed to be: the *best leaders* of the revolution and at the same time its *best servants*. It was with this in mind that Marx said in his 'Address to the Communist League' of March 1850: 'At the beginning, of course, the workers cannot propose any directly communist measures.'[10]

Communism comes not at the beginning of the revolution but at the end, and the Communists are not those who mistake the end for the beginning, but those who want to continue from the beginning to the end. If the Communist Party is not to come to grief at the very beginning, it will thus have to bring into its purview those questions that concern these middle-strata, it will have to treat the national question as something existing, and offer a slogan that brings a solution for these strata, if only a temporary one.

III

What is decisive in everything, of course, for the Communists, is their relationship to the genuinely revolutionary class, the proletariat. It is in their relation to the proletariat that the Communists show their very viability. If the connections of the Communists to those other, semi-proletarian, middle-strata are of a tactical kind, in which a right or wrong attitude can speed up or slow down the revolution, the connection of the Communists to the proletariat is one of principle. Anyone who does not understand the relationship of the Communists to the proletariat, and act accordingly, *ceases to be a Communist*. We would not need to dwell on this question if recent events had not shattered everything that we believed was taken for granted.

'In what relation do the communists stand to the proletarians as a whole?' This is the question that Marx raises in the *Communist Manifesto*, and he goes on to answer it as follows:

> The Communists do not form a separate party opposed to other working-class parties.
> They have no interests separate and apart from those of the proletariat as a whole.

---

10. Marx 2010a, p. 329.

They do not set up any sectarian principles of their own, by which to shape and mould the proletarian movement.

The Communists are distinguished from the other working-class parties by this only:

1. In the national struggles of the proletarians of the different countries, they point out and bring to the front the common interests of the entire proletariat, independently of all nationality.
2. In the various stages of development which the struggle of the working class against the bourgeoisie has to pass through, they always and everywhere represent the interests of the movement as a whole.

The Communists, therefore, are on the one hand, practically, the most advanced and resolute section of working-class parties of every country, that section which pushes forward all others; on the other hand, theoretically, they have over the great mass of the proletariat the advantage of clearly understanding the line of march, the conditions, and the ultimate general results of the proletarian movement.[11]

These paragraphs are the basic law of communism. Everything else is its elaboration and explanation. And on this assumption I would like to examine three questions:

a) *What is the numerical relationship of the German Communists to the German proletariat?*
b) *What are the preconditions for a conquest of state-power by the proletariat?*
c) *How is state-power to be conquered?*

a) *What is the numerical relationship of the German Communists to the German proletariat?*

My object in introducing the following figures from various election-campaigns is not in any way to argue that any action by the proletariat or its seizure of power is possible only after a particular numerical relation-

---

11. Marx 2010a, pp. 79–80.

ship has been established by election or vote. Still less the amusing theory expressed in *Vorwärts* sometime last year that a seizure of state-power by the proletariat would be possible only if 51 per cent of the electors had voted for the proletariat – *Vorwärts* having rebuked some SPD-member for maintaining that, in certain circumstances, a seizure of power by the proletariat would be possible even if only 49 per cent of the 'general population' had voted for the 'dictatorship of the proletariat', as these gentlemen put it. Least of all am I trying to use these figures to indicate the possibility that the aims of the Communists can be realised by elections and votes. I completely agree rather with what Lenin wrote in 'The Elections to the Constituent Assembly and the Dictatorship of the Proletariat':

> Universal suffrage is an index of the level reached by the various classes in their understanding of their problems. It shows how the various classes are *inclined* to solve their problems. The actual *solution* of these problems is not provided by voting, but by the class struggle in all its forms, including civil war.[12]

It is in this sense that I indicate certain figures. It is unfortunate – and not only for this reason – that the first figures that would be needed for this comparison are lacking; i.e. figures from the first general election after the start of the revolution, that of 19 January 1919, which the Communists boycotted. We must therefore start with the *election to the Prussian parliament* of February 1921. The workers' parties received in this election the following votes (rounded to the nearest thousand):

Table 1   Workers' Parties' Votes February 1921

KPD	USPD	SPD
1,156,000	1,087,000	4,171,000

These figures show that, at this time, Communists made up about a fifth of those proletarians who recognised themselves as members of their class. Even together with the USPD, who should certainly not be counted with the Communists, but rather with the Social Democrats, they would make up only a third of these proletarians.

---

12. Lenin 1965a, pp. 271–2.

What is decisive, however, as I will discuss in more detail below, is not this *total* number; I therefore emphasise certain particularly striking examples:

Table 2   Workers' Parties' Votes per Region

	KPD	USPD	SPD
Berlin	112,000	197,000	221,000
Greater Berlin			
(Berlin together with Potsdam			
I and II)	233,000	397,000	564,000
Magdeburg	26,000	48,000	264,000
Halle	204,000	76,000	71,000
North Westphalia	49,000	23,000	196,000
South Westphalia	108,000	84,000	283,000
East Düsseldorf	105,000	84,000	131,000
West Düsseldorf	65,000	23,000	94,000
Rhine-Westphalia			
industrial region	372,000	214,000	704,000

As I said, I shall discuss later on the significance of these figures, and make only the following point here. Comparing the Berlin vote in particular, though this applies also to all other figures, with that for the Reichstag election last summer, it is clear that, following the split in the USPD, as many of its voters turned to the Social Democrats, the party of Noske, as to the Communists. This fact is also apparent from the figures for the Mecklenburg state-election in June 1920 and March 1921. The votes were (in round numbers):

Table 3   Workers' Parties' Votes. Mecklenburg State-Election

	KPD	USPD	SPD
June 1920	1,200	24,500	128,000
March 1921	15,000	2,600	137,000

In this timeframe, the USPD lost 22,000 votes, the Communists won some 13,800 votes, and the Majority-Socialists around 9,000. If we take account on the Communist side what they won from other parties than the USPD, and bear in mind that the Social Democrats would have experienced a loss of votes in this strongly rural constituency without those drawn from the former USPD, we can conclude, as said, that the UPSD voters went more or less equally to the right and left, in so far as they did not vanish altogether (as happened particularly in Berlin).

We have also another measure for the numerical proportion of the Communists to the proletariat, the relationship in the trade-unions. While the election-results do not show a sharp separation of proletarian and non-proletarian elements, and a section of the proletariat finds no expression in the election figures, the trade-unions are purely proletarian, and every Communist trade-unionist is also undoubtedly a member of the Communist Party. The number of KPD members to the number of trade-union members thus gives a maximum figure for the present *numerical* (not intellectual) influence of the Communists on the unionised proletariat as a whole.

Now, the trade-unions affiliated to the ADGB had the following membership:

Table 4   Trade-Union Membership

End 1918	2,866,012
End 1919	7,338,123

There were also 858,283 members of the Christian trade-unions at the end of 1919. At the end of 1919, therefore, some 8.2 million German workers were organised in trade-unions. This figure most likely rose again in 1920, particularly for the ADGB. But, if we take just these figures in relationship to the number of Communists at the start of 1921, i.e. 500,000, it follows that the Communists made up about 1 in 16 of the trade-union organised proletariat, and about 1 in 14 of those proletarians organised in free trade-unions.

This is the numerical proportion, and it is nothing to be afraid of. For, in revolutionary situations, such proportions shift very quickly, while, on top of the numerical influence, there is also, or should be, the intellectual influence.

I shall come on to speak later of this intellectual influence and its significance, also how it is won and lost. Here, I simply want to stress one thing, as we have often put it. There is a certain sense in which, despite the growing Communist organisation and the – at least formerly – growing Communist influence, the situation of the Communists has become more difficult. At the start of the German Revolution, the social reformists of every kind were completely on the defensive. They did indeed have large masses behind them, but their ranks were in disarray; we had free access to them and were able to influence them. Today, however, social reformism has put up a conscious and tough resistance against Communism; here and there, indeed, it has already passed from the defensive to the offensive, and has expelled Communists from their positions. This means that the intellectual influence of the Communists on those proletarian masses that are still undecided or inclined to reformism can no longer be taken for granted. It has to be struggled for.

And, for the time being, it is clear, the Communists are a minority in the proletariat.

b) *What are the preconditions for a conquest of state-power by the proletariat?*

I have already explained above what is not a precondition. It is not a precondition that the majority of the German proletariat have a membership-card of the Communist Party in their hands. Nor is it a precondition that the proletariat has already gone manfully to the electoral urns and proclaimed its readiness on written or printed ballots.

It is not even a necessary precondition that those middle-strata that I referred to above should be Communist or completely in sympathy with the Communists. Certainly, their sympathy means, *in every case*, an extraordinary easing of the task of the proletariat, both *in* and *after* the seizure of power, and circumstances can also be conceived of in which the hostility and refusal of these strata makes the seizure of power impossible. These, however, are matters that, for the most part, arise only in the course of struggle, so that it is hard to lay down rules in advance; applied mechanically, these would only weaken the offensive spirit.

But, leaving these aside, there are indeed certain preconditions for the seizure of state-power. Lenin says in the aforementioned article:

> [W]e have studied the three conditions which determined the victory of Bolshevism: (1) an overwhelming majority among the proletariat; (2) almost half of the armed forces; (3) an overwhelming superiority of forces at the decisive moment at the decisive points, namely: in Petrograd and Moscow and on the war fronts near the centre.[13]

As far as these conditions obtain in Germany, we have already discussed the first of these, a decisive majority among the proletariat, with numerical examples, and will bring up other evidence in due course. The second

---

13. Lenin 1965a, p. 262.

condition, i.e. almost half of the votes among the armed forces, needs no numerical example, being too small for this to be relevant. We have no influence in the army, and whenever we obtain any at all, we always lose it again. We can, however, say that the German army today does not have the *decisive* importance which the army had in Russia. Lenin goes on to say: 'by October–November 1917 the armed forces were *half Bolshevik*. If that had not been the case we could not have been victorious'.[14] The army does not have *this* importance in Germany.

The third precondition is the 'crushing superiority at the decisive moment and at the decisive point'. This standpoint is completely correct. A majority is not needed to win a battle. One need only be in a majority at that point on the battlefield where the decision is made. Nor need one be in a majority to win a war; it is enough to have crushing superiority at the points where battles are fought.

What, then, are the decisive points? For Russia, Lenin described these as follows: the capitals and the military fronts in their vicinity. This last factor is also different for us, for the above-mentioned reasons. There remain the capitals, and especially *the* capital with its government-buildings and central apparatus, which has to be held if state-power is to be seized.

Unfortunately, despite – or should we say 'because of' – the strongly developed nose of some Berlin comrades for any kind of 'opportunism', and their no less strongly developed talent for speaking against it, the Berlin organisation is more or less the worst that we have in the whole Reich. This is evident not just from the election-figures, but also in other ways. In short, these Berlin comrades who are responsible for it have done nothing to achieve *this* precondition for the goal that they strive for more eagerly than all others.

There are also other points in Germany, however, that can be decisive in certain circumstances.

The railways. The situation here is not very different from that of the army. The strong influence that we formerly had has been spoiled time and again by certain stupidities. In these semi-bourgeois and semi-intellectual circles of public officials, we are most strongly revenged for what we have omitted in our dealings with these strata. For all that, however, we do have some influence with the railwaymen, if only in particular towns or districts.

---

14. Lenin 1965a, p. 261.

Then *the industrial districts*. There is no single industrial district in Germany that could lay low the bourgeois state with *one* stroke and force it to capitulate, as Berlin can if the government buildings, banks etc. are occupied. There are, however, two industrial districts that are of vital importance for the state, and that could force it to capitulate after a while: Rhineland-Westphalia and central Germany. As far as Rhineland-Westphalia goes, we have already seen how 372,000 Communist voters are outweighed by 214,000 Independents and 704,000 majority Social Democrats. There can be no talk of a crushing majority here, therefore.

The other area is central Germany. In the Halle district, we had 204,000 Communist voters against 76,000 Independents and 71,000 majority Social Democrats. We had a powerful support and a strong and heroic organisation prepared for sacrifices. *We had* ...

In any case, however, it is clear that, apart from central Germany, which is not decisive in terms of a rapid blow, there is *nowhere* that we have a 'crushing majority'.

Anyone who launches an action *now*, in this situation, for the conquest of state-power is a fool, and anyone who tells the Communist Party that all it needs is to apply itself, is a liar.

c) *How is state-power conquered?*

The conquest of political power by the proletariat is as a general rule (exceptions have already occurred, such as in Hungary) the result of a successful insurrection, whether by the proletariat alone, or supported also by other strata drawn into the revolution. What then are the preconditions for such an insurrection? Lenin says the following in 'Can the Bolsheviks Retain State Power?'[15]

> If the revolutionary party has no majority in the advanced contingents of the revolutionary classes and in the country, insurrection is out of the question. Moreover, insurrection requires: (1) growth of the revolution on a country-wide scale; (2) the complete moral and political bankruptcy of the old government, for example the 'coalition' government; (3) extreme

---

15. Lenin 1964a, p. 134.

vacillation in the camp of all middle groups, i.e. those who do *not* fully support the government, although they did fully support it yesterday.

Here, again, I want to check these preconditions for Germany, and go on to criticise the processes that took place here in recent days.

1) The basic precondition that must be present alongside all others, i.e. a majority for the revolutionary party 'in the advanced contingents of the revolutionary classes and in the country', did not and does not exist in Germany, as we have already seen. Even leaving aside the rural population, which does not play the decisive role here that it does in Russia, the Communist Party ('the revolutionary party') still does not have a majority among the proletariat (the 'advanced contingents of the revolutionary classes').

2) The revolution was not 'growing on a country-wide scale'. Certainly, the advanced section of the working class was growing ever more embittered, the number of unemployed was rising daily, the poverty and misery of the masses was ever greater. But the moment had not yet arrived at which the visible discontent was translated into rising mass-activity; for the time being, as often happens, it was expressed in growing resignation.

3) No one can speak of a complete moral and political bankruptcy of the old (e.g. the 'coalition') government. In Prussia, where the Social Democrats are in coalition with the bourgeois parties, they received almost double the vote of the other proletarian parties together, and more than in June of the previous year.

4) Just as untenable would be the assertion of an 'extreme vacillation in the camp of all middle groups'; the Communist Party had done nothing to make them uncertain, even when such suitable occasions arose as the London *Diktat*.[16]

We believe *no one* in the German Communist Party can have had any doubt about these conditions.

---

16. [The Versailles Treaty in general, which the German government signed in June 1919, was referred to in Germany as '*das Diktat*'; but it seems Levi is referring here to one of the several subsequent attempts by the Allies to enforce the Treaty's provisions.]

What, then, were the preconditions, how did the action come about?

I declare, in advance, that the situation in which the Party finds itself is more difficult than ever before. Whether the KPD can still exist, whether German Communism can still exist as a party, will be decided in a matter of weeks, perhaps days. It is a duty in this situation to address the Party with complete openness and truthfulness; those responsible for undertaking this action must bear this responsibility, just as every last party-comrade. Only in this way shall we manage to avoid supplying new victims to white justice, and the misfortune of what has already happened affecting wider circles than the German Communist Party. In this context, however, truth – the whole truth – is needed.

How did the action come about? It was not the German Communist Party that gave the initial impulse. We do not even know who bears responsibility for it. It became more frequent for emissaries of the ECCI to exceed their plenipotential authority, i.e. for it *subsequently* to emerge that these emissaries did not, in fact, have such authority.[17] We are not, therefore, in a position to ascribe responsibility to the ECCI, even if it cannot be concealed that certain ECCI circles showed a certain misgiving about the 'inactivity' of the German Party. Apart from serious mistakes in the movement against the Kapp Putsch, however, the German Party could not be accused of actual failures. There was thus a certain strong influence on the Zentrale to embark on action *now*, *immediately* and *at any price*.

It was then necessary to justify this immediate action. At the Central Committee session of 17 March, a responsible speaker[18] addressed himself as follows:

> The same is to be said of the general situation as Levi explained at the last session, only that since this report [four weeks previous!! – P.L.] the antagonisms between the imperialist states have sharpened, and the antagonisms between America and Britain have come to a head. If revolution does not lead to a new turn of events, we shall shortly [!! – P.L.] be faced with a British-American war...

---

17. [See Introduction, p. 18. The editor's note to this edition wrongly names the ECCI emissary as Rákosi, who was already in Germany and had triggered Levi's resignation from the KPD-leadership. See 'What Is the Crime?', below, p. 17.]

18. [In the Paul Levi archive, P83/9, the name 'Brandler' is written in the margin of a copy of the pamphlet.]

…[I]nternal political difficulties make it possible that on 20 March sanctions will be sharpened [! – P.L.], while, on the same date, the referendum in Upper Silesia will take place, which with high probability will incite military conflict between the German and Polish imperialists. As far as we are informed, the former French occupation-forces have been replaced by British troops; whereas the French troops displayed a friendly attitude towards Poland, according to our information [! – P.L.] the new English troops have a quite strong position in favour of Germany. The likelihood of matters coming to armed conflict is 90 per cent. The Polish counter-revolution is arming itself, while the German government has been deliberately working for military conflict, as documentary evidence shows, since the beginning of October. The speaker made these documents known to the meeting, remarking that they should not be published…

Our influence will reach beyond our organisation of four to five hundred thousand members. I maintain that today we have two to three million non-Communist workers in the Reich whom we can influence through our Communist organisation, and who will fight under our banners even in our offensive actions. If my view here is correct, than this state of things obliges us to no longer remain in a passive attitude towards tensions in domestic and foreign policy, no longer simply use these external and internal relations for agitational purposes; the present situation rather obliges us to launch actions to change things in our direction.

I declare that, in a party with any self-esteem, a responsible member of the leadership who maintained that, in the time from mid-February to mid-March of this year, antagonisms between the imperialist states had sharpened, and antagonisms between Britain and America intensified, to the point that 'we shall shortly be faced with a British-American war', would be sent off for hydrotherapy. A member of the leadership who, in such a weighty decision, relied on 'secret information', 'documents that must not be published', '90 per cent probability' of a war, in short, a member who gave a report alongside which one by a spy of Weismann[19] would seem a document of historical value, would be immediately removed from his post. If that were not enough, this responsible leading comrade added the fairy-tale of these two to three

---

19. [Robert Weismann, Prussian state-commissioner for public order under prime minister Wirth.]

million non-Communists who would fight with us in 'offensive actions' – *and this was the political basis for the ensuing action.*

For clarification of what an 'offensive action' should be, another responsible member[20] explained:

> What the Zentrale now proposes is *a complete break with the past.* Up till now we had the tactic, or rather the tactic had been forced on us, that we should let things come our way, and as soon as there was a situation of struggle we should make our decision in this situation. What we say now is: we are strong enough, and the situation is so serious, that we must proceed *to force the fate of the Party and of the revolution itself....*
>
> We now have, for the sake of the Party, to take the offensive, to say that we are not prepared to wait until things come our way, until the facts confront us; we want as far as possible to create these facts.... We can to an extraordinary degree intensify the contradictions by leading the masses on strike in the Rhineland, which must sharpen to an extraordinary degree the differences between the Entente and the German government...
>
> In Bavaria the situation is similar to how it was for a long time in Germany, that we had to wait until the attack came from the other side. What is our task in this situation? We have to make sure by our actions that this outbreak comes, if it must come, by the provocation of the local defence-forces...

To which, a third responsible comrade added: 'In conclusion, *we have to break with the Party's former attitude,* one of avoiding partial actions and refusing to give out slogans that might appear as if we were demanding a final struggle...'.

This is the theoretical construction upon which the existence or non-existence of the Communist Party of Germany was put at risk.

One thing, first of all. There are Communists for whom the words 'sharpening', 'coming to a head', 'conflict', etc. arouse certain forcible revolutionary images. What else can be meant, if this speaker expected a mass-strike in the Rhineland to lead to a sharpening of Germany's conflict with the Entente? In the meantime, we have had a test-case. In Düsseldorf, the workers came out on strike, and this strike sharpened Franco-German relations to the point that

---

20. [In the Paul Levi archive, P83/9, the name 'Frölich' is written in the margin of a copy of the pamphlet.]

the French occupation-forces in Düsseldorf returned the German security-police their weapons so that *they* could defeat the strike.

A second 'sharpening' was reported in the press on 4 April. This was in a report from Moers:

> It was clearly on higher authority that the Belgian military intervened on Sunday to protect the non-Communist inhabitants, and when the Communists began to defend themselves, made use of their weapons. The Belgian troops succeeded in restoring calm. In the clashes with the Communists, three trouble-makers were killed and 27 wounded. The Belgians took several prisoners. When the Communists tried to free their comrades, opening fire on the Belgians again as well as throwing stones, the Belgians returned fire. Troop-reinforcements are under way to Moers. The pits have been occupied by Belgian soldiers.

This is the supposed 'sharpening of relations between Germany and the Entente', and, if the speaker at the Zentrale had anywhere in his speech given any thought to the matter, he must have immediately expected that the German government would rouse itself against the Entente because of the shooting of German Communists.

These would-be forcers of fate of the German Communist Party and the German Revolution do at least recognise that there must be a conflict situation, i.e. a situation in which the masses understand that they have to fight and are ready to do so. The 'new tactic', the 'break with the past', however, is that such situations are to be *created*. This is nothing new in itself. We too have always upheld the view that a political party *can*, and a *Communist Party must*, create conflict situations. But it must do so by the *clarity* and *decisiveness* of its positions, by the *sharpness* and *boldness* of its agitation and propaganda, by the intellectual and organisational *influence* that it wins over the masses; in other words, by *political means*. The only new thing that this break with the past of the KPD means is the view that such a conflict situation can also be created by *unpolitical* means, by police-spy manoeuvres, by *provocation*. What is meant here by provocation was revealed by another responsible comrade at another session, while the action was taking place. He said: 'Our view is that, with an intensive propaganda-activity, the peaceful way in which the security-police previously behaved will give way, so that those workers who are not in struggle today will be incited.'

And the same speaker went on to say – this was on 30 March, when the action had long since been lost: 'We must try and achieve a withdrawal in good order, create conflicts, *incite the security-police, incite all counter-revolutionary elements. If we succeed in creating* [! – P.L.] *the movement in this way*, clashes will take place…'

This is certainly something new in the party founded by Rosa Luxemburg; it is a complete break with the past that the Communists are supposed to act like cheap hustlers[21] and provoke the death of their brothers. I would rather not cite the evidence that this last remark is no exaggeration. This, I repeat, was the *new* theoretical basis on which the game began.

The action was launched. For a time, the Zentrale did not have to put its newly acquired theoretical basis into practice. Hörsing got there first.[22] He occupied the Mansfeld district with one success already to his name: the right moment. With the cunning of an old trade-union bureaucrat, he chose the week before Easter, knowing very well what the four-day closure of factories from Good Friday through Easter Monday would mean. Because of this, the Zentrale was, right from the start, a prisoner of its own 'slogans'. It was unable to exploit this provocation of Hörsing's in any way that corresponded to the situation. The Mansfeld workers went on strike. A member of the Zentrale stated at a session sometime later: 'Our comrades in Mansfeld took the slogan of the Zentrale rather too vigorously, and not in the proper sense that was meant. What happened in Mansfeld was an incursion, but not the occupation of factories.'

This depiction is no more than a slander of the battling comrades. If a slogan was given out against the factory-occupation, then can any reasonable person, even a member of the KPD Zentrale, assume it was *not* to be applied against the visible preparations for a factory-occupation, the incursion? And the comrades in Mansfeld interpreted the Zentrale's slogan in this way when they took up weapons. This, too, seems to be contested in the above-quoted passage. Not the first time that the Zentrale did not know what was happening, and only noticed later what slogan it had given out.

---

21. [*Achtgroschenjungen* in the original. See Fernbach 2009, pp. 109–10.]
22. [The Social Democrat Otto Hörsing was governor of Prussian Saxony from 1920 to 1927. On 16 March, he proclaimed a police-occupation of the province, on the grounds that strikes, looting and acts of violence had to be stopped.]

On 18 March, *Rote Fahne* proclaimed the call to arms: 'No worker should give a hoot for the law, but get a weapon where he can find it!'

Rote Fahne launched the movement with this unusual text for a *mass*-action, and it kept up the same tone. On 19 March, it wrote: 'The Orgesch band[23] proclaims the sword. Its words speak naked force. The German workers would be cowards if they did not find the courage and strength to answer the Orgesch band in *its own clear terms.*'

On the 20th, *Rote Fahne* wrote: 'The example of the Halle district, which is answering the challenge of Hörsing with a strike, must be followed. *The working class must immediately take up arms, to confront the armed enemy. Weapons in the workers' hands.*'

On 21 March, *Rote Fahne* wrote: 'Only the proletariat can defeat the infamous plans of the Orgesch bands. It can do so only through united action if it sloughs off the chattering Social-Democratic traitors and beats down the counter-revolution just as it would itself be beaten, *weapons in hand!*'

At the same time, the 'new theory' was making its way through our organisation, with its call for activity and the declaration to attack as soon as possible, be it only by way of provocation. In this situation, the Mansfeld workers took the slogan in the sense that any reasonable person would do so. It is a cowardly slander of the dead heroes, who fell in good faith, to say now that these Mansfeld workers had committed a 'breach of discipline'. No one could believe that, if *Rote Fahne* issued a call to arms, this meant that, for the time being, these arms were to be kept behind the stove. No worker could understand the talk of arms in any other sense than the newspaper's head of advertising did in the issue for 24 March 1921 (supplement no. 139):

The Communists' weapons
consist in the present moment not least in their party-press, which
mercilessly exposes the cancer of capitalism. It is the duty of every
single Communist to take part in this
distribution of weapons
and win new fighters to our cause. Tirelessly strive in the workplace
and with friends for the party-press, so that

---

23. [The Orgesch, i.e. Organisation Escherich, was a national association of home-guards (*Einwohnerwehren*), named after its founder Dr George Escherich, a Bavarian state-councillor, and serving as paramilitaries in crushing the workers' movement.]

the Red Army
of proletarian fighters will receive new recruits each day!

The insurrection in the Mansfeld region thus broke out in an unfavourable week, in a quite impossible political situation, on the defensive from the very first day, without any organisational preparation, *thanks to the toying with insurrection pursued in the Zentrale.*

Evidently, no member of the Zentrale, not even the 'best Marxist in Western Europe',[24] had read or taken to heart Marx's words on the subject:

> Now, insurrection is an art quite as much as war or any other, and subject to certain rules of proceeding, which, when neglected, will produce the ruin of the party neglecting them. Those rules, logical deductions from the nature of the parties and the circumstances one has to deal with in such a case, are so plain and simple that the short experience of 1848 had made the Germans pretty well acquainted with them. *Firstly, never play with insurrection unless you are fully prepared to face the consequences of your play.* Insurrection is a calculus with very infinite magnitudes, the value of which may change every day; the forces opposed to you have all the advantage of organisation, discipline, and habitual authority; unless you bring strong odds against them you are defeated and ruined. Secondly, the insurrectionary career once entered upon, act with the greatest determination, and on the offensive. *The defensive is the death of every armed rising*; it is lost before it measures itself with its enemies.[25]

But events now took their course. The spark sprang from Mansfeld to Hamburg. There were immediately a large number of dead, and we will not judge here whether the 'new theory' had fallen on fertile soil. In any case, the Hamburg comrades were naïve enough to believe that a party-leadership that raised the torch of insurrection knew what it was doing, and that the

---

24. [Apparently, a reference to August Thalheimer, leader of the 'left' faction in the KPD and cultivated at this time by Radek to replace Levi as party-leader, together with Heinrich Brandler and Paul Frölich.]

25. [The series of articles 'Revolution and Counter-Revolution in Germany' appeared under Marx's name in the *New-York Daily Tribune*, and was published in book form in the original English by Eleanor Marx in 1891. These articles are now known to have been written by Engels, and this quote is taken from Marx and Engels 1979, pp. 85–6. The emphasis is that of Levi, who cites a 1919 German edition that still ascribed the articles to Marx.]

leadership meant what it said. They went at it 'tooth and nail'. An express-messenger was sent to tell them that they should put on the brakes. When this was done, they were found to have braked too much. Another messenger came to say they should go easy on the brakes. But, by the time the second messenger arrived, the Hamburg movement was already broken. And, with this, the entire 'action' had essentially reached the end of its strength. The 'action', which originated with *an individual* who had not the least idea of German conditions, and was politically prepared and carried out by unpolitical simpletons, left the Communists holding the can.

It is now the most natural thing in the world – to anticipate a bit – that the commanders of this putsch should seek to shift the blame for the defeat away from themselves. The hunt has already begun for 'saboteurs', 'pessimists' and 'defeatists' within the Party. The gentlemen who undertook this attempt are just like Ludendorff in this respect, and other similar traits can be found as well; they are like Ludendorff not just in finding a poor excuse for blaming *other people*, but also in the underlying mistake they committed. Ludendorff was from the school who believed that war is made 'with the principles of the general staff in command and slavish obedience in the ranks'. This may have worked sometime in the past. In the era of Old Fritz and the Potsdam Guards, it was quite sufficient if the soldiers marched round blindly in squares, and the king's will decided everything. In the era of mass-armies, however, of people's armies, this was no longer enough. The 'moral factor' came increasingly into its own. Great armies are not just a military instrument, but a political one as well. They are linked with the civilian masses by a thousand threads; there is a constant exchange of desire, feeling and thought between the one side and the other, and a commander who is unable to lead his army *politically* in this sense, ruins the best armies – precisely as Ludendorff did.

The same applies to political parties. It works perfectly well for an anarchist club if the will of the leader commands and the believers follow unto death. For a mass-party, one that does not just seek to set the masses in motion but is itself a mass, this is quite insufficient. What must be expected from the Communists is that they rapidly detect struggle-situations, energetically exploit them and bear in mind at all times not just the aim of the present struggle but the final aim as well. No Communist, however, because he belongs to the Communist Party and possesses a membership-card, is therefore obliged, or even in a position, to seek out a struggle-situation where *this does not exist*, and where it is only the will of the Zentrale that, in a secret and invisible conventicle, and for reasons different from those that the proletarians see before their eyes, decides that a struggle-situation exists. The Zentrale is not even as ingenious as the Indian prince who, to show his power over all things, pointed to the sunrise from his tent and said: 'Sun, follow the course that I show you', signalling from east to west. The Zentrale, feeling the same almighty power, rather signalled from west to east. And, in this way, it offended against the basic law by which alone a mass-party can be moved. Only their own will, their own understanding, their own determination, can move the masses; and, given these preconditions, a good leadership is able precisely to *lead*. The Zentrale, however, refused to recognise the conditions in which alone a mass-party, which is a mass among masses, and everywhere connected with the proletariat, personally, at work and in the trade-unions, and accordingly subject to the strengthening and enabling influence of sympathy, or the laming one of hostility or enmity, can fight. And, here, we come back to the question: what should the relation of the Communists to the masses be in an action? An action that corresponds simply to the political needs of the Communist Party, and not to the subjective needs of the proletarian masses, is ruined in advance. The Communists do not have the ability to take action *in place* of the proletariat, *without* the proletariat, and ultimately even *against* the proletariat, especially when they are still such a minority in the proletariat. All they can do is create situations, using the *political* means described above, in which the proletariat sees the necessity of struggle, does struggle, and, in these struggles, the Communists can then lead the proletariat with their slogans.

But how did the Zentrale see the relation of the Communists to the masses? As already mentioned above, it thought, first of all, that it could create the situation by *non-political* means. Then, it had its dead, in Hamburg and the Mansfeld district. But the situation was, right from the start, so lacking in any precondition for action that not even these dead could manage to set the masses in motion. Another means was thus prepared. Issue 133 of *Rote Fahne*, for Sunday 20 March, contained an article with the title: 'Who Is Not for Me Is Against Me! A Word to the Social-Democratic and Independent Workers.' This article, however, explained only the *'for me'*, and only at the end did it tell the workers on what conditions they should collaborate. It reads:

> Independent and Social-Democratic workers! We stretch out a brotherly
> hand to you. But we also say to you, if you want to fight with us, you must

be equally hard not just towards the capitalists, but also to those in your ranks who pursue the capitalist cause, who take the field with the Orgesch bands against the workers, and against the yellow-bellied cowards who lull you to sleep and discourage you, just when the Orgesch are sticking their swords into your breasts.

Consider this. The situation gave the Independent and Social-Democratic workers no reason for action. The genius who proclaimed the action was unknown to them, and a decision by the Communist Party was no reason for them to rise for action without any reason being given. I am sure, indeed, that if they had known the reason, their will to action would have been no stronger. These workers, faced with an action that they completely failed to understand, were given as the condition for their collaboration that they should string up their former leaders from the lamp-post as soon as possible. And, in case they were unwilling to accept this condition, they were given the alternative: 'Who is not *with* me is *against* me!' *A declaration of war on four-fifths of the German workers, right at the start of the action!*

I do not know whether the author of this article is sufficiently experienced to know that he had a forerunner in this line of thought – though this forerunner was at least modest enough so say: 'Who is not for *us* is against us.' He was neither a Marxist nor a socialist; his name was Bakunin, the Russian anarchist, who in 1870 issued an appeal to Russian officers with just this alternative. The *Rote Fahne* author can find Marx's verdict on him, and other related matters, in 'The Alliance of Socialist Democracy and the International Working Men's Association'.[26] It should be noted, in this connection, that the whole attitude towards revolutionary classes of 'who is not for is against' is precisely that of anarchism; the proposition 'Who is not with us is against us' was precisely the favourite motto of both Bakunin and his disciple Nechayev, and it is precisely this general attitude that gives rise to the methods anarchism applies: not to defeat the counter-revolution, but, rather, in the words of a member of the KPD-Zentrale, 'to force the revolution'. Communism is never, at any time, against the working class. This Bakuninist basic attitude, a mockery of everything Marxist, this complete misunderstanding and complete slander of any Marxist attitude of the Communists towards the masses, gave rise to all

---

26. Marx and Engels 1988.

the resulting anarchistic features of this March uprising, conscious or unconscious, desired or not, deliberate or otherwise: the struggle of the unemployed
against those in work, the struggle of Communists against proletarians, the
emergence of the lumpenproletariat, the dynamite-attacks – these were all
logical consequences. All this characterises the March movement as *the greatest
Bakuninist putsch in history to date.*

In other words, a declaration of war against the working class. The Zentrale
seems not even to have noticed this. For a member of the Zentrale already
mentioned also blamed the Mansfeld workers for this 'false start' to the
movement. And there is no word to describe what then happened. To call it
Blanquism would be an insult to Blanqui. For, if Blanqui maintained, in permanent opposition to Marx and Engels, that 'revolutions do not make themselves, they are made, and by a relatively small minority', for him this was, at
least, a minority that carried the majority by force of its example. A writer in
Rote Fahne, however, under the authority of the Communist Party Zentrale,
declared war on the workers at the start of the action, *as a way of drumming
them into action.* And the war began. The unemployed were dispatched in
advance as assault columns. They occupied the factory-gates. They forced
their way into the plants, started fires in some places, and tried to drive the
workers off the premises. Open warfare broke out between the Communists
and the workers. From the Moers district came the following report:

> On Thursday morning, the Krupp Friedrich-Alfred works in Rheinhausen
> saw violent clashes between the Communists, who had occupied the
> plant, and workers trying to get to work. Finally the workers set on the
> Communists with cudgels and forcibly cleared their way in. Eight men were
> wounded at this point. Belgian soldiers intervened in the fighting, separating
> the two sides and arresting twenty Communists. The Communists thrown
> out of the plant returned in greater numbers and once again occupied the
> premises.

Still more shocking reports came from Berlin. As reported to me, it must
have been a terrible sight to see the unemployed, crying in pain from the
blows they received, driven out of the factories and cursing those who had
sent them in there. Now, when it was already too late, when the war of
Communists against workers had already started and the Communists had
already lost, *Rote Fahne* suddenly came out with good advice. On 26 March,
an apparently different editor from the one who wrote the article 'Whoever

Is Not for Me Is Against Me' wrote that there should be no war of workers against workers! This Pontius Pilate washed his hands in innocence.

But enough of this. As if there were not already enough unemployed, new ones were created. The Communists in the factories were in the difficult position of deciding whether they should leave those plants in which they were a minority, and where, accordingly, their strike had not led to a stoppage of work – often not even to any obstruction. The Zentrale's instruction was, in such cases, to remain in the factories. The Berlin secretary wanted the same thing, but there was a text of the Berlin organisation stating: 'Under no circumstances must a Communist go to work, even if he is in a minority.' The Communists thus left the factories, in troops of two or three hundred, more or less. Work went on, and now they are unemployed, the employers taking the opportunity to make their factories 'Communist-free', and indeed with a good number of workers on their side. In short, the 'action' that began with the Communists declaring war on the proletariat, and the unemployed against the workers, was lost from the very first moment; in an action that starts off in this way, the Communists can never make any gains, not even any moral ones.

The Zentrale then had to decide what to do next. It decided to 'step up the action'. An action that had begun misguidedly, in which no one knew what they were actually fighting for, in which the Zentrale, evidently because it could think of nothing else and the trick seemed frightfully clever, fell back on the trade-union demands from the time of the Kapp Putsch (!) – the action, the foolishness, was to be stepped up. It *could* be stepped up. The dead in Mansfeld and Hamburg were joined by the dead in Halle. But even this didn't make the right atmosphere. The dead in Halle were joined by the dead in Essen. After the dead in Essen, the dead in Mannheim. But the atmosphere still was not right. This made the Zentrale increasingly nervous. That was the situation on 30 March, when a member of the Zentrale gave a sigh of relief that perhaps in Berlin the security-police would 'lose their calm' and give the working class a bit of 'incitement'.

It was in the interest of 'inciting' the working class, then, that on 30 March 1921 *Rote Fahne* treated them as follows:

> We say quite frankly to the Independent and SPD workers: the blame for
> the blood spilt lies not just on the heads of your leaders, but on the heads
> of each one of you, if you silently or with just weak protests tolerate Ebert,

Severing and Hörsing unleashing white terror and white justice against the workers, beating down the whole proletariat....

Freiheit[27] demands the intervention of the trade-unions and the Social-Democratic parties. We *spit* on an intervention by these *scoundrels*, who have themselves unleashed the bourgeoisie's white terror, themselves done butcher's work for the bourgeoisie....

Shame and disgrace on those workers who stand aside at this time, *shame and disgrace on those workers* who still fail to realise where their place is.

This was indeed a 'complete break' with the Communist Party's past, 'inciting' the workers into action in this way. There is nothing left here of the spirit of Karl Liebknecht, never mind Rosa Luxemburg, and yet it was felt appropriate, in the issue of *Rote Fahne* for 26 March ('Combat Appeal no. 1') for some wretch (forgive me the harsh word, but I am defending the memory of the dead unable to defend themselves) to write: 'The spirit of Karl Liebknecht and Rosa Luxemburg marches at the head of the revolutionary proletariat of Germany.'

We have enough fresh corpses for 'incitement'; let us leave the old ones in peace.

What followed now was a shocking performance. The Zentrale 'stepped up the action'. Banner upon banner was raised. There was no distinction here between 'old Communists' and those 'new' ones at whom the anointed still turn up their noses.[28] Heroically and disdaining death, the comrades rose up in an unparalleled fashion. In the small towns and villages of central Germany, at the Leuna works, in factories large and small: banner after banner rose up, just as the Zentrale commanded. Banner after banner joined the attack, as the Zentrale commanded. Banner after banner went to their death, as the Zentrale commanded. *Ave morituri te salutant!* Not just *once*, but *dozens of times*, the fate of Leonidas and his three hundred Spartans was repeated in central Germany. Dozens and hundreds of unmarked graves in central Germany speak today to the traveller who passes: 'Tell them, you who have seen us lying here, how we obeyed the law!'

---

27. The newspaper of the USPD.
28. [The 'new Communists', at this point the great majority in the KPD, were those who had joined from the USPD after its Halle Congress in November 1920.]

And the Zentrale? It met in Berlin and 'stepped up the action'. Already, some days before the action was broken off, the votes at one session were five to three for such a decision. But, once again, this majority fell into the ditch of 'slackness', 'opportunism', 'inactivity' that they had dug for others. Against the minority of three who were for 'holding out', the five did not dare to press their view, for fear of being accused of a lack of revolutionary will. Vague 'reports' from three districts that 'something was afoot', that the agricultural workers of East Prussia were 'stirring', were all that was needed. So the call went out again to 'step up the action'. And what were the reasons of the three diehards? I am not certain that all shared the same view, but the reason expressed by one of them was that now that the action was lost, it had to be pursued as far as possible, so that after it was broken off they would have no need to defend themselves against the 'left', but only the 'right'.

What can one say to that? Even Ludendorff pales in comparison, when, with certain defeat before his eyes, he sent men outside his class, class-enemies, to their deaths. But these people sent their own flesh and blood to die for a cause that they themselves already acknowledged was lost, so that their position, the position of the Zentrale, should not be endangered. We are not asking these comrades, with whom we have been through good and bad times for a long while, to do penance for what they have done; only one punishment is appropriate, for their own sake and that of the party in whose interest they believed themselves to have acted: *never again to show their faces to the German workers.*

It was pretty well unavoidable in this anarchist witches' sabbath stirred up by the Communist Party Zentrale that an element should appear that was already the preferred force of Bakunin, discoverer of this kind of 'revolution': i.e. the lumpenproletariat. I should make one thing clear here. I assume – without, but even after, the assurances given – that the Communist Party and its Zentrale had neither officially nor unofficially anything to do with the dynamite attacks of recent time. The Zentrale cannot avoid disavowing such things *publicly*, taking a political attitude towards them, rejecting them *no matter who might be at the bottom of them*. It is forced to do so all the more in that, after its 'complete break with the past', the *obviousness* that formerly prevailed in such matters no longer exists after what we have described above. To come back to the lumpenproletariat, I must remark that love for them had already spread beyond the strict school of Bakunin. A few months ago, I already had occasion to quote a phrase of Engels on the lumpenproletariat, and the danger for Communists in getting involved with it. Some comrades evidently felt this warning was meant for them. Comrade Frölich, in the *Hamburger Volkszeitung*, tried to shake the bush to see what hare was hiding beneath it. Comrade Frölich received some support in this. In an article by Comrade Radek, which has not yet been published and which I do not know whether its author still wants to publish, we read:

> His revolutionary instinct immediately led Comrade Frölich to sense that something rotten was afoot here. Nothing more nor less was at issue than the fact that with the rapid decay of capitalism and the slow development of the revolution, ever greater proletarian masses are being thrown into the ranks of the unemployed, impoverished and lumpen-ised. Anyone who now starts turning up a theoretical nose at these 'lumpenproletarians' in the old Social-Democratic fashion will never manage to mobilise these masses for revolutionary action.

Mark this well: the 'rottenness' that Comrade Frölich sensed with his 'revolutionary instinct' was not the lumpenproletariat, but rather my warning of involvement with it.

I hope Comrade Radek will allow me, as a poor and erring soul, 'lacking clear insight' and only 'in the process of development', since I am a 'revolutionary results-politician', to offer the great Marxist some notes from my weak understanding. Comrade Radek speaks of 'turning up a theoretical nose' at the lumpenproletariat in the 'old Social-Democratic fashion'. The fashion is indeed a very old one. It started already in the first 'Social-Democratic' text there is, the *Communist Manifesto*:

> The 'dangerous class', the social scum, that passively rotting mass thrown off by the lowest layers of society, may, here and there, be swept into the movement by a proletarian revolution; its conditions of life, however, prepare it far more for the part of a bribed tool of reactionary intrigue.[29]

This 'turning up a theoretical nose', therefore, began with Marx, and in his early years at that. The spiritual forefather of this latest Communist uprising,

---

29. Marx 2010a, p. 77.

Mikhail Bakunin, had quite a different opinion. In the previously mentioned text of Marx and Engels, the following quotation from Bakunin is cited:

> Brigandage is one of the most honourable forms of the Russian people's life. The brigand is a hero, a protector, a people's avenger, the irreconcilable enemy of the state, and of all social and civil order established by the state, a fighter to the death against the whole civilisation of the civil servants, the nobles, the priests and the crown.... He who fails to understand brigandage understands nothing of Russian popular history. He who is not in sympathy with it, cannot be in sympathy with Russian popular life, and has no heart for the measureless age-long sufferings of the people; he belongs to the enemy camp, among the supporters of the state.... The brigands in the forests, in the towns and in the villages scattered all over Russia, and the brigands held in the countless gaols of the empire make up a single, indivisible, close-knit world – the world of the Russian revolution. *It is here, and here alone, that the real revolutionary conspiracy has long existed.*[30]

You see how grateful I should be to Comrade Radek. While he accuses me only of 'turning up a theoretical nose' and being 'devoid of clear insight', his lord and master Bakunin is not so sparing with those unwilling to share his heroic robbers' tales. He declares that they 'belong to the enemy camp', they are 'partisans of the state'. Marx and Engels bore this fate of being for Bakunin 'partisans of the state', and I too will have to bear it; for, at present, even Radek's reasons convince me just as little as Bakunin managed to convince Marx and Engels.

What are Radek's reasons? In the lumpenproletariat Comrade Radek sees the 'ever greater masses thrown into the ranks of the unemployed'. This is quite wrong from the start. Unemployment is neither universal, nor is its extent and length anything new for capitalism. It is the constant shadow that accompanies capitalism. No one has ever thought of identifying the 'industrial reserve-army' with the lumpenproletariat. The lumpenproletarians are classless, fall-out from all possible classes and strata. The unemployed, precisely because their unemployment is a constant and inevitable result of their economic condition as sellers of labour-power, are member of the class of

---

30. Marx and Engels 1988, p. 520; emphasis P.L.

sellers of labour-power, the proletariat. They share, and necessarily so, in the life of their class. Through the ties of trade-unions, co-operatives, political organisations and, above all, *political activity*, the unemployed remain proletarians and must remain so. True, prolonged unemployment does indeed declass certain individuals from the stratum of unemployed and push them down into the lumpenproletariat. But this process is precisely encouraged by those who break these connections between the unemployed and their working-class comrades, especially the connection of common political activity between those in work and those without. This is indeed what happened, and not just by sending the unemployed as assault troops against those in work. It happened also by misusing the unemployed, demoralised by hunger and poverty, for methods that are otherwise characteristic of the lumpenproletariat; this meant declassing them and hurling them forcibly (and with worse means than force) into the ranks of the lumpenproletariat.

One might object that, if the Communists ally themselves with all other revolutionary classes, as we have seen above, then why not with the lumpenproletarians? The answer to this is quite simple. The other classes with which the Communists can ally themselves for the purpose of overthrowing the existing state, i.e. the peasants, the artisans, the bourgeoisie when it is still revolutionary, are *classes*. In other words, collections of people who are bound into a social body by their similar relation to the means of social production. *The lumpenproletarians are not a class.* They do not belong to the sellers of labour-power, as do both employed and unemployed proletarians; they are leaves blown from different trees, and if they certainly are victims of an unjust social order, the most damaging loss they have suffered is that they are precisely declassed, classless, and no longer have even what the proletarian still has: the ability to fight as a class for a change in the conditions of which they are victim. Certainly, movements of lumpenproletarians, robber-bands, etc. can lead to a situation that enables Communists to use them *politically* – if the state is greatly weakened. It would be foolish not to make use of such a situation, and 'theoretically wooden-headed' to let such a situation pass simply because it was created by lumpenproletarians. But, as for *involvement* with the lumpenproletarians, Engels's word still holds:

> The *lumpenproletariat*, this scum of the depraved elements of all classes, which establishes headquarters in the big cities, is the worst of all possible allies. This rabble is absolutely venal and absolutely brazen.... Every leader of the

workers who uses these scoundrels as guards or relies on them for support proves himself by this action alone a traitor to the movement.[31]

The big distinction between a fighting proletarian and a 'political' lumpen-proletarian is always this: the fighting proletarian commits even criminal acts for political ends, while the lumpenproletarian commits even political acts for criminal ends.

We have had relevant practical experiences of all this in Germany. The particular characteristics of the German worker have also to be taken into account here. I will spare Comrade Radek the attempt to make a cheap joke here, and say only that, just as the Russian worker has his strong and weak points, so the German worker has his too; and one of the strong points of the German workers, as Engels put it, is that: 'they belong to the most theoretical people of Europe; and they have retained that sense of theory which the so-called "educated" classes of Germany have almost completely lost.'[32]

It is this very particularity of the German workers that makes even an external connection with the lumpenproletariat unfavourable in the highest degree. We gathered our experiences of this in the Spartacus League, in which we decisively rejected the least involvement with the lumpenproletariat, and when in the sudden days of November and December 1918 we did all that we could to shake the lumpenproletariat off our backs, so that it would not colour in any way the opinion the workers had of *us*. In a long struggle, by which I am not referring to our argument with the KAPD,[33] we purified ourselves of this, not without having the experience that the lumpenproletariat far prefers to sell itself to the bourgeoisie than to go with the workers – with the result that the workers took us seriously, our influence among them grew and they gained confidence in us. And, now, the Communist uprising of 1921! Here, I shall just give voice to one individual comrade, with extraordinary experience in railway matters, and belonging not to my school of thought but rather to the 'Berlin' one. He said the following at a meeting on 30 March:

---

31. F. Engels, 'Prefatory Note to *The Peasant War in Germany*', Marx and Engels 1985, pp. 98–9.
32. Addition to 'Prefatory Note to *The Peasant War in Germany*', Marx and Engels 1988, p. 630.
33. [See Introduction, p. 13.]

> The tomfoolery at Ammendorf, and the derailment of a passenger-train, brought the workers against us. Now the railwaymen and the entire personnel come and say: couldn't you at least have blown up an arms train or a military transport? Dresden is just assembling military transports. We should work there with all our forces to prevent these trains being assembled. This prevention has been made impossible by the ridiculous attacks. The government has won the railwaymen to its side. I attribute this to the ridiculous dynamite-attacks. They contributed to it...

This was the effect. And, in passing, I declare it that if *one single* train was prevented from being assembled in Dresden, out of solidarity and an understanding of the situation by the railwaymen, that would have helped the cause of the workers in central Germany, indeed in Germany as a whole, far more than five trains blown into the air.

These are our German experiences. And I would prefer to go astray with Marx and Engels than to find the truth with Radek and Bakunin. It is pertinent here to return once more to the 'old Social-Democratic fashion'. Comrade Radek would be the last person not to know this position of Marx and Engels. I have certainly not told him anything new with all this. This fact, however, casts a peculiar light on this kind of Marxism. I am certainly not a person to accept each single dead or living word with an *'autos epha'* – the master has spoken. What is powerful and overwhelming in Marx's body of ideas, acknowledged even by those who reject this as a whole, is that not only does it recognise and take into account the thousandfold complexity of political and social events, but it brings this diversity back to that simplicity, that singleness, that is peculiar to everything major. It is thus impossible for me, just because it seems suitable, to stuff certain chapters of Marxism into a back pocket and 'turn up my nose' at 'old Social-Democratic fashions'. But this is perhaps because I am a poor simple-minded fellow, 'lacking any understanding', and it takes a greater mind – not that of a 'results-politician' – to make an occasional flying visit to Bakunin, simply because it seems convenient or because an eight-month wait is beginning to have its effect.

How are the Communists to conquer state-power? After making this 'complete break with the past', it would seem, only by *completely fundamentally and irrevocably breaking with this present*, with a state of affairs in which no one knows where tomfoolery ends and political criminality begins. The only thing is to return to the sentence from our party's founding programme:

The Spartacus League will never take over governmental power except in response to the clear, unambiguous will of the great majority of the proletarian mass of all of Germany, never except by the proletariat's conscious affirmation of the views, aims, and methods of struggle of the Spartacus League.[34]

This means first of all the following. Never again in the history of the Communist Party must it happen that the Communists declare war on the workers. Anyone who believes in Bakuninist style that the workers can be driven into action *by dynamite or cudgels*, has no place in a Communist Party.

Never again in the history of the Communist Party must it happen, or even any attempt be made, to 'create struggle-situations' by police-spy manoeuvrings. The Communist Party is a party of struggle, it is glad of the day and waits for the day on which it can fight with the proletariat and at its head, and it works politically and organisationally for this day, seeking to create struggle-situations by *political* means, instead of circumventing them by compromises as the social reformists do.

The Communist Party is only the vanguard of the proletariat, and never a bludgeon against the proletariat; it cannot march out if it has lost its connection with the main force.

This is, first of all, the first precondition for getting rid of the tremendous mistrust that the majority of German workers feel towards us after this crazy escapade. Here lies the greatest damage that the March events of this year have caused. No one should deceive themselves as to the difficulty of this task. Never has the mistrust – to use no stronger word – of the German workers towards the Communists been as strong as it is today. And, yet, we had an infinitely hard struggle to gain a foothold in the working class, organisationally and, above all, intellectually. The fruit of this work has now been destroyed, and it is worth saying openly that *as long as the workers do not regain trust in the Communist Party, there can be no talk of the German Communist Party having the capacity for action.* The *correction* for the March events must therefore be made visibly to those outside, *in a manner that is visible to the workers.* If the Communist Party persists in its *present* standpoint, it will become a sect, sharing

---

34. 'What Does the Spartacus League Want?', in Hudis and Anderson (eds.) 2004, pp. 356–7.

the fate of all sects: reduced to insignificance in numbers and influence within three months.

It is necessary in this connection to make an immediate and energetic start with a *political* leadership of party-business. Here too the tremendous damage wreaked by the movement is apparent. If the Zentrale, instead of fooling itself with 'secret information', had considered the political facts, it would certainly have acted otherwise. In England at this time, the miners' strike broke out. A state of emergency was proclaimed, not unexpectedly. Anyone who followed events on the English coal-market would know what would happen – the whole English coal-export, a pillar of England's world-market, collapsed; since October last year, the United States has exported more coal than England produces; the entire English coal-industry rests on an export-price of 150 shillings, while America is offering coal freight-paid to France and Belgium for 90 shillings. If the Zentrale, instead of rooting through my Reichstag speech of 12 March for 'opportunism', had actually read it, they would have found this already predicted – without any 'secret information'! The blockade of Germany is beginning. Not, as the 'secret information' had it, on 20 March, but gradually. A slow starvation like that in wartime. The conflict between Bavaria and the Reich is opening up, as the Reich has to carry out disarmament. Not because of the Communist uprising, but *despite* it. Indeed, 'the situation is crying out for struggle'. But, through a Bakuninist adventure, in which the Zentrale let itself be inflamed by a putschist hothead, for the sake of 'stepped-up activity', the fighting power of the German proletariat has been weakened, as in the struggles ahead it will not have confidence in the plans of its leaders. 'It would only have needed combining into a united proletarian front in order to conduct the struggle together.' So the Zentrale wrote at the end of its putsch, to show that even after it they had learned nothing. 'Only', indeed. It would *only* have taken the understanding of the Zentrale that the unity of the proletariat is the result of a *political process* and cannot be won by police-spy provocations. It would only have needed the understanding of the Zentrale that it is there for the proletariat and the Party, and not the Party and the proletariat there for *it*. Then we would be in an excellent situation today, strong and armed for struggle. Then we would have been able to say: 'Down with the government!' Instead, we have to be more modest and say: '*Down with the putschists!*'

IV

There still remains in this connection the question of the relations of the German Communist Party with the Communist International. Not only because such a catastrophic defeat for the KPD also affects the International, but because, without going into details, the Executive Committee of the Communist International bears at least a part of the blame.

One thing, first of all. The ECCI saw and still sees a certain danger in the fairly strong anti-putschist attitude of myself and other comrades. It is so disturbed by this that it has sent out its most expert spies and analysts to establish whether there is not already 'opportunism' somewhere or other. It is appropriate to speak quite openly about this and say that this entire approach is incorrect. As far as opportunism and social reformism is concerned, it should be borne in mind that in no country is this so clear, so unambiguous, so unconcealed and so unmistakably crystallised as in Germany.

The German Communist Party and its leading comrades, like the great majority of its members, have emerged from the Social-Democratic Party. The struggle with Social Democracy, internal and external argument with it, was an argument with opportunism. And not just that. Our daily struggle in the press, in parliament, and, above all, that of the workers in the trade-unions and factories, is a constant, living, energetic and successful struggle against opportunism. The great power we have to fight against is opportunist Social Democracy. In such conditions, therefore, there is no great danger that opportunism can be found in the German Communist Party, if it is to be found anywhere. Opportunism *within* the Party is thus a very minor concern.

There is, however, within the Party, a danger of putschism. Comrade Radek least of all needs me to explain how much putschism has already damaged us, as he has followed these things very closely since 1919. I have already perused our literature of the time for quotations. After our arguments with the KAPD, in which they shared our theoretical standpoint, the comrades of the ECCI, and steadily following them Comrade Radek, were of the view that the danger of putschism had now been overcome, and that a bit more 'unrest', as we might put it, could not do any harm. This idea was wrong. The danger of putschism had not been overcome, but was acute, and necessarily became so, at the moment that the majority of the USPD came over to us, not having been through the learning experience that our original Communist Party had. It was now more necessary than ever to keep a firm hand on the tiller against putschism, but the comrades of the ECCI were of a different opinion, and the ship is now on the rocks!

So as to avoid the danger of errors, I shall say something more about putschism.

That what has taken place in Germany, an uprising fired from a pistol against the bourgeoisie and four-fifths of the working class, was a putsch, needs no further word on my part. It is not my view however that every partial action is a putsch. We were against partial actions in 1919, when the revolution was on the decline and any armed movement only gave the bourgeoisie and Noske the hotly desired occasion for drowning the movement in blood. In declining revolutionary situations, partial actions are to be avoided. In rising revolutionary situations, however, partial actions are absolutely necessary. Despite the high revolutionary training of the German proletariat, it can still not be expected – that would need the re-run of a miracle like the Kapp Putsch, but, this time, not misconstrued by the Communists – for the proletariat to stand ready *on one particular day* for the button to be pressed, as a Social-Democratic party-secretary, or Rudolf Hilferding, understands it. If the revolutionary wave rises again in Germany, then, just as before 1918, there will be partial actions, even if the greater maturity of the German proletariat compared with that time will find expression in such partial actions being more powerful and more solid than previously. But, by a partial action, we understand only one thing – the proletarians rising up in struggle in one part of Germany, or a large city, or an economic region. We do not mean that, in one part of the Reich, or in the Reich as a whole, Communists strike or take action. Partial action should always be interpreted in a vertical, not a horizontal sense.

Apart, however, from the different assessment of the putschist danger in Germany, there is a second subordinate difference in the judgement of our activity. Our propaganda, our activity in parliament, and so on, were not considered sufficiently revolutionary. There is no dispute about certain things, for instance the agitational effectiveness of *Rote Fahne*. For the most part, however, here again the complaints of the ECCI seem to rest on a wrong assessment. It would like things to be more 'noisy', as the English say. Here, again, however, we have already gained experience, and its implications are quite different. We, too, at the start of the Revolution, sent out our street-speakers and propagandists to make forceful speeches. They had great success at their first meetings, but, after the second ones, our organisers wrote in to say that we should send other speakers, the workers did not want to hear insults. We must openly say that a large part of the propaganda-literature, appeals, etc. that we receive from Russia, if not actually damaging to us, is not as useful in content as it might be, on account of its excessively robust form. I recall a case in which although the German Zentrale, by a unanimous vote, had declared a certain text inappropriate, it was published all the same over our heads.

It is just the same with the work of the parliamentary group. A Communist parliamentary group would be in dereliction of duty if it did not make proper use of a revolutionary situation, with all means at its disposal. But parliament is the last place in which revolutionary situations can be 'made'. Parliament is the 'mirror-image' of what is happening outside, especially in revolutionary times. A parliamentary group which expressed itself in a constant fit of rage would make itself ridiculous. What it comes down to again is that the German workers are reflective and theoretical. Perhaps far too much so; but they cannot be brought to do something by insults; they have to be convinced. And this is not just our experience in the two and half years' existence of the Communist Party, it is my experience in well over a decade of practical party-work, and the experience of comrades who have spent a long lifetime in this work. It also did not escape Comrade Zinoviev, I believe, when he wrote after the Halle Congress: 'The old school is making itself felt. The work of the best German revolutionaries was not in vain.'

Zinoviev saw how the great effect of his speech at Halle rested precisely on the fact that it was so factual, and avoided any impulsive form.

All this, however, pales before the tasks of the Communist International and the practical resolution of these tasks.

One point, first of all. I believe it is not just in Germany, but everywhere, that the leadership of the ECCI is experienced as inadequate. This is not because we have at its head neither a Marx, as at the head of the First International, nor a Lenin. The problem is one of the great technical difficulties, inadequate postal connection, etc. The ECCI is isolated from Western Europe, its most important region of activity. I believe that the ECCI is by no means the last to feel this. Its solution, however, is most unfortunate, and, on this point, I had to express myself as party-president with some reservation, while now, as an ordinary party-member, I can speak with complete openness. This is the system of confidential agents. First of all, Russia is not in a position to send out its best forces. They have positions in Russia that are not replaceable. Cadres and comrades therefore arrive in Western Europe, each of them with the best will, each full of their own ideas, and each full of an eagerness to show how well they can 'handle it'. Western Europe and Germany thus become a test-bed for all kinds of *duodecimo* statesmen, of whom we get the impression that they are keen to develop their skills. I have nothing against these Turkestanis,[35] and only wish them well; but I often have the impression that they would do less harm with their tricks in their own country.

The position becomes most serious, however, when representatives are dispatched who are quite inadequate even from a human point of view. I come back again here to the Italian events. Comrade Rákosi, after representing the Third International in Italy, then arrived in Germany. He was introduced at the sessions of the Zentrale and the Central Committee as representative of the ECCI. He explained in so many words that in Italy 'an example had been given', and declared both privately and in public that the German Party would also have to be split again. He had indeed brought the Italian division to breaking point with this idea of the need for new splits. The speeches are there in the stenographic record; a hundred witnesses can attest to it. Rákosi, however, reports to Moscow, and what is the Communist International to make of it? The semi-official (or maybe quite official, if still apocryphal) article by Comrade Radek states:

> The attempt (at a further split) exists only in Levi's imagination, basing himself on a supposed expression of the Hungarian Comrade Rákosi, who was the representative of the ECCI in Italy, and who is supposed to have said, in Levi's report, that the German Communist Party would again have to be purged. Comrade Rákosi, who took part in the session of the Berlin Central Committee as a private individual, denies having said anything of the kind. And, even if Comrade Rákosi did say it, he was not authorised to do so.

The utterance reveals the completely frivolous way in which parties, causes and people are played with. Comrade Radek is aware that private individuals have no access to meetings of the Central Committee of the KPD. Comrade Radek declares that Rákosi was not authorised to make such a statement. But Comrade Rákosi was the ECCI's plenipotentiary at Livorno. He gave us

---

35. [See Introduction, p. 18.]

the authentic reasons that led to the split in this form. He gave us reasons, therefore, that could lead to a split in the German Party tomorrow. Rákosi himself drew these conclusions; myself and 23 Central Committee members expressly disagreed with these reasons,[36] and the ECCI then explained that Rákosi was not authorised to make such a statement. Presumably, he was authorised only to carry out a split without reasons. This is a frivolous game being played here; the method of dispatching irresponsible people, who can later be approved or disavowed as need be, is certainly very convenient, but even if it was blessed by long party-tradition, it is fatal for the Third International. I may remark, in passing, that some people are all too hasty in toying with new splits, at least these foreign representatives of the ECCI. I hope I shall not be compelled to give evidence that in German circles close to the ECCI, at least in circles for which the ECCI bears political responsibility, the dreadful defeat of the Party is brushed aside with the words that, if the March Action only led to cleansing the Party of its right wing, the price would not be too high. The comrades now lying dead in central Germany were not told, when they were sent to their deaths, that their corpses would be used as dynamite for the Party. If the ECCI is not able to cast off such unconscionable fellows of this calibre, it will ruin both itself and us.

Comrade Radek's semi-official statement, however, only reveals a further and still more damaging effect of the delegate-system. This is the direct and secret contact between these delegates and the Moscow leadership. We believe that more or less in all countries where these emissaries are working, discontent with them is the same. This is a system like a kangaroo-court. They never work with the Zentrale of the country in question, always behind its back and often even against it. *They* find people in Moscow who believe them, others do not. It is a system that inevitably undermines all confidence for mutual work on *both* sides, that of the ECCI as well as the affiliated parties. These comrades are generally unsuitable for *political* leadership, besides being too little trusted. The hopeless situation that results is that a centre of political leadership is lacking. The only thing of this kind that the ECCI manages are appeals that come too late, and excommunications that come too early. This kind of political leadership in the Communist International leads either to nothing or to disaster. The only thing left for the whole organisation is what we have

---

36. [See Introduction, p. 17.]

described above. The ECCI works more or less like a Cheka projected beyond the Russian frontiers – an impossible state of affairs. The clear demand that this should change, and that the leadership in certain countries should not be taken over by incompetent delegates with incompetent hands, the call for a political leadership and against a party-police, is not a demand for autonomy. In the same passage in which Marx uses the most forceful words against autonomy in the International, he also says:

> Without damaging in the least the complete freedom of the movements and efforts of the working class in individual countries, the International has managed to combine them in an association, and for the first time make the ruling classes and their governments feel the world-embracing power of the proletariat.[37]

The ECCI is in the best position to measure how far removed it is from this ideal situation. The present situation may be good for an international of sects; it is pernicious for an international of mass-parties.

In this connection, I want particularly to mention the seriousness of the decision which this collapse of the German Party poses for the International. For understandable reasons, we cannot go into a detailed discussion of who is to blame. We have to emphasise, however, that the German Communist Party, now endangered in its very existence, for which *in part* the ECCI is to blame, and is at least responsible for, is the only Communist-led mass-party in Europe up to now. The German Communists are faced with the question of life and death, whether they can still maintain their Party as Communist or whether it will collapse into a heap of Bakuninist ruins. It is the fate of revolutionary parties, when the revolutionary process goes quiet, when there are long counter-revolutionary epochs, that they consume themselves; in cases such as these, anarchism completes the fate of Communist parties. No one can see behind the weaving of history, or can measure the diversity of forces according to their strength and aim and constancy: 'no eye that sees the golden scales of time'. It is only from the *symptoms* that the victorious tendency among those in struggle can be discerned. If the Germans do *not* manage to rebuild the Communist Party, if the March affair is to be their fate,

---

37. 'The Alliance of Socialist Democracy and the International Working Men's Association'; Marx and Engels 1988, p. 554.

then it is definite proof that the counter-revolutionary tendencies which we are seeing throughout the world are of longer duration and greater strength than we had formerly believed. If this is our destiny, it is also the destiny of the Communist International.

If we do succeed, however, as we hope and wish, in rescuing the Communist idea in Germany and so proving that there are still revolutionary forces that can seize the hour, let the International not put obstacles in our path if we return to the past of the Communist Party and the doctrine of its founder. She depicted the route we have to take in the following words:

> The unification of the broad popular masses with an aim reaching beyond the whole existing social order, of the daily struggle with the great world transformation – that is the task of the Social-Democratic movement, which must successfully work forward on its road of development between two reefs: abandonment of the mass character or abandonment of the final aim; the fall back to sectarianism or the fall into bourgeois reformism; anarchism or opportunism.[38]

We cannot avoid one abyss simply to fall into the other. Both must be avoided.

---

38. 'Social Reform or Revolution', in Hudis and Anderson (eds.) 2004, p. 165.

What Is the Crime:
The March Action or Criticising It?

Speech at the Session of the
Central Committee of the German Communist Party
on 4 May 1921[*]

Preface

It is exactly one month now since the publication of
my pamphlet *Our Path*. Its overall effects are already
becoming clear.

One effect, almost the only one to outward appearance, is that any street-urchin who calls me a traitor or insults me in any terms he likes sees himself
marching at the head of the German Revolution.
I am happy to grant such revolutionary heroes this
easy heroism, and will not waste words over them.

The other effect, however, I can say already today,
is that, in essentials, my view has already prevailed.
Not only is there no longer any talk of throwing the
'Levites' out of the Party, but the high Zentrale, after
establishing itself as a star-chamber, is happy today to
keep muddling along on a collegial basis; the hilltop
from which these generals dreamed of commanding
the 'offensive' has been abandoned; and time is even

---

[*] The title page of the original edition reads:
Was ist das Verbrechen?
Die Märzaktion oder die Kritik daran?
Von Paul Levi
Rede auf der Sitzung des Zentralausschusses der V.K.P.D. am 4. Mai 1921.

being regularly taken to consider not just the incitement against me, but also the damage that the March Action has done to the Communist Party. Principles have, in the meantime, been adopted that amount to a beheading of the Zentrale that 'made' the March Action, if it is not a contradiction to speak of beheading in the absence of any head worth the name.

Outwardly, however, the Zentrale prides itself on the victory it has won over me; my scalp, it believes, can distract the believers' gaze from the Zentrale's retreat on essentials. And, if the Communist Party has lost everything else, at least the prestige of those responsible for the loss can be maintained. The cracks that these great and small idols of earth and heaven have suffered are not to be seen from outside. And, in this way, the Zentrale and the others involved shirk from acknowledging their error – the *one* favour they could still do for the Communist Party. They think that the more they rail against me, the easier it will be for them to avoid such acknowledgement. We can indulge them: the iron necessity that rules all political activity, especially all political mistakes, will not spare them from sacrificing their prestige on the altar of the Party, against which they have so greatly sinned that they owe greater sacrifices than simply their prestige. And, each day that the Zentrale continues an existence which is fundamentally dishonourable and indeed hypocritical, the more its guilt increases, in line with the damage done to the Party.

It would be unjust not to recognise that, even in the wretchedness of these days, there have been certain beams of light. Many comrades, particularly from the old Spartacus League, have remained true to the cause for which they more than others have struggled for so long. From their mouths I have heard no complaints or hesitations. We all know that the cause of the German Communist Party will soon come to rest again on the shoulders of these *triarii*, and the heavy task will find us all prepared, just as it did before.

15 May 1921

Speech

Comrades! You did not expect me to speak in my defence, and this is not my intention in the strict sense. I do not feel today that I am forced to defend myself; if something is needed, it is, rather, a debate. For the result already seems quite clear to me: we shall go our separate ways, and it is no more than duty on both sides that, after spending a while together, indeed with several comrades having worked closely together for a long time and now dissolving this partnership, there should be a division of the household-goods. I also believe, however, and not only on these grounds, that I should address the content of my pamphlet.

Comrade Pieck said that we basically don't want to speak about the March Action; the only point at issue is a 'breach of discipline'. I say, however, that the only question at issue is whether the March Action was correct.

[INTERJECTION: *'Indeed!'*]

In that case my expulsion is justified.

Or was the March Action rather an error, an extremely ominous error as I and many of my friends believe? In that case, far more would be excusable and justified than what I did with my pamphlet, and so I believe there is no alternative but to come clearly to grips with the essential point: what should be the verdict on the March Action?

But, before I embark on this question, I would like to touch on another matter: the effect that this pamphlet had on the Party. I will concede right away that it did not have the effect I had counted on, and I shall deal with this later on in more detail. But, I should, at any rate, have been able to expect a straightforward and honest debate, not the kind of thing which I shall give you just one example of. Comrade Meyer wrote as follows in the *Rote Fahne* of 15 April:

> In the style of a Social-Democratic party-treasurer or trade-union baron, Levi is completely satisfied with the fact that the number of organised Communists rose from a few thousand in November 1918 to half a million at the turn of 1921: 'No class in the world has ever managed this before.'

What I actually said in my pamphlet was the following:

> In Germany however, in this present revolution, the revolutionary forces are more or less keeping pace with the development of the forces of counter-revolution. This is expressed in two ways. The strength of a revolutionary class, the proletariat, grows in proportion to the strength and number of its clearest, most conscious and decisive vanguard. In November 1918, the Communists in Germany formed a group, but not a large one. In February 1921, they were a force half a million strong. The other phenomenon in which the growing strength of the revolutionary forces finds expression is that the German proletarian class has already received terrible blows in the

two and a half years of the German Revolution. It has lost blood in streams. Once, twice, and again a third time it has suffered heavily from this, yet on each occasion it has taken only a short time for it to rise up again with new forces, with a giant's stature and strength. No class in the world has ever managed this before.

I believe that no fact can show better than the confrontation of these two quotations how comrades who should be serious in judging the question at hand, have dismissed without seriousness or honesty problems so weighty that even the Communist International now writes that they have to be dealt with at the coming World-Congress. They have not yet even managed to give their quotations honestly.

The response I shall probably get now is that I also published minutes of party-meetings, and, again, only in extracts. There are two points I have to make against this. First of all, the charge is raised that I published, off my own bat, minutes of a session of the Central Committee. However, nowhere in the Party is there any doubt that this session of the Central Committee on 17 March was the most serious session in the history of the German Communist Party, and that, never before in such a session – whether for better or for worse – had a decision been made that so greatly affected the life and very being of the Party as did this.

I say, therefore, that keeping such a decision secret from the membership, as the Zentrale has done up till now, is quite monstrous. It is absolutely essential to put full minutes of such serious decisions at the disposal of the membership, to tell the members what is happening, to confide in those who indeed have to carry out the decision what is being done; and so it is no reproach against me, but a reproach against the Zentrale, if it was *I* who was forced to convey the decisive passages to the members of the Communist Party.

[INTERJECTION: *'Why not sooner?'*]

I will explain this exactly to the comrade. I received the minutes on the day I returned from a trip abroad, after the so-called Action was already well under way.

I will say further: I am in good company in publishing minutes, even from a secret session – which that of 17 March certainly wasn't – in a case when the Party faces an emergency. Those comrades who are familiar with Russian history will recall certain events shortly before the Bolshevik seizure of power.

On 21 October (3 November) 1917, i.e. *six days before the insurrection*, Lenin published his pamphlet 'A Letter to Comrades', to convince them of the necessity of an immediate armed uprising. To give his reasoning the necessary weight, Lenin rehearsed in this pamphlet all the reasons that his opponents in the Party, led by Zinoviev, had given against the uprising. In particular, Lenin expressly set down in the pamphlet the information and date that he knew, and wrote in his introduction how on 'Monday morning, October 16 [he] saw a comrade who had on the previous day participated in a very important Bolshevik gathering in Petrograd'. At this secret session, two comrades had taken a negative stand. Lenin wrote:

> The arguments which those comrades advanced are so weak, they are a manifestation of such an astounding confusion, timidity, and collapse of all the fundamental ideas of Bolshevism and proletarian revolutionary internationalism that it is not easy to discover an explanation for such shameful vacillations.[1]

And, on the basis of material from a *secret* session that a comrade had given him, Lenin wrote his flaming attack on the 'vacillators', showing the 'abysmal spinelessness' into which these two comrades had fallen.

The comrades that Comrade Lenin directed himself at here were Comrades Zinoviev and Kamenev, and he obtained his material from a comrade who had attended a secret session.

If the Party is in an emergency situation – and I do not know whether the Bolsheviks at that time were in a direr emergency than the German Communist Party is today – then there is a duty to speak out.

I am asked again, however, why I published these particular extracts and not others, why only these, and why I published them without going to the speakers in question and asking them whether the extracts were correct.

And, here, I already come closer to the nub of the question of how the Action arose. At the end of February or the beginning of March of this year – as I assume you all know – a comrade arrived in Germany who had no previous experience of working in Germany.[2] He had a discussion with Comrade Clara Zetkin, on 10 March, I believe, which made such a devastating impression on Comrade Zetkin that she came to me in a state of consternation to inform me

---

1. Lenin 1964a, pp. 195–6.
2. [Béla Kun. See 'Our Path', above, p. 138.]

of the subject of this discussion, immediately saying that she would in future refuse to talk with this comrade unless witnesses were present.

On 14 March, I then discussed with the comrade in question myself, and in this discussion the comrade not only said the same thing to me as Comrade Zetkin had told me he had said to her, but – and I am sorry to have to remove the aura of originality from the comrades who gave these explanations at the session of 17 March – said *in so many words* precisely what stood in the extracted passages that I published from the minutes of the Central Committee, through to the passage about the impending war between Britain and the United States; the originality is that of the comrade in question. *Every part* of this was explained to me, right through to this and also the bit about provocation, *just as it was to Comrade Clara Zetkin*; even the two or three million who would fight for us in an 'offensive action' was already there.

I gave my opinion about the provocation clearly and unambiguously to the comrade, just as Comrade Zetkin had given hers, and now, comrades, you will grant me the following: on 10 March of this year, Comrade Clara Zetkin heard these ideas about an action which had to be initiated by means of provocation if need be. On 14 March, I heard them, theories which we all agree are foreign to us all and have never been represented previously by anybody in our Party. On 17 March, the leadership met with the Central Committee and the same theories were put forward. Do I then have the right or not to say that there is a causal connection between the two sources? I deliberately say once again today, therefore, and this can and should not be denied by the comrades involved: *the first impulse to this action in the form in which it took place did not come from the German side.*

And now, comrades, it is further said that the action was triggered by Hörsing, and Comrade Pieck, who has said that my pamphlet contains three untrue assertions, though I can only find two of these mentioned in his notes – Comrade Pieck has said that the first untruth is that I wrongly maintained that the action that broke out was the particular action that the Zentrale had in mind with its decisions.

I never said anything of the kind. Indeed, I said just the opposite. To quote again from my pamphlet:

> For a time the Zentrale did not have to put its newly acquired theoretical basis into practice. Hörsing got there first. He occupied the Mansfeld district with one success already to his name: the right moment. With the cunning

of an old trade-union bureaucrat he chose the week before Easter, knowing very well what the four-day closure of factories from Good Friday through Easter Monday would mean. Because of this, the Zentrale was right from the start a prisoner of its own 'slogans'.

I, in no way, said that the action was the one that the Zentrale had intended, I clearly and unambiguously said that the Zentrale was *the prisoner of its slogans*, it could no longer make unimpeded use of the situation Hörsing had created.

There is then a further point that I need to dwell on, one which, perhaps, the members of the German Zentrale are less aware of than I am. It is the question whether there was a causal connection between Hörsing's occupation and the overall action. And what I mean by the overall action, comrades, I shall make more clear to you.

[The speaker argued here that there was a difference between what the Zentrale had ordered as a body, and had to justify politically and legally, and the overall complex of occurrences that accompanied the action, that lay outside the will or even the knowledge of the Zentrale, but *politically* formed a unity with the decisions of the Zentrale. He concluded that, possibly, Hörsing's intervention at the time and place it occurred was only the result of events that formed part of this overall complex lying outside the knowledge and will of the Zentrale.[3] He then continued:]

If the Zentrale said in its appeal for a general strike, after political killings that were not in every case just police-machinations, but of which even the Zentrale in its guidelines for the March Action (*Die Internationale*, no. 4) said that they were 'a sign of despair as to revolutionary mass-struggle' – if, in respect to these things, *the* Zentrale *said*: 'As in 1914. At that time news went out that the French had dropped flying bombs on Nuremberg and were poisoning wells. Today it is trains and public buildings that are supposedly dynamited, the object being to incite hostility against the Communists,' – then *what I say*, comrades, is that anyone like me, who ten days previously had heard theories of provocation unambiguously from the mouth of a legitimised comrade, the same theory then repeated at the session of the Central Committee, followed by the police-occupation, then I have to say, comrades, it takes great optimism to still assume that the one thing has nothing to do with the other,

---

3. [The reference here is to Levi's claim that the ferment in Prussian Saxony was stirred by the KPD's new Zentrale in order to provoke a government-intervention.]

and that it is possible to maintain that it was just the same as in 1914, when there were no flying bombs and it was all merely an invention of the intelligence service and the general staff.

No, comrades, that was a 'false start',[4] and I know it will also be counted as Menshevism, and I will be counted as a Menshevik, but I say nonetheless: *There is also a certain moral dimension that should not be flouted.* A Zentrale that lacks the rock-like conviction of its right, that has at the back of its mind the idea that you have to provoke, you have to *make something appear that is not the case,* such a Zentrale, comrades, has lost the moral power – not to speak of the right – to lead political masses into struggle.

And so, comrades, it was quite clear to me, and remains quite clear, that it was a completely false moral and political attitude to slip into the idea of winning the masses for struggle by any other means than by what actually is the case, to play with the idea of provocation and then finally to end up with the position: 'As in 1914. It was all a pack of lies.'

And then, comrades, what did the Zentrale try and do with this attitude and under its political guidance?

I then come to the point that gave rise to the most weighty allegations – so Comrade Pieck says – that were raised against me. What did the Zentrale intend?

I quote here the Zentrale's appeal for a general strike. It gave out the following slogans:

> Break the violence of counter-revolution with violence!
> Disarm the counter-revolution; take arms, form local defence-groups from circles of workers!
> Immediately form proletarian local defence-groups!
> Secure power in the factories!
> Organise production through factory-councils and trade-unions!
> Make work for the unemployed!
> Secure the livelihood of war-victims and pensioners!
> Struggle to occupy dwellings of the rich and make housing for the homeless!
> Block transports of troops and weapons!

---

4. [The Zentrale, in retreating from its 'putschist' adventure, had described the Mansfeld uprising as a 'false start'. See 'Our Path', above, p. 148.]

Of all this mish-mash of demands that the Zentrale put forward to be realised by a general strike, the last one was more-or-less the only slogan that had a concrete meaning.

And, now, something else, comrades. Now the great charge against me is raised that I deliberately accused the Zentrale of wanting to overthrow the government, or, more correctly, 'wanting to establish the dictatorship of the proletariat'!

Comrade Frölich, in no. 4 of *Die Internationale*, actually made this the centre-piece of his attacks. He extracted from my pamphlet this paragraph: 'Anyone who launches an action *now*, in this situation, for the conquest of state-power is a fool, and anyone who tells the Communist Party that all it needs is to apply itself, is a liar.'[5]

Frölich continues: 'Here we have the basis of Levi's criticism, and this basis is actually the folly and lies. Levi did not manage to adduce a single fact to demonstrate his emotionally charged contention.'

I'm sorry, comrades, but I do have such facts, and, for a start, I will cite them from Comrade Frölich's article in no. 3 of *Die Internationale*:

> In the last there years there has not been a moment at which the government
> has been as weakened as it is now.... This government can be overthrown
> by a fairly strong push, and any new government, whatever its complexion,
> will be an advantage to the revolution, creating clearer conditions. If there
> is the possibility of such a push, then a revolutionary party must lead it.
> Under these conditions, the KPD decided to take the offensive.

I leave completely aside here for the moment the theory that also played a considerable role in the Kapp Putsch of blessed memory, the theory that any other government would be better, that even a Kapp-Lüttwitz government would be better, by 'creating clearer conditions'.

I leave this point completely aside, and will deal only with the point that the KPD went on the offensive in order to overthrow the government.

[INTERJECTION FROM PIECK: '*Certainly!*']

And, now, the comrades say, certainly, we wanted to overthrow the government, but we were not fighting to set up the dictatorship of the proletariat, the rule of the working class, those are two different things. And this is why

---

5. [See 'Our Path', above, p. 136.]

I ask again right away: how did the Zentrale of the KPD pursue the fall of the government?

The Zentrale rejects the idea that it pursued this by armed insurrection; it claims not to have wanted this, and thus to have deliberately confined its slogans to those of a general strike.

Is this your view, then, Comrade Pieck?

And then I return to the question, whether the Zentrale of the KPD bears political responsibility for the armed uprising that broke out in central Germany, or does it not?

I declare that it is no ill-minded slander against the Zentrale on my part if I maintain that, at a certain stage, those workers in central Germany who through their own fault, their breach of discipline, had caused the damage, were attacked as breakers of discipline,

[INTERJECTION: '*Who?*']

Indeed, this was said by Eberlein publicly and in my presence at the Berlin functionaries' meeting.

I say then: Is the Zentrale responsible or not? No one will deny that the Zentrale is at least responsible for *Rote Fahne*. And on 18 March 1921, *Rote Fahne* wrote: 'No worker should give a hoot for the law, but get a weapon where he can find it!'

On the 19th, *Rote Fahne* wrote: 'The Orgesch band[6] proclaims the sword. Its words speak naked force. The German workers would be cowards if they did not find the courage and strength to answer the Freikorps band in *its own clear terms.*'

On the 20th, *Rote Fahne* wrote:

> The example of the Halle district, which is answering the challenge of Hörsing with a strike, must be followed. *The working class must immediately take up arms, to confront the armed enemy. Weapons in the workers' hands.*

And, on the 21st:

> Only the proletariat can defeat the infamous plans of the Orgesch bands. It can do so only through united action if it sloughs off the chattering Social-Democratic traitors and beats down the counter-revolution just as it would itself be beaten, *weapons in hand!*

---

6. [See 'Our Path', p. 143, note 23.]

And, for this reason, I say, comrades, it no longer needed Comrade Z to travel to Mansfeld; these appeals of *Rote Fahne* were sufficient to lay political responsibility for events throughout the Reich on the Zentrale.

I also say that rather than nonsense, it is an unheard-of injustice towards the workers not to gladly take full responsibility for what on the basis of these newspaper-quotations one is indeed responsible for, but try instead to shove it off onto the workers, and burden those who have been struck down with this guilt in addition.

And now, comrades, I am pleased that this call to arms found the Zentrale of the KPD a critic that I don't begrudge them. It was the *Kommunistische Arbeiterzeitung*[7] that wrote the following on 21 March:

> We call on the workers to heed not what they say but what they do. Point out to the KPD people all the shameless tricks they perform daily for the bosses, demand once more from them a solidaristic and unreserved defence against this impudence, demand from them once again the revolutionary destruction of the capitalist economic edifice, demand again revolutionary solidarity with the unemployed, in whom only the ruin of the capitalist sham-economy can arouse new hopes; and fight day after day against the swindle of legal factory-councils, for the building of revolutionary action-executives.
>
> It is high time to call the workers to arm themselves. The real struggle however starts in the factories: only after this does it move on to shooting on the streets.
>
> You KPD-people, are you ready to dare the *final* move? If so, show that you're ready for the *first* move.

Leaving aside the nonsense about sabotaging production, which makes its appearance here as it always does, this whole passage is a *giant measure of political wisdom* compared with the behaviour of *Rote Fahne* and the Zentrale who bear responsibility for the paper. And if you keep repeating to all and sundry, 'No, we didn't want to overthrow the government!', then I have to say clearly that the Zentrale with all its calls to arms obviously meant nothing at all, and I would like to offer the Zentrale – I don't know if further

---

7. [The organ of the KAPD. It was a sore point for Levi that the Comintern had recently given this organisation consultant-status, without even consulting the KPD-leadership.]

opportunities will arise – a word from Sorel: 'Anyone who addresses himself to the people with words of revolution must put his honesty to an exacting test. For the workers understand these words in the sense that they have in their language, and don't go in for interpretations.'

This should have been taken to heart, I believe.

And, now, something else. Did the Zentrale intend the conquest of power or did it not?

[INTERJECTION: *'Of course!'*]

Then I shall read the Zentrale something else from the *Kommunistische Arbeiterzeitung*. This paper, in its issue no. 187, unfortunately without date, wrote the following:

> In the morning-edition of *Rote Fahne* for 15 April, an article titled 'Levi's Road to the USPD' completed their reckoning with the fallen angel. But Ernst Meyer, author of this article, had the misfortune of raising against Levi a charge that, precisely by being a *charge*, bears not so much on the 'scoundrel' as on the present Zentrale of the KPD. Meyer literally wrote: 'He (Levi) assumes that the decisions of the Zentrale and the Central Committee shortly before and during the March Action had the intention of conquering state-power, i.e. establishing a Soviet Germany. In reality, no party-comrade had any such intention either before or during the Action.'

'What a frightful "assumption"!' the *Kommunistische Arbeiterzeitung* continues.

[INTERJECTION: *'Is this your view too?'*]

I'll come to that, Comrade Urban, I won't conceal anything.

'What a frightful "assumption",' the *Kommunistische Arbeiterzeitung* continues,

> As if the revolutionary workers of Germany would seize weapons today without having the goal in mind of conquering political power! Paul Levi's charge-sheet against 'putschism' seems to have kindled such rage in his opponents of the 'left wing' that they have evidently forgotten their own slogans. The *Rote Fahne* also seems to have forgotten that scarcely a week earlier, in a series of articles, it described the March Action with great satisfaction as the start of a 'revolutionary offensive'. Did the German high command take the offensive in March 1918, for example, to conquer a few devastated square kilometres on the Somme, or did it rather think of

striking an annihilating blow at the enemy? Is it possible to expect success in any offensive struggle if at the very start the decision is made to pursue this struggle only to a certain stage? Or isn't it only possible to reach such a stage if the goal is set as far as possible? Anyone who sets out to take the struggle only to a certain line will fail even to reach this line, let alone the final goal. The limit of the offensive is decided in the struggle itself, otherwise the final goal retreats into *infinite* distance. If *Rote Fahne* now has to defend itself against the 'charge' that the March Action aimed to establish a proletarian dictatorship, it would be better if it laid to rest the whole idea of a 'revolutionary offensive'. It would be still better, of course, if the same issue of *Rote Fahne* did not also maintain the opposite of what E.M. deceitfully denies in his leading article. In a report of an unemployed rally that the KPD held in Berlin on 13 April, in fact, a resolution was published which said among other things: 'The problem of unemployment can thus only be successfully solved by the dissolution of the capitalist economic order and the introduction of a socialist one on the basis of the dictatorship of the proletariat. The general strike that the KPD recently proclaimed was also directed towards this goal.'

Which is the right reading, then? Is the leading article decisive or this supplement?

And, now, comrades, Comrade Urban has repeatedly interrupted to ask me whether this is also my own view. Here, I must admit to you, comrades, that once you start applying the purely military idea of 'offensive' and 'defensive' to politics, then this has to be judged in military terms. And, in this case, what the *Kommunistische Arbeiterzeitung* writes is absolutely correct. An offensive such as you had in mind, i.e. the redirection of a large party-body to the attack, such an offensive, carried out by the will of the Party and its leadership, is, in political terms, an impossibility, as I shall go on to explain. It is anarchistic foolishness. But, if you are at all able to think in political terms, then it is certainly possible only with the final victory, the conquest of political power, as its immediate goal. On psychological grounds, it is not otherwise possible. The *Kommunistische Arbeiterzeitung* is quite correct: what brought the weary soldiers out of the trenches once more in 1918 was the hope of a decisive victory. What brought them to their feet in 1914 was the hope of a final victory in six weeks.

As a certain military writer once said quite correctly during the war-aim debates, if someone is to jump a metre, the bar has to be set at 1.05 metres and not 0.95.

The idea of a 'final victory' directly linked with this general attack cannot be separated from the anarcho-syndicalist idea of the general strike or general uprising initiated by decision of the organisation. This point of departure and this final goal are what characterise so-called 'direct action'. And, where I differ absolutely and completely from the KAPD and from the present orientation of the KPD is precisely in that I reject this anarchist belief in miracles and say that it is impossible, a monstrosity, to go from one day to the next from the *defensive* to the *offensive*, from *passivity* to *activity*, or however you like to put it, on the basis of a decision of the Party or a party-body or a particular comrade who sees himself as too much of a genius for words.

And, at this point, comrades, I do indeed arrive at the nub of supposed 'Menshevism', as the term has been recently used: the Party has gone from the *defensive* to the *offensive* and is now on the *attack* and struggling to 'force the development of the revolution'.

If this is so, then the Zentrale, and those who make this undertaking, must, in my opinion, also proclaim this idea with its promise of victory openly and before the masses whom they still seek to win over.

The Zentrale, however, experienced a remarkable difficulty here. At the first moment of the first action on the 'new line' of the 'offensive', the Zentrale issued an appeal which said, among other things: 'The counter-revolution has picked a fight...'. 'The struggle has been forced upon us...'. 'Rise up with us,' it went on to say, 'in common *defence* against this villainy.'

Thus, immediately after the glorious fanfare, when it was already clear how things were going wrong, an attack of embarrassment. No one is prepared any more to acknowledge the glorious offensive.

The Zentrale says, this is not what we intended; the ECCI says, this is not what we intended; the representatives of the ECCI say, this is not what we intended, and so – let the comrades again call this 'sentimentality' if they like! – it is clearly in the final instance the workers who intended it, who gave out the thesis of 'forcing' the revolution, and of transition from the 'defensive' to the 'offensive'.

And, then, something more. I say that the whole idea of 'activity' and 'passivity', of the 'offensive' and the 'defensive', of the 'transition from agitation to action', all these are vain and artificial distinctions, and completely unpolitical interpretations and word-games.

Two months ago – this is how quickly things change – two months ago in this very room,[8] I read out to the comrades a paragraph from Comrade Rosa Luxemburg, without hearing contradiction from any side. It read as follows:

> The conditions for social-democratic activity are radically different. This derives historically from the elemental class struggle. It operates within the dialectical contradiction that here it is only in the struggle itself that the proletarian army is itself recruited and only in the struggle that it becomes conscious of the purpose of the struggle. Organisation, enlightenment and struggle are here not separate moments mechanically divided in time, as in a Blanquist movement, they are merely different facets of the same process.[9]

Here, you have the reasons why I say that the whole idea of transition from defensive to offensive by way of a decision of the Zentrale or of a still higher heavenly illumination is un-Marxist, unpolitical, and cannot reasonably be expected to lead to any other result than a pitiful catastrophe such as we have witnessed.

Indeed, revolutions cannot be made. This is, indeed, the standpoint that formally at least is still represented in our movement, and about which we are finally all agreed.

You are nodding, Comrade Schmidt! Then I will tell you, when I made this simple point to the comrade who gave me the first revelations about the 'new tactic', he replied to me with a smile: 'Is that your opinion? You're still in primary school!'

I tell you, then, revolutions cannot be made. What is it supposed to mean when Comrade Frölich says to you that we now have to 'force the fate of the Party and the revolution'?

---

8. [This would have been on 24 February 1921, when Levi presented the Central Committee with his critique of Comintern policy in Italy, 'The Beginning of the Crisis in the KPD and the International'; above, pp. 92–112. Its rejection by the Central Committee triggered his resignation as party-president.]

9. 'Organisational Questions of Russian Social Democracy', in Hudis & Anderson (eds.) 2004, p. 252. [Levi must have been aware, in citing this passage, that it comes from a text in which Rosa Luxemburg took issue with Lenin's concept of revolutionary organisation.]

This idea is nothing else than that, in certain circumstances, revolutions can be made. And Comrade Meyer, in his *Rote Fahne* article of 15 April 1921, said about what he called our passivity, that it was wrong, a cheek, to appeal to the authority of Karl Liebknecht and Rosa Luxemburg. He would refrain, he said, from the insults that I had so richly distributed.

I am glad, comrades, that *Rote Fahne* still tolerates a certain objectivity and freedom of discussion at least towards the dead, and that on 1 May of this year *Rote Fahne* saw it as timely – very timely, indeed – to reprint an article by Comrade Rosa Luxemburg. She said in this:

> The seemingly sore point of genuine socialist policy in war lies in the fact that revolutions cannot be made on command. This argument should apply both to the attitude of the proletariat on the outbreak of national slaughter as to its present attitude to the question of peace as apology and cover-up of the socialist surrender. But this seemingly decisive 'practical' objection is no more than an escape. Of course, revolutions cannot be made on command. This however is not the task of the socialist party. Its duty is only to 'speak out the facts' at all times and without fear, i.e. to explain to the masses clearly and unambiguously their tasks at a given historical moment, to proclaim the political action programme and the slogans that result from this situation. *Concern for whether and when the revolutionary mass-uprising breaks out, socialism must confidently leave to history itself.* If it fulfills its duty in this sense, then it operates as a more powerful factor in the unleashing of the revolutionary elements of the situation, and contributes to accelerating the outbreak of mass-actions. But even in the worst case, when it initially seems like preaching in the desert, it establishes, as always and unquestionably emerges at the end of the day, a moral and political position whose fruits it will later be able to harvest with compound interest when the hour of historical fulfilment strikes....[10]

Concern for whether and when the mass-uprising then takes place is something that socialism must confidently leave to history.

[INTERJECTION: *'Quite right!'*]

[INTERJECTION: *'When did Rosa Luxemburg write this?'*]

---

10. This quotation is from 'Brennende Zeitfragen', originally published in *Spartakusbrief* no. 8 of August 1917; Luxemburg 1983, pp. 288–9. [The emphasis here is Levi's.]

In 1917, in the fortress at Wronke.

[INTERJECTION BY MEYER: *'That's true, I put the article in the paper.'*]

I acknowledge this lack of partisanship towards the dead.

I say then, whereabouts in this whole line of thinking is there any place for the idea that revolutions can be made, that 'the fate of the revolution and the Party' can be 'forced', by provocation if need be? There is no trace of such an idea! And you cannot tell us that, in this sense, in the sense of these ideas, we have ever fallen into passivity. There was not a moment, and I tell you, Comrade Meyer, this is something that you will yourself acknowledge, the Zentrale of the Communist Party was never passive in the sense of *expressing the demands of the day*, in your day,[11] when it opened its mouth wide and shouted its activity through every alley.

No one can say that mistakes were not previously made, that, in earlier times, before what Comrade Frölich calls the complete break with the tactics of the Party had been carried out, everything had been free from error – we are all fallible – but certainly the Party was never in dereliction of its duty in such a serious and catastrophic way, never trampled its own principles underfoot, at that time.

I say therefore, comrades, that the whole idea of a transition from 'defensive' to 'offensive' carried out by deliberate *decision*, is an idea that is un-Marxist and unpolitical, and cannot bring any political success.

Let me continue. We happen to live in Western Europe in rather different conditions. You know that on the occasion I mentioned, basing myself on quotations from Comrade Rosa Luxemburg, I explained the quite different circumstances in which we in Western Europe have to form Communist Parties.

The Communist Party in Russia, before the Revolution, had to take shape in a social body in which the bourgeoisie was not at all developed, a social body in which the *proper*, natural antipode to the proletariat, i.e. the bourgeoisie, existed only in traces, and where the main enemy opposing it was agricultural feudalism. In Western Europe, conditions are quite different. Here, the proletariat faces a fully developed bourgeoisie, and confronts the political consequences of the development of the bourgeoisie, i.e. democracy,

---

11. [Presumably, a reference to the period after March 1918 when Leo Jogiches had been arrested and Meyer edited the *Spartakusbriefe*, soon joined by Levi and Eugen Leviné.]

and, under democracy, or what is understood as democracy under the rule of the bourgeoisie, the organisational form of the workers takes different forms from under the state-form of agricultural feudalism, which is absolutism.

In Western Europe, therefore, the organisational form can only be that of a mass-party which is not closed in on itself. Mass-parties of this kind can *never* be moved at the command of a central committee, the command of a Zentrale, the only way they can be moved is in the invisible fluid in which they stand, in psychological interaction with the whole proletarian mass outside. They are never moved by a word of command; they move in the movement of the same proletarian class whose leaders and guides they must then be in this movement. The one is dependent on the other and vice versa, and, for this reason, comrades, it was a fateful error, and I shall come to speak of this later, that, after the collapse of this action, the Zentrale did not make the attempt, not at all a revolutionary one, to 'deal with' some of the many questions that are raised.

But I come on now to speak of another matter. This fact, that we, in Western Europe, live in a quite different social body, has given us a complexion that is new in kind. Before the revolution in Germany, the life of the working class was essentially lived in *one single* organisation. This organisation was a firm core within the proletarian class; what lay outside this organisation was indifferent or only in a twilight-state of becoming-conscious. A fundamental change has now taken place in Germany and in Western Europe. In Germany and Western Europe, an overwhelmingly large portion of proletarians are united in workers' organisations that already exist. And, now, comrades, this fact alone brings with it the great danger – by its very existence – of the working class splitting down the middle, so that two sections, for instance the organised and the unorganised, the Communist organisation and the non-Communist organisation, not only confront one another as politically separate bodies, but, in a certain sense, part company as socially separate bodies; one organisation embracing different layers of the proletariat than the other, so that the Communist Party is not what it should be, the organisation of a part of the proletariat – the most advanced part, but a part going through the whole proletariat – but, instead, becomes a part vertically divided according to socially differentiating aspects.

And, comrades, the significance that the relationship of the Communists to these workers' organisations has, I am happy to demonstrate with a quotation from Comrade Radek, who, in his very latest pamphlet,[12] writes: 'It is clear that, in the event that this mass is not brought into motion by some kind of external events that completely shake them up, *we cannot count in Germany on any spontaneous and unorganised movement.*'

This is absolutely and completely correct. Without the heavy organised mass, we will not have large-scale movements, except for particular strokes of luck with which we cannot reckon in our daily work. Our relationship to those workers' organisations becomes the core of our being. It is this that determines the justification of our existence: on the one hand, we have to maintain our specific character and our nature as Communists, while, on the other hand, making the closest connection with these masses of workers.

And, now, comrades: the way that we as Communists are to make the connection with these masses of workers is also something that must be discovered in Germany for the first time. There were two preconditions for this. One of them was that, in purely numerical terms, we reached a strength that allowed us purely mechanically to develop the forces that were required to influence such large masses of workers.

The second precondition was that we now also reached in political terms some kind of connection with these organisations, that we sought to win political influence on them.

We embarked on this path with the 'Open Letter'.[13] This was the first attempt, and it is not a question of whether it was successful or not, whether it could have been done better or worse. But it was an attempt based on the correct sense that it is only possible to approach organised masses of workers if one does not just fight against them, but if one relates to their own ideas, even if these are mistaken, and helps them to overcome the error by their own experience. We must help them in what they understand, and not force them into something that they do not understand.

And this idea, which now, as before, I take as correct and as the only possible one, this idea was fundamentally contradicted by the action of the Communist Party in March 1921. Indeed, I was laughed at, and the object of unpleasant words, when I said that the struggle in March 1921 had become

---

12. [This was *Soll die Vereinigte Kommunistische Partei Deutschlands eine Massenpartei der revolutionären Aktion oder eine zentristische Partei des Wartens sein?* (Hamburg 1921), written in response to the controversy over the Italian split.]

13. [See Introduction, p. 15.]

the struggle of one section of the proletariat against another section of the pro-letariat, and what is still worse, the struggle of one *stratum* of the proletariat against another *stratum*. This was laughed at. Well, *Rote Fahne* sometimes, if seldom, finds the courage to speak the truth, and, in the last few days, it published a report about the trial in Moabit, in which it wrote:

> Five unemployed Communists were brought before the special court of Landgericht Berlin I, presided over by Judge Braun, for calling on their proletarian brothers to stop work, both in the Ludwig-Loewe factory and at the AEG-plant. *Some of them had also been prepared, in view of the unenlightened attitude of a section of the workers, to take energetic measures to close down the factories. To this end they had taken some hand-grenades with them.* The prosecutor claimed that the five accused, who are to be sentenced on Wednesday, had been selected from a larger number of imprisoned unemployed Communists, and as many as *two or three hundred persons are to be tried and condemned in the same manner.*

Comrades, does this not sound like bloody and bitter disdain for all political ideas, like a satire on the idea of proletarian solidarity written by some pamphleteer? And this is printed in *Rote Fahne*, as a factual report or, as it might well think, an embellishment of the events of those March days?

Yesterday, moreover, I heard of another case, and the Zentrale may perhaps like to extend its projects to this case as well.

In Zschornewitz, where the large electricity-plant is situated, the 'order' was given to sabotage the power-station. The workers learned of this 'order' in a way that I do not wish to expand upon. The workers were almost entirely Communist. These Communist workers posted sentries to ensure their work, so that if the sabotage-column had come to the plant, they would have been received with blows and machine-guns not only by proletarian class-comrades, but even by their own party-comrades.

And, comrades, these are not just occasional derailments, they are typical cases that you hear about from all parts of Germany, and they lead to the core of what was wrong with the whole March Action. *It was the action of a small section of the proletariat, with no regard for the other large section.*

And, comrades, here we must ask ourselves once more what the real intention was when such an action was undertaken off our own bat and with our own resources, 'in order to force the fate of the Party and the revolution'?

One idea at work I have already indicated. It was the idea that, by acts of terror and violence, it is possible to create situations that feign to the proletariat the necessity of struggle, instead of pursuing the attempt to prove to the masses the necessity of struggle out of the existing objective conditions, without cheating, which is in no way needed.

That was one idea. It was present in those who believed in the miraculous effect of provocation. The other idea then is an idea that I have up to now not come across in any publication of the Zentrale, but which I am confronted with ever more frequently in my discussions with members outside. The comrades mostly understood the action in these terms: yes, we Communists are called to give the masses an example, to go ahead of them and draw them into struggle.

This is not just almost literally what I have heard from the mouths of comrades, it is also the classic Blanquist formula of the determined minority. This idea has also led with logical necessity to the only result which such theses and slogans can lead to in a country with strong workers' organisations that are consciously reformist, the result that these strong workers' organisations stand as a closed front against the minority that wants to 'demonstrate' revolution.

And, now, the comrades who support this kind of revolution write of our supposed opportunism. No, the opportunism is actually to be found somewhere else. I would like to read you the following quotation:

> In actual fact the connection between socialist opportunism and the revolutionary adventurism of terror has much deeper roots. The former and the latter both render history an account before the payment date. In the effort to artificially accelerate the birth, they bring it to a miscarriage. Both terrorist tactics and parliamentary opportunism shift the centre of gravity from the mass onto representative groups, on whose talent, heroism, energy or sense of timing the entire success depends. In both cases, broad corridors are needed that separate the leaders from the mass. At one pole, the 'combat-organisation' shrouded in mystery; at the other, the secret conspiracies of parliamentarians, to benefit the stupid party-masses against their will.[14]

The comrades will know who wrote these words against this kind of politics. It was Comrade Leon Trotsky.

---

14. [This quote does not seem to exist in any English edition of Trotsky's writings, and the same holds for the further quotes below.]

And, now, something else, comrades. Partial actions will happen. I spent a few words on partial actions in my pamphlet, and Comrade Frölich has even appealed to the heavenly father to exorcise their diabolical content. He said that, by partial actions, I understood something quite other from what the Executive understood and intended to be understood by partial actions. He and they meant partial actions for *partial goals*, whereas I meant partial actions in terms of territory.

There you have it. And, if Comrade Frölich had considered the question more maturely, he would have managed to recognise that I was forced to speak precisely about this latter kind of partial action; for it was this form of partial action, i.e. partial actions in geographical terms, that gave us the greatest problems in Germany up till now, this was the form that bled dry the great movement of 1918–19, when one geographical region after another was beaten down.

And these too were partial actions in which the Zentrale threw our best organisations into the breach, not seeing and not concerned whether the rest of Germany would be in a position to follow the action.

It was also necessary for me to talk about partial actions in this sense because there has been no lack of theorists who have again defended this kind of partial action, despite the 'heavenly father'.

And, now, comrades, something else. There must have been something in mind. It is said now to be the task of the vanguard to make an action in order to 'hasten the revolution'.

I have here a quotation that runs as follows:

> The proletarian vanguard is intellectually won over, that is the main thing. Without this it is impossible to take even the first step towards victory. But from this point to victory is still a long way. It is impossible to conquer with the vanguard alone. To throw the vanguard alone into the decisive battle, before the whole class, the broad masses have come round either to direct support of the vanguard or at least to a benevolent neutrality towards it, and the complete inability to support its opponents – *this would be not only stupidity, but an actual crime.*[15]

---

15. *'Left-Wing' Communism – An Infantile Disorder*, Lenin 1964b, pp. 92–3.

The man who wrote this is fortunate that he is not already counted as one of the 'Levites', though he might well be in the future. It is Lenin.

And, now, comrades, what we experienced is that the Communist Party was thrown into the battle alone and cut off from the masses. We saw how our best organisations went into disaster. The best organisations were destroyed and entire large organisations could not be moved at all. What occurred here was nothing but a tragedy. In almost the whole of Germany, apart from Hamburg, it was impossible to bring the organisations into life. It was just impossible for them to obey a ridiculous decision, any more than water will flow uphill on command.

And, here, comrades, to say that the Party has brilliantly understood the action and only my pamphlet is to blame for the failure is just childishness and a untruth towards the comrades.

[INTERJECTION FROM PIECK]

Ah, Comrade Pieck, how modest you are now! Whether the damage ascertainable at this point is small or large I shall confidently leave to your better judgement in this regard. But I believe, Comrade Pieck, that I can, in a certain sense, claim the ability of seeing the tendency that is present and assessing to an extent the results to which this leads.

[INTERJECTION FROM PIECK: *You see things in too dark colours!*]

To which this leads, Comrade Pieck? I don't need to let my imagination get out of hand. I will read you something else:

> In the attempt not to lose influence over the active elements of the workers at a time of defeat for the mass movement, a section of the Bolsheviks sanctioned in the name of Marxist doctrine the tactic of piracy, expropriations, etc., in which only the anarchist dissolution of revolutionary psychology found expression. On this basis, the inclination to conspiracy that the Bolshevik fraction of the Party particularly displayed in the period before the [1905] revolution came to full development. Things were done behind the back of the Party that had nothing to do with the political life of the masses and by their very nature escaped party-control. Adventurist elements permeated the party-organisations. Responsible party-offices were frequently entrusted to individuals who proclaimed their organisational ability in a sphere that lay outside the party-movement. Independence from any kind of workers' organisation, heroic speculation on 'good luck', undertakings that were kept secret from party-comrades of 'second grade' – all this developed an

unrestrained individualism, contempt for the 'conventionalities' of party-status and party-morality, in short a political psychology that in its nature was quite foreign and hostile to the atmosphere of workers' democracy. While the Hamlet of Menshevik criticism, oppressed by the contradictions of political development, responded to the question of the Party's existence with a liquidationist 'not to be', the authoritarian-centralist Bolsheviks, under the pressure of the drive for *self-preservation*, sought to separate the Party from the class, the Duma fraction from the Party, the centre of the fraction from its periphery, and with fateful necessity this led to forcing its entire political practice into the Stirnerist formula of 'the individual and his individuality'.

The more deeply the wave of mass arousal ebbed, and disorganisation in the ranks of the Bolsheviks advanced as a result of the unreserved withdrawal of the intelligentsia, the more sharp was the mistrust of some elements of Bolshevism against everything outside their own fraction, and the more clear the expression of the tendency to maintain the workers' organisations in subordination by means of decrees, reprimands and ultimatums 'in the name of the Party'.

These elements, the so-called ultimatists, knew only one means to keep the Duma fraction or the legal workers' organisations under the influence of the Party: the threat to turn their backs on them. The boycott-tendency that pervades the whole history of Bolshevism – boycott of the trade-unions, of the Duma, of the local councils, etc. – the product of sectarian fear of 'ferment' in the masses, the radicalism of 'irreconcilable abstaining' – congealed in the time of the third Duma into a particular current within Bolshevism, which in its turn displayed different shadings: from complete, anarchist-hued rejection of any parliamentary activity through to a certain disdainful and thoughtless tolerance of this activity.

Things that you already see indications of today – you will not deny this, Comrade Pieck – and the person who described this was again Comrade Trotsky.

And, now, comrades, it is again said, or will be, that, of course, the Bolsheviks, or the bureau of the ECCI, support the publications against me; so they can't be wrong.

Yes, indeed, the ECCI, at least outwardly, has assumed the role of God on the sixth day of creation, when He looked at all the work He had done, saw that it was good, and blessed it. And, over and above this act of the Lord God on the sixth day of creation, the ECCI also sent out simultaneously and by return of post its curse against those who did not share this satisfaction with all its works.

This is how it looks to outside appearance. And, yet, there is no doubt, comrades, that not a single Bolshevik accepts this story. There is no doubt what can be read between the lines – i.e. 'even if Paul Levi was right...'

Oh yes, I know this tactic, it's an old trick. At the point when you have to defend yourself against unwelcome critics, you attack them with double force, so that it escapes notice, at least to the stupid, how the critics are really correct.

And I'm also well aware of the reason why the ECCI intends to reserve the final decision about these problems of practical anarchism, which are in no way as recent as the Executive presents them, to the Third World-Congress. Quite simply because it is assumed that the German Party that has acted so stupidly will finally also manage to punish this stupidity. In this way, it intends to keep the substantial decision in its own hands, without preventing the immediate resolution of the matter.

But, comrades, in principle, this whole method of deciding on such serious party-questions by shifting decision from one body to another, or from one conventicle to another, is completely in line with the underlying idea from which the March Action arose, i.e. that just as stupidities are committed in conventicles, so their correction can also be achieved by conventicles.

If anything at all is to be learned from the March Action, this can only be done if the masses get to know the errors and discuss them in the broadest and freest context.

[INTERJECTION FROM KOENEN: 'It's you who've prevented this!']

No, Comrade Koenen, it's you who didn't want it. You could have done this as well as the personal attack on me, that didn't stand in the way of the substantial debate.

[INTERJECTION: 'As you did with Radek's letter in Heidelberg!']

I am not exactly sure what this interjection is trying to say, but I shall try and answer.[16] The letter from Radek that was read out in Heidelberg, I received from the comrade who is sitting here just half an hour before the start of

---

16. [The KPD Conference of October 1919. See Introduction, p. 10.]

the Congress and thus just before I read it out. The comrade will vouch for this herself. I am also quite well aware what it means if Radek, who in two years of operating in world-history displayed the Heidelberg Congress as a moment of glory, suddenly wants to know nothing more about Heidelberg, at a time when new hope is being placed in the KAPD. I am happy to grant Radek these moments of glory that he prided himself on as long as they were indeed seen as glorious, just as I shall also be happy to offer him the fig-leaves behind which he may like to conceal whatever he thinks necessary to conceal.

So, comrades, I come back to the point from which I started; for the method adopted even in the liquidation of the March Action shows how the Party intends to remain faithful to a basic attitude that is un-Marxist and anarchistic. And that it does intend this, comrades, I deduce from another point. I already felt this for a long time, and comrades from the Zentrale, I have been with you too long not to know that you were not happy either. And if this feeling of mine needed confirmation, it has received this by the principles that were presented yesterday and have also been adopted. For how you plan to reconcile the March Action with these principles, which *for me are too opportunist*, is a puzzle. Every sentence of these principles knocks your March Action on the head.

The principles speak quite clearly, and if I listen to your inner voice, as I have long been accustomed to do, it was rather you telling each other: 'We messed up once, now we must defend the prestige of the Zentrale. We won't let this kind of thing happen again.'

People who think in these terms have another thing coming. It is possible to stumble into error. What is not possible, however, is to try and cheat your way out of an error, such a catastrophic error as has been committed, by adopting principles in which you swear on the one hand to remain fast and true to the established line – for the sake of prestige – while on the other hand denying this action – in order to return to reason – and then think: 'Time won, everything won; it won't trouble us any more.'

No, comrades, the spirits you have conjured up, you (to the Zentrale) won't get rid of so easily, and the Party won't get rid of them either, unless it finds the strength to express quite clearly, unambiguously and sharply the errors that have been committed, to characterise them, to say everything, to the last detail.

[INTERJECTION: *'Without you!'*]

Without me! I am glad, Comrade Koenen, that – in better form than me – *you* will be the man to expose the mistakes without embellishment. I am happy for you.

But, comrades, now I come to the question as to why I wrote my pamphlet.

One point, first of all. It has been said that the time of publication was the most unsuitable time conceivable. On this point, I would like to put the facts straight. The Zentrale has charged that I reported its speeches at the Central Committee meeting of 17 March without asking permission of the Zentrale members. Here, too, however, the Zentrale has had an unfortunate accident. In its resolutions-document, it embarked on a public defamation of a comrade, without first asking the comrade what he had to say. Now, you, Comrade Pieck, in your speech today have said that I wrote the pamphlet at a time when the struggles were still under way; in your document, it was even said that the pamphlet was *sent to press* when fighting was still under way. This is not correct. The struggle was officially broken off on the evening of 31 March –
[INTERJECTION]
– alright, on 1 April, but the decision was already made known to me on the evening of the 31st. I say, therefore, that, on 1 April, the call to break off the 'action' went out across the country. I wrote my pamphlet on 3 and 4 April, and it was certainly no small superficial thing that Comrade Pieck – indeed the author of the expulsion document – equates 'wrote' and 'sent to press'. On 7 April, the session of the Central Committee –
[INTERJECTION]
– I maintain that, at that time, a request to listen to me and my criticism was twice put to a vote and rejected; critics were not wanted or needed. And, a day after I heard the catastrophic news that the Zentrale and the Central Committee were persisting in their mistakes in a resolution, I sent the pamphlet to press, and it appeared on 12 April. On 12 April, when the pamphlet appeared, there were no longer any struggles under way anywhere in the German Reich.
[INTERJECTION: *'The action of the counter-revolution was still under way!'*]
Indeed, Comrade Koenen, it will be under way for a good while yet.

So, the pamphlet appeared on 12 April. At that point, all the struggles were over, and it was impossible to wait until the last man was condemned in the last corner of the Reich. The danger seemed to me too great for this, as it still does. If such catastrophic mistakes as were committed are not *rapidly and sharply repaired*, then they eat their way in.

And, now, the comrades will ask me whether my sharp attack on the Zentrale was necessary. On this, I would like to say a further word, not because it is fundamentally of such great significance, but because it nonetheless shows the spirit from which this expulsion-document emerged. Comrade Pieck says in so many words: 'The worst however is this: Levi has sown distrust against the Zentrale and against the representatives of the ECCI.' Indeed, I did so, and I plead guilty of this lèse-majesté. I will even go so far as to say that in my pamphlet I intentionally went beyond sowing distrust –

[INTERJECTION: *'Listen to him!'*]

– I am concealing nothing, I am not defending myself. The Party had abandoned its old ways, it had run into disaster, there was only one kind of repair that was able to prevent at a stroke further outbreaks of the disorder, i.e. a kind of surgical operation, and this was not a method of sowing distrust against the Zentrale, but rather of exposing and denouncing unrestrainedly the whole political crime, the whole betrayal of the Party's former principles: this was the operation needed, and this I am content to have intended and done.

[INTERJECTION FROM MEYER: *'You voluntarily gave up the leadership!'*]

Indeed, Comrade Meyer, that is something I already did on the foundation of the Party.[17] I always said that *you* perhaps had the better ideas, and I hope that your left wing, what calls itself the left wing and sees itself as specially chosen, will take up the leadership. Are you making this into a reproach against me? What kind of opposition is it that does not take pride and rejoice each day that it can turn its ideas into practice and take responsibility for this practice? I despise this fine kind of opposition *which complains about its task*. I know why you are complaining. You want us to be the donkeys on which this opposition can learn to ride, and this is a role I am not prepared to play.

[INTERJECTION FROM KOENEN: *'That is what you are now trying with us!'*]

---

17. [It is the foundation of the VKPD by the merger with the USPD left that is referred to here. Levi was indeed elected co-chair, but resigned a few weeks later. See Introduction, pp. 17–18.]

No, I shan't do this, although, Comrade Koenen, the role it would give you would perhaps be a good one.

I say, therefore, this was the sickness! If someone does not see a sickness, then self-evidently they must forcibly oppose the attempt to root out the sickness. And, for this reason, this is the key point that we are disputing. And since I see absolutely no prospect that at this point in time any of you here will see that this is a sickness, or will see how it is the ruin of the Party – because you do not see this, you are right therefore to expel me. But then, Comrade Pieck, you can spare yourself such antics as 'sent to press on the 3rd/4th, given to the USPD on the 7th'; tricks of this kind can confidently be dispensed with.

And all such fine phrases as the 'joy of our enemies' can also be dispensed with. You did the same thing once before, Comrade Pieck. During the Kapp Putsch, I sent my well-known letter from prison to the Zentrale, which was no milder in form than my present pamphlet. You know how that letter in its day was published against my will in the *Kommunistische Internationale*. When I heard of the intended publication – I was then in Petrograd – I immediately contradicted it and explained that the letter was not mean for the public. And, at that time, it was Zinoviev who said that, if a party makes such catastrophic stupidities as the German Communist Party did during the Kapp Putsch, then criticism of it is not a private matter. And so the letter was published against my wishes, and the ECCI wrote about it:

> The passionate tone of the letters – especially the letter of Comrade Levi, which he wrote in a prison-cell – is only too understandable. Our enemies will naturally make hay with these disagreements within the KPD. Let them do so! We Communists have never been afraid of self-criticism.

At that time, you members of the Zentrale held back from printing the issue for three months, bothered about your prestige and the 'joy of our enemies', but the ECCI said: 'A fig for your concerns, the criticism must be made!', and published the issue of the *Kommunistische Internationale* off its own bat.

And do you believe, comrades, that if the ECCI did not now have a particular position, for different reasons, against its critics, and against myself in particular, and if it agreed with the criticism, as I believe it actually does, does any of you believe that the ECCI would have then said a word against the publication of my pamphlet? Oh no, it would have distributed laurel-leaves if it had any to distribute.

Another objection is made to me that Rosa Luxemburg's attitude in the January uprising of 1919 was completely different. Yes, I agree. I would never compare myself with Rosa Luxemburg, but what is the difference here? I am told that Rosa Luxemburg had also been against that action, and yet she wrote articles and appeals. You also know, Comrade Meyer, that I too was against the movement at that time, but I also wrote leaflets and articles. And why was this? From the quite different standpoint that it was great masses that were going astray, and not a small conventicle of leaders who were driving the non-straying masses to disaster, and, at that time, there was a genuine, large-scale, powerful and spontaneous mass-movement, with more workers assembled in the Berlin Tiergarten than the number involved this time in the whole of Germany.

And – Comrade Meyer, you were no longer there, I believe – but I think that Comrade Pieck was at the session in the Puttkamerstrasse when we came into conflict with Karl Liebknecht over his attitude. You will remember how stubborn Karl Liebknecht was, and how it was Leo Jogiches who made the proposal, already at that point, *during* the action, to publish a sharp declaration in *Rote Fahne* that quite clearly dissociated us from Karl Liebknecht and would declare that Karl Liebknecht no longer represented the Spartacus League with the revolutionary shop-stewards. You know very well how strongly Rosa Luxemburg rejected Karl's behaviour, and you know how sharp her criticism was; and she came out with her criticism the moment the action came to an end, she would not have waited until the last prisoners of the January uprising were condemned, which was not until June.

And I believe, Comrade Pieck, you are also aware that Comrade Rosa Luxemburg even had the idea at that time that it was no longer possible to work with Karl Liebknecht, so strongly did she reject his behaviour. The reason she wrote nothing more was not because she believed that such criticism was a matter for history and not of political struggle, it was rather because death took her pen away.

And now, comrades, a few words about the International. It is certainly no accident that the Levi case has had a certain effect throughout the International; quite unconnectedly and spontaneously, here and there in almost every country, comrades have declared their solidarity with me. And I can say that it was not everywhere the weakest heads who did so. Just as, in Germany too, I can confidently say that it is not the weakest heads who share my path.

It is quite clear, then, that the crisis against anarchism that has now opened in Germany is something that the entire Communist International will have to overcome, and so the Executive Committee of the Communist International that reproached us German Communists for passivity will be forced to reflect on its own political activity.

Indeed, how exactly did the ECCI act? It is deeply saddening to see how, in these last weeks of the greatest European crisis since 1914, the Second International has been back in sight with its false words, reformist appeals and litanies. But it has shown itself and appeared on the political stage.

And the Communist International? It had time to insult me as an infamous liar, and Radek had time to write a pamphlet against me, in which he proved to a hair that I am the German Serrati, that the Serratists and Levites are the worst of all political scoundrels and it is high time to warn against them and take a distance from them.

But any trace of political leadership in such a serious political crisis from the 'active' Communist International we have seen less of than at any time in its existence. There have just been appeals that come too late, and excommunications that come too early, and a few pots of filth exchanged with Jouhaux: this is the activity of the Communist International!

[INTERJECTION FROM REMMELE: *'Then you must be at the head!'*]

No, no, Comrade Remmele, I don't want to be at the head, even if perhaps, without taking pride in it, I am a match for some who play so big a role today. I never, I believe, misread a situation so catastrophically as Comrade Zinoviev for example misread the situation in October 1917, when *he* declared the Bolshevik seizure of power a senseless putsch – I never laid down my party-mandate during an action that was so decisive as that October action of 1917 was for the existence of the Bolsheviks, and never acted as Zinoviev did at that time, to appear later on as a great accuser against 'Mensheviks' and 'breakers of discipline'.

And this absolute passivity of the ECCI in the last year has done the cause of Communism more damage than any 'Menshevism'. Just remember how radiant a year ago was the allure of the Communist International. And think what it is today! A powerful moral resource has been wasted, it has just about managed to carry through the split from reformism, and when the task is to build up Communist parties it threatens to come to grief because of its passivity and inability.

For, comrades, on this point I am completely clear: this crisis for the Communist International, which has begun with my case, or rather the case of the German Communist Party, is under way throughout the world, and I have already read you quotations about the development of the Russian Revolution in periods that, as no one would deny, are very similar to our present experience in Germany. But with one distinction, that this present crisis in Germany is not simply a German crisis, but connected with the International by more than just individuals and outward appearance.

The Russian comrades will thus persist for a time in their struggle against the 'Mensheviks', against those they call 'Mensheviks', not always in good faith, and I am happy at least that now it is quite different people who are falling under the notion of Mensheviks, people in whose company I am happy to be seen.

It is absolutely not the case, as Radek writes in his latest pamphlet, that Rosa Luxemburg once went astray and 'stood with the Mensheviks'. I can demonstrate that this aberration of Rosa Luxemburg was not some disturbance of her ideas that lasted three or four months, as little as it was a momentary disturbance of Clara Zetkin that she stands alongside me, or the result of personal connections with me, as Zinoviev and Radek have the good taste to put it.

The International and the German Party will have to fight against signs of decay that are typical phenomena of a period in which the revolution goes into retreat and cannot be redirected to an offensive by decision of a party-body. In this connection, I shall say one thing quite expressly, that, today in Germany, conditions are different from how they were in Russia in 1906. Even if the political revolutionary movement is on the ebb, the world-economic crisis persists and is growing stronger, with no sign of its being overcome. And this also means that the basis is present, that it can happen not just after ten years, but, in a matter of days, that the defensive, the ebb, turns back to the offensive, the flood. Not by a decision of the KPD that the revolution now has to embark on the offensive, but because, as a result of economic and political development and facts, history – and not provocation, history alone – brings the masses into struggle.

And, until you understand and accept this, you will break your teeth trying to force history, until the German Communist Party, whose task was to prepare each hour with propaganda and organisation, is hopelessly compromised and reduced to an anarchist club, while the masses are scattered and muddled.

This is the experience that we have from the Russian movement in its ebb years. But the German masses cannot, of course, learn everything from the lessons that the Russians give us by their history – nor by their more or less rousing words. What Trotsky wrote remains true:

> Each country had and still has to win Marxism for itself afresh, if it is to possess it. The international character of the socialist movement is shown not only by the fact that each country draws lessons from the experiences of the more advanced country, but also by the fact that it repeats its mistakes.

The mistakes of the Russians, which they themselves then recognised as mistakes and eradicated, we, for our part, have richly repeated. There are, of course, comrades who believe that the dose of stupidities is still not large enough, new and stronger doses are needed. You will decide today to do what law and legislator command, and decree my expulsion. I will not sink into oblivion, but we shall see, and see soon, who is right and by which path you will once more return to the theories and methods that were formerly those of the Spartacus League, the German Communist Party and the Communist International. Whether *you* (to the Zentrale) will still be in the ranks at that point is another question. For, if the masses never make mistakes without profit, leaders never make mistakes without being punished.

Closing words

Comrades! Despite the lengthy arguments directed at me, I shall be brief.

The first question directed at me is, what would you have done if it was up to you to decide? I have indeed argued that the possibility existed that, when Hörsing triggered the action, this was not without a certain connection with various earlier events. If this is so, then, naturally, the question is not answerable at all, as I would in no case have taken political responsibility for these preceding events.

But, assuming that Hörsing's intervention was a completely unoccasioned provocation, then I must confess that, in the face of a provocation by the enemy, I am inclined to avoid contact, as I tell myself: the enemy provokes when it suits *him*, and if it suits the enemy, then *in most cases* – not a hard and fast rule – everything says that the occasion does not suit us; for me, therefore, the possibility must exist of stepping aside so that the blow aimed at me in an unfavourable situation meets empty air, or reaches its target in a situation where conditions are more favourable to me.

I am personally of the view that, if Hörsing's police-action really was a provocation, then in the situation it itself described, eight days before Easter, the Zentrale should not have accepted the provocation.

And, further, assuming that despite everything, whether we wanted it or not, the Zentrale had to accept the provocation – I completely contest that this was and is the case, quite in opposition to the 'offensive' – but, assuming this was the case, what should the Zentrale have done? Indeed, Comrade Radek has already given us some explanations in his timely pamphlet:

> [Hörsing's] incursion necessarily followed, given the former work of the Party. The tactic of the 'Open Letter', if it was not a simple trick, demanded, before we stepped into action, making clear to the masses that it was not our fault if we were required to take a special action of our own. The needs of the situation thus demanded that we turn once again to the trade unions and Social-Democratic parties and ask them: 'Do you want to defend the miners of central Germany together with us or not?' Since the government-action in central Germany was initiated by the Prussian interior-minister, the Social Democrat Severing, since it was pursued by the Social Democrat Hörsing at the behest of the bourgeoisie, our task first of all was to require the Social Democrats to openly acknowledge this blow against the workers, and secondly to require the Independents to come clean to the workers whether they intended to stand in a common front with the Orgesch and Severing, or with the miners of central Germany.

All this was neglected, which already deals with a large part of my criticism. But what Comrade Radek has not perceived, or does not want to acknowledge, is, and I repeat this, that it is simply not true that the Party was forced to go into action *at this point*, forced to hasten along great impending actions. The action as a whole was of course not planned by the Zentrale, the action of the Communist Party was also not planned for the Easter week; I still maintain, however, that Hörsing's action was only a counter-move in the context of a larger action, and responsibility for it rests with those who rashly triggered this counter-move. It is no good dealing in offensives and then talking of a shameful attack, no good playing with provocation and refusing to acknowledge the consequences.

[THERE FOLLOWED HERE MORE DETAILED INFORMATION ON THIS POINT]

And then further. I have been reproached with having a love for the KAPD, and, in the same breath, that my whole temperament has always led me to struggle against the Left. I do not know how these two charges can be combined, but there is something correct in them. It is true that I believe the KAPD, i.e. the anarchist tendencies, have done us great harm in the revolution, and I have struggled against them – but *one thing* I do acknowledge: if, at any time, I was to do KAPD-type politics, then I would ten times over prefer the KAPD with its rascally politics, as it is ten times more genuine and honest than KAPD-politics dressed up in frock-coat and horn-rimmed spectacles.

Everyone now says that we should learn from our mistakes. But I must say then that I am most eager to hear what mistakes the March Action is now seen as having involved. It may be that this rather delicate question will be dealt with in a more select circle than that into which I am admitted, but Comrade Schmidt has already repeated that the lessons are that we have to learn the strictest discipline and the strongest leadership. In other words, the mistakes that led to the failure of the March Action were purely organisational: a stricter discipline, a stronger leadership, and next time everything will work out fine.

For the further instruction of Comrade Schmidt, I can also read him something written in the *Kommunistische Arbeiterzeitung*. This appeared in no. 191:

> In this way the practice pursued on the basis of the mass-party thesis has been proved false by the practice itself. At the same time, the exaggerated, quite external idea of the possibilities of *party-discipline*, with which it was believed the masses could be ordered around as will-less tools of their leaders, one way today and a different way tomorrow, has been proved false.
>
> Perhaps now the Communist International is gradually understanding what the KAPD meant when it always spoke of a party welded firmly and absolutely together into a unity, even if a small one. Not that the party should be as small as possible, but it should never attempt to become a mass-party at the *cost* of clarity and unity.

[INTERJECTION: *'Is that your psychology then?'*]

Yes, Comrade Schmidt, that is the psychology of people who are clear that you either build a political party on the principle of individual selection, in which case you get a *small* – and I repeat this a hundred times – dedicated party ready for sacrifice, but not a proper *party*, rather a *sect*. It can and will show military discipline, mindless obedience, in its small ranks. But, if you want to have *masses* in a party, then you can never manage to move them by the commands of a military leadership, at the behest of a Zentrale, and because a conventicle of leaders has so decided; you can only move them according to political principles, because the party is a political and not a military body. And if you can learn no better lesson from the March Action than a need to improve and strengthen 'discipline', you show that you have in fact learned *nothing* from the March Action.

Comrade Schmidt has argued with extraordinary acuity that my situation in the Party was already untenable from its foundation. Indeed, it was not my ambition to join the Zentrale at that time. Perhaps, I confess, I made a mistake by joining the Zentrale, after struggling to avoid this as long as I could, when I gave in to the pressure of other comrades including Comrade Schmidt. Perhaps, at that time, when Brandler stood up and demanded my expulsion if I did not accept being voted on to the Zentrale, I should have left the premises and said that in the face of this kind of threat there was nothing for me here.

But what was the 'untenable situation'? This is quite clear, one need not be any political genius to see it not just today, but already at that time, as clearly as I did. As you all know, I already stood in a certain opposition to the Executive in Moscow, and as I differed from this on many things, I did too on the Twenty-One Conditions.

Why was this? Because, as I said, if these masses are separated from the USPD on the basis of a purely organisational procedure, then this separation will be an organisational escapade and not a process of political education. And it gave me a certain satisfaction, if no real pleasure, when Zinoviev himself in his Halle speech was the first to declare with regret that the debate was so largely an organisational rather than a political one.

The large masses of the USPD thus came over to us unschooled. I wanted to set sharper conditions than the Twenty-One, but *political* conditions and not *organisational* ones, and because these masses from the USPD had no clear political ideas in the debate, they came to us with false hopes, with the idea that now we're with Moscow, Moscow will do everything, now we have a great centralised leadership over us, now the revolution in Germany must move forward.

This was quite clearly a KAPD-mood, and Comrade Schmidt will not want to contest the fact that, at that time already, in discussions with him, I recognised it, and he and I were agreed about its dangers. My position towards these currents was clear, I also formed my opinion in our long experience. I am firmly convinced that we would have been able to overcome the KAPD-current within the Party, if all of us who had this experience had remained united, firm and determined, especially if the old Spartacus League had remained intellectually together.

Already at that time, however, the old Spartacus League had broken apart – and this is not a reproach against anyone. Competition for the highest degree of 'revolutionariness' had begun, and so it was, I confess, not only the mood in the Party that caused me to want to withdraw from the position of president, it was the clear desire not to have to take part in this competition. In Moscow, I was told every day of the KPD's passivity; what then is more understandable than the honest desire to let the 'more active' people into the leadership. But the activists already played at that time – no, I won't use any sharp term – they played the extraordinary game that they are still playing today.

'It was fateful for the Party', Comrade Schmidt says today, that we departed in February, and the Left took the helm. Indeed, either people have a definite idea what they want when they call themselves the 'left wing', in which case they should also show what they want, or else keep silent. But how can you, Comrade Schmidt, and how can any other comrade say that we were wrong if we let the 'leftists' take the helm. There is no political current with the privilege of stopping short with words of opposition; the culmination of any opposition is leadership; the opposition that reproaches its opponent with letting it take the lead is a fine opposition. Indeed, it is just as I previously said: you wanted me to be the beast on which the 'left wing' learned to ride.

Comrade Schmidt goes on to say, comrades, that I was the representative of the International in Italy. Firstly, that is untrue. The ECCI, and Comrade Zinoviev, refused to send me as representative to Italy, something that I was not unhappy with either at the time or now. But the reason such a fuss was made about the Italian question is that we did not want to burn bridges with the Serrati group.

And what happened after all this fuss? They were invited to the Congress in Moscow! And how were they treated in Moscow? In Moscow, discussions were held with the Italian workers, and an attempt made to win them for the

International and for a break with the reformists; and if you read my various articles and speeches, you will see in each case *precisely this same idea*. In order to do this, what was needed was not the fuss that had been raised about us, it could be more easily done by listening to us. Here, again, it is only the same tactic from Moscow: if someone has made a mistake, then attack three times harder the person who criticises the mistake while satisfying them in substance. It is the tactic you use to maintain your own infallibility, and you can perhaps still even find some people on whom this works.

To go on. Comrade Schmidt proclaims that in Moscow they spit on our slogan of unity! Indeed, there has been a great deal of spitting today. In the March Action already, spitting was a favourite cause. Every other day we 'spat in the eyes' of those Independents and Majority-Socialists whom we needed for the action.

Yes, comrades, it may be that the comrades in Moscow spit on our slogan of unity. Comrade Schmidt must be aware of this. The slogan however was, for many weeks, the slogan of the German Communist Party; we raised it already with the 'Open Letter' and focused on it ever more as international questions sharpened. True enough, we are sinful people and perhaps on this point went long and deeply astray, as never happens to more capable heads. But then it was not the task of the ECCI to spit on us, the task of the Communist International was rather to take the initiative itself, to convey to us something of the more illuminated spirit of its small bureau, so that we could acknowledge our sins, and the ECCI should have made its own views clear in Western Europe. Nothing is gained by spitting on our slogans in Moscow, rather by making a calm and pertinent criticism and explaining what we could do better.

I will just add one final point.

What was the reason I published my pamphlet? I must remind Comrade Schmidt of one thing. The Tenth Congress of the Russian Communist Party took place, if I am not mistaken, on 6 March of this year, and on the 15th we received reports in Europe in which Zinoviev declared: 'We have opened the struggle against Levi.'

If the Russian comrades proclaim a struggle, I am not so childish as to be unaware what this means. And I was also well aware, when the Action was broken off in Germany, that it cannot have been a slip of the tongue on the part of an ECCI representative when already during the action he declared that if it led to a 'cleansing' of the German Party of its 'right wing', then the action was justified. And the Zentrale at this time also confirmed this, by deciding on 'organisational measures' when the action was broken off.

The Action was then broken off 'with organisational measures' and, on the same day already, Comrade Richard Müller and Comrade Wolf were summoned by the high synedrion and dismissed from their posts. I am not that simple-minded not to know what this means. A few days later, they were expelled, and after Müller and Wolf were expelled, Comrade Däumer was expelled on account of his letter. And then a few more were expelled, and, before too long, it was my turn.

Honoured comrades, this is a game I don't go in for. So, I said openly and frankly: if you want to drive out the 'Levites', then I am man enough to place myself with my business-card and my political views at the head of the 'Levites'. If you want to purge, I will not let you expel me on the basis of an organisational provision. For we want to know why we are separating, I owe this to you and to myself. And this is no attack in the rear; it is the highest revolutionary duty, if a Party goes so *far wrong* as ours has, for *someone* to speak the truth; I do not want the Party to make once again the same mistakes it has made now, but if it does, then let there be someone who does the same as I have.

And then it has been said: 'But not in public.' What kind of attitude is this? I have already explained why as I see it there is no other way. The Central Committee, in its infallibility, refused to listen to me. I was not invited and not summoned, and a request to hear me was rejected by the comrades in their godlikeness. But, quite apart from this, it is a completely false attitude that Communists can sort out their mistakes in a quiet little room. The errors and mistakes of the Communists are just as much a component of the political experience of the proletarian class as their achievements. Neither the one nor the other can or should be withheld from the masses. If they made mistakes, they did not make these for the Party, and even if the Party collapses as a result – if *this* is the only way in which the proletariat can draw the lessons from experience – then it has to be so, as the Party exists for the sake of the proletariat and not the other way round.

And, once again, the comparison with Rosa Luxemburg. Certainly Rosa Luxemburg did not write a pamphlet against putschism. She no longer had the chance to do so. But when a similarly catastrophic collapse of the old Social-Democratic Party took place, Rosa Luxemburg did write a pamphlet, which was no gentler than mine –

[INTERJECTIONS]
– and the comparison *holds good to the last detail*. The old Social-Democratic Party suffered just the same catastrophic fall into opportunism in 1914 as the present Communist Party has into anarchism.

One final word. Comrade Pieck has already said that the bankruptcy of the Party is something that he simply cannot imagine. I rejoice at this optimism. Here, I will just read out this passage: 'In conspiracy as in the Duma, Russian Social Democracy performs the same work: it enlightens the workers and unites them. It can do so better or worse, but one thing is clear: on this path mistakes can certainly be made, but on this path there is no bankruptcy.' And Comrade Trotsky then explains how, if the road of Communism is abandoned, if the Party is gripped by anarchism, then the end is bankruptcy and necessarily so.

I will not go into the many prophecies with which the last hour was filled, we shall see the end of the road on which you are set, and await the result.

Letter to Lenin (1921)*

Esteemed Comrade Lenin,

The situation that has now arisen in Germany leads me to offer you my view of matters. To anticipate one point: in my reflections on these things, the fact that I resigned from the leadership of the Communist Party plays no part. For anyone familiar with my inclinations knows that I experienced this withdrawal from the leadership of the Communist Party as welcome rather than the opposite, and so I am also, I believe, in a position to judge the situation in Germany without any ill feeling; all the more so, indeed, in that the relatively slow course of events in Germany often caused me to consider whether other men should not take over the leadership of the Party, and to see this in no way as unwelcome. But the leadership that the Party has now will lead, in the space of six months at most, to the complete collapse of the Communist Party, and this fact leads me – and the whole seriousness with which I see the situation forces me – to address myself to you. I assume that as well as press-reports, you will have had information whose content I do not know. I would like then to give you my own presentation of events.

You know that, four weeks ago, a comrade from the Comintern was sent to Germany.[1] I myself had

---

* This letter, dated 27 March 1921, is translated after Beradt (ed.) 1969, from a copy in the Paul Levi archive.
1. [This was Béla Kun. See Introduction, p. 18.]

only one single interview with him – about ten days ago. Before me, he had discussions with members of the Zentrale, the content of which I do not know, but can only infer from his interview with Comrade Clara, which was nine days before he met with me. The content of the discussions with me and with Comrade Clara, who gave me a report immediately, was as follows: the comrade explained that Russia finds itself in an extremely difficult situation. It is unconditionally necessary for the burden on Russia to be relieved by movements in the West, and, for this reason, the German Party must immediately step into action. The VKPD now counted half a million members, and this would make it possible to put one and a half million proletarians on the streets, enough to overthrow the government. The struggle should, therefore, immediately begin with the slogan: overthrow the government. Both Comrade Clara and I stressed to the comrade that we also understood and recognised the difficult situation of Russia; even if we did not know the details, and that, quite apart from any immediate difficult situation, we were also committed to shortening the time as much as possible in which Russia stands in a certain sense alone. But we both shared the view that it would be no help, but, rather, a most serious blow to Soviet Russia, if we launched actions in Germany that would not lead to victory but, instead, to a defeat of the movement in Germany. The comrade, however, was firm in his view of launching actions right away, including what he called 'partial actions', and on his advice and at his pressing, the Zentrale called a meeting of the Central Committee on 17 March last, in which 'the workers' were called to embark right away on actions for a series of demands that were raised there, at the head of which was 'overthrow the government'.

Events then took the following course: on 17 March, the meeting of the Central Committee at which ideas or instructions for the comrades dispatched were given as a guiding line. On 18 March, *Rote Fahne* switched to the new decision and called for armed struggle, without first saying what the objectives were, a note that it maintained for some days. This, and other indications from the ECCI-representative, were the only political preparation for what then happened. A few days later, Hörsing, the prime minister of the Prussian province of Saxony, took certain measures in the industrial zone of central Germany that were partly of a general political nature, though partly also directed against the workers there who were strongly Communist. I could not estimate, at that point, whether the strikes that the workers there began were spontaneous or not. At all events, these spontaneous strikes were not only supported right away by the Party, as a matter of course, but made into the starting point for an action that went far beyond the context of the workers directly involved.

Here, it turned out that the judgement on the situation that Comrade Clara, myself and many other comrades stood by was the correct one. The situation in Germany is in my view as follows: just as Germany's whole relations with the Entente, the whole 'post-war', had begun in a certain sense to stagnate, so the relationships of classes in Germany had begun, in a certain sense, to stagnate, in the sense that the existing contradictions did not immediately lead to open confrontation. Despite this stagnation, however, there was a certain concentration of forces within the bourgeoisie, while the corresponding revolutionary forces were being created with the growing strength of the Communist Party and its internal consolidation. Just as the postwar-situation was steadily moving towards a critical resolution, so the time seemed to us also to be drawing ever nearer at which class-relations in Germany would also become critical again. And our view was that it was precisely from those conflicts of the post-war that a situation would very shortly arise in which class-antagonisms in Germany would move from stagnation into openness. On the basis of this idea, our tactic was that we had, at the present time, to show the masses the goal that could lead them out of the coming postwar-crisis, and it was in this perspective that we put forward the slogan: 'Alliance with Soviet Russia'. Our view was that the masses, who had, up till now, been drawn with apathy and resignation behind the hopes for an understanding with the West, should be shown the way to the East, so that on the day that they awakened from their illusions they would necessarily as it were follow this other way. On this assumption, we held that, at the present time, we should not go beyond the slogan 'Alliance with Soviet Russia', because, beyond this slogan, it seemed to us impossible to pull into motion those masses in Germany who do not directly belong to the Communist Party. It seemed to us that, if we succeeded in bringing the masses into movement with the slogan 'Alliance with Soviet Russia', which the proletarian class can understand, everything else, the fall of the government and whatever might come from this, would follow of itself. The most important thing seemed to us for the moment to start bringing the masses into movement again by actual partial demands.

Our view therefore was that the decisive thing was to reach the proletarian class as such – leaving aside petty-bourgeois milieus, etc. Those comrades who are at the moment leading the movement in Germany had a different

idea. They believed it would be enough to put the Communist Party in movement with a 'partial action'. They accordingly chose their slogans according
to the needs and perceptions of the Communist Party, and selected slogans
that quite naturally went much further than ours. The comrade who now represents the ECCI in Germany took the position that *this* is what was meant by
partial action, and that partial actions were needed at this point in Germany.

I do not share this view. The German Revolution will not emerge from the
stagnation in which it finds itself at the moment with one great blow, but
there will, rather, be partial actions, i.e. the proletariat of certain large cities
or industrial areas rising up. Partial actions of this kind we have to promote
and support. What I do *not* mean by partial actions is that the Communists
of certain areas, or of the whole Reich, undertake private actions; since *party-
actions* of this kind, as opposed to proletarian actions, we said, would lead to
what did indeed happen, i.e. the end-result of the action just described. Not
a struggle of the proletariat against the bourgeoisie, but a struggle of Communists against the overwhelming majority of the proletariat, which, in this
situation, not only confronts the Communist Party without sympathy, not
only with a certain hostility, but directly in open conflict as enemy to enemy.
I believe that no further proof of the correctness of this contention is needed,
if you have read the recent issues of *Freiheit* from these days. It is not news to
anyone that the right Independents are scoundrels, but that they dare to call
so openly and undisguisedly for active struggle against the Communists in
an action shows how the mood of the great majority of the proletariat in this
action was one of open and active hostility against the Communists.

So much for the verdict on the movement, as I see it. This action has not
only done damage in central Germany to partial actions that are really possible, partial actions in the best sense of the term, but it has also, in my view,
destroyed the fruit of two years of struggle and two years of labour by the
Communist Party in Germany. It took two years of tiring work to anchor the
Communist idea firmly in the masses, not only in organisational terms, by
the creation of a Communist Party that is numerically large enough that it is
important alongside the other major workers' organisations in purely numerical terms, but also – after many misunderstandings – to have communism
and the Communist Party grasped by the broad proletarian masses intellectually, so that these masses saw the Communists as their leaders. We had to win
the trust of the proletarian class. Our 'Open Letter' in January this year was
completely in this sense, so that, after numerically reaching the appropriate

strength, we could deliberately attack the second part of our work, or, at least, make a start on it. Not only is this now destroyed. But, in my view, we are now back where we were two years ago, as we have succeeded in getting into a position of open hostility to the major workers' organisations and the majority of the proletariat.

I do not want to go into details about the numerical proportion of Communists within the working class. I only want to stress that, apart from central Germany, where the Communist Party is in a numerical majority, there is not only no district in Germany where the Communist Party has such a majority, but, above all, no district that is so essential for the state that by an action there the Communist Party could right away damage the bourgeois state, let alone destroy it. We are thus led to collaborate and work together with the proletarian class as such, and we can only consider ourselves as a vanguard [*Vortrupp*][2] if the proletarian class comes into action itself; we must also remain in a reasonable relationship with these masses in terms of mood, if we don't want to shut out for a long period the possibility of gaining ever greater influence among these masses.

I see the situation of the Party if it continues this policy, i.e. continues party-actions *without* regard to the entire proletariat and *in certain circumstances* against the whole proletariat, as follows: the Communist Party is getting into an increasing and sharp contradiction not only to the overwhelming majority of the proletarian classes, but also to all other strata that are important for the revolution. The Communist Party itself will split, because even the masses who are in our party and are undoubtedly brave fighters ready for sacrifice, will not, in the long run, be able to withstand this break and the hostility of the whole mass of the proletarian class. And, just as the sympathy of the proletarian class strengthens and increases the power and capacity not only of the Communist Party but of each individual Communist, so the antipathy and even open hostility of the proletarian classes reduces and cripples the power and ability of the Party and of individual comrades. Two or three more actions like the present one, actions that the proletariat perceives as directed against it, actions undertaken by the Communist Party, will even lead to the risk that they actually are directed against the proletariat and the proletarian

---

2. [On the distinction between *Vorhut* (advance-detachment) and *Vortrupp* (front-rank), both often translated in English as 'vanguard', see below, p. 236, note 19.]

class: then the Communist Party will lie broken on the ground, and we will have to begin to build up again what remains in far more difficult conditions.

I shall only mention one point as to the harm that has been done us for the moment. Not only have we spoiled a favourable situation, so that, in the coming foreign-policy crisis and the struggles of the bourgeoisie internally and externally that will result from it (occupation of further regions by the Entente, rising unemployment, closing of factories, stoppages of supply, new taxes, reduction of wages, etc.), we shall stand in an extraordinarily tense relationship to the proletariat and no longer enjoy the trust of the proletarian class: on top of this, we have handed the bourgeoisie precisely what they needed in order to relieve their difficult situation. What presses the bourgeoisie above all is the Entente's demand for disarmament, and what it most needs are things that will appear in the eyes of the Entente as proof that disarmament for the German bourgeoisie might not be in the interest of its preservation as a class. If the German government had led the action, and not the Communist Party, it could not have had any other outcome than it did.

Since I see the situation of the Communist Party as not only difficult, but possibly fatal, since I see a danger to the very life of the Party, I am turning to you personally, not knowing to what extent you are familiar with details of the policy of the Communist International, with the request for you to consider the situation for yourself and possibly act accordingly. I do not think, for my part, of personally confronting this policy of the Communist International in Germany. I already made clear my position to the representative of the Executive, and said that I would do nothing to this action, for, after recent events, I am now only too aware that they are only too willing to hear my views in this way, in order to use the occasion to brand me as an opportunist. I have therefore, apart from the last conversation with the representative of the Executive, taken no steps against the Executive's policy, and simply now see the results. I will also now go no further than perhaps writing a pamphlet in which I present my view, but not put forward ideas for either the Executive or the future leading bodies in Germany. The comrades who bear this responsibility should not feel themselves inhibited by me. But, in these days and weeks that will be decisive for the German Party, I would also like to have not neglected anything, and this is the reason why I am approaching you and ask you, in the event that you agree with my arguments, if only partly, to undertake whatever seems appropriate to you.

With Communist greetings!

The Demands of the Kommunistische Arbeitsgemeinschaft*

The First National Conference of the KAG unanimously passed the following declaration:

The KAG does not aim to found its own party, it rather believes that, given the self-inflicted fate of the KPD and the diminished respect of the Communist International, the future development of a large revolutionary mass-party will take place not by way of a split but rather by way of coalescence. If the KPD maintains the policy that it adopted at the last Central Committee meeting, if it conducts this policy honestly and not to achieve tactical party-interests, then, in due course, there will be no difference between it and what is wanted by the overwhelming majority of USPD-workers and a large part of honest and revolutionary SPD-workers.

If a large revolutionary party is to arise organisationally from this situation, and if the KPD is to play a decisive role in this, then the following preconditions must be met, which would restore the respect and confidence of the masses that it needs:

---

* Translated after Beradt (ed.) 1969. [On the Kommunistische Arbeitsgemeinschaft, see Introduction, p. 23.]

1) Complete material independence from the Communist International;
2) All literature appearing from foreign Communist organisations (including organs of the Communist International and the Red Trade-Union International) to be placed under joint control of the German party-leadership;
3) Security from all open or concealed organisational interventions by the ECCI alongside, outside or against the organs of the German section;
4) Establishment in its programme of a policy that makes possible the collaboration of all revolutionary workers in Germany, with express renunciation of all putschist attempts along the lines of the March Action;
5) Establishment of a trade-union policy that irrespective of all revolutionary aims maintains the organisational unity and coherence of the German trade-unions.

Part Three

The Soviet Question

Letter to Clara Zetkin[*]

Dear Comrade Clara,

In your letter of 21 September, you seem to make two separate assumptions, and I am afraid I must say that neither of them are correct.

First of all, I am not sulking[1] in any way. I believe that none of those who came with me[2] share that view. I could assure my confessor that there is no trace in me of anger or even indignation at some 'injustice' suffered. I completely 'glow with good cheer', and hope that this will not be a 'most blessed and sweet foretaste of death'. Nor am I in any way bothered about what 'Radek says' or 'Zinoviev says' or 'Bukharin says'. I have the ability – this may be a failing or a virtue – to rapidly separate myself inwardly from people so that they become something objective and natural for me, like a chair or a cab-horse. In this respect, you can be assured, dear Comrade Clara! The ranks of opposition will not be disturbed from my corner, and least of all out of personal resentment.

---

* This letter, dated 23 September 1921, is translated after Beradt (ed.) 1969, from a copy in the Paul Levi archive. [Zetkin had written to Mathilde Jacob for material for a proposed edition of Rosa Luxemburg's works (which would not include Luxemburg's pamphlet on the Russian Revolution), then to Levi when Jacob referred her to him.]

1. [The German expression is *die gekränkter Leberwurst*.]

2. [Presumably, those who left the KPD with Levi, not all of whom joined him in the Kommunistische Arbeitsgemeinschaft.]

Secondly, you see no material ground for a critique of the Bolsheviks, and still maintain that we should go on keeping silent. It is doubtful to me whether we were right to remain silent for so long. But this is something that we no longer need to decide.

There are two things that I see: on the one hand, the complete turnaround in Bolshevik policy since March. This is a fact not contested *on any side*. Secondly, the present situation must be seen as – relatively – permanent. As far as Russia is concerned, and as far as the revolutionary situation in Antwerp is concerned. If we were now to keep silent, we would not reach Russia and would commit a deadly sin against communism. I tell you openly, dear Clara, the baggage that the Russians are now burdening communism with is something that we communists in Germany – God forgive me if I still count myself among them – could scarcely carry, even if we still had a Communist Party – God forgive me if I don't count the present one as such. But, when communism in Germany and Europe is in the condition that it is now – you see, I don't raise the question of blame – this baggage will be the end of us.

The Russians have a convenient method. Anyone who says anything is a Menshevik. I see it as a timely need to look into the *deepest* sources of the Russians' mistakes, in purely ideological terms, and to show how, in my opinion, these mistakes arise from a view of Lenin's that Rosa Luxemburg combated about twenty years ago – both for the sake of the cause and as a convenient method for distancing myself from Menshevism. How necessary this is has also been brought home to me by the fact that Lenin himself now presents the articles that I wrote, for example, as Menshevism. Lenin really should know that Menshevism is something completely different, as I shall try to show. And I believe that, all things considered, Rosa had a more profound difference with the Mensheviks than with the Bolsheviks. In my view, dear Comrade Clara, you are equally unjust to Rosa, if not more so, in ascribing all this simply to misunderstanding and bad information – Rosa was very well informed – or even personal ill-feeling.

Someone with such a coherent world-view as Rosa, however, is always and everywhere the same – whether writing the Spartacus programme or criticising the Bolsheviks, whether writing articles or books, whether giving a speech or making tactical decisions: they are *always the same person* and it is some consolation that this is how it is or was.

For these reasons, I believe it would do violence to Rosa's legacy if we were now to deal with this question from the point of view of temporary Russian difficulties. On certain questions – this cannot be denied – Rosa was opposed to the Bolsheviks, and it is precisely these questions that the course of the Russian Revolution has brought to the fore, and – I believe – strikingly confirmed Rosa's conceptions.

There are statements enough in Rosa's final literary document, the Spartacus programme, and no one knows better than I do whom these were aimed at.

To publish Rosa's writings silently ignoring this opposition or even without discussing it – because of temporary difficulties – would mean: firstly, abandoning such criticism once and for all, as these difficulties will remain as long as Russia stands alone in its present situation; secondly, abandoning a path that the dead Rosa already indicated to us in her lifetime, and that – in opposition to many of Lenin's views – history has confirmed; thirdly, it would mean destroying the whole wonderfully unitary picture of Rosa's world outlook. I see this as completely intolerable, both with respect to Rosa, *and* with respect to the communist idea, which needs a certain recovery after its various baths of steel.

Introduction to Rosa Luxemburg's Pamphlet
The Russian Revolution

Preface

I believe that I am right, in every respect, to publish this pamphlet. Its origins are as follows. In summer 1918, Rosa Luxemburg sent the *Spartakusbriefe* articles from her prison in Breslau, in which she took critical issue with the policies of the Bolsheviks. This was the period after Brest-Litovsk, the time of the *Zusatzverträge*.[1] Her friends saw their publication as inopportune at that time, and I agreed with them. Since Rosa Luxemburg stubbornly insisted on their publication, I travelled to see her in Breslau in September 1918, where, after long and detailed discussion in the prison, though I did not convince her, she agreed to refrain from publishing a recently written article against Bolshevik tactics.

In order to convince me of the correctness of her criticism, Rosa Luxemburg wrote the following pamphlet. She informed me of the broad lines of its content from prison by way of a trusted woman-friend,[2] remarking that she was busily at work writing a detailed critique of what had happened in Russia. 'I am writing this pamphlet for you,' Rosa

---

1. [The *Zusatzverträge* [supplementary treaties] that the Soviet government was compelled to sign on 27 August 1918 recognised effective German suzerainty over Finland, Ukraine and Georgia. The collapse of the German army less than two months later put paid to these treaties.]
2. [Mathilde Jacob.]

Luxemburg added, 'and if I convince only you, I shall not have done this work in vain.' As material for the pamphlet, she used not only German newspapers, but all the Russian newspapers and pamphlets that had reached Germany through the Russian embassy, and that trusted friends had smuggled in to her in prison.

I expect two reproaches: from some people, that I am publishing it only now, and, from others, that I am publishing it already, indeed publishing it at all (the pamphlet was indeed condemned to the flames by a certain party).[3]

As for the timing of publication, it goes without saying that this was independent of differences that I have had with the Bolsheviks on a well-known occasion. In my view, the timing is firstly determined by the fact that the rule of the Bolsheviks in Russia is more secure now than at any previous time, and as secure as it can be so long as the Western proletariat does not relieve Russia from its isolation. And, secondly, it is determined by the fact that the present Bolshevik policy involves the most serious consequence for the European workers' movement, and that everything must be done to promote independent criticism of Russian developments. Only those who think critically are able to separate truth from lies, the permanent from the accidental, the gemstone from the rubble.

This publication therefore seems to me both possible and urgent.

Rote Fahne will cry 'anti-Bolshevism!'. That is something I cannot prevent, it is up to its editors.

As is readily apparent, the pamphlet is not complete. There are certain passages where the train of ideas is sketched only lightly, though still clearly. I would have liked to have added a faithful development of this summary, but have refrained from this so as not to leave room for any misunderstandings. There are just a few quotations that in the manuscript were given only by

---

3. [According to Clara Zetkin, who devoted a short book to rebutting the content of Luxemburg's pamphlet, Leo Jogiches advised her after Luxemburg's death to burn the manuscript, though Zetkin makes clear that this was not from unwillingness to offend the Bolsheviks, but because Luxemburg had not had access to sufficient material in prison, and intended, in due course, to write a fuller critique of Bolshevik policy. The accusation was also made that Levi, in reproducing a copy of Luxemburg's text, had not accurately published her original manuscript, which had not yet been found. In the event, when this eventually reappeared in 1929, it turned out to be only marginally different from the version Levi published.]

headwords and that I have inserted literally here, as the author intended by leaving space for them.

In my introduction, I have preferred to cite almost exclusively Lenin or Trotsky. I fear that this could give the impression that my intention is to 'chafe' Lenin. Nothing could be further from my mind. I have basically cited him because the Russian Revolution and its works should be judged after the great men who lead it, rather then the scribblers: neither its Narcissus nor its Thersites.

Paul Levi

Frankfurt a. M., 14 November 1921

Introduction

> It is glorious to be even a complaint on the lips of the beloved...
> – Schiller, *Nenie*

I

There can be no doubt that the world working class finds itself in a serious crisis. And it would be superficial to see this crisis as simply that, here and there among the workers, differences of opinion have arisen, which, at a party-level, confront one another in desirable or undesirable forms. That would not in itself be bad, and would not be felt by the working class as a crisis, if there were not a real crisis as well. The working class the world over emerged from the War in a state of extreme distress. It had sacrificed its sons and brothers by the million, and this was its reward: millions upon millions of unemployed, depressed wages, the collapse of even the paltry shelter that the proletariat of the capitalist world possessed before the War. A development such as we see today is certainly unprecedented in history: not like the case of the Roman *proletarii* who over a number of generations fell from the level of dignified life to the depths of the sewer, but that, in a handful of years, five at the most, a change occurred that could only make the time before the War seem like a paradise. This was not Adam expelled from paradise to live on the earth, but millions who at least lived on the earth as best they could who are now driven under the ground.

Is it any wonder, then, that millions are now set on socialism? That they expect from it a miracle that no one can provide? But is it any wonder, too, if now, precisely in this situation, when socialism cannot give the hungry bread from one day to the next, cannot give the thirsty wine, and when only the clearest and most open speech can open the eyes and ears of the proletariat to what *its own* task is, it is doubly hard for them to see disappointment precisely where they formerly believed that the boldest step towards socialism had been taken? We should not conceal any of this from ourselves: if today, in the West, we learn of speeches by Lenin, decrees of the Council of People's Commissars, in which the masses see not the road to communism but, rather, the road to capitalism (and no speeches or addresses can help this), it is no wonder that the editors of Communist papers or the central leaderships of Communist parties are in despair. These are things that are not simply settled by the editors of *Vorwärts* making spiteful remarks or acting as clever dicks: 'we always told you so'. They are processes that shake the whole working class very deeply, from Social Democrats to Communists, and do not trigger feelings of triumph anywhere, but rather a dull feeling of doubt: not about the correctness of Communist policy in Russia, but about socialism in general. Take the German working class, for example. In one direction, they see the Social Democrats joining up with Stinnes:[4] 'forward to capitalism'. And, on the other side, they see the Communists, who previously identified themselves with every stroke of Soviet Russian policy, but, now, find Lenin also saying 'forward to capitalism'. The two antipodes of the workers' movement are united under the same battle-cry. We fear that the Russian Communists have not completely recognised the whole ominous tragedy that their latest policy contains for the whole world. The Soviet government has committed itself, in a note to the governments of the Entente, to pay the Russian debts from the tsarist war- and prewar-period. It may be – we are unable to judge – that the position of the Russian state requires this. And we also need not mention several billions in treasure, which perhaps means that the Russian national economy is not so poor and the Anglo-French not so rich. But we do need to speak of the moral asset that the international working class loses when it sees the decline of a visible sign of resistance against all-powerful capitalism.

For the fact is that the Russian Soviet Republic, scoffed and scorned by some, loved and praised by others, was, at all events, perceived by *all* proletarians as the first heroic assault against the citadel of capitalism. Its existence

---

4. [The industrialist and conservative politician Hugo Stinnes, who pioneered 'co-operation' between trade-unions and employers at this time.]

was for everyone a living sign that the existing powers of capitalism are not eternal. It was for *all* proletarians the *first* attempt to shape the world in a *proletarian* sense, and it was, therefore, the greatest moral factor that the world workers' movement had ever possessed. We who believed that we had to place our weak forces on the side of the Russian Revolution from its very first day, believe that we can now also say without ambiguity: we see the eternal achievement of the Bolsheviks in the fact that they strove to be this from the first days of the Russian Revolution. Their greatness is not just that, from the first day, they secured the achievements of the revolution that made possible the development of social forces in Russia, by placing at the head of the revolution the one class whose aims lie in the future, that they secured their present victory by struggling for a future still to be attained. It was rather that, with a Faustian drive, the Bolsheviks pointed into the distance, pointed beyond the present world and showed how all their work was only partial so long as the forces of the world-proletariat did not help to support it. 'My field is the world' was their motto from the first day. It is true that the proletarians of the world did not come to the aid of the Russian Revolution either as rapidly as many expected, or in the way that some sought. But, as an arousal, a call, as a magnet for the proletarian forces of the whole world, Soviet Russia exerted a power greater than anything previous. By proclaiming in Russia and hence to the world 'for the first time the final goals of socialism as the immediate programme of practical policy', and, in this way, as the historical task demanded, basing its whole policy on the world-proletariat and its revolutionary arousal, by fearlessly choosing the steepest path in life without bending the knee, and with unshakable resilience directing all thoughts to the victory of the proletariat, the Bolsheviks will remain unforgotten by the proletariat into the furthest future, they will 'be imperishable and shine'.

This high task, however, which history entrusted to them and which they themselves were happy to undertake, lays special responsibility on the Bolsheviks, not only towards the Russian proletariat but also to that of the world. Their actions are subject to criticism, and they should be so both in Russia and abroad. As to the suitability of the measures with which they refused this criticism in Russia, we shall later say a few words, and Rosa Luxemburg already expressed herself on this. But, in so far as the Soviet Russian Republic is unable to do prevent this criticism by force, it does so by defaming any difference of opinion as 'opportunism' or 'Menshevism'. Rosa Luxemburg quite

unambiguously distanced herself from 'Menshevism' in her text, but an outcome emerged all the same that she already suspected in her judgement on
the policy of the Bolsheviks at that time. We do not delude ourselves that the
same slogans will not also be used against the present text. But this cannot
prevent us from what we see as necessary, all the less so in that the frequent
use of these words has certainly made them no more dangerous, and that we
have the conviction grounded on facts that not too many of those who have
the word 'Menshevik' on their tongues connect it with a corresponding idea.
All the less can we be stayed, when precisely the crisis in which the workers
of the world find themselves today demands that we take a critical distance
from events in Russia. Only if we take the trouble to find out whether there
are things wrong in Russia and what these may be, where the sources of the
mistakes lie, will we be able to show the masses that *despite* this, the way to
socialism is the only way that leads to their deliverance. We hope that, in this
way, we shall keep and win thousands for socialism who will otherwise be
lost. Criticism of Russia practised today is balm for the proletarian movement.
And, even if this criticism goes too far here and there – we hope this is not
the case in the following lines – those at whom this criticism is aimed should
value it in the words of Frau Fönss in her last letter to her children: 'If you had
loved me less, you would condemn me less now.'[5]

II

Since February 1921, the policy of the Bolsheviks has undergone a complete
reversal.[6] Concession after concession, compromise after compromise. We
believe we cannot be reproached as people who saw communism as something built in the radiant blue of the sky, presented to the proletariat of
any country or the world like a Christmas gift with the alternative 'this or
nothing'. Compromises are something that cannot be avoided: it would not
be revolutionary to forget compromise, to harness the powers of the proletariat to what is possible, no more than to praise to the grieving people the
compromises made by 'princes' – parliamentarians, ministers – as the work

---

5. [The heroine of a popular story by the late nineteenth-century Danish writer
Jans Peter Jacobsen.]
6. [Following the Kronstadt revolt and the Tenth Party Congress, the Soviet government took the turn that came to be known as the New Economic Policy.]

of a higher dispensation. A compromise that is uncompromising thus has two preconditions. One of them is that the nature of the compromise is not concealed, but openly denounced as being weak and halfhearted, the other is that, beyond the compromise, the goal to be pursued by the masses is kept before their eyes.

Are the measures taken by the Bolsheviks since February of this year compromises? There has not yet been any unambiguous declaration about this, and it is advisable, therefore, to compare these measures with the original intentions of the Bolsheviks. We have already mentioned above how Rosa Luxemburg described the task of the Bolsheviks as necessarily self-imposed.

Lenin himself previously defined this task as follows:

> That is why we are faced with a new and higher form of struggle against the bourgeoisie, the transition from the very simple task of further expropriating the capitalists to the much more complicated and difficult task of creating conditions in which it will be impossible for the bourgeoisie to exist.[7]

We need only compare this description by Lenin of the task in January 1918 with what is contained in his recent statements:

> While the revolution in Germany is still slow in 'coming forth', our task is to *study* the state capitalism of the Germans, to *spare no effort* in copying it and not shrink from adopting dictatorial methods to hasten the copying of Western culture by barbarian Russia, without hesitating to use barbarous methods for fighting barbarism...
>
> One way is to try to prohibit entirely, to put the lock on all development of private, non-state exchange, i.e., trade, i.e., capitalism, which is inevitable with millions of small producers. But such a policy would be foolish and suicidal for the party that tried to apply it....
>
> Inasmuch as we are as yet unable to pass directly from small production to socialism, some capitalism is inevitable as the elemental product of small production and exchange; so that we must utilise capitalism (particularly by directing it into the channels of state capitalism) as the intermediary link between small production and socialism, as a means, a path, and a method of increasing the productive forces.[8]

---

7. 'The Immediate Tasks of the Soviet Government', in Lenin 1972, pp. 244–5.
8. 'The Tax in Kind', in Lenin 1965b, pp. 335.

I do not believe that we need to add to this first quotation any reminiscences from Russian history: there were people who spoke in this vein without having gone through the Marxian school.

I rather believe that this comparison, which can be extended further if you like, is sufficient for the purpose we have set ourselves here: to show, that is, that the goal of the Bolsheviks in 1918 was to create conditions in which capitalism could no longer exist and in which it could no longer return to life, whereas, in 1921, it was to create conditions in which capitalism, as state-capitalism if possible and, if not, then as private capitalism of the common-and-garden kind, could make a return.

There is one thing however that we can admit right away. Nothing at all is proved by this kind of comparison. What goals it is really revolutionary to pursue never result from a more or less 'radical' conception. Only primitive Communists of the kind of Béla Kun and his German followers (unless they have since unlearned this) say: general insurrection, and anything less is evil. In reality, the revolutionary or counter-revolutionary character of any goal does not result from the *words used*, but rather from their historical context. Those who, in Prussia in 1910, for example, demanded mass-demonstrations with the aim of 'universal suffrage' were far more revolutionary than it would have been to demand 'on top of this' workers' and soldiers' councils. So too, from these different goals proclaimed by the Bolsheviks in 1918 and 1921 we cannot directly draw conclusions, but must, rather, go back to the historical context out of which these goals arose.

III

Lenin seeks as follows to make the concessions to capitalism palatable:

> The concessionaire is a capitalist. He conducts his business on capitalist lines, for profit, and is willing to enter into an agreement with the proletarian government in order to obtain superprofits or raw materials which he cannot otherwise obtain, or can obtain only with great difficulty. Soviet power gains by the development of the productive forces, and by securing an increased quantity of goods immediately, or within a very short period.[9]

---

9. 'The Tax in Kind', in Lenin 1965b p. 345.

It is completely understandable (though perhaps not completely accurate) for a Communist writer to present the process in this way. How would a protagonist of capitalism present the process? In exactly the same words, but the other way round: 'Soviet-power,' he would say, 'is a power unable to develop the productive forces, not immediately and not in a sufficiently short time. The capitalist takes advantage of this; he enters into an agreement with the proletarian power in order to obtain extraordinarily high profits. Etc.'

No one will contest the fact that the two sides are both right, but that the capitalist does not need to give any explanation of his view of things – for his very nature always demands extraordinarily high profits – whereas the Communist's presentation of the matter needs explanation.

What, then, was the development on the basis of which the Bolsheviks came to set themselves this (capitalist) goal, in contrast to the socialist goal of 1918?

We shall Lenin speak for himself:

> *First*, with the 'whole' of the peasants against the monarchy, against the landowners, against medievalism (and to that extent the revolution remains bourgeois, bourgeois-democratic). *Then*, with the poor peasants, with the semi-proletarians, with all the exploited, *against capitalism*, including the rural rich, the kulaks, the profiteers, and to that extent the revolution becomes a *socialist* one...
>
> We carried the *bourgeois revolution to its conclusion*. The peasants supported us *as a whole*. Their antagonism to the socialist proletariat could not reveal itself all at once. The soviets united the peasants *in general*. The class divisions among the peasants had not yet matured, had not yet come into the open.
>
> That process took place in the summer and autumn of 1918. The Czech counter-revolutionary mutiny roused the kulaks. A wave of kulak revolts swept over Russia. The poor peasants learned, not from books or newspapers, *but from life itself*, that their interests were irreconcilably antagonistic to those of the kulaks, the rich, the rural bourgeoisie. Like every other petty-bourgeois party, the 'Left Socialist-Revolutionaries' reflected the vacillation of the people, and in the summer of 1918 they split: one section joined forces with the Czechs (the rebellion in Moscow, when Proshyan, having seized the Telegraph Office – for one hour! – announced to Russia that the Bolsheviks had been overthrown, then the treachery of Muryavov,

commander-in-chief of the army that was fighting the Czechs, etc.), while the other section, that mentioned above, remained with the Bolsheviks.[10]

And Lenin expressed his ideas elsewhere in still more sharp, concise and precise terms:

> The proletariat must separate, demarcate, the working peasant from the peasant owner, the peasant worker from the peasant huckster, the peasant who labours from the peasant who profiteers. In this demarcation lies the *whole essence* of socialism.[11]

This is a point that Rosa Luxemburg already dealt with in her critique. One thing, of course, must be made clear: in one respect, she too has been disproved. The Russian *muzhik*, once the distribution of land had taken place, did not crawl behind his stove and let the republic be a republic and the revolution a revolution. When the revolution was threatened, the revolution that had given *him*, the peasant, land, the Russian peasant stood up and defended it no less heroically than the French peasant of 1793 defended his. To this extent, therefore, he proved to be a useful support of the Soviet republic. Indeed, he even went so far in his courage that in passing he also corrected another mistake that Rosa Luxemburg noted in the policy of the Bolsheviks; he finished with the 'self-determination of nations', in so far as it was a useful means of attack against the peasant's revolutionary gains.

On one other point, as well, history has criticised Rosa Luxemburg's criticism. She feared a 'chaotic, purely arbitrary kind' of land-distribution on two grounds: first, the sharpening of class-contradictions within the peasantry instead of their equalisation in the direction of socialism, and, along with this, the sharpening of the contradiction between peasantry and industrial proletariat. On both points, the Bolsheviks, on the basis of the possibility offered by their chosen resolution of the land-question, were in a position that they *hoped* for the first (which Rosa Luxemburg *feared*), so that they could deal with the second by means of the first.

History decided between this fear and hope. Here is what Lenin says on this subject:

---

10. 'The Proletarian Revolution and the Renegade Kautsky', in Lenin 1974, p. 300.
11. 'Economics and Politics in the Era of the Dictatorship of the Proletariat', in Lenin 1965a, p. 113.

The middle stratum of the peasantry is now far more numerous and decisive than previously, the contradictions have attenuated, and by distribution the utilisation of the land has become more equal, the rich peasants have forfeited their predominant position and have even been largely expropriated. In Russia more than in the Ukraine, and to a lesser extent in Siberia, but by and large statistics show us quite beyond doubt that the village has been levelled: in other words, the sharp antagonism between rich peasants and resource-less small peasants has been adjusted, everything has become more equal. We have now by and large to deal with a middle peasantry.'[12]

It is not a burning question today, therefore, to decide what was correct from a socialist point of view: the hope or the fear. For the fact on which both fear and hope were based has disappeared. The Bolshevik calculation, which counted on and hoped for continuing and rapidly intensifying class-antagonism within the peasantry, so that from this burning struggle the power could be drawn to continue the revolution in the direction of socialism – this calculation went awry. The distribution of land led to a levelling of class-contradictions on the land: where, formerly, kulaks and muzhiks, big peasants and village-proletarians, confronted one another, there is now 'by and large a middle peasantry'. Which means that the resolution of that first contradiction – village-proletarians against rich peasants – does not resolve the second – peasants against industrial workers. Quite the contrary. Where the industrial proletarian, three years ago, could still find understanding and help in the countryside, today he finds the broad and unitary stratum of middle peasants with their hereditary-ownership psychology (even if they, formerly, had nothing to apply this to) and their holy terror against anything touching their recently acquired property, whether the touching comes from Lenin or Denikin. At night, they see all cats as grey. This means, in other words: the contradiction between industrial proletarians and owners of land has infinitely deepened; the common factor that bound the urban and rural proletarians together has gone, and what remains is only the will to possession, on the one hand, and the will to socialism, on the other.

---

12. Lenin 1921a, p. 7.

Do the strivings of the Russian peasantry today contain even a *single* social-ist feature? A feature that would facilitate and support the continuation of the Russian Revolution to its socialist goal? Lenin himself judged this peasantry correctly, when he wrote:

> Peasant farming continues to be petty commodity production. Here we have an extremely broad and very sound, deep-rooted basis for capitalism, a basis on which capitalism persists or arises anew in a bitter struggle against communism. The forms of this struggle are private speculation and profiteering versus state procurement of grain (and other products) and state distribution of products in general.[13]

This characterisation of the peasantry, i.e. the stratum of the peasantry in Russia today, is completely correct. It is just not quite comprehensive. The peasantry is not the only basis of operations of capitalism against Russian communism – there are others in Berlin, in Paris, in London, in Warsaw, etc. – nor are speculation and profiteering the only measures that are con-ducted on this basis. Speculation and profiteering are burdensome and dangerous weapons that the peasants possess, but they are not deadly. The peasants in Russia, as generally in every country with a preponderant peas-ant-stratum, possess something more dangerous. One weapon acts as a ham-mer, and the other as a hydraulic press; one strikes immediately, the other is slow but certain in its effects. This second weapon is the withdrawal of the peasant and peasant-production from the market. This is the condition that Rosa Luxemburg describes with the words 'it condemns the revolu-tion to its enemies, the state to decay, the urban population to hunger'. The peasant withdraws like a snail into household-economy. In the long run, a state that has big cities with industry and an urban proletariat cannot with-stand this pressure. The hammer, however, that the Russian peasants hold in their hands is insurrection. They have learned in several wars to defend an encroachment on their property by armed uprising. We believe that the effect of these two methods was threatening when the Bolsheviks decided on the radical change in their policy early in 1921. And, with this fact, we return to answering the question that we raised initially: was the Bolshevik

---

13. 'Economics and Politics in the Era of the Dictatorship of the Proletariat', in Lenin 1965a, pp. 109–10.

aim in 1918 or in 1921 the revolutionary one – not in words but in its historical context – revolutionary in the sense of 'lying in the direction of the underlying preconditions for a later socialist reform'? And, here, there can be no further doubt as to the answer. In their historical context, in their tendency, objectively, these measures of the Bolsheviks against, or rather towards, the peasantry are not revolutionary but counter-revolutionary, taken for the benefit of a class that has dissolved all ties with its armed comrades of 1918, which is unitedly, determinedly, unshakeably anti-socialist and counter-revolutionary. It was not otherwise that Lenin judged those strivings that – just like the Kronstadt rebels – came to light under the slogan of free trade: 'Here the petty-bourgeois democratic element broke through with slogans of free trade that were directed against the dictatorship of the proletariat.'[14]

In this way, Lenin deals also with objections that were raised against these contentions from another source. 'Spektator' says in a polemic against Otto Bauer:

> Has he, Bauer, recommended for example the socialisation of small or medium-sized businesses, or the nationalisation of trade? Not at all. Why then, if the Soviet government refrains from socialising these, does this mean right away a return to capitalism?[15]

The answer is not difficult, according to what has been said above – the relativity of the value of political measures. There are many measures that can be taken, or goals set, which are a minus in relation to the socialisation of trade and yet are revolutionary, i.e. lie in the direction of the socialist final goal. A measure enforced by capitalist forces, the peasants, which abolishes a previous – possibly premature – revolutionary measure, is not a step in the direction of socialism, but, rather, one in the direction of capitalism.

IV

'But we have maintained the rule of the working class, the dictatorship of the proletariat!' This is, indeed, the objection with which all those largely uncontested contentions are supposedly paralysed. It is also the point at which the Communist is presently distinguished from the 'Menshevik' (these

---

14. Lenin n.d., p. 27.
15. Spektator 1921, p. 10.

characteristics of differentiation are not permanently fixed), the 'loyal opposition' from the 'other side'. We believe, therefore, that particular care has to be devoted to this argument.

We believe that we get to the core of the dispute if we bring in the following explanations of Lenin. He starts by quoting literally the following sentences from Kautsky:

> The term, 'dictatorship of the proletariat', hence not the dictatorship of a single individual, but of a class, ipso facto precludes the possibility that Marx in this connection had in mind a dictatorship in the literal sense of the term. He speaks here not of a form of government, but of a condition, which must necessarily arise wherever the proletariat has gained political power. That Marx in this case did not have in mind a form of government is proved by the fact that he was of the opinion that in Britain and America the transition might take place peacefully, i.e., in a democratic way.

Against this, Lenin gives the following definition of the concept dictatorship:

> Dictatorship is rule based directly on force and unrestricted by any laws. The revolutionary dictatorship of the proletariat is rule won and maintained by the use of violence by the proletariat against the bourgeoisie, rule that is unrestricted by any laws.

Lenin then adds the following explanations to this definition:

> Kautsky finds it necessary to interpret dictatorship as a 'condition of domination'...because then revolutionary violence, and violent revolution, disappear. The 'condition of domination' is a condition in which any majority finds itself under...'democracy'! Thanks to such a fraud, revolution happily disappears!...It is patently absurd to draw a distinction between a 'condition' and a 'form of government'. To speak of forms of government in this connection is trebly stupid, for every schoolboy knows that monarchy and republic are two different forms of government. It must be explained to Mr Kautsky that both these forms of government, like all transitional 'forms of government' under capitalism, are only variations of the bourgeois state, that is, of the dictatorship of the bourgeoisie.
>
> Lastly, to speak of forms of government is not only a stupid, but also a very crude falsification of Marx, who was very clearly speaking here of this

or that form of type of state, and not of forms of government. The proletarian revolution is impossible without the forcible destruction of the bourgeois state machine and the substitution of a new one which, in the words of Engels, is 'no longer a state in the proper sense of the word'.[16]

After comparing one view against another in this way, I believe it is possible to say the following. The whole weakness and untenability of Kautsky's definition of the concept of dictatorship, and the correctness of Lenin's criticism of it, spring to the eye. For history does not take place in 'conditions'. Certainly, the 'conditions' created by the development of the economy, i.e. social stratifications and stabilisations, always receive a certain kind of visible expression. But what is historically and politically decisive is *the act* by which a change of condition becomes visible as distinct from the previous one. 'Conditions' are always changing beneath the cover of the state, the cover of the form of government; we ourselves are witness to how far they can depart from their point of origin and come into contradiction with the – by and large – rigid 'form of government', yet without the contradiction becoming flagrant. So long as social forces do not tear apart the 'conditions', this cover, they are no more to the politician than the hares not yet caught are to the hunter. And, so, Kautsky's theory contains the great danger that it directs attention from the stage of political action into the wide realm of a 'philosophy of condition', social-philosophical contemplation, a land of sky-blue tranquillity. *Politically*, this amounts to a softening of the bones.

If we now turn to Lenin's commentary, and particularly his definitions, we can note right away a characteristic that is typical of many of his statements: they are somewhat reminiscent of Heraclitus 'the obscure' of Ephesus, and it is not always easy to establish what in fact he means.

It belongs to the very essence of Lenin that he should bridle the horse precisely on the opposite side from Kautsky, and begin with what is *historically* and *politically* decisive, i.e. the visibility and organisational form of the dictatorship of the proletariat. And, in this connection, Lenin makes a distinction that, I believe, gives a very deep insight into his train of thought. He distinguishes – and this very distinction is pertinent – between 'form of government' and 'form of state'. The form of government, for him, is something of

---

16. 'The Proletarian Revolution and the Renegade Kautsky', in Lenin 1974, p. 237.

subordinate importance. Monarchy and republic are simply a different garb for the same essence, the dictatorship of the bourgeoisie. It is different with the form of state. The task of the revolution is to shatter the bourgeois state-machinery and put the proletarian form of state in place of the bourgeois form of state. To this extent, I believe, all revolutionaries will agree with Lenin. The only question, however, is this:

Is there a form of proletarian state that secures the rule of the proletariat by its very existence, or is a change possible under the cover of the proletarian form of state, of such a kind that it is no longer proletarian but other forces that become decisive?

Lenin himself, as far as I know, never posed this question so sharply, and did not answer with this acuteness. So it is not a question of equating his view right away with the first alternative – although, on the basis of his polemic with Kautsky, this may well be the case – but we can only try to show how in fact his whole conception of the soviet-state and its significance derives from this first formulation.

What is soviet-power? We can select three of the various definitions that Lenin gave of it in his published works:

1) 'Soviet power is nothing but an organisational form of the dictatorship of the proletariat, the dictatorship of the advanced class, which raises to a new democracy and to independent participation in the administration of the state tens upon tens of millions of working and exploited peoples who by their own experience learn to regard the disciplined and class-conscious vanguard (*Avantgarde*) of the proletariat as their most reliable leader.'[17]

2) 'The Soviet government is the *first* in the world (or strictly speaking, the second, because the Paris Commune began to do the same thing) to *enlist the people, specifically the exploited people, in the work of administration*.'[18]

3) Eight lines further on, Lenin writes:

   The Soviets are the direct organisation of the working and exploited people themselves, which *helps* them to organise and administer their own

---

17. 'The Immediate Tasks of the Soviet Government', in Lenin 1972, p. 265.
18. 'The Proletarian Revolution and the Renegade Kautsky', in Lenin 1974.

state in every possible way. And in this it is the vanguard of the working and exploited people, the urban proletariat, that enjoys the advantage of being best united by the large enterprises; it is easier for it than for all others to elect and exercise control over the elected. The Soviet form of organisation automatically helps to unite all the working and exploited people around their vanguard, the proletariat.

One point first of all. In these definitions, as in countless others, there are three levels to distinguish: 1) the mass of the exploited and oppressed, i.e. the mass of industrial proletarians and (at that time) peasants; 2) the front-rank [*Vortrupp*] of the mass of exploited and oppressed, i.e. the urban industrial proletariat; 3) the advance-detachment [*Vorhut*] of the industrial proletariat, i.e. the Communists.[19]

This basic separation, which is maintained throughout Bolshevik literature, has the result that each of these three levels has its own circle of tasks, and that it is an essential task to maintain the connection between these three circles.

As far as the circle of tasks is concerned, what results from the passages quoted above (which could be increased at will) is the following: 1) The task of the advance-detachment, i.e. the Communists, is, by discipline and consciousness of the goal, to show themselves the most reliable leaders of the proletariat. 2) The task of the front-rank, i.e. the industrial proletariat, is to establish technically the apparatus of the proletarian state, to maintain and control it, i.e. what Lenin expresses incompletely in the words 'to elect and exercise control over the elected'. 3) The task of the broad mass of oppressed is – and here Lenin's terminology notably vacillates – 'to be enlisted in the work of administration', or 'to learn by their own experience to regard the disciplined and class-conscious vanguard of the proletariat as their most reliable leader'.

By simply listing these three different stages and circles of tasks, we can turn immediately to the second question: what connection can and does exist

---

19. [The German editions of Lenin that Levi cites here use both *Avantgarde* and *Vortrupp* to translate the Russian авангард, depending on context, whereas English translations stick to the one word 'vanguard'. But Levi is true to Lenin in making a conceptual distinction between 'the авангард of the mass of exploited' (i.e. the industrial proletariat) and 'the авангард of the proletariat' (i.e. the party). *Vorhut*, which Levi prefers to the rather artistic-sounding *Avantgarde*, is the standard military term (Clausewitz) for a small unit that goes ahead to scout or occupy a key position, the less well-defined *Vortrupp* being the front-rank of the main force.]

between these circles? On this point, I believe, there has been among the Bolsheviks only a single point of view, since the start of the Russian Revolution.

Lenin says at the place just cited: 'The Soviet form of organisation automatically helps to unite all the working and exploited people around their vanguard, the proletariat.'

And Trotsky writes:

> The revolutionary masses found their direct representation in the most simple and generally comprehensive delegate organisation – in the soviet.... The soviet embraces workers of all undertakings, of all professions, of all stages of cultural development, all stages of political consciousness – and thereby objectively is forced to formulate the general interests of the proletariat.[20]

The means of connection is thus the soviet. And, yet, there is a difference between Lenin's formulation and Trotsky's. While Trotsky sees the *advantage* of the soviets, even their *essence*, in the fact that they are comprehensive, a totality, for Lenin, they are a means that 'offers the masses the possibility', that 'enlists' the masses. For Trotsky, therefore, according to this definition, the essence of the soviets is destroyed if they lose their totality. Lenin speaks only of the 'possibility' of participation. Doubtless, he has before his mind a case in which the masses make no use of this possibility and yet the soviet-system still functions. For him, the proletariat clearly breaks down into two sharply separated parts: one part that 'enlists' and the other part that is 'enlisted', and the connection between these two parts, as shown by the image of enlistment or the very frequently used image of the 'lever', is taken from the realm of mechanics. For Lenin, both parts of a separated existence are possible: the advance-detachment of the proletariat, which established the soviet-system and is its bearer, can live and exist, and carry the soviet-system forward, until the great mass of those offered a 'possibility' make use of it, having 'learned by experience' to see in them 'their most reliable leaders'; the broad layer of exploited and oppressed, the majority and the rearguard, the object to which the 'lever' is applied, on which the leverage is used until the day when they recognise the blessings of the 'possibility' offered them in the soviet-system and the faithful guardianship of their 'most

---

20. Trotsky 2008, chapter 7.

reliable leaders', and catch up what was formerly the advance-detachment. Like a dedicated mother, the advance-detachment in the soviet-system sews a shirt and waits – patiently or otherwise – until the child can wear it. As long as this is not the case, the mother remains a mother and the shirt a shirt, the advance-detachment an advance-detachment and the soviet-system the soviet-system.

Do we do Lenin an injustice with this depiction? I do not think so. He is a coherent man who has remained one and the same for decades. And what, twenty years ago, was the object of a purely literary controversy between him and Rosa Luxemburg, what appeared at that time in the confined context of a struggle over organisational form, has today had to submit to a test on the great scale of world-history. The greatest revolutionary movement in world-history has decided on the Lenin-Luxemburg controversy of 1904, in which the standpoint of each side can be seen in the following lines from Rosa Luxemburg:

> From the standpoint of the formal tasks of social democracy as a party of struggle, it appears from the outset that the party's battle-readiness and its energy are directly dependent on the realisation of centralism in its organisation. But in this context the specific historical conditions of the proletariat's struggle are far more important than the standpoints of the formal requirements of any organisation of struggle.
>
> The social democratic movement is the first movement in the history of class societies to be premised in its very aspect and in its whole development on the organisation and the independent direct action of the mass.
>
> In this sense social democracy creates a completely different type of organisation from the earlier socialist movements, e.g. those of the Jacobin-Blanquist type.
>
> It appears that Lenin underestimates this when he writes in his book that the revolutionary Social Democrat is really nothing but 'the Jacobin indissolubly linked to the *organisation* of the *class-conscious* proletariat'.[21] It is in the organisation and class-consciousness of the proletariat, as opposed to the conspiracy of a small minority, that Lenin sees the exhaustive distinctions between social democracy and Blanquism. He forgets that this implies a

---

21. [Luxemburg's 1904 essay in *Die Neue Zeit* contained an explicit reference here to Lenin's *One Step Forward, Two Steps Back*.]

complete reappraisal of our organisational concepts, a completely new concept of centralism, a completely new notion of the mutual relationship between organisation and struggle.

Blanquism was not premised on a direct class activity of the masses and did not therefore require a mass organisation. On the contrary, as the broad popular masses were supposed to emerge onto the battlefield only at the actual moment of revolution, while the preliminary activity consisted in the preparation of a revolutionary coup by a small minority, a rigid distinction between the people appointed to this specific task and the popular mass was directly necessary for the success of their mission. But it was also possible and attainable because there was no inherent connection between the conspiratorial activity of the Blanquist organisation and the everyday life of the popular mass.

At the same time both the tactics and the precise tasks of activity were worked out in advance in the minutest detail, determined and prescribed as a definite plan, because they were improvised off the cuff and at will, with no connection with the elemental class struggle. As a result the active members of the organisation were naturally transformed into the purely executive organs of a will that had been predetermined outside their own field of activity, into the instruments of a central committee. This also gave rise to the second characteristic of conspiratorial centralism: the absolute blind submission of the individual organs of the party to their central authority and the extension of the latter's powers right to the very periphery of the party organisation.

The conditions for social democratic activity are radically different. This derives historically from the elemental class struggle. It operates within the dialectical contradiction that here it is only in the struggle itself that the proletarian army is itself recruited and only in the struggle that it becomes conscious of the purpose of the struggle. Organisation, enlightenment and struggle are here not separate moments mechanically divided in time, as in a Blanquist movement, they are merely different facets of the same process. On the one hand, apart from the general basic principles of struggle, there is no ready-made predetermined and detailed tactic of struggle that the Central Committee could drill into the social democratic membership. On the other hand, the process of struggle that creates the organisation stipulates a constant fluctuation in the sphere of influence of social democracy.

From this it follows that social democratic centralisation cannot be based either on blind obedience or on the mechanical submission of the party's militants to their central authority and, further, that an impenetrable wall can never be erected between the nucleus of the class-conscious proletariat that is already organised into tightly knit party cadres and those in the surrounding stratum who have already been caught up in the class struggle and are in the process of developing class-consciousness. The establishment of centralisation in social-democracy on these two principles – on the blind submission of all party organisations and their activity, down to the smallest detail, to a central authority that alone thinks, acts and decides for everyone, and also on the strict separation of the organised nucleus of the party from its surrounding revolutionary milieu, as Lenin advocates – therefore seems to us to be a mechanical transposition of the organisational principles of the Blanquist movement of conspiratorial circles to the social democratic movement of the working masses. And Lenin characterises this point of view, perhaps more astutely than any of his opponents could, when he defines his 'revolutionary Social Democrat' as a 'Jacobin linked to the organisation of the class-conscious workers'. In fact, however, social democracy is not linked to the organisation of the working class; it is the working class's own movement. Social democratic centralism must therefore have an essentially different character from Blanquist centralism. It can be none other than the authoritative expression of the will of the conscious and militant vanguard [*Vorhut*] of the workers, vis-à-vis the separate groups and individuals among them; it is, as it were, a 'self-centralism' of the leading stratum of the proletariat, the rule of its majority within the confines of its own party organisation.[22]

We are today in a position, on the basis of the experiences of the Russian Revolution, to draw the practical lessons from this literary controversy. But, before we do so, we would like, first of all, to deal to a certain extent with the forms that Lenin's conception of the dictatorship of the proletariat has led to.

---

22. R. Luxemburg, 'Organisational Questions of Russian Social-Democracy', in Hudis and Anderson (eds.) 2004, pp. 251–3.

V

We have seen how the soviet-government is a form of state that was established in Russia following the smashing of the Russian feudal form of state by the victorious proletariat.

Not much has yet been said beyond the form of state in itself and the 'possibility' it gives for the broad proletarian masses to take part in the life of the state. The question is, rather, whether various 'forms of government' are also possible within this 'form of state', just as the state-form of the bourgeoisie is conceivable with a very varied range of forms of government (republic, monarchy, parliamentarism, etc.). Without (as far as we know) Lenin having investigated and replied to this question, it would seem from various statements of his that his answer is an affirmative one.

For a start, the masses and their participation in the soviet-system are for Lenin only a 'possibility'. A possibility, however, is not a solid basis on which a state can be built. The firm wall that supports the soviet-edifice is the advance-detachment of the proletariat, i.e. the Communist Party, and, in the first stage of the Revolution, in any case, the Bolsheviks – also quite rightly, at the start – reckoned that the front-rank, i.e. the industrial proletariat, would also take an active part in it. But, because the participation of the majority is only a possibility, which gives the industrial proletariat no security, relations between the only fixed point, the advance-detachment, on the one hand, and the front-rank and the majority on the other, must be variable.

Lenin says about this:

> Dictatorship does not necessarily mean the abolition of democracy for the class that exercises the dictatorship over other classes; but it does mean the abolition (or very material restriction, which is also a form of abolition) of democracy for the class over which, or against which, the dictatorship is exercised.[23]

It follows from this that the form of government under the soviet-system can initially vary through a greater or lesser degree of democracy, vis-à-vis both the dictating and the 'dictated' class.

---

23. 'The Proletarian Revolution and the Renegade Kautsky', in Lenin 1974, p. 247.

Abolition of democracy for the bourgeoisie is necessary, but the degree is not determined. At all events, 'the question of depriving the exploiters of the franchise is [a purely Russian question], and not a question of the dictatorship of the proletariat in general.'[24]

> It would be a mistake, however, to guarantee in advance that the impending proletarian revolutions in Europe will all, or the majority of them, be necessarily accompanied by restriction of the franchise for the bourgeoisie. It may be so. After the War and the experience of the Russian revolution it probably will be so; but it is not absolute necessary for the exercise of the dictatorship, it is not an indispensable characteristic of the logical concept 'dictatorship', it does not enter as an indispensable condition in the historical and class concept 'dictatorship'.[25]

We shall go on to see that Rosa Luxemburg did not represent this point of view, and what were her reasons for this. Here, we would just like to emphasise that, according to Lenin's doctrine, the dictatorship of the proletariat does not have to mean 'completely' an abolition of democracy for the ruling (proletarian) class. The general *rule*, however, that results from this conception, will be the abolition of democracy *also* for the proletarian class.

What we then have is a great Ego that reigns over all, that hands out a tolerable measure of democracy, not too little, not too much, to the 'ruling' as well as the ruled class – this 'Single One' who can say of himself 'that he alone holds in his hands/the fullness of all right,/and allots the several peoples/according to his sight?'[26]

We have already indicated above the role that falls to the Communist Party, the advance-detachment, in this connection. But this does not exhaust all the possibilities. For, perhaps the Communist Party itself falls into that unbounded realm of 'possibilities'. Lenin thinks along just these lines:

> There is, therefore, absolutely *no* contradiction in principle between soviet (*that is*, socialist) democracy and the exercise of dictatorial power by individuals. The different between proletarian dictatorship and bourgeois dictatorship is that the former strikes at the exploiting minority in the

---

24. Ibid., chapter 3.
25. Ibid., chapter 3.
26. [A reference to Hölderlin's poem 'The Unique One'.]

interests of the exploited majority, and that it is exercised – *also through individuals* – not only by the working and exploited people, but also by organisations which are built in such a way as to rouse these people to history-making activity. (The soviet organisations are organisations of this kind.)[27]

With this, the dictatorship of the proletariat is placed on a completely new footing. Democracy or no democracy, party or no party, advance-detachment or no advance-detachment, one individual or several: all this is compatible with the dictatorship of the proletariat, which is characterised by two aspects, a subjective and an objective one: the subjective aspect, that the dictator dictates 'in the interests of the exploited majority'; the objective moment, 'that it is exercised...not only by the working and exploited people, but also by organisations which are built in such a way as to rouse these people'.

From only a brief indication of how Rosa Luxemburg's views on this subject were quite the contrary, we can thus maintain that, even under the soviet-system, i.e. the form of state specific to proletarian dictatorship, the most varied forms of government are conceivable. From free democracy, under certain circumstances even for the bourgeoisie, through to the strict dictatorship of an individual.

It goes without saying that, in this system, compulsion plays a considerable role. For all mechanics ultimately is based on the application and expression of forces, and it also goes without saying that force accordingly plays its role, right up to its most extreme forms in terrorism. I do not intend here to go into the forms in which compulsion is expressed in Russia, but confine myself to a few remarks on Germany. We can happily admit that the use of the sharpest means, even terroristic ones, is a necessity for those struggling for their lives, as the Bolsheviks often did, and has to be recognised as such even by those who do not see it as the finest blossoming in the development of state-power. In Europe and Germany, however, terrorism has, in places, been made into a true religion, and there are Communists who see the characteristic sign of this in a daily sacrifice on the altar of Huitzilopochli. We need not conceal from ourselves that this glorification of terrorism is nothing at all but a sign of great weakness combined with the consciousness of this weakness. The boy who

---

27. 'The Immediate Tasks of the Soviet Government', in Lenin 1972, p. 268.

is wrongly beaten by a bigger boy spends days wallowing in images of the bloody revenge he will take 'as soon as...'. We cannot even see an advance in the revolutionary will of the working class when fantasies of this kind are deliberately given new fuel, and we believe it is only doing a service to the revolutionary movement to oppose such childishness clearly and unambiguously. Rosa Luxemburg had no time for this 'Redskin' romanticism. She also clearly expressed her view of terrorism, and it is no accident that the programme of the Spartacus League contains simply and sensibly the following words: 'The proletarian revolution requires no terror for its aims; it hates and despises killing.'

Any well-informed person knows what she had in mind.

VI

We can now turn to the question that we left above: what are the practical results of Lenin's view, as this was sketched above in the quotation from Rosa Luxemburg?

We have to go back to February of last year, which saw a fundamental change in the Soviet republic in this connection. We have already seen above how, in that month, the Bolsheviks' view of how to resolve the peasant-question took a different tack from their previous conception, and how they had to put their relationship to the peasantry on a new basis.

The same month, however, the Bolsheviks also found themselves forced to take a new look at their relationship to the proletariat. The story that a few 'well-informed' people are retailing in Germany, that the Kronstadt uprising was the work of tsarist officers with French money, or of a few Mensheviks, is extremely naïve. It may well be that some tsarist generals were at work behind the Kronstadt sailors – we do not know. It may well be that 'Menshevik' slogans played a role in the Kronstadt uprising – we do not know. But there is one thing that we do know for sure, which is that neither tsarist generals nor French money nor Menshevik slogans are a sufficient explanation of how it was possible that the *most loyal sons of the revolution*, the most devoted supporters of the Bolsheviks, who had so long been the élite of revolutionary fighters, proven in a hundred battles, rose up against those whom they formerly supported. This fact can only be explained by a profound crisis within the proletariat itself, a serious conflict that has arisen between the 'advance-detachment' and the 'front-rank', perhaps indeed within the 'advance-detachment' itself. We would have evidence for this even if the Kronstadt uprising had not been a visible indication.

I would like to offer here some quotations from those days, all taken from *Russische Korrespondenz* (year 2, no. 3 & 4).

Karl Radek writes:

> Most of the remaining workers, in these particularly difficult moments, saw the Communists as slave-drivers demanding ever new sacrifices from them. This gave rise to a tension between a section of non-Communist workers and the Communist Party and Soviet government.
>
> One of the most important tasks of the Communist Party in the present situation is to reduce right away this gap between the vanguard and the rear, or indeed to reconcile it.

A draft resolution published in the same issue:

> Among these unhealthy phenomena are the bureaucratisation of the leading party-apparatus and the lack of a functioning systematic connection with the mass of party-members, as well as the visible tendency to divide the Party into upper and lower strata, workers and intellectuals, or to reduce the role of the Party. These phenomena together prepare the ground for syndicalist deviations that endanger party-unity.

From the draft theses presented by a group of active functionaries:

> With the purpose of drawing broad masses of the Party into questions of party-life, raising their level of understanding, developing their initiative and autonomy, the system of detailed and open discussion must be made into a principle, in the party-press as well as in party-meetings, so that all tendencies and groups within the Party are offered the full opportunity of making their position known.
>
> In order to be able to attract the advanced strata of the proletariat organised in our party for the sake of building it up, to establish direct connection with the masses and cleanse the leading party-organs (central committee, government-committees, etc.), these organs must consist of at least two-thirds workers.

This means the following: at the same time as the Bolsheviks had reached a critical stage in connection with their relationship with the peasantry, there was trouble among the industrial proletariat itself. The cause of this was quite simple: the distance between the Communist Party and the broad mass had grown so great that the Party threatened to suffocate from it. 'The Party,' Zinoviev complains, 'in a certain sense lacks oxygen. This oxygen is the non-party masses.'

This was the central problem for the Tenth Congress of the Russian Communist Party. We have already explained elsewhere how all the debates of this congress were dominated by the attempt to solve this problem by *organisational* methods, and we can only judge the positive and negative aspects of these attempts after learning their intention and methods from the following explanations.

The theses adopted by the Congress state:

> The Communist Party of Russia has to realise the dictatorship of the proletariat in a country in which the peasants form the great majority of the population. Now that the peasants are no longer threatened by a restoration of landed property, the realisation of the dictatorship of the proletariat comes up against new difficulties. A successful realisation of this dictatorship is only possible in the presence of powerful trade-unions and mass-organisations, solid in their will and efforts, which are open to all proletarians at the different stages of development of their class-consciousness.

I would like to recall here the words of Lenin quoted above, that the dictatorship of the proletariat is characterised by the fact that it strikes its blows in the interest of the exploited, and the further fact that its measures are carried out through the organisations that are in a position to arouse the broad masses and raise them to historic creation. *At that time*, the soviets were characterised as organisations of this kind. It is quite clear that this task is now ascribed to the trade-unions.

This means, on the negative side, that the soviets have played out their role; the soviets are shattered, because the classes that they formerly brought together in unity, peasants and workers, no longer have anything in common. The new organs that the dictatorship seeks for itself are organisations of the industrial proletariat. The *organisational* basis of the dictatorship has narrowed. It is only still supported (in theory) on what was previously the front-rank, and is bending its practical efforts to bring this front-rank, which is already almost lost, up to the advanced detachment.

'We overlooked,' says Zinoviev,[28] 'that a turning point was approaching that was leading us into a general crisis, and that the trade-unions will function as the most important lever [!] in leading us out of it, in helping the Party to overcome the crisis.'

And, two pages later, following his complaint about lack of oxygen, he says: 'The trade-unions form to a certain degree such a reserve [!] of oxygen.'

If this already demonstrates how even the state-form of soviet-republic and the possibilities it offers provide no guarantee as to the class-content of the soviet-republic, and that, under the roof of the soviet-republic (and not only of the bourgeois republic), the class-content can alter, the following presentation will offer definite proof of this.

VII

In February 1921, the situation of the Bolsheviks was as follows: they had lost the support of the proletariat, as is shown by the debates at their Tenth Party Congress. They had lost the poor peasants who had been their former support among the peasantry; these had all become middle-peasants and opponents of any Communist policy. The onslaught was coming from both sides: from the proletariat in Kronstadt, and from the threat of peasant-uprisings. The Bolsheviks, in fact, lacked a class-basis and held out due to the force of their organisation – a force that cannot hold out for long. The Bolsheviks were forced to quickly decide for one class or the other. At this point in time, they stayed with the stronger battalions, i.e. they started by pacifying the peasants. There is no need to list here the whole chain of concessions that have been made to the peasants since February this year – the tax in kind in place of the grain-monopoly, the introduction of free trade, the restoration of private enterprise; they are now seeking to rebuild the entire edifice that they themselves demolished three years ago. It is not only in economics that the Bolsheviks are abandoning their old goals. They are also doing this in their ideas.

---

28. Sinowjew 1920, p. 309.

Lenin writes:

> it is not directly, by way of enthusiasm, but with the aid of personal interest, personal self-interest, with the help of economic calculation, that we shall rebuild a firm bridge that will lead via state capitalism to socialism in a small-peasant country...[29]

This, of course, sounds quite different from what Lenin said for example in 1918:

> Without the guidance of experts in the various fields of knowledge, technology and experience, the transition to socialism will be impossible, because socialism calls for a conscious mass advance to greater productivity of labour compared with capitalism, and on the basis achieved by capitalism. Socialism must achieve this advance in its own way, by its own methods – or, to put it more concretely, by Soviet methods.[30]

And it sounds quite different from what Lenin said in 1919:

> As well as this, the proletariat must go ahead of the whole mass of working and exploited people, as well as all petty-bourgeois strata, in initiating this new economic construction, by creating a new social context, a new labour discipline, a new organisation of labour, which realises both the latest results of science and capitalist technology, and carries through the mass cooperation of goal-conscious workers, in socialist mass production.[31]

These are, of course, the tones that led Lloyd George to say with biting irony early in 1921: 'My honourable friend Mr Winston Churchill would also have spoken in these terms.'

We can say, with certainty, in these circumstances what, in the light of this policy, will come of the other attempt to build a base among the workers, by the organisational 'lever' of the trade-unions. Zinoviev, I believe, already anticipated this when he said, though in a different connection: 'If this policy of concessions becomes a fact, and thousands of workers are employed in the concession-enterprises – will the trade-unions not also have their particular task to fulfill?'[32]

---

29. Lenin 1921b.
30. 'The Immediate Tasks of the Soviet Government', in Lenin 1972, p. 247.
31. Lenin 1920, p. 18.
32. Sinowjew 1920, p. 309.

This is incontestably true, and we come directly to the point if we take this line of thought to its conclusion. 'The concessionaire,' Lenin says, 'is a capitalist. He conducts his business on capitalist lines, for profit...'

What is the task of the trade-unions? Is their task to say: 'work for the capitalists who makes high profits, but thanks to these high profits the basis will be laid on which one day our government can introduce communism'? Or should they say to the workers: 'don't work for the capitalists and their profit, cut back their profit, capitalism is hell'. They can say one thing or the other. In the first case, they become an accessory to the capitalists; in the second case, they will come into conflict with the capitalists, the concessionaires will summon help from those that gave them the concessions. And then?

No, we have to face the facts: there are two classes in Russia that are irreconcilable. On the one hand, the peasant-capitalist class, with the industrial- and merchant-capitalists temporarily on its shoulders. On the other hand, the proletariat. There is just as little prospect in Russia of an armistice or reconciliation in the class-struggle immanent in society as there is anywhere else, and the party that seeks to reconcile, that seeks to give to capitalism what is capitalism's and to the proletariat what is the proletariat's, will be the first to be shattered in this struggle. The Bolsheviks are seeking to give to capitalism *for now*, in order to save the proletariat *for the future*: what the proletariat has to save for its future however, cannot be given it by a party, no Santa Claus can place it on the Christmas tree. The proletariat will conquer its future by its own struggle, in which it grows and strengthens itself. And the party that strikes it for the sake of the present moment, disarms it for the future.

'The working class has only to set free the elements of a new society that are already developed in the womb of the collapsing bourgeois society.' That is Marx's formulation of the task of the victorious proletariat.

We need no one to tell us that the Russian concessionaires with their surplus-profit, the Russian hucksters and speculators whose emergence no one can now prevent, are 'elements of a new society', or that it is for the sake of 'setting them free' that the Russian workers have made such great sacrifices.

What then is left of the 'dictatorship of the proletariat'? Nothing. Nothing of its objective aspects, nothing of its subjective ones. The Russian concessionaires are not measures to be 'realised by the masses of workers and exploited', except as the objects of exploitation.

But what about the subjective aspects? This is what the whole present line of argument of the Bolsheviks seems to depend on. For it is still the Bolshevik

Party that stands at the head of the Russian Soviet Republic, the party that has done more than any other for the world-proletariat, for the world-revolution. There still stand at its head men with such unimpugnable judgement, devotion and fidelity to the proletarian cause as Lenin and Trotsky. On the day that altered circumstances permit, they will be the first to put an end to all concessions to capitalism, which are just as distasteful to them as to anyone else. All this is true. We need only raise one objection: Lenin and Trotsky could die; who will be their successors? For one thing is certain. All the old Communists who witnessed the growth and development of the Bolshevik Party may be firm and unshakeable: but, in the big party of today, they are only a small proportion. And the great mass of the Party? Here, we come to the most profound mistake in Lenin's argument: the idea that you can seal off a party, nurture it like a culture in a laboratory, preserve it unaltered, even improve it, by one 'purge' after another, that you can erect a dividing wall between it and the broad masses who are part of the process. The Party is a part of social being, and a party that carries out this policy of concessions for only a few years will reflect the spirit of this policy, not that of revolution.

And, so, we return to the question from which we started out: the soviet-system is not a recipe that guarantees always and in all circumstances the character of developing *proletarian* power. It is only the most favourable form in which the proletariat continues its class-struggle. If it abandons class-struggle, even in the Soviet Union, then the forces of its enemies grow stronger. Even under the soviet-system, the dictatorship of the bourgeoisie (or of the peasants) can erect itself over the proletariat. And should we wait to continue the struggle for the proletariat for the day when this is possible? I am afraid that Bolshevik policy is postponing such a day until the distant future.

VIII

Before we go into any more detail on this point, I would like to sketch Rosa Luxemburg's position on the question, as can be seen quite evidently from her whole position in the present text.

I believe that the profound opposition between the Bolsheviks and Rosa Luxemburg cannot be made any clearer than by pointing out the following: for the Bolsheviks, the proletarian revolution is a process that takes place with a system of advance-detachment, front-rank and mass. The advance-detachment makes use of the 'lever', needs the 'oxygen-reserve', pulls 'forward'. A system, in short, in which the higher circle acts with mechanical means on the lower. Nothing is more characteristic than this: when, in early 1921, the Bolsheviks lost their connection with the proletarian masses, which the soviet-system had previously produced, they pondered as to a form of organisation, and decided that the trade-unions would now be the 'lever'.

What was Rosa Luxemburg's view of the development of the socialist social order? She says:

> The socialist system of society should only be, and can only be, an historical product, born out of the school of its own experiences, born in the course of its realisation; as a result of the developments of living history – just like organic nature of which, in the last analysis, it forms a part...[33]

At the bottom of her consistent soul, she knew no divisions and walls. For her, the universe was a living process of becoming, in which leverage and oxygen-reserves cannot replace the workings of nature, in which the struggle, striving and contention of human beings, the great struggle that is incumbent on individuals, generations, strata and classes, is the *form* of becoming. This did not mean she did not want people to struggle because everything happens of itself, she rather wanted the most active struggle, since this is the most active form of becoming.

Rosa Luxemburg's judgement of Bolshevik policy follows directly from this basic attitude of hers. Was she a democratic church-mouse who did not want a hair of anyone's head to be touched unless by legal authority? Certainly not. She knew how to wage struggle as struggle, war as war, civil war as civil war. But she could only conceive of civil war as a free play of forces, in which even the bourgeoisie was not forced into cellars by police-measures, because it is only through open struggle that the masses can grow and recognise the magnitude and difficulty of their struggle. She did not seek the annihilation of the bourgeoisie by savage terrorism, by the monotonous work of the executioner, any more than the hunter seeks to annihilate the prey in his wood. It is in struggle that the game grows stronger and larger. For her, the annihilation of the bourgeoisie, which she also wanted, would be the *result* of the social transformation of the revolution.

---

33. R. Luxemburg, 'The Russian Revolution', in Hudis and Anderson (eds.) 2004, p. 306.

If combating the bourgeoisie in a police-fashion was already alien to her point of view, there can be no doubt how she would have judged such measures against sections of the proletariat. Certainly, she took every kind of reformism to be an error, a serious diversion for the working class. She fought it wherever she could. In Germany, she was the creator and leader of the struggle against reformism. In the work published here, she likewise sharply fought reformism. But, in the last analysis, this entire struggle is summed up already in the words with which she concluded her article in *Neue Zeit* in 1904: 'the mistakes that are made by a truly revolutionary workers' movement are, historically speaking, immeasurable more fruitful and more valuable than the infallibility of the best possible "Central Committee"'.[34]

It is true that the Menshevik workers made mistakes in Russia. We certainly believe that they did not understand the lofty task of the year 1917, and that, subsequently, they often vacillated. But no one can contest the fact that, despite the burden of these mistakes, they were part of the great revolutionary mass of workers who stood in 1917 against the tsar, in 1918 against the Czechoslovaks, in 1919 against Kolchak and Yudenich, and in 1920 against Wrangel. They made mistakes, perhaps some of them took steps that were incompatible with the existence of the Soviet republic. These had to be punished; that is the law of life for all states. But to banish parties as parties, as tendencies, from the surface by police-measures, to remove them from the light of day, was, for Rosa Luxemburg, an impossible idea: not for the sake of the reformists, but for that of the revolution and the revolutionaries themselves, who can also triumph inwardly only if they combat mistakes freely. For the experience that revolutionaries gain from the struggle against reformism cannot be replaced by any leader, police-force or Cheka. They have to gain this experience in their own struggle.

We believe that these underlying ideas, which already lay at the root of the debate between Lenin and Rosa Luxemburg in 1904 and have now faced each other on a gigantic scale, have been tested by the history of the Russian Revolution. We believe that Rosa Luxemburg, on the basis of this idea of hers, saw with prophetic eyes the rocks on which the ship of the Soviet republic has now suffered such heavy damage.

---

34. R. Luxemburg, 'Organisational Questions of Russian Social-Democracy', in Hudis and Anderson (eds.) 2004, p. 265.

We have already indicated the critique that she made of the Bolsheviks' land-policy: 'It piles up insurmountable obstacles to the socialist transformation of agrarian relations'.[35]

> The Leninist agrarian reform has created a new and powerful layer of popular enemies of socialism in the countryside, enemies whose resistance will be much more dangerous and stubborn than that of the noble large landowners.[36]

We have seen how this happened. The effects are certainly even more serious than Rosa Luxemburg foresaw. She had in mind the resistance that the peasants would put up to the transformation of agrarian relations. The way things have turned out, though, the peasants are in a position to reverse the transformation of industrial relations.

Here, we believe, lies a second mistake that Rosa Luxemburg found fault with, and which she was still more eager and passionate to pursue than the first one.

> With the repression of political life in the land as a whole, life in the soviets must also become more and more crippled. Without general elections, without unrestricted freedom of the press and assembly, without a free struggle of opinion, life dies out in every public institution, becomes a mere semblance of life, in which only the bureaucracy remains as the active element.[37]

We have seen how, in 1921, when the great push forward of the peasants came, a struggle that the Bolsheviks themselves had long seen coming, they were precisely concerned to re-establish life among the working masses. The soviets were dead. They no longer formed even the mechanical connection between advance-detachment, front-rank and mass, still less did they form that great totality that Trotsky speaks of, in which 'the movement takes charge of itself as a whole'. They were burnt-out cinders. And the trade-unions are now to be their emergency-replacement, since they are the only

---

35. R. Luxemburg, 'The Russian Revolution', in Hudis and Anderson (eds.) 2004, p. 291.
36. R. Luxemburg, 'The Russian Revolution', in Hudis and Anderson (eds.) 2004, p. 293.
37. R. Luxemburg, 'The Russian Revolution', in Hudis and Anderson (eds.) 2004, p. 307.

organisation in which there are still large masses of 'non-party' workers. Non-party? Is there a more serious reproach than that in the Russian proletariat, which since 1905 stood as a shining model for proletarians everywhere, and will remain so for all time, there are, after four years of proletarian rule, an overwhelming mass of 'non-party' workers? Have these really remained uninterested? Do they stand indifferent and with lowered heads when their life is at stake, which they have so often won on the battlefield? Have they become indifferent, or are they shy of saying what they think? Do they guard their tongues or has the revolution become obnoxious to them, so that they are 'non-party'? Is not each one of them a living reproach? However that may be, the Russian Revolution and its leading party have not been able to connect these masses with the fate of the Revolution. They stand aside, not in the ranks of the fighters. Public life is dead. The spirit of democracy, which alone forms the breath of the masses, is dead. A rigidly centralised party, a splendid central committee, a wretched bureaucracy, move over the waters. Below, all is waste and empty. And, so, the pressure from the peasants did not encounter a strong, lively, vigorous, enthusiastic proletariat. It found a vanguard that had no majority behind it. And this determined the fate of the vanguard.

'Dictatorship of the proletariat.' Now we can see what this is. It is not something that happens in broad regions of social philosophy. It is not a patented form of state that contains a secret power within it. It is the state-power that has been conquered, so long as the will, the force, the enthusiasm, the confidence in victory of the proletarian class stand behind it. It is, at the same time, a condition and a form of state, the one expressed in the other. It is kernel and shell at the same time, and where the kernel and shell vanish, the 'dictatorship of the proletariat' is at an end.

The envigorating air of this prospect of victory, and of the will of the proletarian class, would thus, we believe, have made it possible to avoid many of the obstacles that have inflicted such bloody wounds on the Russian Revolution. For, in the final analysis, the life of a great people consists not only in arithmetical magnitudes and in forces to be calculated mechanically. How did it happen – if it is permissible to compare small things with great – that, on 10 November 1918, when the German working class was *without* an organisation and could show only the sadly withered beginnings of a future organisation, that Erich Ludendorff was forced to become Erich Lindström, Crown-Prince

Rupprecht fled to the protection of the Spanish embassy, and the *Kreuz-Zeitung* removed the Prussian cuckoo from its masthead, whereas three years later, under a 'well-ordered republic', Erich Lindström again became Erich Ludendorff and saviour of his fatherland, Rupprecht had gone from Spanish to German again and was pretender to the throne, and the *Kreuz-Zeitung* again stood 'with God for King and Fatherland'? Not simply because the German Republic cannot do what it does not even want to: but because it does not have and cannot have that victorious revolutionary 'authority' which even the lamentable German Revolution possessed in its first beginnings, and which chased its enemies into their hiding places by force of this 'authority'. This is the 'horror of revolution'. But where this powerful force of the class evaporates, in time the substitutes must also fail – concessions on the one hand, organisation on the other, and police-measures in both directions.

These things do not just have measure and number; there is a spirit that must prevail over everything, and only the proletarian revolution can raise this to the historical and moral magnitude in with which it can accomplish its great task.

IX

Anyone who writes in these terms writes a piece of their own heart. For, time and again, the great tragedy of the Russian Revolution is that, in the last analysis, all its mistakes and all its errors were possible only because it saw itself as the first link in the great world-struggle, and because the world-proletariat left it in the lurch. And, yet, we believe that *reproaches* are not enough, it is, rather, a duty to see things as they are. We cannot 'make' the 'world-revolution' in Europe, not with our own forces and not with friendly support. It was precisely, as Rosa Luxemburg stressed, the great wager of Bolshevik policy in its first phase, that they put such great store on 'the readiness for action of the proletariat, the force of the masses, the whole will to power of socialism'. Not only was this the *intention* of Bolshevik policy, it was also in fact the *fruit* of this policy. No previous event in the world took hold of the minds of millions of proletarians, no act ever gave wings to the development and rise of the proletariat, as Soviet Russia did by the very fact that it existed, by the fact that it maintained itself, by the fact that despite all its actual or supposed errors, all party-criticism and contention, the proletarians recognised its burning and unquenchable will to the

victory of the world-proletariat. It cannot be contested that this development
has been interrupted because of reasons that are only partly to be sought
within Russia. But, precisely this situation, extremely difficult and critical
for the workers' movement of every country and for every workers' party,
requires double attention in a place from where great benefit and great harm
can proceed. We will not immerse ourselves in details here, but simply take
one example. German capitalism is encroaching on the railway-companies.
With the rise in social and political antagonisms in Germany, who knows
at what point great social battles may erupt? Perhaps on the railways: all
the organisations of railwaymen have declared themselves ready to use any
means necessary. The basic question may be that of private capitalism or
public ownership. But what should the German workers respond to Stinnes,
if he reads them Lenin's article in *Rote Fahne* which says: 'Personal interest
increases production'?[38]

The Russian Revolution remains a valuable treasure for all workers, as they
recognise in it – even if they see mistakes – the clearest, most determined
and most unambiguous representation of proletarian being and proletarian
future. The Russian Revolution would no longer be able to play this role if it
lost this feeling among the workers.

The Bolsheviks have one thing in their possession: the greatest moral asset
that the working class has ever assembled. No one who went through the
years 1918, 1919 and 1920 will contest this. We have already lamented elsewhere how this asset was, in part, *uselessly* squandered, in a way that can
never be restored. If it were to be totally lost, there may be people who will
take this with an easy heart. We believe that the workers of the whole world
would be spiritually impoverished, and that it might take the work of decades
to rebuild what existed in 1918.

---

38. Lenin 1921b.

Introduction to Trotsky, *The Lessons of October**

I

It is not immediately apparent why the following essay of Trotsky's should have had – and is still having – such an effect on the Russian Communist Party, perhaps also on the Russian state. This is a historical discussion along with a critique – not excessively sharp – of the errors made at the time by the present leaders of the Communist International, but, as these have also meanwhile admitted their errors, that is not enough to explain the excitement; after all, even the saints of the Catholic Church get to heaven not thanks to their innate virtues, but by overcoming their inherent faults. This critique deals with things past, and where it does tackle more recent matters, it does not, in our opinion, even start from correct assumptions. And, finally, in these more topical parts, the criticism does not even refer to Russian affairs, it is rather German problems that are brought up, ones that have a great effect on the Russian situation. In our opinion, these are apparent contradictions for which the German reader requires an explanation.

---

* This German edition of Trotsky's book, *1917 – Die Lehren der Revolution*, was published by E. Laub, Berlin 1925.

II

Trotsky still maintains that, in October 1923, there was a situation in Germany that would have enabled the Communist Party to take power, if it had had a leadership as determined as that of Lenin in October 1917. It is quite understandable why Trotsky should make this assumption. The war in the Ruhr had been lost. Something had happened that we can confidently say was unlike anything in modern history, perhaps in history in general. A nation had been dragged through a horrific war lasting for four years, a war whose suffering only increased as it ended. On human judgement, one would surely believe that the lesson had sunk in: only the pike bites on the hook a second time, which supposedly shows it lacks feeling. The Germans – the nation most full of feeling, as we know – bit a second time. The war in the Ruhr was waged after the recipe of the World-War. Again, we had a struggle over principles, a struggle over the sacredness of treaties and all the rest of it. But this second war was waged by the German government with more inhumane means than those with which the Kaiser's government fought the World-War. The World-War at least had a trace of something honourable about it, as far as the German bourgeoisie was concerned. You shot the 'enemy' dead, and got on with plundering your own people only as a kind of sideline. In the Ruhr conflict, this side-effect became a shameless end in itself: the French were little bothered by the whole business; on the contrary, the longer the thing lasted, the greater their chance of establishing themselves permanently in the Ruhr. The domestic effects, on the other hand, were devastating. Perhaps nowhere have all social relations been so completely undermined in the short space of a few months as at this time in Germany. Out of the sea of tears that the Ruhr war involved, a tiny layer of capitalists arose with increased economic power and an increased lust for power; they began to make a fearful selection in their own capitalist ranks. The early fruits of inflation faded, and the 'honest' capitalists who had not understood in good time the opportunities for robbery that the Ruhr affair offered came to grief. The middle class, both commercial and intellectual, lost its economic basis. The workers saw a reduction in their wages in gold-pfennigs, and, along with their economic basis, this put paid to all their organisational structures, trade-unions and co-operatives. There was, we can indeed say, a much stronger social convulsion than that which underlay the events that Trotsky describes. And, so, Trotsky's assumption has a certain logic behind it: since the human race did not die out, at the end of this kind of social catastrophe, some kind of power must remain that will form a new structure. We can even follow Trotsky in a further assumption: logically, there must be at end of such a catastrophe a different force than that responsible for its origin; if the bourgeoisie were responsible for the Ruhr catastrophe, it is only logical that at its end the proletariat should arise as the commanding power.

Trotsky is only mistaken on one thing, but this mistake is essential. It is not necessary for this force to be that formed by the Communist Party, simply because formerly, in a comparable situation in Russia, Lenin wagered and won, simply because the German Communist Party belongs to the Communist International, and perhaps because – we do not know whether Trotsky also shares this third premise – Grigorii Zinoviev is at the head of this Third International. For, even if all three preconditions were correct, even if the German situation had been completely similar to the Russian, if the Communist International were the most error-free organisation ever existing, and if Grigorii Zinoviev were a politician of magnitude and not the ass of European fame that he is – even if all this had been the case, the KPD would still not have won a legitimate title to present itself at the end of this catastrophe as the one state-structuring force. Such a title can only be won by a superior and well-considered politics, not simply by saying 'We are the Communists'. The Bolsheviks themselves could not take power in October on the basis of declaring that they held themselves to be chosen, but only on the basis of the particular politics that they had pursued from April to October. This politics alone gave them their legitimation.

In the tragic circumstances of Germany, it would not even have been hard to pursue such a politics. We had, as I said, the experiences of the World-War behind us; it was only necessary to demonstrate how the war in the Ruhr was a shameless robbery of everyone in Germany except the capitalists, and that the end of this policy could only be that those strata of society who had suffered would turn against the bearers of this policy. In this situation, which would have been an incontestable stroke of luck for the Communists if they really were Communists, there emerged those know-alls and super know-alls who determine the fate of the Communist Party. Karl Radek in Moscow gave his Schlageter speech, and you could see his glasses sparkle with enthusiasm from Moscow to Berlin. Comrade Zinoviev gave it his blessing: no 'national nihilism' could be tolerated in Communist ranks. And, if 'slogans' like these were issued at the top, you can imagine what effect they had down below. For the law of exaggeration from top to bottom is as valid in the Communist Party as in all similar institutions, just like the army. If the people in Moscow spoke in these terms, anyone can imagine how this was echoed lower down, when the district sergeant-majors Remmele,[1] Koenen[2] and Ruth Fischer[3] repeated what they had heard from such an illustrious source; not to speak of the petty functionaries in Saxony, Thuringia and the Rhineland. And the result of all this was that, at the end of the Ruhr-war, we did not have a strong proletarian force, but rather a nationalist-communist stench that poisoned the whole of Germany. With the same right that the Communists laid claim to the inheritance of a foundering Germany, so did the National Socialists: one lot presented themselves as national-communist, the other as communist-national; the two things were basically the same. Both staked their claims almost simultaneously; one lot in Saxony, the other in Munich. *Both* claims were rejected by history; certainly not because it sought to approve or maintain the existing situation, but simply because the people who raised their claims to the inheritance were not at all the chosen ones. We are no apologists for the past or the present; we see an end coming. But a dictatorship of Muscovite army and Austrian sexual pathology! A generous fate preserved us from this, and rightly so – historically, politically and morally.

And so we believe that in this particular assumption Trotsky's starting-point is not correct.

---

1. [Hermann Remmele was a KPD Reichstag deputy and Zentrale member at this time.]

2. [Wilhelm Koenen was a member of the KPD's Central Committee.]

3. [Ruth Fischer (born Elfriede Eisler) was cultivated by Radek as the leader of the left opposition to Levi, and gained the leadership of the KPD in 1924 with the support of Zinoviev, displaced in her turn by Thälmann. Her book *Stalin and German Communism*, written in American exile, brought her a dubious celebrity.]

III

If Trotsky's criticism is incorrect as far as its factual assumptions about German conditions in 1923 are concerned, it is all the more incomprehensible how it can have had such a powerful effect in Russia. In order to understand this, we believe that two particular features of this criticism have to be borne in mind.

First of all: the criticism places the person of Lenin in a supposed political situation, and measures against this hypothetically acting Lenin the actual person of Zinoviev. This expresses a peculiarity of the present intellectual life of the Russian Communist Party. We should make clear right away that no one can suspect us of wanting to make light of Lenin's achievement. Those people who use Marxian turns of phrase but can still see in the whole Russian Revolution nothing more than a magnified Communist putsch, are completely foreign to us and our point of view. Lenin's achievement is great and will always remain so: it was he who, for the first time, confidently faced the problem of the 'seizure of power by the proletariat'. The majority of Western socialists feared this problem like the Medusa's head. And, instead of formulating and considering this problem in specific and concrete terms, they indulge in all kinds of nice vague expressions about democracy, coalition, intermediate stages and other fine things, which, at the end of the day, amount not to revealing but rather disguising the problem. Lenin, on the other hand, had long been familiar with this problem and set out to solve it. Whether the solution found in Russia was the correct one for Russia, and whether it is directly applicable to all other countries, is a quite different question: even those who, like ourselves, do not agree with this, do not in this way diminish the magnitude of Lenin's achievement. Columbus is rightly remembered today as the discoverer of America, even if he believed he was sailing to the Indies.

But this recognition of Lenin's magnitude, which no one reproaches the Communists for and which many share with them, leads to two phenomena whose dangers we can also recognise in Trotsky's work. One of these is the rise of a Lenin philology, similar to the Goethe philology in Germany or the Pandects literature of the middle ages. In every particular situation, the sentence from Lenin is quoted – by volume, chapter, section and paragraph – that fits the given situation, or, often, does not fit it. Instead of living criticism, we have *autos epha*, the master has spoken. Trotsky not only cites Lenin's words in this way, he does so with a certain roguish justification, using Lenin's words to confront the present bodily claimants to Lenin's spirit. And, in the same vein, his opponents Zinoviev, Kamenev and Stalin bring up all Lenin's works, words and hints to refute Trotsky: the *Tausves Jonsof*[4] has not yet been written, but we can be sure that it will be.

If Lenin's person is thus at the same time both fossilised and raised to the heavens, the same thing takes place with his works. We said that Lenin's greatness was that he tackled a problem most people shied away from touching even theoretically. What raised him above the rank of other Marxists is what he achieved organisationally. These facts then led the more thoughtless of his successors to see only this organisational aspect. This is a very convenient method for dealing with all political problems. All political problems can then be solved by playing around with organisation, and it is not just real children's brains that are most successful and inventive in play, but the brains of political children as well. The history of the German Communist Party can show this. This childish impulse to play generally issues in military formulae and terms: the 'dear little ones' love nothing more than donning their helmets and brandishing their swords.

We almost have the sense that Trotsky himself, though he should be protected against this by his past – as the early debates between his group and Lenin's were in this very area – is exposed to this danger. It is no slight to the founder of the Red Army to say that he is fond of military images; they come readily to his mind. And yet, what does it mean if even Trotsky, time and again, talks almost in Zinoviev's style of separate periods of strategy and tactics, how one period gives way to another, etc.? What are tactics, other than the sum of measures required to attain a given military objective? Tactics without strategy do not make a campaign, not even a manoeuvre; strategy without tactics is an unwritten book. This has to be borne in mind, if we are to understand how senseless it is to transfer these military concepts to the proletarian class-struggle. The proletarian class-struggle does indeed have an objective: the liberation of the proletariat, the defeat of capitalism. As we

---

4. [*Tausves-Jontof* was a celebrated commentary on the Talmud, more widely known through the reference in Heinrich Heine's 'Disputation': 'If the Tausves-Jontof's nothing,/What will guide us? Woe is me!'.]

know, this objective is not reached by a pitchfork-revolution,[5] but only by the overall movement of the proletarian class. In this context, the particular movements and struggles of the class are not technical, tactical measures, but form part of the objective itself. If this idea is dismissed and tactics separated from strategy within the class-struggle, does not this make Communist politics of recent years quite ridiculous? What 'tactical' measures did this bestow on us? We had the united front, then splitting the trade-unions, then, when this came up against a brick-wall, getting together again? And the objective of 'strategy'? This was nowhere to be seen; these tactical movements showed so little planning that war-commissar Trotsky would no doubt have dismissed any general who chased the Red Army troops so aimlessly around on the Russian parade-ground. In reality, the proletarian class-struggle has no strategic or tactical objective in the military sense, and anyone operating with these ideas operates wrongly.

IV

These particularities and peculiarities – not of Lenin's, but of Leninism – have already been frequently mentioned. They only acquire their importance here in combination with the other fact that the whole struggle over Trotsky's book is waged not about a Russian question but a German one. And, yet, everyone is aware that at the root of it lie very serious differences over Russian questions, differences that divide former comrades-in-arms. What the Bolsheviks basically have to decide is essentially the following. The European revolution that was the assumption behind the Bolsheviks' action has not happened. To our mind, the fact that the Bolsheviks made this assumption is not to their detriment but to their honour; it was a socialist duty to base their politics on this likelihood. And there is no point today in asking who is to blame for the European revolution not happening, what was lacking in the West and what in Russia itself. The fact that this event did not happen is unchanged, and is forcing the Bolsheviks to certain consequences. There must be a certain

---

5. [This expression seems to have originated with Adler's review of Bernstein's *Evolutionary Socialism*, in which he accused Bernstein of caricaturing the Marxist concept of revolution.]

settling of accounts between them and the stratum that reaped the first reward from the Russian Revolution, the Russian peasants. This may take place by way of an internal transformation of the Bolsheviks, it may take place by the way of democratic education of peasant-forces, it may take place by way of a violent uprising by the peasants: but the Bolsheviks cannot avoid certain conclusions, and everything that agitates the Russian Communists at this time ultimately turns around when and how the decision will be made.

And, in the face of this problem, are the Bolsheviks battling over past affairs and German problems, completely ignoring their own? It seems to us as if the Bolshevik movement is, in a certain sense, returning to its origins here. None of us have ever really understood the Russian workers' movement of earlier years. This took place in different forms from the European. It developed on the ground of a feudal absolutism. The forms of expression of the European workers' movement elsewhere, where it grew on bourgeois-democratic soil – parliament, trade-union, press, party, co-operative – were almost or completely foreign to it. It lived in illegality and therefore developed in literary forms: the stations of its development – aside from the events of 1905 – were resolutions and splits on account of resolutions. No European workers outside of Russia would have understood a split on account of a resolution.

We were always inclined to see these phenomena in the Russian workers' movement from the passive side, to understand them as the heavy burden of persecution. Today, we are in a position to see these things, as it were, from the active side. The Bolsheviks are, as they themselves proudly say, the only legal party in Russia. They alone have freedom of press and assembly, they alone have freedom of speech. But freedom that exists just for one, a single person or a single party, is precisely no freedom. The freedom of one individual already existed for a long time in Russia: Ludwig Börne already said that there was the greatest freedom in Russia because only one person had it; the larger the number who share, the smaller the portions are. In reality, however, this greatest freedom of one is a single unfreedom: the freedom that the Bolsheviks, like the tsars, claim for themselves reduces the amount of freedom for others and, in this way, loses all its qualities. And the Bolsheviks thus suffer the same burdens from their freedom as they once suffered from their unfreedom. Because their freedom has no correlative it loses all connection to reality, becomes mere paper, and in place of real political life and the welter of views that creates this we have literature and resolutions. The history of the

Bolsheviks in recent years proves this, as likewise does the effect of this book; without this, its effect in Russia would be quite incomprehensible. And, here, it seems to us that the Bolshevik movement has reached an 'ad absurdum' point, which we already indicated a long time back: not only rigid persecution, but also rigid rule, condemn people to the life of a sect, and thus ultimately to political negation. In this sense, Trotsky's book may be of decisive significance, for who can be more aware of this than Trotsky, who in those days, ten years ago and more, pointed out with considerable scorn and irony, and on good grounds, these dark sides of Bolshevik thinking?[6] And, here also, in all likelihood, lies the international significance of Trotsky's book. In an international workers' movement that will arise anew from the embers of the last decade, and on a higher level than ever before, the Russian workers' movement will certainly not be absent: this book seems to us to be a sign of how the real interest of the workers destroys the will of an emperor, even an emperor who has made the *Communist Manifesto* a national sacrament.

28 December 1924

---

6. [Levi probably had in mind Trotsky's pamphlet of 1904, *Our Political Tasks*.]

The Retreat from Leninism*

The present heavy bureaucratic régime in the Party reflects the pressure of other classes on the proletariat.

The above words were spoken by Leon Trotsky – unfortunately only in May 1927. It was already time to express them in 1921: perhaps the Kronstadt guns in March that year anticipated the language that Stalin now speaks, and the language-teacher then was Trotsky himself. Yet the question today is not how long the Russian opposition went along with the misguided policy of the Party, what was the point that forced it into opposition, and how far it itself created the preconditions for the situation that it suffers under today. As regards the tragedy that has befallen Russia, we must content ourselves with establishing what is now the case there and what it means.

I have stated very often that the interest of the proletariat and that of the land-owning peasants are opposed to one another. The Bolsheviks made two mistakes. The first was that, with their peasant-policy of 1918 that allowed the land-hungry peasants and rural workers to become landowners, they created the basis for the intensity of opposition that

* This essay appeared in Levi's weekly *Sozialistische Politik und Wirtschaft* on 8 July 1927.

is manifest in Russia today. Perhaps, in 1918, the Bolsheviks could not have done anything other than give the land to the peasants. Perhaps, if they had not made this concession, the movement would have done away with them: at the least, the peasants would have taken the land in any case. But, from the theoretical point of view, from the standpoint of socialism, handing them the land was a mistake, and a second and bigger mistake followed. If handing over the land was, in practice, unavoidable, despite theoretically wrong, the Party should have recognised this in its statement of aims. But, instead of doing this, it made a theory out of its mistake: the theory of the solidarity of interests between workers and peasants. This was already the case under Lenin. And his successors have made it into canon-law.

Yet, both for Marxists and for anyone with some knowledge of history, it was clear what kind of solidarity this was. If there really were a solidarity of interests between property-owning peasants and non-owning workers, European history over the past three centuries would be incomprehensible. The Bolsheviks believed that they could bridge this disharmony between the two classes, overcome it, by putting both as it were into a single retort. This retort they called soviets, and, in the soviets, the contenders were combined, just as for believing Catholics spirit and body are combined in the host that they swallow. Such a mistake is quite incomprehensible for politicians coming from the school of Karl Marx: there is, unfortunately, *no* form of state that can do away with existing class-antagonisms; for the form of state is the expression and result of class-antagonisms and not their cause. If there were forms of state that could do away with such class-antagonisms, it would impossible to understand why the whole business could not simply be settled by a coalition-government. Indeed, the pretence of class-solidarity in the context of actual class-antagonisms is – historically speaking – more tolerable in the form of a coalition-government than in that of a soviet-government along Russian lines. For a coalition-government destroys the illusion of class-solidarity, contradictions open up again, and the coalition flies apart into its natural components, so that parties that were previously crippled in the coalition regain their natural functions. In the Russian model of the soviet-form, however, we experience precisely what we are experiencing in Russia today. The contradictions previously did not have a form: they are seeking their form in the single existing party, the party is dividing into fractions and splinters, with the effect that people who were formerly called friend and leader are now called traitor, and, eventually, the comrades involved will face the rifles of their comrades of yesterday. In countries where this mistake is experienced in the form of coalition-government, the crisis is already resolved when this flies apart and we then have the beginning of recovery: in the soviet-régime, the severe crisis is only beginning, and if illusions are certainly destroyed, the independent functional forms of the different classes have not yet been found. This is the situation in Russia. Because the worker is pummelled by the peasant, Stalin and Bukharin have to pummel the opposition.

If the functions of the party-leadership and the opposition in Russia are thus clear to the close observer, for the masses in Russia all this is still concealed, and, for most of them, indeed, an incomprehensible discussion about China; and the opposition in Russia – we have to say – is also unclear about the starting point of its opposition. Either it is really unclear, or it does not want to speak out. It follows from what has been said above where the underlying seat of this evil lies. This 'solidarity' between workers and peasants, however, is the real kernel of so-called Leninism; it is in this way that Leninism is supposed to have developed beyond Marxism. In actual fact, we can grant Lenin only one point – certainly no small one, and that already makes him a great man: that he recognised the particular conditions for seizing power in Russia, that he showed how to create new forms of state, and once again made the concept 'dictatorship of the proletariat' not just a phrase but a reality again, even if only for a short time. But the generalisation of all this beyond Russia and into Leninism, the canonisation of tactical moves in a particular situation, is just as much a mistake as the canonisation of the tactical or strategic turns of a field-marshal. The Germans came unstuck by canonising the Schlieffen strategy of 1914, just as the Bolsheviks are now doing with Lenin's tactic of 1917. No, we must say it openly: Lenin remains, Leninism is over. Lenin failed in believing that he had taken Marx to a further stage. We could say: nowhere has the correctness of Marxism been proven more terribly than in the end that Leninism is heading for.

After Ten Years[*]

I noticed then a sacred work of stone
Two men with callused hands bore it along.
Bid I them stay? I, Ulrich Hutten? No!
'You men, now lay this idol low!'
As I moved near they heard my call resound,
They threw, and something precious hit the ground.
– Carl Friedrich Meyer, *Hutten's Last Days*

When the Bolsheviks seized power in November 1917, they created overnight the greatest political fact there has ever been in the history of the proletariat, in the thousands of years that there have been proletarians. Christianity did indeed win the souls of slaves around the Mediterranean basin, the enthusiasm of the Crusades swept Europe like a storm, kings and rulers built empires, united peoples, led armies and changed countries: but what are all these as against the fact that the a bunch of conspirators, poor devils and émigrés under Lenin's leadership, seized power and possessed from one day to the next what no one had previously possessed: not only trust, but affection, love, and the seemingly unshakeable belief that the sun was beginning to set on the capitalist world? The hope of the distant future became an immediate promise. Was it the generals and statesmen who

* *Sozialistische Politik und Wirtschaft*, 4 November 1927.

brought the World-War to an end? The end of the World-War came when the German workers, who had told themselves for a year, amid their horrors, that the Russians had the right idea, finally went and did what the Russians had done. Then the War was at an end. There was certainly no way in which the Bolsheviks performed a greater historical service than by giving international solidarity – something previously just celebrated at international congresses and in festive greetings – visible form in this way for the first time. If anyone today asks what international solidarity is, they have only to look at that heroic deed: the inspirational example of a people raising up the hearts of the tired and defeated, giving back courage to the disheartened, calm to those in despair, pride to the humbled, humanity to the dehumanised, and doing this not with money and messages, not with decrees and resolutions, but with the mysterious mental power of heroism; and those united by such ties doing the same across trenches and frontiers. This is international solidarity. And as long as there is a proletarian history, and when the glowing cheeks of boys and girls are no longer inspired by the famous deeds of kings and rulers, but rather by the deeds of those who come from the people and struggle for the people, then the act of the Russians, the act of Lenin and the men around him, will remain unforgotten: they have built a memorial in the hearts of coming generations that is more enduring than bronze.

Will there be any trace in those future days of what lies today like a black ribbon over the splendid spectacle played out in Moscow today? Certainly not. We read in the newspapers that thousands of people, famous and unknown, representatives of art, literature and science, for the most part important in their own eyes though unknown to the outside world, have travelled to pay their respects to the new Russia. Ordinary workers have indeed been invited, to come out of their humble dwellings and dark factories and behold the miracle: but who can deny that, where, ten years ago, millions of hearts were aflame, today it is paid agitators and journalists who produce tiresome jubilee-speeches and articles from their dry bones: without enthusiasm, swing, power or vigour. And the thousands who make these visits are no longer attracted by the glorious force that captured them ten years ago, but rather by a dumb statue – rigid, unapproachable and terrifying, like all idols.

This process of ossification, how what existed in 1917 became what exists in 1927, is, like its beginning, both the most remarkable and passionate phenomenon in proletarian history. There is no need to repeat here developments that have been so often pointed out: how the very conditions for the victory of the Russian proletariat – its connection with the peasants – gave rise to the limitations of this victory. But we can stress, as we have so often done, that it was beyond the capacity of the Russian proletariat to free itself from these terrible fetters, and that the movement of the European proletarians was needed to achieve what the Russians could not do alone. There is also no purpose in indicating today the point from which the Russians can be blamed, our duty is only to show what is the case. The proletarian rising of 1917 is at an end, leaving some people disappointed and others embittered, some with a heavy head and others with insulting words. There is a rift even in the ranks of those who carried out the work of 1917 and whose deed is therefore writ-ten in the history-books; those who, yesterday, sat side by side will soon be divided by prison-walls and perhaps more, perhaps by that silent realm from which no one has returned since the time of Orpheus. We know how hatred for the present rulers of Russia exaggerates things: but, if the masters of the Kremlin, in reviewing their situation at this time, see hatred even where this is unjustified, they could still say as Frau Fönss once wrote to her grieving children: 'If you had loved me less, you would hate me less today.'[1]

Hatred or love, joy or pain: the picture of 1917 has turned to stone, and the working class, which is not cut out for idol-worship, has to take leave of these idols. We know we are the object of suspicion by the Russian Party: the only worthy celebration is that which unites Russia's great past with a great future. But it is worthy to bear in our hearts the memory from ten years ago, yet keep in mind the great goals of the workers that no longer have a place in Russia but will find their realisation from the determination and strength of those who have a life-and-death need to fulfill them: the proletarians of the world.

---

1. [See above, p. 225.]

Approaching the End*

> I dreamed I came to heaven's gate
> And found you there, my sweet!
> You sat outside next to a spring
> In which you washed your feet.
> Though all was wondrous gleaming white
> You wiped without a rest,
> And with amazing haste began
> To start your work afresh.
> I asked: 'Why are you bathing here
> With cheeks so wet with tears?'
> You said: 'Because I fell so deep in dirt
> With you in bygone years.'
>
>   – C. F. Meyer

The final act of the tragedy is approaching with frightening speed. The rattle of chains, the echo of shots, may be the final sound that gives the world notice of the fate of the Russian opposition; politically, the question is already fully developed, and the result cannot be in doubt. The present government in Russia, and the section of the Party with which this is identified, will triumph over the opposition with the same right as the Thermidoreans did over the Jacobins: Stalin has behind him not only the party-apparatus, the strongest number, but the class-interest and active will of a hundred million

---

* *Sozialistische Politik und Wirtschaft*, 18 November 1927.

peasants. And Trotsky, what does he have behind him? As far as we can get a picture of things from the unreliable reports: the old Bolsheviks, the core of the old party, the one-time group of conspirators, and perhaps a few thousand workers – even ten or a hundred thousand. But certainly not *the* working class of Russia. This is destroyed, broken up into groups and fragments – some are state-employees, some have wandered away, some are quibbling know-alls, people who discuss theses: everything but a cohesive working class, strong enough to resist, even for a short time, the forceful counter-revolutionary tendency of the peasantry. If this is how things stand, the case is then decided as far as material victory is concerned. Yet does material victory bother us socialists? Certainly, we prefer it to defeat, but we can withstand defeat, for the workers' revolution is not the work of a single day or a single battle, and we can measure the temporary character of defeat by placing it in the context of the overall proletarian movement. If we are in the right, in the context of the overall movement, then even a serious defeat is nothing more than an itch on the skin. And so, for us, the issue of Trotsky is not resolved by the question whether he is stronger than Stalin or vice versa, nor by whether he has the working class behind him or not. The only question for us today is whether he has with him, as well as a few thousand people, the ideals of socialism, whether he and his cause have a great future before them as well as a great past behind. This alone is the question that decides our position towards the Russian opposition.

The issue in Russia has been no secret for many years. It has been known for half a decade and more. I can cite a few sentences here from an article I wrote in July 1922, at the very beginnings of the NEP – for the sake of a check:

> It will probably be argued that the Russian Communist Party will even be up to this task [i.e. of preserving the proletarian character of the Soviet state], that the granting of capitalist concessions is a matter for the Soviet government and not the Russian Communist Party as such. This kind of view is refuted not only by the fact of a personal union between the one and the other in all decisive functions. It is also refuted by the very ideology of the Russian Communists, for whom the dictatorship of the proletariat can only ever mean the dictatorship of the Communist Party. It is simply impossible to pursue the policy of the Communist Party and the proletarian dictatorship according to a system of double bookkeeping. At the moment that the Communist Party seeks to overcome the dialectic of history by,

on the one hand – in the Soviet state – bending to the capitalist interest, and on the other hand – in party-work – to the proletarian interest, at that moment this dialectic turns against the Communists themselves; they will be torn apart by the contending forces. This is the karma that prevails over any party and any government. From this point of view, we see the present policy of concessions as a fateful one, and marking the beginning of the end of the Russian Communists (even if people's commissars remain).

There is nothing to be added here. The moment at which this dreadful law begins to operate has arrived: anyone who still keeps a spark of communism in their soul has left the Party and must leave it. The old guard, who withstood tsarism for so many difficult years, who held high the ideals of socialism in poverty and squalor, in prison and banishment, have again come together to fight desperately for the lost paradise. They stand there empty-handed, the sweetness of power has escaped them, and they would like to believe they are back where they were in 1905: at the foot of the great revolutionary hill. If only this was the case!

They did have one thing at that time. They had fame and credence with the masses that they were the coming liberators of the proletariat. Every worker in Russia, and every peasant, knew that, on one side, was the tsar with his butchers, on the other, the socialists, the liberators. And every gallows that was built, every shot that echoed, every sigh, every complaint, every cry of pain from the prisons, simply carried the fame of the Russian Social Democrats onward from town to town, from village to village. This was the great and imperishable legacy that the Social Democrats – with the Bolsheviks to the fore – brought with them from the first Russian Revolution, and with which they won the victory of 1917.

Has the opposition in Russia today still kept or won something of this? Perhaps one of them just a bit. Trotsky – it is true – was the first person, already at the start of 1922, to see the dangers and warn against them. But, for a long time, he kept solidarity with the government and responsibility for it. And, as for the others: Zinoviev, Radek and company. Were they not the loudest in their cries and shouts against Trotsky's criticism? Was it not Radek, as early as 1921, who stirred up antagonism in Germany towards Trotsky and other critics, and made himself the grand inquisitor of the sacred doctrine of NEP?

But everyone makes mistakes, people said; these people may have made mistakes in the past, now they are doing the right thing. This is certainly true. But it is impossible for them to do the right thing, as they are never able to gain a perceptible distance from the Soviet power whose actions they championed for so long. What are they doing today? Putting forward theses about Russia's defeat in China, about the Anglo-Russian Committee in England.[1] It may be that their theses are right. But what a terrible recognition of their situation; with this too they believe they are still in 1905, when they, the motley crew of yesterday and today, masters only of a distant land in the future, formulated theses in little splinter-groups, and one group distinguished itself from another like black from white. Today *theses* have paled, they are no longer a differentiating sign, ten years after powerful deeds were written in the heavens in letters of flame. Theses are no longer a platform: the men who today gather round the theses of the opposition and believe they are doing something when they produce ten-pfennig pamphlets, forget that these are outgrown and how their historical greatness contrasts with their present smallness.

No, both sides in Russia, the Stalinists on the one hand, because of their betrayal – to use a favourite Bolshevik word – and the others because of their actions and mistakes, will no longer be the generation to set aside and correct the mistakes of the Russian Revolution. Marx's fearful prophecy is truer of them than it was when he wrote: 'The present generation is like the Jews that Moses led through the desert. Not only has it a world to conquer, but it must perish to make way for the people who have grown up for a new world.' They went along too far with Stalin; nothing any more will cleanse them.

It is not in Russia that this generation will grow up. The entire heavy responsibility for the future lies again on the shoulders of the European proletariat. It will again be from our own ranks that the men will arise who will be great revolutionary leaders of coming struggles. Who will be able to shoulder such a burden of responsibility?

---

1. [This would particularly refer to Trotsky's 1927 articles 'The Struggle for Peace and the Anglo-Russian Committee', and 'The Chinese Revolution and the Theses of Comrade Stalin'.]

The most terrible tragedy of the proletariat is not without its satyr-play. The Central Committee of the German Communist Party, a dozen secretaries in Rosenthaler Strasse in Berlin, at their green baize table, by a warm stove, with salaries and pension-plans, pass a resolution in which they demand 'the most severe measures' against those whose hands they had previously eaten from, people in relation whom, despite everything, they do not have the stature of a mouse in relation to an elephant. Enough to make anyone feel ill!

Return[*]

1907. On a January day, one of those transports set out: a group of grey detainees, a group of soldiers, a few officers busy giving orders in their rasping voices. A prison-door opens, the day gets under way, and ends not with freedom but with the infinite Siberian loneliness, an immensity all around that is like a second prison. One of this troop is Leon Trotsky: his guard are tsarist soldiers, his clothing that of a prisoner, his chains those of barbarism, and what is really his is only the star on his breast. When he reached Siberia he could write in his diary:

> Everything in Siberia is still as it was five or ten years ago, and yet at the same time so much has changed. Not only the Siberian soldiers, but also the Siberian *cheldonii* (peasants), who discuss political questions and discuss whether 'all this' will soon be at an end. Our driver, a youngster of thirteen – he assures us he is already all of fifteen – keeps singing out loud 'Arise, ye starvelings from your slumbers...' The soldiers threaten to report the singer to the officers, but good-naturedly...

1928. Another rising, not in St Petersburg, now called Leningrad, but in the old unchanged Moscow: prison-clothing may have been abandoned,

* *Sozialistische Politik und Wirtschaft*, 13 January 1928.

but, otherwise, things are just the same. Soldiers and officers, no longer the tsarist bandits but Red Army men, no longer the St Michael's cross but the red star; after the rising, they lead a group of some few dozen people to Siberia, where the infinite expanse is a prison, and, in the midst of this small handful, is the man who founded and built up the Red Army: Leon Trotsky. And, once more on the way, soldiers and driver sing aloud and hum: 'Arise, ye starvelings from your slumbers...' But the lips of the men being exiled remain sealed, and in their eyes is only the fire of hatred; for the song being sung has changed from a song of rebellion to a state-anthem, and the men are prisoners of the state, the state that they carried in their heart, one could say, when they took this journey for the first time twenty years ago. It was perhaps only in the French Revolution that people sitting behind bars, or on their way to the guillotine, heard the song of their torturers in their ears, a song that they, the tortured, had once created and sung. What Trotsky must recognise on this road is the difference between that time and now: this is the terrible tragedy of a lost revolution. And if it had only been defeated in the way that it triumphed – if its strong wings had been clipped by a visible arrow, if an enemy-bullet had struck its heart, it would have fallen with its honour intact. But, now, it is those who have defeated the revolution who are singing, and their songs sound like scorn in the ears of those who are now once more prisoners. This is the most frightful of tragedies, and Leon Trotsky and his friends now have the occasion to measure its full depth.

There is no need here to discuss how much the 'guilty' themselves are to blame. What has now happened had been predictable already for a long time; already when Karl Radek hurled thunder and lightning as the representative of the gods, we could see that it would end like this. If it were now only Zinoviev and Radek, Trotsky and Kamenev and a few more who are being sent to Siberia, we could console ourselves with some of those proverbial words of wisdom that the petty-bourgeois philistines have at their disposal in such cases. In reality, however, it is impossible to overlook that everything that is happening here will serve the bourgeoisie as material to use against the whole workers' movement. Because the Russian movement, in its early days, was a part of the world-movement of workers, and because it had an influence on the workers of the whole world, its fate is shared by us all. And this is the result of so much tiring effort, so much pain and sacrifice, so many battles and victories, so much night-time study, the result of a movement that sought to reshape and liberate the world, that, after ten years' government, a 'proletarian' movement stands precisely at this point, has not a halfpenny of understanding more or less than the tsarist government, so that it too can do nothing better than exile people to Siberia – simply that the tsar had his enemies exiled with their own flesh and blood, their partners. Who will be surprised that, in the light of these results, the bourgeoisie are rubbing their hands, just as they rubbed their hands when Emil Höllein[1] explained how beheading and hanging are perfectly moral, as long as they take place in a proletarian state.

For the working class, it is a fearsome warning, to take account of their situation and to recognise what is at the bottom of this fearsome event. The attempt has been made to place the blame on the concept of 'dictatorship of the proletariat'. If the Bolsheviks had done nothing more than practise the dictatorship of the proletariat, they would never have come unstuck as badly as they did. But they did something else. They did not practise the dictatorship of the proletariat against an enemy-class, but began first of all to 'guide' the proletariat, then to 'lead' it, then to correct it, then to discipline it, then to exercise it, then to command it, then to bully it, then to torment it, then to terrorise it, in the name of this 'dictatorship'. In this completely misguided and upside-down theory of the 'role of the Party', the omnipotence of a central committee in the Party, the divinity of a few bonzes, lies the beginning and the end of what is happening now in Russia. It is not socialism and not the proletariat that have collapsed in Russia, rather the doctrine that has been practised. The proletariat is a great and powerful body, more powerful in its forces than any other class. What this strong body needs in order to rule, *the will* to power, no one can give it, it must create it itself out of the thousandfold play of a thousand tiny cells, each of which has its own life. This is the meaning of *democracy* within the working class and within the party, to form such a will *in this way*. The Bolsheviks believed that they could go straight to heaven with the wisdom and omnipotence of a 'central committee', but, instead of heaven, they have ended up in the Siberian tundra. What they have exiled there is not just three dozen 'oppositionists', but their own party-history.

---

1. [Emil Höllein, KPD deputy in the Reichstag since 1920, and, from 1921, editor of *International Press Correspondence*.]

Part Four

The German Republic

The Murder of Erzberger*

DR. DEPUTY LEVI: Ladies and gentlemen, one might actually be surprised that the murder of former deputy Erzberger should have aroused such great indignation and deep shock in Germany. For we have to say that the murder of Erzberger is nothing unusual or new – neither in the fact of the murder, nor with respect to the milieu involved.

['*Very true!*' FROM THE COMMUNISTS][1]

Very many people have been murdered since November 1918, murdered by the political Right.

['*Very true!*' FROM THE COMMUNISTS. – DENIAL FROM THE RIGHT]

During the Revolution not only were members of left parties murdered, and particularly friends of ours, but murder has already made its way previously into the ranks of the Centre. I recall the Catholic lay brothers in Munich.

---

* Reichstag speech of 1 October 1921 (*Reichstagprotokolle*, vol. 351, p. 4705ff.) [The Centre Party politician Matthias Erzberger, despite having drafted the German war-aims of September 1914, publicly attacked the war-effort in 1917 and called for a negotiated peace. He headed the German delegation that signed the armistice on 11 November 1918, and, as finance-minister, endorsed the Versailles Treaty in 1919. Branded by the Right as one of the 'November criminals', he was murdered in Baden on 26 August 1921 by members of Organisation Consul.]

1. [Levi spoke on behalf of the KAG group of thirteen deputies who had left the KPD with him, only two of their colleagues remaining in the Party. In the parliamentary report, they are still jointly referred to as Communists.]

[*'Very true!'* FROM THE COMMUNISTS]

Who were murdered in a bestial and shameless fashion, and whose murderers found judges whose verdict amounted to an instigation to new murder.

[LIVELY AGREEMENT FROM THE COMMUNISTS]

The forces that have the murder of Erzberger on their conscience, those who carried it out, have been an essential component of the structure of German society, of the German social order, since the outbreak of the Revolution. To the great surprise of all those gentlemen who, in these three years, have enjoyed the support of these social forces, these gentlemen did not see what for anyone who thinks historically is self-evident: that, one day, these social forces were bound to gain a life of their own, and turn with historical necessity against everything that stood in their way, including those who had believed themselves to be the masters of these social forces.

[*'Quite right!'* FROM THE COMMUNISTS]

Which classes, which strata, which social forces have been so greatly pampered in the three years of the German Republic? They are the old military strata, the same generals who, for four years, waged murder abroad, the same lieutenants who, in some cases with a personal courage that is not to be denied, served in the front-ranks, but partly also lieutenants and others who believed they best served their fatherland during the War by a fine life at headquarters: quite a large stratum, whom you could almost view with a certain sympathy when the War came to an end; they were then socially uprooted, their existence had been undermined. These social forces, just like large strata that are separated from their class on the proletarian side, socially uprooted and necessarily assuming lumpenproletarian features, these forces on the side of the right necessarily become lumpenproletarians when there are uprooted, and it is they who have been deliberately cultivated by Noske for three years and used in the service of the Republic, and who now have perfected their work.

Herr Bernstein[2] gestures that this is not so. Then I will just remind you of a word of Noske's – he is still in the Party, is he not? – that he uttered one day in cold blood, I believe in the National Assembly: 'If I have to defend myself, I don't ask who comes to my aid; anyone is welcome!' You will not deny,

---

2. [Eduard Bernstein, the founder of 'revisionism', had opposed militarism before 1914 and was one of the founders of the USPD in 1917, though among the first to return to the Majority-party in 1919.]

Herr Deputy Bernstein, that this was precisely the statesmanlike principle on which your party-colleague Noske based himself, and that this very statesmanlike principle became the principle of your party, as long as it was in a leading position to conduct the business of the German Republic.

['*Very true!*' FROM THE COMMUNISTS. DEPUTY BERNSTEIN: '*That is wrong!*']

And, so, it is a particular social force from which the German Republic drew support that has now turned against the Republic. But all these forces in themselves – for they are few in number and without a social foundation – would not be able to work the evil that they are still working today in Germany, if they did have not still today an extremely close link into the ranks of the bourgeois parties.

I don't know, if I look from right to left, where I should draw the line.

['*Very true!*' FROM THE COMMUNISTS]

There is a common feeling of nationalism, and I would ask Herr Deputy Scheidemann to consider, when he uses this word for love of the fatherland – and the word seems recently to please him very well, as I heard it from him the other day, two weeks ago – if Herr Deputy Scheidemann and his party-colleagues bear this word so deep in their hearts and are always using it, to consider how this feeds the ideology, I would say, that forms the common tie between all the bourgeois parties and those circles that today everyone in this house wants to shake off. Karl Marx, who is certainly not unknown to Herr Deputy Scheidemann, and has not been completely shaken off, despite the Görlitz Congress,[3] said that the proletarians have no fatherland, and what they do not have cannot be taken away from them.

[DISTURBANCE AND SHOUTS FROM THE SOCIAL DEMOCRATS]

Indeed, Herr Deputy Bernstein, there is nothing you need to tell me; I know perfectly well that the sentences that you don't like either don't exist in Marx or were slips of his pen.

[DISTURBANCE. DEPUTY BERNSTEIN: '*Marx said the opposite, the workers have to defend their country!*' – INTERJECTIONS FROM THE COMMUNISTS AND THE RIGHT]

I recall the comedy of justice in connection with the Arco case,[4] a comedy performed not only in court but also outside, where students demonstrated

---

3. [The programme that the SPD adopted at Görlitz in 1921 to replace the Erfurt Programme dropped the concept of class-struggle.]

4. [Count Anton Arco-Valley, the officer who murdered Kurt Eisner in 1919, was condemned to death, his sentence being commuted to life-imprisonment and sus-

in support of the murderer of Eisner and the Bavarian government celebrated the reprieve of his murderer. This is cultivation of the murder-mentality, cultivation on the part of the authorities.

[SHOUTS FROM THE COMMUNISTS: '*And Pöhner will be the judge again!*']

Yes, Pöhner[5] will be the judge again, the same Pöhner who calmly tolerated Arco being celebrated for years in Munich, precisely from where the murderers were recently dispatched against Erzberger, being celebrated as a national hero in poems, postcards, posters on walls and columns. Herr von Pöhner wanted to see nothing and did see nothing.

I would like in this connection to ask the Reich government something, though it is not represented here today. What is its position on this matter? Just an outward look at the legal prosecution for the murder of Erzberger gives the impression that something very odd is going on. I am aware that the Baden authorities – I believe on 2 September, reached Munich at 11 am, but, at 8 am, the murderers had already been put on the train.

I would therefore have liked the Reich government to answer the question whether it had directed its attention to the point that there was undoubtedly here a connection between the murderers and their associates on the one hand, and certain circles in Munich on the other, who were aware of the arrival of the Baden authorities, or, to put it clearly, the only place that would have known about this, the Munich police-headquarters under the direction of Herr Pöhner.

['*Very true!*' FROM THE COMMUNISTS]

If I have shown, as I believe, that there are deep inner connections between the murderers and the milieu from which they came on the one hand, and the structure and external organisation of the German Republic on the other, it is truly putting the cat among the pigeons to entrust the defence of this republic now to the German civil service and to laws of the Republic that are applied by those who formerly, whether deliberately or otherwise – we can leave this undecided – were accomplices of the gentlemen who carried out the murder. And, here, I believe that, if the German Republic can and should be main-

---

pended in 1924 (when he was evicted from his cell to make room for Hitler); he was pardoned completely in 1927.]

5. [Ernst Pöhner, the Munich police-chief in the early 1920s, then minister of justice in 1923. Hitler planned to appoint him Bavarian prime minister in his attempted putsch of November 1923, and he was condemned to five years' imprisonment.]

tained, the saying of old Sallust, that states can only be maintained by the forces that created them, is true for it as well.

And it is a logical and historical law that this creation of the German proletariat cannot be maintained without the forces of the German proletariat.

I would like to say a word here on our position as Communists towards the question of the German Republic. For perhaps some people found it rather unexpected when the previous speaker, Frau Zetkin, also avowed her recognition of the German Republic in this enthusiastic and honest fashion. It goes without saying – this we do not deny – that the German Republic has no more eternal value for us Communists than does any other existing form of government.

[SHOUT FROM THE RIGHT: '*Neither for us!*']

But we do not need Tillessen[6] and company to abolish it again. We do not see it as a form of government with an eternal value, and we are convinced that the social ills of our time can only be healed in a form of government that offers the creative forces of the proletariat freer room for development than a bourgeois republic can.

['*Very true!*' FROM THE COMMUNISTS]

We also believe – and this is a point on which we differ from the gentlemen of the Social Democrats – that the forces of the German proletariat in November 1918 and the following months were strong enough that a form of government could have been created which, while it could not yet have brought in socialism and communism – perhaps you [TO THE SOCIAL DEMOCRATS] are right here – would, at all events, have provided the forces of the proletariat with freer room for development than the form of the present state.

['*Quite right!*' FROM THE COMMUNISTS. – SHOUTS FROM THE SOCIAL DEMOCRATS]

I would like to say to the gentlemen who have made such loud interjections that it is, I believe, uncontested that the Social-Democratic Party, already on the next day after the overthrow, i.e. on 10 November 1918, acknowledged the republican form of state that exists today, and, from this first day, limited and fettered the forces of the proletariat so that they would remain within the bounds of this party's programme.

---

6. [Heinrich Tillessen, one of the two murderers of Erzberger. He had already taken part in the Kapp Putsch, and was sentenced to three years' imprisonment for the murder of Erzberger, though he only served part of this term.]

[*'Very true!'* FROM THE COMMUNISTS]

We are convinced that the transformation of present social relations, a goal which is also apparently that of the Social-Democratic Party, cannot take place in the framework of the present republic. And, for this reason, we also acknowledge at this point our belief in the dictatorship of the proletariat, as we have always done. By the dictatorship of the proletariat we understand – and, here, we mark a sharp difference from all those who have some other kind of belief and understand, by the dictatorship of the proletariat, the command of some very energetic and clever minority – a form of government in which the will of the producers, i.e. of the millions working out there, is decisive, and in which a democratic form does not give the possessing classes the possibility of sabotaging the will of these millions of producers.

Despite this understanding, we do not deny that the present form of government possesses for the proletariat a value to be defended in relation to the past form. From this point of view, therefore, without denying our future goal, we insist that we do defend the democratic republic even in the form in which it exists today. We emphasise that the true defence of this republic can only take place if a united front – to use this favourite term – of the proletariat is established at least on these concrete questions, which can be the most urgent ones in certain historical situations.

I am glad, in this connection, that the honourable previous speaker, Frau Zetkin, has stressed this point here,[7] and, in her explanations, has completely distanced herself from the idea that it is the task of the Communists to take certain energetic measures against the proletariat itself, to exert a pressure on the proletariat so that it does certain things which, at present, it does not want to do – whether one is sorry about this or not. It is also not the task of the Communists to establish this united front in such a form that, as is said in certain documents that are certainly familiar to the previous speaker, the Communists pull certain parts of the proletariat into struggle even when it is clear that the forces are insufficient. This is not the united front of the proletariat. We rather see, despite all differences that we have about the way forward and particular circumstances – I don't know to what extent we differ on this point also from the Social Democrats, even about the goal – that the united front can only be possible if there is unity and unanimity about the most urgent

---

7. [Clara Zetkin had remained in the KPD after the break with the 'Levites'.]

questions of the day, the most necessary tasks of the proletariat, and, from this view of ours as well, there also results the whole difference in our position towards the Republic, which, for us, is as little an ultimate goal as it is for the gentlemen of the Right, and distinguishes us from other parties.

It has indeed become popular recently to cast Communists and German nationalists together as apostles of Right and Left, and the Reich Chancellor[8] also maintained yesterday that the 'common measure' here is that one strikes left and the other right. But there is an absolute distinction between our view of violence and that on your side [TO THE RIGHT], namely that you, in contrast to us, are trying to go back to something that previously existed, and you want something that is historically impossible, so that you are not able to call on forces whose victory is certain. And, for this reason, because of the deep impotence to which history has condemned you, you seize hold of all methods that historical impotence customarily applies, the methods of terror, of personal violence, of assassination.

These are the methods that necessarily grow out of your historical situation.

We have a more pleasant aspect. We are not trying to return to something past, but forward to something coming, something superior to what exists today. We know that the masses and history bears us and our goals forward, and, for this reason, we can renounce assassination and the like, as we shall be victorious without this.

['Bravo!' FROM THE COMMUNISTS]

---

8. [Joseph Wirth of the Centre Party was the chancellor at this point.]

The Needs of the Hour*

The Kommunistische Arbeitsgemeinschaft has come
to an end. It was never a party and never intended
to be one. We are in a party once again. We are
again in the setting that is 'naturally ordained' to
embrace everything proletarian, outside of which
politics ceases and political hydrotherapy or mysti-
cism begins. We have joined the Independent Social-
Democratic Party without any false cheering, and
believe we can assume from more than one sign
that such cheering is also absent on the side of our
present party-comrades. On both sides, the step was
taken in the knowledge that it is *one* of the steps – not
the final one – that had to be taken in order to reach a
different organisational configuration of the overall
proletarian movement. How necessary this is, how
the present organisational form, or rather formless-
ness, presents an extreme danger, that of the crip-
pling and retreat of the proletarian movement for
perhaps a number of decades, is clearly understood
by all those who have their place in the proletarian
movement. But, as to *how* this change can be brought
about or striven for, ideas are equally unclear, and
discussion of this is the real issue behind all discussions and divisions in the proletarian camp and the
German proletarian parties.

---

* Published in Levi's weekly *Unser Weg*, no. 7, 1922.

Rote Fahne makes hay while the sun shines. The 'decomposition of the USPD' was a juicy morsel for it, and it has nothing more to say. But this very question is being discussed in the USPD with greater eagerness and attention than in other parties, and dust is flying here too. Nowhere, until now, has the discussion led to the forms that are customary with the Communist Party in such cases. Not once has the word 'traitor' been heard, there have been no mass-excommunications or bannings, and no one has yet declared that someone else is a spy who has wormed their way into a party or organisational position. Because there are none of these side-effects, despite the existence of a serious problem, *Rote Fahne* calls the process one of decomposition, whereas, if all these side-effects were present, they would be able to speak of a 'purge', 'concentration', 'consolidation of the party', etc. So this debate is still under way, and we declare that we do not lament we are joining this party at a time when such a debate is under way, which forces everyone to take a position towards a question that is the most important one facing the workers' movement at the present time.

As already said, we see the *kernel* of the debate within the USPD as lying in the need felt to change the organisational form that divides the working class into three parties. Everything else that is discussed in this connection, the question of coalition-policy, 'practice' or 'agitation', compromise over taxation or not, are only questions that have to be discussed in order to work out on what lines this organisational change should proceed.

We need not repeat here that we recognise the necessity for a combination of proletarian forces; we have made this point clear more than once in the past year. The workers' movement, particularly in Germany, cannot endure the way it is now, and it will not endure in this way. This is not a conclusion we draw on any ideological grounds. The fact that the KAG has joined the USPD, and that some comrades have left the USPD, all clearly indicates that the German proletarian movement is not on its natural bed, but still in flux and recomposition.

But two different ideas are possible as to *how* the restructuring will happen, and we should distinguish these. One of them is organisational, which we see represented by Kautsky. Kautsky has not welcomed our entry into the USPD very warmly. He spoke of the return of a handful of bankrupt communists. One might contest the tastefulness of this expression, but such aesthetic questions are beyond discussion. At most, the usefulness of this expression could be debated; for we believe that the path Kautsky recommends and is perhaps also following may bring him into a position in which he will be himself protected by a greeting of this kind only by the fact that the editors of *Vorwärts*, as has to be recognised, are careful and rarely tasteless. Those who believe today that the unification of USPD and SPD is merely an organisational act, a decision for a party-congress or a leadership-conference, in our view take no account of the conditions of the German workers' movement and succumb to illusions. The opposition in the German workers' movement today is not an organisational but a political one, with not only a political present – on coalition-policy, for example – but a history that, though only eight years, has been highly eventful, vigorous and full of sacrifice – and unfortunately, neither past nor present can be set aside by a stroke of the pen, a mere organisational measure.

The change in the organisational situation of the workers' movement can only be brought about by political means and in a political way, just as it came about through political conditions and continues to depend on political conditions. We believe that it can be taken for granted here that a change in these conditions does not just consist in recognising the – real or apparent – fact that the Social-Democratic Party is at present the strongest component of the workers' movement, and accepting its political programme and tactics so as to alter conditions 'politically'. This attempt is one of those purely organisational attempts that we already mentioned, simply that it is not a paragraph about organisational status that would be changed, but, rather, a paragraph in the party-programme. We believe, rather, that a change in political conditions will arise first of all from an increased understanding by the proletariat of its class-situation. What did the 'split' in the proletariat arise from? From the fact that broad layers of the proletariat lost sight of their enduring proletarian class-interest in the fog of nationalistic phrases, in the rush of 'national' enthusiasm, and sought their fortune in a war-situation that is now completely in the past. How can this split be overcome? By recognition of the fact that *all* workers, those 'victorious' in the War as well as those defeated, the Social Democrats 'victorious' in the Revolution, just like the 'defeated' Communists – are all, in actual fact, defeated, and confront an exploitative and ravening capitalism that exploits and oppresses everyone *more* than it did before the War.

Only a basic recognition of this can be the basis for unification, and this basic recognition needs, first of all, as its first precondition, to create a political situation that finds the workers' parties as parties of a *single* class in its natural community: a class-community against the capitalist parties, and expressed in parliamentary terms as opposition. It is completely inconceivable that a unification of the proletariat could take place in any other situation and under different preconditions. Parties can pass away, break up, be destroyed or collapse: without these basic preconditions, any change in party-terms will never take the form of a genuine unification of the political effort of the proletarian class.

Anyone can acknowledge these principles, no matter how much or how little of its particular tenets the USPD needs to abandon in order to prepare the ground for the unification of the proletariat. We believe that insisting on this basis, even in a situation that is more devoid of prospects than the present situation seems to be, is not simply a politics of agitation. We also believe, however, that defending this basis is an extremely real and fruitful policy, and serves the immediate and urgent aims and goals of the working class. For, if we said above that common recognition of the class-situation of the proletariat as the only defeated party in the World-War was the precondition, we can go on to say that acknowledgement of this fact amounts to a considerable advance in relation to both Right and Left. The mere fact that, in recent days, the executives of the three Internationals have been meeting together[1] is – whatever the 'practical' outcome – a sign of advance in this recognition. How rapid and strong this advance will be can be judged by someone who wagered on the possibility of such coming together a year ago. The recognition has grown on *both* sides – that of Moscow as well as that of the Social Democrats.

A year has gone by since Moscow tried its March putsch, and pronounced bans and prohibitions, excommunications and curses, on those who did not believe in the unsurpassable appropriateness of this kind of victorious forward march. How times have changed. To recognise this, read, for example, Clara Zetkin's article in *Rote Fahne* of 2 April, in which she welcomes the meeting of the executives and in which we are happy to note two things: that it is now safe to express *non*-Bolshevik views in the Communist International, and

---

1. [From 2 to 5 April 1922, representatives of the Socialist International, the Communist International, and the International Working Union of Socialist Parties (see p. 98, note 5) met in Berlin to discuss the possibilities of unification.]

that Clara Zetkin makes use of this opportunity with her customary enthusiasm. She writes:

> The precondition for what should be is the open and unrestrained expression of how things now are. That is, the impossibility of bringing together the supporters of the three great tendencies of the workers' movement nationally and internationally in a unified organisation *at the present time*. The differences that separate them on questions of principle and tactics are too great....
>
> We had to separate, nationally and internationally, in order to concentrate nationally and internationally the power that has to be united if the proletariat is to be victorious in this struggle. Unity and cohesion of all who want proletarian revolution and are determined to struggle for it coolly and calmly, and with bold judgement.
>
> This can only be achieved by unity in a common struggle for defence against the pressure from the bourgeoisie of all countries to impose on the proletariat both the burdens of the War and the costs of rebuilding the shattered economy. Action, not discussion, must be the sign under which the international discussions proceed.

We do not conceal from ourselves for a moment that this is not and cannot be the view of the Moscow International, and we must even reckon with the possibility that Clara Zetkin herself, however hard she finds this personally, will have, for the sake of discipline, to express, from time to time, a different viewpoint. But however this may be, and even though one swallow does not make a summer, we learn here from an authoritative Communist source, for the first time:

> that *at the present time* (we emphasise) unification is not possible,
> that what is necessary is 'unity and cohesion of all who want proletarian revolution and are determined to struggle for it coolly and calmly, and with bold judgement'. Nothing more, therefore, about the Twenty-One Conditions, but a single condition, and reasonably well put;
> that what must follow will be through 'common struggle for defence against the pressure from the bourgeoisie of all countries'.

This is very true, and, in fact, an immense departure from all Bolshevik phrases, a change that can only fill us with satisfaction. A satisfaction not reduced but strengthened by the added sentence: 'Action, nor discussion, must be the sign under which the international discussions proceed.' For no one, least of all a woman with such a lofty train of ideas, can fail to conclude that if the word here and in the present situation is 'action', this cannot be anything remotely similar to the ideas of Zinoviev and Béla Kun, but, rather, a long, tough struggle, over years or even – we hope not – decades, conducted with all parliamentary and non-parliamentary means, including trade-union, economic and others. Whoever seeks a common struggle for the situation in which the proletariat finds itself today, and seeks to make use of the situation, must keep clearly in mind – as Clara Zetkin undoubtedly does – that neither the situation will change from one day to the next, nor will the common struggle end tomorrow, but that both the situation and the common struggle are to be envisaged for a lengthy period, and – as everything suggests – will not be suddenly terminated.

We do not blind ourselves to the fact that nothing corresponding to this can be reported from the right wing of the workers' movement. We do not draw from this the conclusion that, because on the Right there is stronger resistance to this kind of unification of the proletarian class, it is necessary, in order to reach an 'agreement', to make that much more in the way of concessions in this direction. It is not always good policy to do this kind of thing. Often, it is far better to be strong and able to wait. We do not believe there is any occasion for a loss of nerve. We need not attempt a magic change in the SPD or inject it with a deadly pathogen. The dialectic of history will not be cheated, and will do its work. It must and will divide labour from capital and bring labour together with labour, and in this way create the first precondition that will lead to the real unification of the working class, making a future virtue from the needs of the hour.

Why Are We Joining the United Social-Democratic Party?*

I

The World-War, born out of imperialist lunacy, came to an end in a capitalist witches' Sabbath. The struggle for the 'freedom of nations', for the welfare of 'oppressed peoples', for 'healing the world the German way', found its grotesque conclusion: absconding potentates, runaway generals, in other words shouting and screaming, on the one hand, hate-filled 'national liberators' greedy for land and people, on the other – this is the true picture of the ideals that capitalism proclaims. On both sides of the frontiers, poverty, squalor and the rising impoverishment of the working masses remain the same. After a brief period of false economic boom, the bloody losses that the working class suffered from the War have been followed by the leaden misery of unemployment and hunger. In England, France, Italy and America, the proletariat enjoy no victory. It is the bourgeoisies who have triumphed. Our brothers, for their part, have been beaten on all sides. But the proletarians of Germany do not feel the fate of defeat any the less. If they are not unemployed, the lash of hunger drives

---

* *Unser Weg*, no. 16, 1922. [The United Social-Democratic Party or VSPD was formed by a merger between the USPD and SPD in September 1922; the two Reichstag fractions had already merged in July. In 1924, the united party took the name of the old SPD.]

them to work each day, a work that gives them not a fraction of the scanty wages of the prewar-time. In those days, though the proletarian condition was too poor for them to be able to fully develop their mental and moral powers, they could at least clothe their children, start a home, escape once a week from the gloomy sea of buildings, and build up a steadily growing wealth of knowledge from newspapers and books. Those days are gone. The shirt that the youngest boy needs, the pair of shoes for the eldest, the jacket that the husband needs for work, the bread and potatoes that the housewife has to put on the table – each of these is a tragedy repeated a million times each day. The maintenance of life and with it the ability to work, training and therefore the quality of work, nutrition and thus a successful new generation of the proletarian class, are all on the decline. This is the result of the Great War, this is the conclusion to the liberation of nations. The German proletarians bore a great deal until this came to an end. They showed infinite patience, and, when the burden of war became intolerable to them, they cast it off.

The outbreak of revolution divided the German proletariat more than the outbreak of war had done. At that time, there was a battle of opinions, but, now, there was a battle with weapons. Many people, ourselves included, believed that the end of the international capitalists' war against the workers was bound to turn into a war of workers against capitalists; they believed that it was a proletarian duty, trusting in the great international wave of proletarian revolution, to anticipate the goals of socialism; and, to this belief, they sacrificed their careers and often their lives. It is idle today to go into how this happened. Those of us who shared this belief have been defeated in Germany. No one can say whether, if we had been victorious here in Germany, the international power of socialism would have been great enough to change the fate that burdens Germany and the world today, whether it would have been possible also to arouse the proletarians of other countries to follow this example. We can say only one thing: those who were of a different opinion from our own also failed to achieve the goal of their hopes. The German Republic is not firmly established. The united German state is threatened by monarchist rebels. A counter-revolutionary Reichswehr is robbing it of free breath. A rebellious caste of officials lames its arms and legs. Cowardly assassination creeps like poison through its veins. On all sides, monarchists both secret and overt wait for the moment when the improvement of the external situation will facilitate a coup d'état. The one thing that the Revolution has brought the

German workers is in danger. This is the hour when German workers find themselves together in protecting the single common thing that they have left. Proud, at the end of the horror, to have achieved the Republic, the basis for a broad development of their class in the struggle for socialism, the German workers find themselves together in defending this, in the knowledge that further strife and contention about what might have been possible in a different situation will not help one or the other party to maintain the little that we have left from 9 November 1918. No one's dreams and hopes of that time have been fulfilled: but, as the day of the first great movement of the German proletariat, its first clearly visibly victory, the German workers remember it and stand by its fruit, the German Republic – despite everything.

II

The loyalty of the German workers to the German Republic, and the will to protect and preserve it with all means, is not just Platonic. This loyalty does not live off memories, neither of previous times nor of 9 November 1918. The German Republic, as a part of the history of the working class and a first achievement of its struggle for liberation, can only be preserved as long as it remains an essential part of the striving of the working class. If the German Republic loses this living connection with the struggling working masses, it will be lost. It can only be maintained by the force by which it was created. From this point of view, it is the first requirement of a socialist workers' politics to purge the Republic of all those elements that, in the eyes of the workers, and rightly, are perceived as something alien and hostile. The judiciary that scoffs at the Republic and its laws, the state-officials who turn these laws into their opposite, the governments that abuse the Republic's own laws against the Republic, the officers who whip up soldiers, the sons of the people, against their own people – a socialist party has to combat these not with speeches and resolutions, but with concrete and directly effective measures, and not only because of an immediately threatening danger, but to show the working class the extent to which it is in a position to fill the Republic with its spirit. The public spirit of the Republic must be a social one. In its food-policy, in the tax-system, in caring for victims of both work and war, in foreign policy and in justice, in the police and in public works – in none of these can we have 'socialism' from one day to the next, but we can force the overall direction to be from the bottom up and not from the top down. It is in this that the working class sees the essence of its participation in the Republic. And the Social-Democratic Party will be able to hold together working class and Republic, the one for the other, only if it leads a clear, determined, and unambiguous policy for the working class and makes it its foremost concern to serve the working class as a whole. No sacrifice of temporary advantages, no renunciation of momentary imagined results will offset the great, lasting and enduring success that the working class, the first class in the state, the class of the future, sees the Social-Democratic Party as *its* party.

Such a clear and unshakeable workers' politics does not mean that the Party should show no interest in other classes and strata as well as the industrial proletariat. More now than ever, perhaps, we witness the collapse of large strata of society. The middle classes were ruined by the War and post-war; currency-devaluation has finished them off. Capital gives ever more scanty protection for a small and middling independent existence; like an avalanche, the big economic forces are overwhelming the smaller ones. The large stratum of bourgeois intelligentsia have fallen into hunger. The civil servants, who used to stand sharply against the working class, are shaken in their economic position and thereby also in their mental position. Such major social forces, having become fluid, can be both a danger and a reinforcement. They can be a danger if they go along with the forces of reaction, as can easily happen given their thousand-fold mental ties with the past. But they can be a reinforcement, if their many capable and necessary individuals turn to the cause of the working class. There is no greater danger, however, than that these strata should lose faith in the cause of the working class, that the feeling should creep upon them that this too offers nothing more than anything else. A clear and determined working-class politics, based in the first place on the industrial proletariat and its future, will also be able to win these circles. We shall simply be true to a part of our old belief that socialism, which is the *work* of the workers, is not just the cause of the workers alone, but of all humanity.

The Social-Democratic Party, however, as a party of the working class, will not be able to deny its character in the struggle for the working class itself. The unification that is now taking place will not embrace all the workers' parties. It will leave the Communists outside. We do not ask – and would indeed oppose – concessions being made to the Communists and their politics, which today makes them a tool of Russian national-capitalist foreign policy. We believe that a socialist workers' party must not refrain from criticising what is going on today in Russia, and what will discredit socialism for generations if it remains uncriticised. But, despite all their errors, the German Communists are a part of the German working class, and will not be its worst part if they devote themselves to the liberation-struggle of the proletariat with the same zeal and dedication with which they are struggling for Russian foreign policy today. To bring them into the ranks of the workers' party, and really win them for the cause of socialism that they believe they are serving today, is a task for the Social-Democratic Party. It cannot succeed in this task by isolation and organisational measures, which only arouse in the Communists the bitter feeling of rejection and keep them in their sideline position; success in this task can only be achieved by a clear and determined working-class politics, and by attracting the Communists to participate in the framework of the whole German workers' movement. There may well be mistakes and disappointments: but the task can only be solved in this way, and it has to be solved if the German workers' movement is to be free of the last obstacles in its own ranks.

III

It is a tragic fate that the first great and visible success of the German working class should have fallen at a time of severest economic shortage and collapse. There is no point in lamenting this fact; the task of politics is to recognise existing difficulties and take measures to overcome them.

The task of the Social-Democratic Party is a double one. It must protect consumers against usurious exploitation of any kind. It must not allow usurious profits to be made in the unregulated – even by capitalist standards – chaos of commodity-circulation, profits that do not have their origin in production or distribution costs, but simply in the fact that commodities are not to be found where they are needed. It must take the sharpest measures against those who plunder the national economy by buying and selling currency; it must make trafficking in the most necessary articles, especially foodstuffs, an impossibility. The Social-Democratic Party must not forget, however, that punitive measures are not enough to overcome an economic system. The usurer stands behind capitalism like the shadow behind the donkey. A genuine struggle against usurious exploitation of the people is possible only by a planned organisation of purchasing with the help of co-operatives. The situation of consumer-cooperatives has to be given privileged regulation by public law. They have today become more than ever a condition of existence for the broad masses, and the state has to value them as such. All the more so, in that the consumer-cooperatives today, growing and strengthened, will no longer be the enemies of small independent businesses. These are threatened with extinction today from a different direction. A planned organisation of purchasing will help to protect many of these businesses from the usurious exploitation that they are impotent in the face of today.

This alone, however, I see as insufficient for our present situation. The most serious oppression, the worst burden for the working masses as well as for the small independent businesses, is today the depreciation of the mark. This takes from the working man the taste of his sorely earned bread. All measures have to be taken to control the depreciation of the mark, and no domestic measures should be discounted just because this depreciation is *also* the result of international factors. Production has declined under the effect of the War, in agriculture, industry and commerce. This is a most serious development. The fall in production directly involves the danger of further oppression and more serious exploitation of the proletariat.

Take the productivity of agriculture first of all. After a certain apparent blossoming, with the conversion of gold-based mortgages into paper-marks, agriculture today faces the most serious problems, especially for the small and intermediate peasants. The peasant sells his harvest in autumn. He has to live for a year on the sale of the harvest, as well as buying machines and fertiliser in spring. The same lot affects him as the working man. The money that he earns in autumn has lost a portion of its value by spring, when he goes to buy means of production. The big farmer, with his ties to the banks, can protect himself against the depreciation of the mark, the small and intermediate farmer cannot. The small and intermediate farmer cannot put the same amount of fertiliser into the soil the next year, let alone a greater amount; so the yield declines. What does this mean? It means a slippage back from intensive to extensive cultivation, it means less bread. Here a wide field of activity opens up for rural co-operatives. Here is the possibility, by way of co-operatives, to win the peasants for the workers, the countryside for the town, and pull the peasants away from the forces of reaction that threaten to attract them.

Just as important is the question of raising industrial production. No more than agriculture is this purely an organisational question; it bears still more clearly the features of class-struggle. A society cannot accept a collapse in production; it would die from it. All means must be employed to struggle for an increase, and the workers must be conscious that, if this increase in production is not achieved at the cost of the bourgeoisie, they will seek to achieve it at the cost of the proletariat. The eight-hour day, one of the social gains of November 1918, will then be the object of class-struggle. We are certain that the German working class will deploy all means against an encroachment on the eight-hour day, but the point is not to wait until the bourgeoisie attack it, but to wage preventive struggles that tackle the question of raising production not on the ground of the proletariat but rather on that of the bourgeoisie. The organisation of trade, the production of the mines, of the metal-industry and all places of actual production, must be controlled by the workers. The working class must notice where attempts at monopoly lead to workplaces being shut down, where black-marketeers shift production abroad, where mines are worked uneconomically, where factories operate against one another instead of in co-operation. A new and unsuspected field of activity opens up here for the organisations of the working class, for the trade-unions and the factory-councils associated with them. These, and likewise the working class organised in them, will outgrow in this way the role of work-*taker*,[1] and thus achieve a part of the realisation of socialism, fending off present hardship and preparing future victories. In no other way can either the trade-unions or a workers' party resolve the question of increasing production. Empty formulae such as 'extension of working hours' and 'working more' sacrifice more than just the long-term interest of the working class, they do not even help against the present distress. For, to a certain extent, the worker is also in a position to move from intensive to extensive cultivation, i.e. to live worse, go without more in the way of cultural goods and live a lumpen existence; there is a great danger that things will go in this direction, in a situation of shortage of food,

---

1. [The German word for a waged employee is *Arbeitnehmer*, literally 'work-taker', and for an employer *Arbeitgeber*, 'work-giver', a curiosity that Engels already remarked.]

housing and clothing. But, if the worker is shown that the spirit of socialist order is making its way into the economy, that his own work benefits not just a few capitalists and speculators, this will arouse gigantic powers even in workers who have suffered as much in recent years as the Germans have.

We will not make peasants into socialists, or the capitalist economy into a socialist one, from one day to the next. But, more urgently than ever, the world is crying out for new forces that can drive the machinery which capitalism has built but which it is now prepared to let rust. The working class can provide these forces, and socialism shows it the path to do this; to take this path boldly now is the greatest and most difficult task that the Social-Democratic Party has to tackle.

IV

The ending of the World-War brought with it a complete transformation of the world-picture. What is really important is not that empires have collapsed on the old land of Europe, that a dozen or more new states have been created, that oppressed peoples have been freed and freed peoples oppressed, that villages, towns and provinces have been swapped back and forwards like old carthorses, that black Senegalese watch over the Rhine and German generals maintain that they 'stand fast', that a League of Nations manages cities and territories like an administrator of bankrupt property – jokes of this kind are not decisive. Big and powerful states, whole continents, have emerged from the obscurity in which they formerly lived. The United States and the English colonies made their decisive entry into world-history for the first time, and it was with their collaboration and largely according to their will that the fate of Europe was decided. In this way, the situation that had existed for thousands of years has been changed, and in all likelihood for good. Since the days of the Roman Empire, the western part of the continent has been the nerve-centre of the world. It was from here that the lines went out to all countries, from here that the world was 'discovered'. And, from here, the world was formed: the European way of life and European culture put paid to old forms; old civilisations such as Japan and China, or India, acquired European forms, major old-established civilisations, whole peoples and races bit the dust in America. But, now, the new continents are turning against the old. The colonial countries, with their great extent and economic resources, have strong, conscious and powerful peoples of their own; they are contributing now to determine the fate of the world. The World-War effected in a few years what might otherwise have been the work of generations: the world's centre of gravity has moved away from Europe: the great Anglo-American or Anglo-Saxon community has stepped into the legacy of Old Europe.

It goes without saying that this change cannot but have the greatest influence on Europe and on the European workers' movement. The question of Europe has become a secondary question on the world-scale. But it does not cease thereby to be one of the most dangerous. The peace that ended the World-War is no true peace. It left old European questions unresolved, such as the struggle for the Adriatic and the Aegean. It created new centres of crisis with the fragmentation of western Russia. And, above all: with the rise of French power on the continent, French policy has slipped back onto old lines: the opposition between continental France and an England that dominates the ocean and the French coast. Japan, that stands in conflict with England and America for the Pacific, and the future imperialist Russia with its Asian and European claims – this is the reality of the New Jerusalem that the heralds of war conjured up for us a thousand times.

Germany's position in these conditions is doubly difficult. Not only is Germany involved in all the contradictions and dangers, since it is part of the capitalist world that has produced these dangers: the mantrap of the Versailles Treaty directly chains it to all crises that arise anywhere in the world. Its relationship with Poland entangles capitalist Germany in all the difficulties that will arise from a future capitalist Russia. The Versailles Treaty makes Germany a plaything of Anglo-French antagonism. Towns on the Rhine are exchanged for Arab tribes, Western coal-seams for Turkish *vilayets*. The meddling of the Bavarian reactionaries in Tirol and Hungary is stoking up the Adriatic conflict. From the very ruins of war, new flames are shooting up on all sides, and each wafting flame singes the German skin.

The task that the German proletariat confronts is a hard one. At least at this time the German Republic does not present a danger of war, in the sense that the old Germany did; the German bourgeoisie have had their nails cut, and even the biggest mouth of a defeated general cannot kill a single French soldier. But there is no security that this is how things will remain. This is the first concern of the German working class. The second is that of doing away with the Versailles Treaty, which hits the German bourgeoisie hard, but the German proletariat still harder.

The German working class is aware of the fact that neither the one task nor the other can be completely solved by it alone, but only depending on the sympathy and actual political forces that it manages to arouse in its class-comrades of other countries. It can only succeed in this by measures at home. The struggle against reaction, against loud-mouthed generals and swaggering field-marshals, against the stupidities of a military caste defeated on the field, against the secret and open sabotage of the Republic by officials of all ranks – a visible struggle of this kind to strengthen the Republic and against the return of the old Germany is the most important weapon of the proletariat in foreign policy. The world must know that *this* Germany is standing firm, and the German working class must keep in mind that every regimental parade causes just as great a harm internationally as every general placed before the court is a benefit. It is unfortunate that much of what the German working class needs to do off its own bat is demanded by the Versailles Treaty, but this should not keep the German working class from doing what is needed. Over and above the Versailles Treaty, the German working class must overcome the harsh legacy of the War. The ruins in France still bristle against the sky. To get rid of them and rebuild human dwellings is a task not only in the interest of peace in general, but one most highly suitable to bring German and French proletarians closer together. We hope that the reconstruction of northern France will be acclaimed by the French proletariat and its parties, and that they will do their part to avoid this appearing as the trophy of victorious militarism. Only in this way and by working in this spirit can the working class in Germany hope to receive from the hands of class-comrades in other countries what it needs: protection against the oppression that it has to suffer from its own masters as well as from foreign ones.

We believe that, to put an end to German suffering, it is necessary to conduct an active proletarian foreign policy. We still believe that it was not the least service of the Russian Revolution that, for the first time, it raised and shaped the will of the international working class above mere sentiment. This work of its collapsed, and could only collapse, in so far as the Russian Revolution collapsed into Russian reaction. But the basis on which the Russian Revolution founded its international work has remained. The masses suffer the results of the War internationally. The proletarians see more clearly than ever in their history how the suffering of the one is the suffering of the other. Hunger in Germany means unemployment in England and America, militarism in France means heavy taxation and exploitation in England as well as Germany. The War did not bring peace, but new dangers of war. Europe is stumbling from conference to conference, from crisis to crisis. We know the dance of death that led up to 1914. No one wanted it, all sides participated in it. The capitalist world, impotent to restrain itself and the monster it has created, is being driven towards new abysses. Internationally, and to the extent that the centre of gravity of world-politics has been shifted to the Anglo-Saxon world, to the English working class in particular, the proletariat must pursue an independent politics internationally, something that Marx already declared in 1864 was possible and necessary. It is not festivals of fraternity that we demand. But the unification of the workers of Germany must be the starting point for a new organisation of the working class at the international level, and for carrying out a politics of the working class and of humanity: a politics against capitalist wars, against militarism, against the oppression of nations, a politics for the union of the creative forces of the world in the work of peace and civilisation.

We know that the German working class can no longer be decisive for the workers' International to the degree that it was before 1914. It has finished playing this role. But its authority and the respect it enjoys are still great. Combatting the reaction it faces at home, boldly shaping the fate of the creative forces in Germany, peasants as well as workers, newly forming their ranks, can strengthen this authority even today, and exert a lasting influence in the ranks of the international proletariat, whose will alone can relieve the suffering of the German proletariat and give the world peace. May the United Social-Democratic Party rise to the task that history has placed before it.

V

This, we believe, is the framework in which the policy of the United Social-Democratic Party has to move in the coming years. This is a programme, not talk about theoretical questions: it is simply an attempt to recognise the urgent needs of the proletariat, and to connect the struggle for these needs with the great struggle to fulfil the task of the proletariat, i.e. socialism. Many people will ask whether the possibility exists for the United Social-

Democratic Party to really apply such a programme, not seeking a republic of councils tomorrow, but at least presupposing the constant living activity of the proletarian masses and their party. We know that many people raise this question, and many of these answer in the negative, some seeing even seeing a positive answer as tantamount to abandoning their past. In the Social-Democratic Party, they say, there are these people and those who have done this and that to us. This cannot be denied, not even glossed over, but it makes the decision about the fate of a class dependent on the decision about the fate of individuals. It could be that those individuals who opposed one another in recent years can no longer work together: in which case, they have to give way, so that the working class can live. And, if the working class wants to live, it has to unite. Already some years ago, when the revolution arrived powerful and strong, and seemed as if it would grow still stronger, we warned that if a reaction came that bowed down the working class, this should not lead to sectarian splits, but, rather, to a concentration of the working masses and their parties. The reaction did come, and drove down the working class deeper than we feared. We believe that, in every worker's heart, the idea trembles today that, if the workers' parties do not stand together, they will fall together. But is not this 'unification at any price', unification in sin instead of unification for the good? Neither the working class nor the workers' party is a ready-made product, a finished thing. Only once in history has a single attempt been made in this direction, with the famous Twenty-One Conditions, 'legalese' as we called it at the time and still call it today. The working class and the workers' party are products that change historically, they are living creatures that live their own lives, and what they are depends on those who are in them. Who would maintain that the workers in Germany, those in the SPD and those in the USPD, are the same today as they were in 1914? Who would maintain that those in the KPD are the same as in 1918? The school of these years was rough and hard, and in no one has it failed to leave its traces. The German working class, despite everything, has experienced in this years something greater than did the two generations who worked at the task of socialism. To connect this experience with the traditions of the past and the expectations of the future, acting in an understandable way, and indicating the unending future, this is the task of the Social-Democratic Party.

The Assassination of Rathenau

Reichstag speech of 11 July 1922[*]

DR DEPUTY LEVI: Ladies and gentlemen,

[DEPUTIES OF THE GERMAN NATIONAL PEOPLE'S PARTY LEAVE THE CHAMBER. SHOUTS FROM THE LEFT: '*The cowards are leaving! Hefferich[1] is running away!*']

The German people, in my view, are not an exuberant people, and not inclined to political excesses. If they have a political weakness, it is perhaps that they are all too much inclined to gentleness, caution and forgiveness,

['*Very true!*' FROM THE INDEPENDENT SOCIAL DEMOCRATS]

a fault that the German people and the German proletariat showed in 1918. From this point of view, we can only welcome it if gentlemen such as Herr Deputy Graef (Thuringia) regularly demonstrate to the full public eye the hypocrisy, meanness, shamelessness and deceit, the brazenness of the German National group of murderers here in the German Reichstag. This can, to our mind, only serve to make things clear to the German people and show them how even the bullets that struck Rathenau are not the last ones, and were aimed at the German people and not just its ministers.

---

[*] Reichstag speeches of 11 July 1922 (*Reichstagsprotokolle*, vol. 356, p. 8417ff.) and 15 July 1922 (*Reichstagsprotokolle*, vol. 356, p. 8595ff.) [Walter Rathenau, industrialist and politician, was a founder of the German Democratic Party after the War, and, in 1922, foreign minister. He was assassinated on 24 June 1922 by two officers linked to Organisation Consul.]
1. [Karl Hefferich, founder and leader of the Deutschnationalen Partei.]

['*Very true!*' FROM THE INDEPENDENT SOCIAL DEMOCRATS]

[AGREEMENT ON THE LEFT]

The law that we have assembled here to pass was prompted not by one act of murder but by several, and we accuse publicly from the tribune of the Reichstag, before Germany and the world, the German National Party,

['*Quite right!*' FROM THE INDEPENDENT SOCIAL DEMOCRATS AND COMMUNISTS]

German nationalist circles,

['*Quite true!*' FROM THE LEFT] in a broad and wide ramification of being responsible for the deliberate murder of German ministers.

[RENEWED AGREEMENT ON THE LEFT. SHOUTS FROM THE GERMAN NATIONALISTS]

Deputy Graef has spoken about the position of the Social-Democratic Party and social-democratic parties in general towards individual terror and political murder. I believe that, on this subject, a word can be added: political murder is old, political murder in itself is as old as people have a political constitution.

['*Quite right!*' ON THE LEFT]

I believe I can remind the gentlemen who are working so hard on the Right that we all very likely attended a school in which we were told about Harmodios and Aristogeiton, and this memory brought a flush to all our cheeks as young people. There is probably no one who did not read with excitement, in their younger days, the drama of Wilhelm Tell. Yes, gentlemen, political murder exists, and there are situations where new and unfamiliar ideas, where a world that is coming and has to act against a declining world, also expresses itself in political murder.

But this is not what we are dealing with here. There was never, I can say, apart perhaps from dim and distant times, a political tendency, a party, that deliberately placed political murder as a tool in the service of its will. No political party has ever previously done this; socialism never did anything like this. Socialism did not even do so in the cases to which Herr Deputy Graef referred, where excesses took place, for example in the struggles of 1919. Certainly, we are aware of the fact that there were also excesses at that time, and a few – two, three or five, I do not know how many – citizens perhaps lost their lives. These excesses were paid for in blood: for these four or five, dozens, hundreds and thousands lie in their graves.

['*Very true!*' FROM THE INDEPENDENT SOCIAL DEMOCRATS]

We did not make a philosophy out of these excesses, any kind of new religion; we assumed them for what they were, acts of rashness by an excited popular mass that got beyond itself. This is not what we are facing here. Here it is not a question of over-excitement or emotion, it is not a question of masses who lose sight of boundaries in their passion.

['*Very true!*' ON THE LEFT]

What we have here are cold-blooded, coolly calculating murderers who plan their actions around the green baize tables of a bar.

['*Very true!*' FROM THE INDEPENDENT SOCIAL DEMOCRATS]

Here we do not have individual terror, not a tyrant who has tormented his people and is shot, here we have a deliberate killing of people in whose hands the German Republic has placed its fate, for better or worse.

['*Quite right!*' FROM THE INDEPENDENT SOCIAL DEMOCRATS]

Here, we do not have assassinations of individuals; we have a major state-conspiracy, led in large clubs and societies, that is seeking to throw the whole people into chaos by way of murder, to kill, murder, destroy with the 'spiritual' weapons of lead, as it has no others.

[INTERJECTION FROM THE GERMAN NATIONAL PARTY: '*Nothing to do with us!*' – LIVELY CONTRADICTION AND INTERJECTIONS FROM THE FAR LEFT]

You have nothing to do with it? You are hand in hand with people who are wading up to their knees in the blood now flowing in Germany!

[VIGOROUS AGREEMENT FROM THE FAR LEFT]

That is what it's about!

It is from this point of view that we approach this law, and I can confidently say that we have also been concerned from our point of view to make the limits that the law draws as tight as possible.

Our intention has been to tackle nothing except political assassination, and the cultivation of an atmosphere without which political assassination cannot exist.

Herr Deputy Graef made the reproach that I am happy to take on board, that I spoke in the committee of a court for philosophies or a revolutionary tribunal. Ladies and gentlemen, if we are speaking of the German Revolution and a revolutionary tribunal that it should establish, we can do so with all the reservation with which the German Revolution can be called a revolution at all.

['*Very true!*' FROM THE INDEPENDENT SOCIAL DEMOCRATS AND COMMUNISTS]

The German Revolution was not a revolution of the kind that gives the world a quite new and original ideal content.

['*Quite correct!*' FROM THE COMMUNISTS AND INDEPENDENT SOCIAL DEMOCRATS]

The German Revolution, in its beginning and end, took place within the framework that the German Revolution of 1848 set for it. It essentially remained in this framework. But, even within this framework, it had its work to fulfill. It had to catch up with the settling of accounts between the rising bourgeoisie and the still standing feudalism that was neglected in 1848. It had to fulfill the neglected task of 1848. And, to this extent, it is true that, among the bureaucracy and the judiciary, which has been pervaded for decades by a tradition of feudalism, inculcated with the world of ideas of German feudalism – in this mental universe, even the modest ideas of bourgeois democracy have their enemies and barriers.

['*Very true!*' FROM THE INDEPENDENT SOCIAL DEMOCRATS]

These barriers must be torn down. I say calmly that this will not be possible in the forms of the judiciary up to now. The judiciary, cultivated over decades in a content that is hostile even to bourgeois democracy, is rigid and can only be broken, and new principles and a new world-outlook can only be created, if we succeed also in creating new forms of court that help the new ideas to overcome the old ideas from the late eighteenth and early nineteenth centuries.

['*Very true!*' FROM THE INDEPENDENT SOCIAL DEMOCRATS]

It is in this sense that we demand not a court for heresies or auto-da-fés. We do not demand that people who have done nothing wrong should be hanged or burned at the stake. But we do demand that the law that we make should be applied with all severity and pitilessness, in the awareness that we have to defend a new age and a new form of state, applied against those who stand against the new form of state and are trying to restore old, declined and forgotten things.

['*Very good!*' FROM THE INDEPENDENT SOCIAL DEMOCRATS]

From this point of view, what is of decisive importance for the law in general is the relationship that lay people – who do not have to be socialists, but at least have to stand firm and unshaken on the ground of bourgeois democracy – take part in the process of judgement. The position of these forces in the court will be of decisive importance for our position towards this law.

Ladies and gentlemen. Herr Deputy Graef has again indicated, with a certain condescension, the popular masses standing outside, and the threats that we make by indicating those popular masses. Indeed, ladies and gentlemen, we do indicate the popular masses, and, in recent days and weeks, great masses have come out and filled the streets, larger in many places than during the Revolution.

['*Very true!*' ON THE LEFT]

If the government does not recognise the command, and if the German Nationalists are every one of them blind, the popular masses, perhaps unconsciously, instinctively feel that their fate is being decided here.

Ladies and gentlemen, we can therefore not take a definitive position towards this draft-law in the present situation. Our definitive position depends on what happens in particular to the other draft laws for defending the Republic. This draft-law is, in and for itself, a part of the work, it is incomplete and does not meet our desires. The failings that it has can only be improved if both this law itself and the additional laws that are indisputably needed to apply it are given a form that we wish.

Ladies and gentlemen, you do not like threats, and I like still less to utter them. We will do our share of the work needed to carry through the demands that are raised not by us but by those broad masses. We shall say to you what we have to say, we shall try to make you listen, and if you do not want to listen we shall do our best to see to it that the millions speak for themselves, [*Very true! on the Left*] and you will hear their call, repeated a million times, the call of the Reich Chancellor that 'The enemy is on the Right!'[2]

[VIGOROUS APPLAUSE FROM THE INDEPENDENT SOCIAL DEMOCRATS]

Reichstag speech of 15 July 1922

When the 1914 catastrophe broke over us, we had the striking vision before our eyes of the complete collapse of the entire German state-body – diplomatic, military, administrative. And, at the moment when it had to measure itself against the great democracies of the West, those great democracies who, in a free state-system, were able to attract the best minds for the state, it was shown that the Prussian Junker was too petty and narrow-minded for the world that had grown up outside.

['*Very true!*' FROM THE LEFT]

---

2. [Josef Wirth was the chancellor who had said this.]

And, now, German democracy is faced with a task which I believe is equal in difficulties to any in history. The German Republic has to be constructed in external and domestic circumstances that have no comparison in terms of difficulty. Without a democratic tradition, without the possibility of external support, domestically amid very severe social struggles, not only struggles of the workers against the bourgeoisie, but struggles of the cities against the countryside, a state-system has to be constructed that at this point is still without the weapon it needs; for this weapon, the civil service, does not want to serve, does not want to be of service.

['*Very true!*' FROM THE INDEPENDENT SOCIAL DEMOCRATS]

A task of tremendous difficulty.

I have already tried in the committee to make clear to my colleagues the difficulty of the whole situation, in the extraordinarily profound words of Ranke, which he wrote in a quite different connection, but which I believe give a full picture of our own situation. Ranke said:

> If one conceives for a moment the entire body of officials of a monarchy under a republican constitution, it will be immediately apparent what difficulties there would be in keeping them together under the grip of the state, exerting a strict control and establishing a strong central power in the midst of free and equal citizens. How can this be possible without giving freedom an entry, without giving free rein to individuality and parties?

Ladies and gentlemen, I believe that the whole great difficulty of this moment, and the task which we face, is described in these words.

What then is the ideology that rises from these circles of civil servants – certainly not all of them, but at least a minority – and strives against the law, speaks and fights against it?

It is the ideology of the democratic rights of officials. The ideology says, as it were: we have the freest democracy, so the German official must also be able to do what he wants in the name of democracy. Ladies and gentlemen, people who speak like this show to our mind that they understand nothing about democracy.

['*Very true!*' FROM THE INDEPENDENT SOCIAL DEMOCRATS]

Democracy means no less the fulfilment of duties than does monarchy or any other kind of state; it is just that the fulfilment of duties is different under democracy. It is not the conviction that, if someone does not do their duty, someone higher-up comes and gives them a clout round the ear, but, rather, the deep conviction that each person in their place has to work for the good of the whole, that all officials perceive it as their primary responsibility to serve the whole state-system, a conviction that in all other states is firmly rooted in history and tradition, in the harsh revolutionary struggles that those states have waged for their free constitutions. You [to the Right] lack this tradition. You were content enough with the Revolution, seeing it as the end of a 'fraud', and now believe you can swing back and forth between your convenience and the possibility, at the expense of the state and with its resources, and in its officials, of injecting its bloodstream with poison.

['Very true!' FROM THE INDEPENDENT SOCIAL DEMOCRATS]

Ladies and gentlemen. It is quite clear that, as Ranke says, without giving freedom an entry, it is certain that the new civil service that democracy and the Republic require cannot be formed. As well as this, we are, above all, of the view that a civil service cannot be formed by taking away freedom, simply under the rod. The government cannot believe it has done its duty sufficiently by creating a new law about civil-service discipline and acquiring strong disciplinary powers. No civil service can be created just by discipline. The creation of a new civil service is in the largest part also a task that cannot be solved in the civil service itself, but rather in the secondary schools, in the education of young people,

['Very true!' FROM THE LEFT]

by the attraction and cultivation of new forces, including those to whom the civil service and an official career were formerly closed.

['Very true!' FROM THE LEFT]

If the government continues to draw its officials from the circles that formerly provided recruits for officialdom, it will come to grief.

['Very true!' FROM THE LEFT]

In its own interest, in the interest of bourgeois democracy itself, and doubly and triply in our own interest, that of giving democracy a social and socialist form, it is a vital necessity to have recourse to different milieus. It must be possible to place the very many forces coming from the working class in the service of the Republic, and make creative use of these for the good of German democracy.

['Very true!' FROM THE LEFT]

I recall here that today, even if there are very few workers' academies, there are large organisations, people's school-organisations, people's educational organisations, that offer the state the possibility and resources to attract people from a different background and spirit than the milieus from which the old German and Prussian officialdom was recruited.

['*Very true!*' FROM THE LEFT]

Without this living influx from new and rising social classes, without the most vital participation of these forces, and without the skill and strength of the government to attract minds and capacities from these milieus that are ready and able to construct a democratic state and a republic and fill it with new spirit and new points of view, to make the state humane and socialist, you will not achieve your objective. You will do so only if you draw your helpers, your recruits, from the broad masses of the workers. There, in the working people, lie the roots of the force of German democracy.

['*Very true!*' FROM THE LEFT]

The working class created German democracy, and the old saying goes that states are only maintained by the forces that created them. The working class created German democracy; only the living forces of the German workers can maintain this state.

[VIGOROUS CHEERS FROM THE INDEPENDENT SOCIAL DEMOCRATS]

The Situation after Rathenau's Death*

I

The murder of Rathenau, still more than that of Erzberger, more than the many grisly deeds of the German counter-revolution, has passionately aroused
the mass of working people. There can be no doubt
that the masses who demonstrated after the death
of Rathenau were large, even larger in many places
than on 9 November [1918], which so many people
laugh at today, and so many forget. The anger was
great and remains great; the feeling of rage among
the German working class has lasted longer than
before. There is no single opinion as to the possibility of expressing this rage. Some people believe that
they can raise the actions to the level of a general
strike, with the *proclaimed* aim of carrying through
measures to protect the Republic, but whose real
aim, should it succeed, lies well beyond this; others
believe that the street-demonstrations have already
given sufficient expression to the force that the proletariat is in a position to apply at this time in fur-
thering its political demands. But, however this may
be, everyone does agree, as far as we can see, that
whether greater or lesser, this show of force will
not lead to a 'revolution'. On the right wing of the
working class, this prognosis is made from inclina-
tion, on the left wing from understanding. Even *Rote*

* *Unser Weg*, no. 12/13, 1922.

Fahne has essentially conducted its campaign in the last few days under the slogan: dissolve the Reichstag, a demand that can be fulfilled completely in the present framework, and it thereby betrays a recognition that the present movement does not have the strength to go beyond bourgeois democracy, beyond the Republic. A revolutionary movement, i.e. one that is proletarian both in terms of the forces behind it and in its content and aim, cannot be carried out in Germany alone. Not that we mean, as many people used to say, that one country has to wait for the others: a revolutionary-proletarian movement may very well begin in Germany, but a mass-movement beginning in Germany – such as we had and have now – can only become proletarian-revolutionary under international circumstances that are favourable to proletarian revolution. At the present time, this is not the case: the opposite is rather more true. Internationally, capitalism is in the process of reconstruction, as we have already very often stressed, and, politically, revolution has given way to reaction. There is no country where this does not hold true. Neither England, nor France, nor America, nor Italy: the resulting movement is a general one, and is most clearly shown in the country that stood at the head of the revolutionary movement and carried its banner – in Russia. This *general* situation defines the circle within which any mass movement has to move today. By natural necessity today, mass-movements in Germany can only have *defensive* aims, they can only seek to maintain what the movement of 1918 brought. What the movement of the German working class from 1918 to 1920 did not accomplish cannot be obtained in the period of decline that began in 1921. Later years will bring it, restoring the international situation and the relationship of capital and labour to what it was in 1917–20, only on a larger and clearer scale, and with greater maturity.

II

At an earlier point in time, we believe when the first signs appeared that the star of revolution was setting in the sky, we pointed out that the German working class would go through the years of reaction in a different condition from the Russian working class of the years 1906–12. The Russian movement, up to the revolution of 1917 – except in 1905–6 – was not a mass-movement. The milieu of those caught up in the movement was numerically small, and it had no legal forms of expression. In the West, however, in the capitalist countries, and especially in Germany, in countries with a workers' movement that had half a century of tradition, the workers' movement exists even in a situation when impatient people see stagnation, and its organisations – political, trade-union and co-operative – contain the life and development of the working class itself. The ideological oppositions that necessarily exist in the working class, between reform and revolution, are contained in these organisations in the way that the soul is contained in the body. All ideas acquire reality only to the extent that they take hold of organisations; if revolution rises and the opposition between ideas rises with it, this has its effect on the organisations. But, if revolution declines, though the opposition of ideas does not decline with it, the topicality of these oppositions does decline, the organisations are less moved, they fall back into a condition of apparent lifelessness in which it is often hard even to observe them breathing.

This corrective of mass-organisations is something that the Russian movement did not possess. In this movement, it was the intellect that ruled, completely detached from the masses. The movement existed not in organisations but in resolutions. This is not to say anything *against* the Russian movement. It assumed the form that it had to assume given the conditions of the country, and in this form it performed great things for the workers' movement. In its detachment from all matter, it saw the problems of the proletarian revolution more sharply, and clarified them more completely, than did the workers' movement of any other country. We all recognise today the profound importance that the Russian debate had in the time before and after the first revolution. But, just as the movement was an intellectual one, so it was one marked by strife. It did not have the heavy mass of workers and their organisations, which binds the intellectual contending parties and keeps them together.

On these considerations, we already said at that time, that the Russian reaction would be marked by contention between socialist groups, while the German reaction would result in the concentration of the working class.

We need not shy away from saying, again today, how, at that time, we conceived the concentration of the workers' movement and the particular role of its left wing in this connection. The extent to which this role was not fulfilled, and the reasons for this, is outside discussion today. But the fact remains that, even in the ranks of the Communists, a recognition is growing that, by standing outside the major workers' organisations, they are standing outside the world. And, this time, we even have to allow it to the Moscow leaders of the

Communist movement that they have grasped the German situation more quickly and surely than the German leaders have. In their appeal of 8 July, the Moscow Communists demanded unconditionally that the German Communists should stand together with other workers' organisations. Unfortunately, the warning came too late, two days after the Germans had manoeuvred themselves out of the workers' community – perhaps more by bad luck than ill-will.[1] This outcome is something that we thoroughly regret from our point of view. The felt need to stand together, the common defence against even the last gains of the Revolution being taken away, is a general one, and, if particular branches of the workers' movement are removed from this task or remove themselves, any action, at least outwardly, loses its class-character and gains a party one. It is not so easy to win respect with a face crippled on its left side; this is not at all the divine image.

III

The problem that remains to be settled after the murder of Rathenau is, as we said, that of defending the Republic. The last crisis showed that the Republic does not have reliable support in the bourgeois parties. In so far as these stand by the Republic today, the reasons lie not in the constitution of the parties themselves, but rather in the influence of a few individuals. The life of a few individuals is not a rock on which you can build. It is the workers who are republican today, and the defence of the Republic can only be undertaken by the workers. The question then is this: can the German Republic be defended by the workers, given the state in which the workers' movement is today? We believe there is a widespread sense that it cannot. The struggle between the different workers' parties lames them all. The parties all suffer, and especially so the trade-unions; these are becoming visibly more politicised, and their strength, which is several times that of the workers' parties, is inhibited because they cannot connect *their* political will with any *one* political party. This is not the least of the reasons why we are sorry that the Communists have been expelled again from the front in which they

---

1. [This refers to the attempts made to create a united front between the KPD, SPD and trade-unions, around demands for banning the right-wing leagues and purging the state-apparatus.]

joined. It is precisely the strong force of the trade-unions that must serve the purpose not of blurring ideas in the working class, but of subjecting its organs to a common goal.

All the more so, in that the 'defence-of-the-Republic' question cannot be solved as a 'thing-in-itself'. In the last few weeks, we have frequently heard the view that the Republic must first be secured; the social constitution of the Republic can follow later. Nothing could be more false. A state exists only by virtue of the interests that classes have in it. The German Republic has no certified right to eternal life. It does not even have behind it the tough force of historical tradition, which can temporarily maintain a state in existence even if the supporting classes falter. The German Republic only deserves to live if it is freshly won each day. In other words, only a social, socialist constitution of the German Republic will be the firm tie that binds the German working class, which today maintains the Republic, to it permanently.

If this idea is correct, it is then quite clear that the preservation of the German Republic is a part of the class-struggle, in which the social element must be to the fore and not lag behind. And, if this struggle is to be great and vital, no member can be lacking.

The Reich and the Workers*

I

The war in the Ruhr has completed what the World-War began. In social terms, it has completed what the World-War only cautiously announced with its war-profiteers and polonaise gowns: above a very broad base of half-starved proletarians working short time and petty bourgeois and intelligentsia who have lost their livelihood, who have nothing left in life but a memory of former times, there reigns a clan of super-capitalists, small in number, tough in their will, frightful in their weapons and over-flowing in economic might. 'They have power in their everlasting hands and can use it as they please.'[1] The state-power of the Reich has paled to a shadow. Like plants without chlorophyll, its decrees and commands sprout from a barren soil. No one reads them, no one knows them, no one counts them, no one heeds them. The state-form is breaking apart. Unrepresented, without the deceptive cover of state-authority and legal form, the social forces of the popular body are coming to light; something that often has its effects unnoticed, only as a secret weaving of history, is becoming visible reality: the class-struggle – we could almost say, in

* *Soziale und Politische Wochenblätter*, 12 October 1923.
1. [A paraphrase of Hölderlin's verse 'The Unique One'; see above, p. 242.]

the 'pitchfork'[2]-sense – is becoming not only the principle of political events, but their actual form.

This is one thing that the war in the Ruhr has given us. The other is the ruination of what was known as 'Bismarck's work'. The political unification of the Reich has been put in question, as well as the continued adherence of large parts of the country to the German political and economic community. What Clemenceau could not attain in 1919 at the height of military triumph, the French have been given by the war in the Ruhr. There are many men buried in the Paris Panthéon who performed great services for the cause of the French state; most of these services would pale by comparison if the French government were to decide in the near future to prepare a place of honour there for Reich Chancellor Cuno. For what many have sought to achieve since Richelieu, Cuno has succeeded in doing.

II

In this time of state-decay, it is as if an old chapter of German history were being replayed. The overweening powers of the economy already stifled the state once before: but what took the German feudal lords of the middle ages almost six centuries, from the Declaration of Rhense to the peaceful death-rattle of the Reich under Napoleon, has happened now in six months. Bit by bit, these feudal lords on an industrial basis have demolished the wall of the Reich's power: they have destroyed the power of taxation by depreciating the currency, the means of state-power by organisations hostile to the state, the unity of the state by financing separatism and related tendencies in Bavaria and the Rhineland. They have taken everything away from the state; in the six months of the Ruhr conflict, they 'lost' billions in gold, they stole the shirt off the back from the Reich and its citizens: now that there is nothing more to be given, they are running to the French in order to try and come to an agreement with them. The old German misery, repeated a dozen times in German history. But another misery is also repeated: just as in the middle ages, the damaged idea of the Reich took refuge with the peasants, who rose up not least for the sake of a strong power that would guarantee

---

2. [See above, p. 263.]

their protection against plunderers, so, today, the idea of the Reich finds its only refuge with the workers. Not out of love for the Reich or any or its organs; simply for the ridiculous reason that only a strong Reich power is in able to offer them protection against these highway-robbers, only a strong state-power can secure them the basis of social existence, which the German working class won in the struggles of two generations and which it now sees being torn away. And, so, the German working class finds itself facing a double task: to preserve the Reich and to defend its own social existence.

III

It is historically perverse to believe that any class will defend any kind of state for the sake of its fine constitutional clauses. If a rising class finds a form of state that runs counter to its vital interest, then it bursts this form of state asunder. If a form of state is newly created and does not suit the vital interests of the class that created it, then the form of state decays. Several examples can be given from nineteenth-century France. The Bolsheviks, too, have been forced to bow, and largely adapt the social content of their new state-system to the vital interests of the class that is most powerful in this new state: the peasants. The German Republic was created by the workers. This proposition is defended in all proclamations about 9 November as an occasion of festive commemoration. But, sadly, nothing more than this. For it seems to us that what really divided the workers at the time of the Revolution was that people were not clear about the consequences of this statement. It was the view of the Social Democrats of that time that the foundation of the Republic, the form of state, was *one* thing, while the social content of this new state-system would only be found later. They saw the form of state as primary and the social content as secondary. The other section of the working class thought differently. Their belief was that the achievement of the Republic was only a part of the great social struggle, that the Republic would prosper if the workers were victorious on the social level, but would perish if economic ideas were not fulfilled. In the debate within the working class, the former tendency had the upper hand; the question is whether it was historically in the right, and it seems to us that the day has come when it has been proved historically wrong. Once again, however, the problem has arisen and has to be decided: this struggle is no longer in the smoke of gunpowder, as in the tragic days of January 1919, the question is being decided in stormy, yet – in relation to the magnitude of the question – small discussions in the context of our party. The majority decided as it did on the previous occasion. Once again, the majority of our fraction sacrificed the social question in order to save the democratic one, it surrendered the content for the form. And what it surrendered was a great deal. Everything has been placed in the hands of a directorate in which the Social-Democratic Party plays only a minor role in terms of numbers and influence: the achievements that made up the history of the old German Social Democrats, and those brought by the Revolution – the social legislation and the eight-hour day, the factory-council legislation and political freedom – all this has been abandoned, it is an empty form that a bold *condottiere* can shatter tomorrow, or German super-capitalism mould anew to its advantage. Everything has been taken from the workers in order to preserve the Republic; and, by doing so, a surer grave has been dug for it than if a monarchist corps had been formed; it has not brought the Republic new enemies, but it has taken away from it its friends.

IV

History does not proceed by way of formulae. If we say that what the SPD Reichstag fraction has done amounts to burying the Republic, this does not mean that this burial is inescapable. Establishing and securing the Republic is not a thing-in-itself, but, rather, one part of the forceful struggle for social-ism, in which the working class can indeed be pressed back, but can never succumb, so that this end is not certain. The struggle goes on. But we believe it is time to devote a few words to the nature and means of this struggle. It seems to us as – to bring back this old word from storage – a parliamentary cretinism has formed in the leading ranks of the Party, but of a very different kind from what used to be characterised by this term. In its former sense, this meant the tendency that sought to win state-power by parliamentary means in the old state with its existing structure. We have never subscribed to this conception, but it did have a certain relative sense. For, whoever had the state in their hands did indeed possess a formidable machine. The parliamentary orientation of our leaders, however, is mistaken not only in that state-power in general cannot be won by such means; it is also mistaken in that, even if the state were won with all parliamentary means and ruses, what they would have in their hands would be a helpless and fragile thing. For, this is a state stripped of its richness and colour. It is no longer the all-powerful organisation of the ruling class's might: the bourgeoisie has deliberately not set out to remove the parliamentary position of the Social Democrats, but rather to create extra-parliamentary means of power for itself. The bourgeoisie has been very good at combining parliamentarism and anti-parliamentarism, while we always talk past each other in the circle of our fraction whenever the question of such a synthesis comes up. And, here, it is indeed only too true what Comrade Hilferding said at the Berlin district party-conference: the others are better led. A precarious position in a precarious state – that is what five years of revolution have brought the working class.

And, yet, we believe that the deep pessimism, the absolute hopelessness, that Hilferding expressed in Berlin and very likely Wels[3] also in Brussels, is not justified. It would be frivolous to present the situation of the working class in a rosy hue, but to present it as lost without a struggle strikes us as no less dangerous.

V

What does the working class have in the way of active forces, and how can it defend itself?

If the Reich is weak and decaying, its component parts are becoming stronger again. These parts are not all bound for the same infirmity that has struck the Reich as a whole. In two states at least, Saxony and Thuringia – the extent to which this has succeeded or not is something we need not discuss here – the proletariat has in principle grasped that synthesis between parliamentarism and anti-parliamentarism for which we have striven in vain in the Reich. Certainly, the relationship is not so favourable here as it is unfavourable in the Reich. For, the bourgeoisie in these states has not confined itself to such a hopeless kind of parliamentarist modesty as our party has in the Reich. But, in any case, the proletariat there has managed to gain strong positions of power for itself both in the state and alongside it: a look at our members in those parts of Germany will show anyone who wants to see how different a spirit

---

3. [Otto Wels was the chair of the SPD from 1919, and was to make a famous speech in the Reichstag session of 23 March 1933 against Hitler's 'Enabling Act'.]

prevails there. There, our ranks show a rare feeling for the state and power. There our comrades learn daily what it is to be a *state*, and it is only in the light of this reversal of psychological relations that the complaints of the bourgeoisies of Saxony and Thuringia can be understood. Still, no bourgeois in Saxony has been hanged, and none arbitrarily imprisoned; their houses have not been seized and their moneyboxes remain unopened. If they nevertheless complain and moan, it is because their *'dulcis consuetude imperandi'* – the sweet habit of rule – has been broken.

We shall refrain here from discussing in further detail what the existence of such positions means for the German proletariat as a whole, and do so only by taking a negative example. Saxony and Thuringia have not separated from the Reich, and the position of the proletariat here is not uninfluenced by the politics of the Reich by and the Social-Democratic Party in the Reich as a whole. But we have seen how the position of the Social-Democratic Party in the Reich is a fictitious one, while that in Saxony and Thuringia is a real one. A leadership of our party as a whole that refuses to see such things thereby overlooks a fundamental essential change in the make-up of our party. And, in the long run, it must expose our party to shattering experiences, all the more so as the position of the proletariat becomes stronger in those states than the existence of the entire party in the well-heated offices of a shadow republic.

These states, however, as they step increasingly into the foreground of proletarian politics, have taken a step forward, one that we believe is both promising and of symptomatic significance: Social-Democratic and Communist workers have come together in a common government. We would perhaps share the scepticism of so many people about this if we saw it only as organisational co-operation for a particular purpose. What the Communist Party has generally lacked up to now is a sense of reality. It had learned from Marx that all history is the history of class-struggles, it had learned from Marx and Lenin that class-struggles are also waged 'by other means', but it had not learned from Marx and Lenin that even the finest 'class-struggle' is, just like the joys of war, an act of politics, and that it is played out in the context of *existing* political conditions, even if these are in the process of transformation. And, so, its policy of class-struggle was far less a struggle than a war-game, it abandoned reality and indulged in wild leaps in which soon no reasonable person could follow it. But here, in Saxony and Thuringia, they are connecting themselves and their politics with existing conditions. In a context that was clearly not foreseen by former congresses and their theses, the working class finds itself united in the exercise of power, on the stony ground of capitalism and in very great danger, but ready despite or because of this to defend what it has. We are convinced – whether defeats occur or not – that this day marks the start of the reunification of the German proletariat.

In this way, however, in state- and organisational terms, Saxon and Thuringia have acquired a central importance for the proletariat. And the task of the Party and party-comrades in the Reich directly follows from this. We will not get into the realm of prophecy, but it would be wantonly light-headed not to take into account that the power of the Reich is completely exhausted and that the day is coming when a party will no longer be measured by its 173 deputies in parliamentary seats, but, rather, by the heads that it has outside, and the means of power at its disposal. We believe this shows that the Party has to catch up in a few weeks what it has neglected over several years.

The task is hard, but not unsolvable. But there is one condition without which it cannot be solved. There must be from bottom to top the belief in the party that victory is still to be struggled for, and the will to win. No army, party or class has ever been victorious if its leaders have given up the game as lost before it begins. We recall in these days the last half year of the USPD and the deep pessimism that spread in its ranks from the top down. This pessimism, it can today be said, was not justified. Many of the best people from that time are still in place today. It seems to us, however, that what happened at that time may be repeated today. And then we would certainly see the future in dark colours, and many Achaens will be killed for the sins of their kings.

The Defenders of the Republic*

I

In 1909, a Prussian Junker, von Oldenburg-Januschau, declared in the German Reichstag that, if it pleased the Kaiser, one lieutenant and ten men would suffice to get rid of this parliament once and for all. A storm of indignation swept across Germany. Hundreds of newspaper-articles and leaflets, thousands of meetings, protested against this 'Junker cheek'. For several years, this provided rich material for agitation. No one wanted to stop protesting against the idea that an overweening Junker should dare to give a mature people and its freely elected parliament such a challenging box on the ear. But, as was said at the time, Germany was precisely an *authoritarian state*, the constitution a mere façade; what we had, in reality, was the personal régime of an emperor with pretensions of grandeur, not a people's state in which Junkers like Oldenburg-Januschau would be impossible, and that, if one of his kind did indeed dare to make such a threat in the parliament of a people's state, he would be driven out, and given an answer that he would have to accept.

* *Soziale und Politische Wochenblätter*, 30 October 1923.

II

This was, as we said, in 1909. In the Reichstag of an authoritarian state, with a grandiose fool on the throne. Fourteen years later, a squad of soldiers appeared at the ministerial building of one of the German federal states; the band played the Hohenfriedberger march. They came to a halt and the troop positioned machine-guns, *one officer and four men* made their way rapidly into the prime minister's office. They released the safety-catches of their rifles outside the doors, and while the four soldiers made ready to fire, the officer went into the prime minister's room, indicated the armed force and commanded him immediately to leave his post. The minister constitutionally appointed to his position by a constitutionally elected parliament had to give way to brute force. The other ministers were dismissed from their posts in the same fashion. The parliament was closed, and the deputies prevented from entering the building. And the Hohenzollern, this time round, was the president of the German Republic, Fritz Ebert, defender of the Weimar constitution, obliged by oath and handshake to defend the constitution and watch over it so that it would be altered neither by brute force not by ill-intended political interpretation. But those who were prevented by force from their constitutional work, who were expelled by the threat of rifle-fire from the positions that the will of the majority of the people had placed them in, were not opponents but defenders of the constitution to which they had sworn allegiance. These were not monarchists but socialists, republicans, with millions of German men and women behind them, who had shown themselves ready more than once and again today to defend the republican state not only with words but also with their lives. For these events did not take place in Bavaria, where the constitution has been trodden underfoot for weeks, but in Saxony, precisely the most secure heartland of this constitution. It was not in Munich, where the government is in open revolt against the constitution, but in Dresden, that the appointed ministers of a free republican state were treated like criminals and driven from their posts. In the name of the constitution of the 'freest state in the world'. In the name of a president who is not only a republican but a socialist! And in the name of a cabinet with three Social-Democratic members, who gave their assent to an action which is almost unprecedented in history.

III

A number of excuses may be sought and found. But no power in the world will absolve the de facto leadership of the Social-Democratic Party from responsibility for the horrific events in Saxony. The party-leadership shares the blame for this illegal and unconstitutional act of violence, for it gave its agreement to the proclamation of the state of emergency. It shares the blame, as its appointed ministers contravened the fundamental rights of the constitution and gave complete power to seven monarchist generals. It shares the blame, as it covered its ministers when they gave a Reichswehr pervaded with elements hostile to the constitution its orders to march into Saxony. It shares the blame, since the man who in the last analysis has to order all these violent measures, Reich President Ebert, is a member of the Social-Democratic Party, and the Party has covered with its name every measure of this high-placed man. Is all this in the interest of the socialist movement, in the interest of upholding the German Republic? There may be a subjective belief, but it is naïve, or still worse, it is stupid, and, in politics, stupidity is worse than a crime. Who is happy about the coup d'état against Saxony? The republicans? They experience shame and revulsion. It is in the camp of reaction that we see triumph and jubilation, among the enemies of the working class, who saw a bastion fall that they did not even need to storm themselves, as others did the job, indeed those who were supposed to support it. 'The initiative of the Reich Chancellor[1] worked in Saxony like a hawk in a henhouse', trumpeted the paper of the extreme nationalists, the *Deutsche Zeitung*. It is right. Before the brutal use of force, we had the machinery of lies sowing confusion and error, and it was not the counter-revolutionaries who set this in motion. The counter-revolution used an admirable strategy. Under the slogan 'defence of the Republic', almost all the positions were destroyed that stood in the way of the reactionaries, in order to restore respect for the 'authority of the Republic' they are being trampled down and overturned until neither authority nor republic exist any more, and monarchy and reaction can install themselves all the more comfortably in the now empty building. What the high dignitaries of the Republic have been doing in the last few weeks for

---

1. [Gustav Stresemann of the German People's Party had recently replaced his Centre Party predecessor.]

the supposed protection of the Republic is so much a work of the devil that the reactionaries themselves could have done no better. These statesmen deserve a monument to them erected by Ludendorff.

IV

What has been destroyed in recent weeks will not be rebuilt in months, perhaps even years. And the worst of it is that all this was not lost in open struggle with reaction, but that the Republic and its red heart, the working class, was disarmed and unable to defend itself. The Republic is committing a coup d'état against itself, it has carried out a successful putsch against itself in Saxony. It will now do the same in Thuringia. The counter-revolution in Germany is developing according to programme, it does not even need to dirty its fingers, others are doing this for them. It does not need to increase its power, as the Republic is seeing to it that thousands of its own supporters are abandoning it each day, growing apathetic and indifferent in the face of anger, pain and revulsion at such actions. And, so, reaction is growing as the Republic steadily mortifies itself and commits harikiri, one suicide after another. Still more: the Republic is killing its children by letting them succumb to desperation or, like the Saxon workers, shooting them down, as if hungry proletarians were the country's only enemy. Twenty-three deaths on Saturday alone in Freiberg, over thirty seriously injured and groaning in pain in the hospitals. All of them suffering proletarians, in despair at this leadership, and because they yearn for better days, for creative activity, they are dying, or shot and maimed. And no mourning, not even a rousing protest in this country, which seems to be in its final convulsions, despairing for its future and for this reason triumphantly proclaiming like a lunatic that its horrific acts are victories. Is German right injured only when the 'national enemy' spills German blood, is it only cause for mourning when Germans are shot by Frenchmen? Are there only parliamentary announcements and tolling bells when Germans fall victim to the French at Essen? Is the blood of Saxon workers, spilled by Germans themselves, worth less than that which flowed on Good Friday in the Rhineland as a consequence of French actions? Incapacity and crisis are the characteristics of this republic blessed with Stresemann as chancellor. What happened in Saxony has only one precedent: Belgium in the Great War. If it was not possible to defeat the enemy in the World-War or beat Poincaré in the Ruhr, there must still be a victory, even if it is this bloody victory over the Saxon proletariat. But such victories will kill the Republic, as the Kaiser's Germany died from its 'victories' in the World-War.

After the Oath*

> All these fractions of the party of Order, each of which had its own king and restoration *in petto*, in turn enforced the joint rule of the bourgeoisie in opposition to the usurpatory and mutinous desires of the rival pretenders: they enforced that form of society in which particular claims of the various parties were held in check and neutralised – the republic.
>
> – Karl Marx, *The Class Struggles in France*

So, Herr von Hindenburg has sworn. There stood the field-marshal in his glory, spread before him the black-red-gold flag, beside him the delicate little Löbe,[1] and around him – in our German fashion – laurels and sky-blue hortensias. The new president took the leather-bound book and read the formula of the oath as this stands written in the article of the constitution. Around him stood the chosen representatives of the German people united in their tribes, admiring and listening. They were also musical souls, and the most musical were our friends from the Centre and Democratic parties. And when it was all over, they raised their eyes full of confidence, having noticed the particular emphasis with which the new president had spoken of the republican

---

* *Soziale und Politische Wochenblätter*, 14 May 1925.
1. [Paul Löbe, SPD deputy and president of the Reichstag from 1920 to 1932.]

constitution and popular sovereignty: it was 'much noted' that in his oath –
sponte sua sine lege[2] – he added an additional solemn word of his own. This
was for the sake of the Democrats: already in the Tuesday evening-papers,
the persistently blind could ascertain from the sound of his words and his
handshake – 'I feel by the press of your hand, my son, the sign of nobility' –
that the man honestly meant what he said. There is nothing false about such
a speech. They simply reached a conclusion that can be taken for granted.
Scoundrels have been relatively rare in world-history. When Cesare Borgia
bumped off his various cousins, brothers and brothers-in-law he was surely
gripped by the idea of a higher duty, just as Napoleon was when he had the
French youth bleed to death in Spain and Russia. When Bismarck falsified the
Ems telegram, he was no less convinced that his action was for the salvation
of the German people than Hindenburg was when he opposed an immediate
peace in 1917. Subjective honesty really can be taken for granted, rather like
the faithfulness of a woman – absolute at any particular moment.

So we do not see the question of the future of the German Republic as a
question of the honesty of the president, but must rather seek more solid characteristics. In the past weeks and months, we have repeatedly said that we
continue to see the security of the republican form of state as relatively great,
now that the stratum that has proved strongest in present-day Germany has
seen and found the Republic to its advantage. But it seems important at the
present time that, not only have circles of the big bourgeoisie quite openly
made their peace with the Republic, but circles far beyond this that are certainly not those of heavy industry. Hindenburg is certainly not a representative of heavy industry in terms of his origin and way of thinking. He did not
come to be presidential candidate with their blessing, but, rather, against their
will. It was other 'fractions of the party of Order' that placed him on their
banner, and it was in the name of Hindenburg that they all then united in
recognising the republic.

We believe that the words of Marx that we quoted above fully enlighten
this apparently absurd situation. What holds all these people together is the
will to preserve bourgeois society in general; each bourgeois fraction is neu-
tralised in the formula of the Republic, but each still maintains its own aims.
And, given the present superiority of heavy industry, and the visible bless-

---

2. ['Of his own will, without legal requirement.']

ing that God has bestowed on it under the Republic, the Republic would be *absolutely* secured if politics were an absolutely logical science. But politics is not logical in the way that mechanics is. The politician can count on the tendency of a political development as a constant; but it would be misguided to confuse the tendency with the present situation. The tendency of historical development under capitalism is towards the republic and 'democracy'; but the present situation can often run counter to the tendency. Let us take the example that Karl Marx gives here. The political tendency in France was undoubtedly towards the bourgeois republic, since 1848 and even since 1789, and yet this tendency was interrupted several times, before 1848 and again soon after, apparently refuted by monarchical experiments; only in 1871 did the tendency become an enduring political form.

What then, if we are seeking to learn from history, was the condition that allowed the French reactionaries in 1851 to go against the tendency and install a monarch? The working class was shattered. Its movement had been partly drowned in blood, and partly taken a petty-bourgeois pacifist line. The workers had ceased to be an object of fear for the bourgeoisie. At the moment that a common rule over the proletariat was established beyond doubt, Louis Napoleon could make his monarchical coup d'état with the help of the petty bourgeoisie. The main thing, the continued existence of bourgeois society, was unchallenged.

It is not hard to draw parallels with today. We have repeatedly stressed in the past what forces there are in the bourgeoisie for the Republic, and what against it. We do not believe that the contradictions within the bourgeoisie will attenuate: the taxation-problem, and especially the problem of commercial treaties and customs-duties, will only sharpen the contradictions between its four groups: agriculture, extraction, manufacturing and trade. It is all too possible, and indeed certain, that a danger to the republic will arise from these struggles *if the bourgeoisie as whole has forgotten to fear the proletariat*. Then, and only then, can its conflicts of interest rise to the point of a change in the form of state, and then the present anti-republican tendencies will make headway.

We believe that this should define the position of the proletariat and the proletarian party. It was only necessary in recent days to think back to the past, in order to understand how the bourgeoisie breathed a sigh of relief; what an outcome by divine providence! Yes, what an outcome, though where the finger of God ends and human frailty begins is a different question. But we should draw bold conclusions from what has happened, for the sake of a better future. What did the coalition-policy cost us? Not only the office of president, not only so many positions of power that the proletariat possessed. *It cost us the fear of our adversaries.* And, yet, eight million socialist voters, ten million proletarian voters, are still a powerful force. *May they learn to be fearsome and feared.* Then, the Republic will be in good hands, in better hands than with the emotional vocal chords of Herr von Hindenburg.

References

Beradt, Charlotte 1969, *Paul Levi*, Frankfurt: Europäische Verlagsanstalt.
—— (ed.) 1969, *Zwischen Spartakus und Sozialdemokratie*, Frankfurt: Europäische Verlagsanstalt.
Borkenau, Franz 1962 [1937], *World Communism*, Ann Arbor: University of Michigan Press.
Broué, Pierre 2005, *The German Revolution 1918–1923*, Historical Materialism Book Series, Leiden: Brill.
Fernbach, David 2009, 'Editorial Introduction to Paul Levi's *Our Path: Against Putschism* and *What Is the Crime: The March Action or Criticising It?*', *Historical Materialism*, 17, 3: 101–10.
Gruber, Helmut (ed.) 1967, *International Communism in the Age of Lenin*, New York: Fawcett.
Hudis, Peter and Kevin B. Anderson (eds.) 2004, *The Rosa Luxemburg Reader*, New York: Monthly Review.
Jacob, Mathilde 1999, *Rosa Luxemburg: An Intimate Portrait*, London: Lawrence & Wishart.
Lenin, Vladimir I. [n.d.], *Die gegenwärtige Lage Sowjetrusslands*, Berlin: Frankes Verlag.
—— 1920, *Die grosse Initative*, Berlin.
—— 1921a, *Das Verhältnis der Arbeiterklasse zum Bauerntum*, Berlin: Frankes Verlag.
—— 1921b, article in *Rote Fahne*, 30 October 1921.
—— 1964a, *Collected Works*, Volume 26, London: Lawrence & Wishart.
—— 1964b, *Collected Works*, Volume 31, London: Lawrence & Wishart.
—— 1965a, *Collected Works*, Volume 30, London: Lawrence & Wishart.
—— 1965b, *Collected Works*, Volume 32, London: Lawrence & Wishart.
—— 1972, *Collected Works*, Volume 27, London: Lawrence & Wishart.
—— 1974, *Collected Works*, Volume 28, London: Lawrence & Wishart.
Luxemburg, Rosa 1983, *Gesammelte Werke*, Volume 4, Berlin: Dietz Verlag.
—— 1984, *Gesammelte Briefe*, Volume 5, Berlin: Dietz Verlag.
Marx, Karl 2010a, *The Revolutions of 1848*, London: Verso.
—— 2010b, *Surveys from Exile*, London: Verso.
—— 2010c, *The First International and After*, London: Verso.
Marx, Karl and Frederick Engels 1979, *Collected Works*, Volume 11, London: Lawrence & Wishart.
—— 1985, *Collected Works*, Volume 21, London: Lawrence & Wishart.
—— 1988, *Collected Works*, Volume 23, London: Lawrence & Wishart.
Morgan, David W. 1975, *The Socialist Left and the German Revolution*, Ithaca: Cornell University Press.
Nettl, J. P. 1966, *Rosa Luxemburg*, Oxford: Oxford University Press.
Quack, Sybille 1983, *Geistig frei und niemandes Knecht*, Cologne: Kiepenheuer & Witsch.
Sinowjew [Zinoviev], G. 1921, *Zwölf Tage in Deutschland*, Hamburg.
Spetkator 1921, *Der neue Kurs in der Wirtschaftpolitik Sowjetrusslands*, Berlin: A. Seehof & Co.

Trotsky, Leon 1945, *The First Five Years of the Communist International,* Volume 1, New York: Pioneer.
—— 1975, *The Struggle Against Fascism in Germany,* Harmondsworth: Penguin.
—— 2008, *Terrorism and Communism,* London: Verso.
Weber, Hermann 1993, *Die Gründung der KPD,* Berlin: Dietz Verlag.
Zinoviev, G. 1920, article in *Russische Korrespondenz,* year 2, vol. 5.

Index

ADGB (Allgemeiner Deutscher Gewerkschaftsbund), 133
Adler, Viktor, 263n, 322n
agriculture, 301–2
    See also peasants
anarchism, 120, 147, 164, 196, 205
Arbeiter-Unionen, 99
Arco-Valley, Anton von, 47n, 285–6
arming the proletariat
    during Kapp Putsch, 85, 88–9
    during March Action, 143, 174–5

Bakunin, Mikhail, and Bakuninism, 120, 147, 151, 153
Barth, Emil, 35n
Battleship Potemkin, 29
Bauer, Gustav, 81
Bauer, Otto, 232
Bavaria, 140, 322, 329
    See also Munich Soviet Republic
Bebel, August, 38
Belgium, 331
Beradt, Charlotte, 2–3n
Berlin, 40, 132, 135
Bernstein, Eduard, 9, 263n, 284–5, 322n
Bismarck, Otto von, 322, 334
Blanqui, Louis-Auguste, and Blanquism, 148, 180, 238–9, 240
Bolshevik Party
    adventurism in, 188–9
    approach to peasantry, 126, 128, 253, 264, 323
    and electoral participation, 39–40, 189
    historical place of, 224, 250
    in 1917, 15, 106, 135, 170, 196, 258, 269
    See also Communist Party, Soviet
Bordiga, Amadeo, 15–16
Borkenau, Franz, 12
Börne, Ludwig, 264
Bornstein, Josef, 29, 30
bourgeoisie
    contradictions within, 335
    and democracy, 182–3

dictatorship of, 233, 235, 250
and German Republic, 44, 333, 334–5
Hungarian, 71, 72
international position of, 54, 211, 304
and militarism, 81, 82, 114
and November Revolution, 42, 44, 121
organisation of forces by, 114–16, 208
and proletariat, 87, 335
Russian, 182
in Saxony and Thuringia, 325
and SPD, 44, 115
in Western Europe, 182
and World-War, 296
Brandler, Heinrich, 18, 138–9, 201
Brecht, Bertolt, 29
Broué, Pierre, 9n, 16
Bukharin, Nikolai, 15, 268

Cachin, Marcel, 108n
capitalism
    initial Soviet stance toward, 226–7
    international reconstruction of, 317
    and public ownership, 256
    Soviet concessions to, 24, 223, 225, 227–8, 232, 248–9
    state-capitalism, 226, 248
    and usury, 301
capitalists, see bourgeoisie
Catholic Centre Party, 35n, 333
centralisation, 57, 69, 107, 254
    Luxemburg on, 238–9, 240
Cesare Borgia, 334
Chartist movement, 60
Churchill, Winston, 248
civil servants, 125, 299, 314
class-struggle, 87, 302, 320
    and history, 197, 326
    Lenin on, 326
    political nature of, 262–3, 326
    and socialist activity, 239
    and soviet-system, 250
Clemenceau, Georges, 3
coalition-government, 7, 84, 137, 267–8

Milton Keynes UK
Ingram Content Group UK Ltd.
UKHW050243050324
438897UK00030B/537